NORT
STATE BC
DEPT. OF C
LIBRARIES
P9-ARN-709

Lifetime Speaker's Encyclopedia

Vol. 2

by Jacob M. Braude

Prentice-Hall, Inc.

Englewood Cliffs, N. J.

LIBRARY OF CONGRESS
CATALOG CARD NUMBER: 62-18248

Ninth Printing..... January, 1969

PRINTED IN THE UNITED STATES OF AMERICA

53653-X

Contents

4930. Prayer is not a substitute for work; it is a desperate effort to work further and to be efficient beyond the range of one's powers. It is not the lazy who are most inclined to prayer; those pray most who care most, and who, having worked hard, find it intolerable to be defeated.

—GEORGE SANTAYANA

4931. Prayer isn't something that we do, and then stop doing. If we are really praying we carry our prayers with us wherever we go; it is a disclipline. It is an art that can be learned. Whenever a thought comes to you, that thought can immediately be translated into prayer.

—WILLIAM FITCH

4932. Prayer that craves a particular commodity, anything less than all good, is vicious. Prayer is the contemplation of the facts of life from the highest point of view. It is the soliloquy of a beholding and jubilant soul.

—RALPH WALDO EMERSON

4933. John Wanamaker, who in addition to being one of America's greatest merchants served in a high governmental position, was asked: "What was your most glorious hour?" "It was," answered Wanamaker, "when I was a child and my mother took my two baby hands and folded them in prayer as she pointed me to God."

—A. GORDON NASBY

4934. As an alienist, and one whose whole life has been concerned with sufferings of the mind, I would state that of all the hygienic measures to counteract disturbed sleep, depression of the spirits, and all the miserable sequels of a disturbed mind, I would undoubtedly give the first place to the simple habit of prayer.

—DR. T. BULKLEY

4935. Prayer is not only asking God for what we want, but rather the way to learn to trust Him, to ask that we may know His will, and do it with all our strength. If we can really do our work, whatever it is, as well as we can in God's sight, it will become His work, and we can safely leave the issue in His hands.

—LORD HALIFAX

4936. It wasn't exactly that the seven-year-old disliked going to church. His chief objection was the long pastoral prayer. So he was naturally apprehensive when his father asked the visiting minister to say grace at dinner. But the prayer was brief and to the point. In pleased surprise the youngster looked up and observed: "You don't pray so long when you're hungry, do you?"

4937. In a discussion of how best to pray, there was some difference of opinion as to whether one must kneel, or stand with head reverently bowed, or if it is permissible to be comfortably seated. Finally a wise old minister said, "The most fervent prayers are said lying down. Most people wait until they are flat on their backs before they turn to prayer, and believe me, the prayers they say at that time they really mean."

4938. Any form of prayer is like the key that opens a door. How small a key it may be, taken from an inner pocket, a key grown smooth from much handling. Responding to its turning, the door opens slowly—into what stillness, down what avenues of radiance, only the one who prays knows; but the experience, no matter how long or short, is not unmarked in our lives.

—ELIZABETH YATES, *Your Prayers and Mine* (Houghton, Mifflin Co.)

4939. O God, whom the world misjudges, and whom everything declares! listen to the last words that my lips pronounce! If I have wandered, it was in seeking thy law. My heart may go astray, but it is full of Thee! I see, without alarm, eternity appear; and I cannot think that a God who has given me life, that a God who has poured so many blessings on my days, will, now that my days are done, torment me forever!

—*The last prayer of Voltaire*

4940. On the night of July 10, 1943, General Eisenhower watched the vast armada of 3,000 ships sailing across from Malta to the shores of Sicily for a great battle. The general saluted his heroic men and then bowed his head in prayer. To an officer beside him, Eisenhower explained: "There comes a time when you've used your brains, your training, your technical skill, and the die is cast and the events are in the hands of God, and there you have to leave them."

—CHARLES L. ALLEN

4941. A PRAYER

God keep me child-like
  And not too wise;
Let wonder, not wisdom,
  Each dawn fill my eyes.
That the world I must live in
  Keep fresh its delights

And I a small Alice
Amongst its strange sights.

—MARY BALLARD

4942. In a little town in the French Pyrenees is a shrine celebrated for miracles of healing. One day shortly after World War II an amputee veteran appeared there. As he hobbled up to the shrine, someone remarked: "That silly man! Does he think God will give him back his leg?"

The veteran, overhearing, turned and replied: "Of course I do not expect God to give me back my leg. I am going to pray to God to help me live without it."

4943. PRAYER

Prayer changes things, prayer changes you.
It changes people and the things they do.
Prayer is the key to the storehouse of God,
Opening new ways He would have you trod.

Prayer is the stairway to heaven above,
The most direct route to His wonderful love.
Prayer is important, we need it today.
Prayer is a privilege—so why don't you pray!

—EDITH WOOD

4944. On the eve of his history-making bout with James J. Corbett, heavyweight champ Bob Fitzsimmons was entertaining a friend in his hotel suite. During their conversation a murmuring feminine voice was heard in the next room. The friend lifted his eyebrows inquiringly.

"That's my wife," Fitzsimmons explained. "She's praying for me to win."

"Oh, and I suppose you pray, too?"

"My wife is more devout than I am," replied the champ, shaking his head. "If He won't do it for her, He certainly won't do it for me."

—GLORIA HELLMAN

4945. The British statesman, Gladstone, used to tell friends about a neighbor's little girl who really believed in prayer. When her brother made a trap to catch little sparrows, she prayed that it might fail.

Suddenly her face became radiant as she pondered the problem, and for three days she prayed hard. Her faith was so absolute that her mother asked her one morning, "Julia, why are you so sure your prayer will be answered?"

Julia smiled. "I know that my prayer will be answered," she said, "because I went out three days ago and kicked the trap to pieces."

4946. We thank Thee for this place in which we dwell; for the love that unites us; for the peace accorded us this day; for the hope with which we expect the morrow; for the health, the work, the food, and the bright skies that make our lives delightful; for our friends in all parts of the earth, and for our friendly helpers in this foreign isle. Give us courage and gaiety and the quiet mind. Spare to us our friends, soften to us our enemies. Bless us, if it may be, in all our innocent endeavors. If it may not, give us the strength to encounter that which is to come, that we be brave in peril, constant in tribulation, temperate in wrath, and in all changes of fortune, and down to the gates of death, loyal and loving one to another.

—Robert Louis Stevenson

4947. He asked for strength that he might achieve; he was made weak that he might obey.

He asked for health that he might do greater things; he was given infirmity that he might do better things.

He asked for riches that he might be happy; he was given poverty that he might be wise.

He asked for power that he might have the praise of men; he was given weakness that he might feel the need of God.

He asked for all things that he might enjoy life; he was given life that he might enjoy all things.

—*The Speaker's Book of Illustrative Stories,* edited by Maxwell Droke (Droke House)

4948. A MAN'S PRAYER

Teach me that 60 minutes make an hour, 16 ounces a pound, and 100 cents a dollar. Help me to live so that I can lie down at night with a clear conscience and unhaunted by the faces of those to whom I may have brought pain. Grant that I may earn my meal ticket on the square, and in earning it I may do unto others as I would have them do unto me. Deafen me to the tingle of tainted money. Blind me to the faults of other fellows and reveal to me my own. Guide me so that each night when I look across the table at my wife, who has been a blessing to me, I will have nothing to conceal. Keep me young enough to laugh with little children and sympathetic so as to be considerate of old age.

And comes the day of darkening shades make the ceremony short and the epitaph simple: "Here lies a man."

—*Author Unknown*

4949. Prayer is the ladder upon which the soul climbs to Heaven. To get into fellowship with God we must approach Him through prayer, and make known our wants to Him. Prayer is the soul's incense; the offering up to God of our dearest wishes and sweetest hopes, in the spirit of pure, trusting faith. What returns our Father makes, we may not even guess: sometimes He answers us speedily, sometimes it is best that we should wait, and ask again and again before our request is granted: sometimes our plea is denied—and we often live to thank Him that many of our prayers were not answered. Rest assured, that when or how the answer comes, God's love is always the same.

—IDA SCOTT TAYLOR

4950. GIVE ME

Give me work to do,
Give me health,
Give me joy in simple things,
Give me an eye for beauty,
A tongue for truth,
A heart that loves,
A mind that reasons,
A sympathy that understands.
Give me neither malice nor envy,
But a true kindness
And a noble common sense.
At the close of each day
Give me a book
And a friend with whom
I can be silent.

—S. M. FRAZIER

4951. Don't forget to pray. Go to God for things you need, and ask in simple faith for temporal and spiritual blessings. God is abundantly able to give: He is generous, He is willing; why not tell Him your wants? He is your Father, you are His child, and it is your right to confide in Him, to believe in Him, and to be dependent on His bounty. You cannot see Him, but His inward peace assures you He is near. You cannot hear the sound of His voice of footsteps, yet in the hallowed silence when you lift your heart to Him, you feel His sacred Presence, and cling to His promises by faith. Commune with Him in the dewy dawn of the morning; gather from Him strengthening manna for the day; let a little prayer run upward to Heaven during your busiest moments; and seek again the Throne of Grace when the curtain of night is hung over the sleeping world. O there is no time that you do not need prayer!

—Ida Scott Taylor

4952. A young aspirant came to an old monk and complained that though his own life had been wholly given up to good works he had not been able to attain peace.

The old monk told the young man to bring some water in an earthen vessel from a shallow pool. The water was turbid.

"Let it remain still," said the old man. After a time the mud and sand settled down to the bottom of the vessal and the water was perfectly clear.

"See," said the aged statesman, "your own life hitherto has been like that turbid water, and the more activities you performed, the more disturbed and restless your own mind became. But if, on the contrary, you give yourself over in silence for a while to a life of prayer, your heart will become clean and pure like this water."

The young man took the advice of the aged ascetic, who himself had practiced what he preached, and thus he found a new vision of God and a new peace within his own soul.

—Charles Freer Andrews

4953. PRAYER FOR EVERY DAY

Make me too brave to lie or be unkind.
Make me too understanding, too, to mind
The little hurts companions give, and friends,
The careless hurts that no one quite intends.
Make me too thoughtful to hurt others so.
Help me to know
The inmost hearts of those for whom I care,
Their secret wishes, all the loads they bear,
That I may add my courage to their own.
May I make lonely folks feel less alone,
And happier ones a little happier yet.
May I forget
What ought to be forgotten; and recall,
Unfailing, all

That ought to be recalled, each kindly thing,
Forgetting what might sting.
To all upon my way,
Day after day,
Let me be joy, be hope! Let my life sing!

—*Author Unknown*

Preaching—Preachment

4954. He who lives well is the best preacher.

—MIGUEL DE CERVANTES

4955. There are many preachers who don't hear themselves.

4956. Let those who do not practice all they preach stop preaching long enough to catch up.

4957. The difference between preaching and the practicing of the Gospel is this,—the former scatters the seed, the latter gathers and distributes the harvest.

—REV. WILLIAM SCOTT DOWNEY

4958. No man practices so well as he writes. I have all my life long been lying till noon; yet I tell all young men, and tell them with all sincerity, that nobody who does not rise early will ever do any good.

—DR. SAMUEL JOHNSON

4959. An earnest young minister, eager to improve his sermons, bought a tape recorder and recorded one of his Sunday morning services. After supper that evening he set the recorder, seated himself in an easy chair, and awaited the playback.

The opening prayer, scripture reading, and matters of the day all came forth just as he would have wished them. Then came the sermon.

When he awoke some time later the choir was starting the closing hymn.

4960. TO THE PREACHER

Preach about yesterday, Preacher!
The time so far away:
When the hand of Deity smote and slew,
And the heathen plagued the stiff-necked Jew;

Or when the Man of Sorrow came,
And blessed the people who cursed His name—
Preach about yesterday, Preacher,
Not about today!

Preach about tomorrow, Preacher!
Beyond this world's decay:
Of the sheepfold Paradise we priced
When we pinned our faith to Jesus Christ;
Of those hot depths that shall receive
The goats who would not so believe—
Preach about tomorrow, Preacher,
Not about today!

Preach about the old sins, Preacher!
And the old virtues, too:
You must not steal nor take man's life,
You must not covet your neighbor's wife,
And woman must cling at every cost
To her one virtue, or she is lost—
Preach about the old sins, Preacher!
Not about the new!

Preach about the other man, Preacher!
The man we all can see!
The man of oaths, the man of strife,
The man who drinks and beats his wife,
Who helps his mates to fret and shirk
When all they need is to keep at work—
Preach about the other man, Preacher!
Not about me!

—CHARLOTTE PERKINS GILMAN

Prejudice

4961. Prejudice is the reason of fools.

—*Old Proverb*

4962. Prejudice, which sees what it pleases, cannot see what is plain.

—AUBREY DE VERE

4963. Better a man with paradoxes than a man with prejudices.

—JEAN JACQUES ROUSSEAU

4964. Prejudice: weighing the facts with your thumb on the scales.

4965. Drive prejudices out by the door, they will re-enter by the window.

—Frederick the Great

4966. There are times when a man's imagination takes unfair advantage of his true knowledge.

4967. Some people are so prejudiced they won't even listen to both sides of a phonograph record.

4968. Next time you run across racial or religious prejudice just ask what color skin God has and which church He belongs to.

4969. Prejudices are seldom overcome by argument. They are not founded on reason, therefore cannot be destroyed by logic.

4970. They who, without any previous knowledge of us, think amiss of us, do us no harm; they attack not us, but the phantom of their own imagination.

—Jean de La Bruyère

4971. Prejudice is a mist, which in our journey through the world often dims the brightest and obscures the best of all the good and glorious objects that meet us on our way.

—Earl of Shaftesbury

4972. Prejudices, it is well known, are most difficult to eradicate from the heart whose soil has never been loosened or fertilized by education; they grow there, firm as weeds among stones.

—Charlotte Brontë

4973. Prejudice leads to discrimination, it is true, but it is also true that discrimination leads to prejudice. Discrimination may be the father as well as the child of prejudice.

—Otto Klinberg

4974. If George Washington were alive today he would have no chance of being elected President of the United States. He would find himself bitterly opposed by the following elements:

The American Legion and the Daughters of the American Revolution because he was a known radical of revolutionary tendencies; by the New Dealers and the Fair Dealers because he believed in the Constitution and rugged individualism; by the Methodist Board of Prohibition, Temperance and Public Morals because he loved life, liberty and the pursuit of happiness and kept the best cellars in Virginia; by the Roman Catholics and the Missouri Synod Lutherans because he was a Mason.

He would be opposed by the National Association for the Advancement of the Colored People because he kept slaves; by the Communists and other radicals because he was an aristocrat and a capitalist; by the aristocrats and the capitalists because he believed in the rights of the common man; by the United Nations and the internationalists because he warned of foreign entanglements; by the isolationists and hundred-per-centers because he entered into a treaty of alliance with France and welcomed Lafayette, von Steuben and Kosciusko as his allies; and by the conservationists and the Amalgamated Fruit Growers of America because he chopped down the cherry tree.

—*"If Elected, I Promise . . ."*
by John F. Parker
(Doubleday)

Premature—Prematurity

4975. Never ask pardon before you are accused.

—*Old Proverb*

4976. Do not praise the fairness of the day until evening.

—Solon

Preparation

4977. Before everything else, getting ready is the secret of success.

—Henry Ford

4978. A barber always lathers his customer before he shaves him.

Preparedness

4979. Preparation for war is a constant stimulus to suspicion and ill will.

—James Monroe

4980. Prepare for emergencies, but don't put up your umbrella until it rains.

—ARNOLD H. GLASOW

4981. Forewarned, forearmed; to be prepared is half the victory.

—MIGUEL DE CERVANTES

4982. To be prepared for war is one of the most effectual means of preserving peace.

—GEORGE WASHINGTON

4983. Unless a man has trained himself for his chance, the chance will only make him ridiculous. A great occasion is worth to a man exactly what his antecedents have enabled him to make of it.

—W. MATTHEWS

4984. Though a soldier, in time of peace, is like a chimney in summer, yet what wise man would pluck down his chimney because his almanac tells him 'tis the middle of June.

—TOM BROWN

Present, The

4985. The trouble with our times is that the future is not what it used to be.

—PAUL VALERY

4986. Let ancient times delight other folk; I rejoice that I was not born till now.

—OVID

4987. There isn't any "now." By the time you've said the word your "now" is "then."

4988. It is better to love today than tomorrow. A pleasure postponed is a pleasure lost.

—A. RICARD

4989. Shallow men speak of the past, wise men of the present, and fools of the future.

—MME. DU DEFFAND

4990. He who governed the world before I was born shall take care of it likewise when I am dead. My part is to improve the present moment.

—JOHN WESLEY

4991. Our grand business undoubtedly is, not to *see* what lies dimly at a distance, but to *do* what lies clearly at hand.

—THOMAS CARLYLE

4992. Let us . . . quietly accept our times, with the firm conviction that just as much good can be done today as at any time in the past, provided only that we have the will and the way to do it.

—ETIENNE GILSON

4993. An able man, who has something regular to do here and must toil and struggle to produce day by day, leaves the future world to itself, and is active and useful in this.

—JOHANN WOLFGANG VON GOETHE

4994. Today is the only time we can possibly live. Let's not turn it into a physical and mental hell by aimless worry about the future. Let's also stop fretting over the blunders we made yesterday.

—DALE CARNEGIE

4995. Try to be happy in this very present moment; and put not off being so to a time to come: as though that time should be of another make than this, which is already come, and is ours.

—THOMAS FULLER

4996. To be of one's own time—nothing seems easier and nothing is more difficult. One can go straight through one's age without seeing it, and this is what has happened to many eminent minds.

—THEOPHILE GAUTIER

4997. Make use of time, if thou lovest eternity; know that yesterday cannot be recalled, tomorrow cannot be assured: today only is thine; which, if thou procrastinate, thou losest; which, lost, is lost forever. One today is worth two tomorrows.

—FRANCIS QUARLES

4998. There is no moment like the present. The man who will not execute his resolutions when they are fresh upon him can have no hope from them afterward: they will be dissipated, lost, and perish in the hurry and scurry of the world, or sunk in the slough of indolence.

—MARIA EDGEWORTH

4999. Abridge your hopes in proportion to the shortness of the span of human life; for while we converse, the hours, as if envious of our pleasure, fly away: enjoy therefore the present time, and trust not too much to what tomorrow may produce.

—HORACE

5000. One day at a time,—this is enough. Do not look back and grieve over the past, for it is gone; and do not be troubled about the future, for it has not yet come. Live in the present, and make it so beautiful that it will be worth remembering.

—IDA SCOTT TAYLOR

5001. As yesterday is history, and tomorrow may never come, I have resolved from this day on, I will do all the business I can honestly, have all the fun I can reasonably, do all the good I can willingly, and save my digestion by thinking pleasantly.

—ROBERT LOUIS STEVENSON

5002. Some statistically minded individual, reflecting on the increased complications of our present-day living, has pointed out that an average man today has 484 wants, as against 72 a century ago. Of these, 94 can be classed as necessities. When wants were fewer there were only 16 necessities. One hundred years ago, according to the statistics, there were about 200 different articles being offered for sale. Today the total is far above 32,000.

5003. Men spend their lives in anticipations, in determining to be vastly happy at some period or other, when they have time. But the present time has one advantage over every other—it is our own. Past opportunities are gone, future are not come. We may lay in a stock of pleasures, as we would lay in a stock of wine; but if we defer the tasting of them too long, we shall find that both are soured by age.

—CHARLES C. COLTON

5004. Dream not too much of what you will do tomorrow,
How much you will work perhaps another year;
Tomorrow's chances you do not need to borrow—
Today is here!

Boast not too much of mountains you will master,
The while you linger in the vale below;

To dream is well, but plodding brings us faster
To where we go.

Talk not too much about some new endeavor
You mean to make a little later on;
Who idles now will idle forever
Till life is done.

Swear not someday to break some habit's fetter
When this old year is dead and passed away;
If you have need of living wiser, better
Begin today!

—*Anonymous*

5005. THE STARTING POINT

If you want to be happy, begin where you are.
Don't wait for some rapture that's future and far.
Begin to be joyous, begin to be glad,
And soon you'll forget that you ever were sad.

If you want to be happy, begin where you are.
Your windows to sunlight and sweetness unbar;
If dark seems the day, light a candle of cheer,
Till its steady flame brightens each heart that comes near.

If you want to be happy, begin where you are.
Tune up daily discords, till out of their jar
New harmony rises, rejoicing and sweet,
And onward, in music, go ever your feet.

If you want to be happy, begin where you are.
God sets in each sky Heaven's joy-bringing star.
Live bravely beneath it, through cloud and toward light,
And under its radiance your path shall be bright.

—PRISCILLA LEONARD

Presidency, U. S.

5006. I shall be a happier man in my retirement.

—JAMES K. POLK

5007. I'd rather be in the grave than in the presidency again.

—GEORGE WASHINGTON

5008. Never did a prisoner released from his chains feel such relief as I shall in shaking off the shackles of power.

—THOMAS JEFFERSON

5009. If you are as happy, dear Sir, on entering this house as I am on leaving it, you are the happiest man in the country.

—JAMES BUCHANAN (*to Lincoln*)

5010. I feel like the man who was tarred and feathered and ridden out of town on a rail.

—ABRAHAM LINCOLN

Pretense

5011. Intentions which die are pretensions which lie.

—*Old Proverb*

5012. Be what you are. This is the first step toward becoming better than you are.

—JULIUS HARE

5013. People used to want to be rich, but now they seem satisfied just to live as if they were.

Pretense, False

5014. YOU TELL ON YOURSELF

You tell on yourself by the friends you seek,
By the very manner in which you speak;
By the way you employ your leisure time,
By the use you make of dollar and dime.

You tell what you are by the things you wear,
By the spirit in which your burdens bear,
By the kind of things at which you laugh,
By the records you play on the phonograph.

You tell what you are by the way you walk,
By the things of which you delight to talk,
By the manner in which you bear defeat,
By so simple a thing as how you eat.

By the books you choose from the well-filled shelf;
In these ways you more, or less, tell on yourself.

So there's really no particle of sense,
In an effort to keep up FALSE PRETENSE.

—*Author Unknown*

Pretension

5015. The desire of appearing clever often prevents our becoming so.

—FRANÇOIS DE LA ROCHEFOUCAULD

5016. Where there is much pretension, much has been borrowed: nature never pretends.

—JOHANN KASPAR LAVATER

5017. It is no disgrace not to be able to do everything; but to undertake, or pretend to do, what you are not made for, is not only shameful, but extremely troublesome and vexatious.

—PLUTARCH

5018. Librarians at the Pittsburg, Kansas public library were curious when a woman asked for the discarded jackets from new novels, biographies, and scientific works. She explained that she had a lot of old schoolbooks at home. By putting the new jackets on them and locking them behind the glass doors of her bookcases, she could impress her visitors with her comprehensive library of the newest and best books!

Price

5019. The real price of everything is the toil and trouble of acquiring it.

—ADAM SMITH

5020. Anybody can cut prices, but it takes brains to make a better article.

—ALICE HUBBARD

5021. There is hardly anything in the world that some man cannot make a little worse and sell a little cheaper, and the people who consider price only are this man's lawful prey.

—JOHN RUSKIN

5022. An Italian journalist once asked of the Grand Vizer of Turkey: "Would your highness consent to the sale of Crete?"

"Certainly," replied the potentate, "anyone can have it at the price we paid for it—twenty years' war."

5023. When a business firm attempts to mold its whole policy to meet the prices of its competitor that business is entering a labyrinth, the center of which is the chamber of despair. Highest quality never can be given nor obtained at the lowest prices. If a price must be sacrificed, quality must be sacrificed. If quality is sacrificed society is not truly served.

—H. T. GARVEY

Pride

5024. The nobler the blood the less the pride.

—*Old Proverb*

5025. There is no pride like that of a beggar grown rich.

—*French Proverb*

5026. There is such a thing as a man being too proud to fight.

—WOODROW WILSON

5027. A man may have a just esteem of himself without being proud.

—*Old Proverb*

5028. We can believe almost anything if it be necessary to protect our pride.

—DR. DOUGLAS A. THOM

5029. Pride is to the character, like the attic to the house—the highest part, and generally the most empty.

5030. There was one who thought he was above me, and he was above me until he had that thought.

—ELBERT HUBBARD

5031. There is a certain noble pride through which merits shine brighter than through modesty.

—JEAN PAUL RICHTER

5032. Men are sometimes accused of pride merely because their accusers would be proud themselves if they were in their places.

—William Shenstone

5033. Pride is a great urge to action; but remember, the pride must be on the part of the buyer. On the part of the seller, it is vanity.

—James R. Adams

5034. Pride has a greater share than goodness of heart in the remonstrances we make to those who are guilty of faults; we reprove not so much with a view to correct them as to persuade them that we are exempt from those faults ourselves.

—François de La Rochefoucauld

5035. Pride may be allowed to this or that degree, else a man cannot keep up his dignity. In gluttony there must be eating, in drunkenness there must be drinking; 'tis not the eating, nor 'tis not the drinking that must be blamed, but the excess. So in pride.

—John Selden

Pride, False

5036. Many people fail to make the adjustments which life requires of them, because they have too much false pride to seek the help of others, who have met the same difficulties and surmounted them.

—Philipica

Principle—Principles

5037. I often think no man is worth his salt until he has lost and won battles for a principle.

—John Marsh

5038. We have always found that, if our principles were right, the area over which they were applied did not matter. Size is only a matter of the multiplication table.

—Henry Ford

5039. One thing I certainly never was made for, and that is to put principles on and off at the dictation of a party, as a lackey changes his livery at his master's command.

—Horace Mann

5040. He who floats with the current, who does not guide himself according to higher principles, who has no ideal, no convictions—such a man is a mere article of the world's furniture—a thing moved, instead of a living and moving being—an echo, not a voice.

—Henri Frèdèric Amiel

Printing

5041. Every school boy and girl who has arrived at the age of reflection ought to know something about the history of the art of printing.

—Horace Mann

5042. The oldest printed book is the *Constance Missal* printed by Johann Gutenberg about 1450. Printing in the U.S. began in 1638 at Harvard Academy.

5043. Printing is the adjunct of civilization, for through it we receive the bulk of the world's intelligence. It is the chief means in the transmission of knowledge from age to age and era to era. It is the art that preserves all others.

—Catherine Talbott

5044. Printing is a good business. It is clean, honorable, respectable. It is celebrated as a trainer of men for higher stations in life. It has many inspiring traditions and legends. It combines the need for knowledge of everything under the sun: mathematics, mechanics, language, spelling, grammar, color, composition, salesmanship; there is indeed no limit to the accomplishments that are required of the printer. The printer is brought into contact with all other vocations and professions. No vocation or profession can really exist without the printing-press. From text-books to novels, from pamphlets to newspapers, from tickets to tax-bills, no man can evade the printed word.

—Henry P. Porter

5045. A PRINTER'S PRAYER

To the Great Printer Who Prints in all the colors of the rainbow, and Whose Type Faces are stars and clouds, autumn leaves and sunbeams, snowflakes and flowers, this is my prayer:

That I may SET UP my life to the MEASURE of a man; that I may have the courage, win or lose, to follow the RULES of the game; that I may POINT my life towards the things that count; that I may LOCK UP within my heart idle tales, gossip, and words that hurt; that I may MAKE READY for the opportunities to serve that come my way; that I may REGISTER in my memory the splendor of sunsets, the glow of friendships, the thrill of great music, and the mental life of inspiring thoughts; that I may PRESS forward in the spirit of adventure towards new horizons of achievement; that I may WORK AND TURN out worthy accomplishments; that the IMPRESSIONS I make on the white pages of time may encourage, cheer, and inspire all those who cross my path; that I may BIND together in my own life all those positive qualities that make for happy, creative, triumphant living; and finally, O MASTER OF PRINTERS, help me to avoid the disgrace of making PI of my life and guide me safely around the yawning mouth of the HELL BOX.

—*Author Unknown*

Private Ownership

5046. As soon as government management begins, it upsets the natural equilibrium of industrial relations, and each interference only requires further bureaucratic control until the end is the tryanny of the totalitarian state.

—ADAM SMITH

5047. This country has achieved its commercial and financial supremacy under a regime of private ownership. It conquered the wilderness, built our railroads, our factories, our public utilities, gave us the telegraph, the telephone, the electric light, the automobile, the radio and a higher standard of living for all the people than obtains anywhere else in the world. No great invention ever came from a government-owned industry.

—GEORGE B. CORTELYOU

5048. I am convinced that much better results can be obtained from operating organizations which are responsible to a competent private management and boards of direction which must show economical operation, adequate upkeep, good public relations, and a profit than can possibly be secured from a national bureaucratic or a local political organization which is responsible to a constantly changing, short-lived political administration without any financial responsibility as to the result.

—HENRY EARLE RIGGS

Problem—Problems

5049. Everything is much simpler today; instead of solving a problem, you just subsidize it.

5050. When presented with a difficult and ticklish problem we can do one of two things. We can attack the person who brought it, or we can attack the problem itself. The easier action, of course, is to abuse the person. That diverts attention from the problem and sets up temporary blame for its existence. The more difficult action is to attack the problem itself and try to find a solution for it. This may require intelligence, courage, and decision, but in the end it is the only action worthy of a man.

—*Nuggets*

Procrastination. See also Delay

5051. Procrastination is the thief of time.

—Edward Young

5052. One of these days is none of these days.

—*Old Saying*

5053. He that resolves to mend hereafter, resolves not to mend now.

—Benjamin Franklin

5054. "Waiting for times to get normal" means never doing anything.

5055. A kindness put off until tomorrow may become only a bitter regret.

5056. All of us are going to do better tomorrow—and we would, too, if only we started today.

5057. Men who hang around waiting for something to turn up, should begin with their own sleeves.

5058. It's easier to get folks to agree to do better tomorrow than to get them to do their best today.

5059. He who puts off until tomorrow what he should do today eventually will get out of doing at least one day's work.

5060. At one time or another we are all convinced that the hardest way to do a thing is to put it off until tomorrow.

5061. No man ever sank under the burden of the day. It is when tomorrow's burden is added to the burden of today that the weight is more than a man can bear.

—George MacDonald

5062. How mankind defers from day to day the best it can do, and the most beautiful things it can enjoy, without thinking that every day may be the last one, and that lost time is lost eternity.

—Max Müller

5063. Procrastination usually results in sorrowful regret. Today's duties put off until tomorrow give us a double burden to bear; the best way is to do them at their proper time. "Never put off until tomorrow what you can do today," is a good old maxim: you will find it a reliable rule to follow, and by closely adhering to it you will be saved a great deal of trouble, sorrow, and regret.

—Ida Scott Taylor

5064. We forget that every good that is worth possessing must be paid for in strokes of daily effort. We postpone and postpone, until those smiling possibilities are dead. Whereas ten minutes a day of poetry, of spiritual reading or meditation, and an hour or two a week at music, pictures, or philosophy, provided we began now and suffered no remission would infallibly give us in due time the fullness of all we desire.

—William James

5065. DO IT NOW!

If you have a task worth doing,
  Do it now!
In delay there's danger brewing,
  Do it now!
Don't you be a "by-and-byer"
And a sluggish patience-trier;
If there's aught you would acquire,
  Do it now!

If you'd earn a prize worth owning,
  Do it now!
Drop all waiting and postponing,
  Do it now!

Say, "I will!" and then stick to it,
Choose your purpose and pursue it,
There's but one right way to do it,
  Do it now!

All we have is just this minute,
  Do it now!
Find your duty and begin it,
  Do it now!
Surely you're not always going
To be "a going-to-be"; and knowing
You must some time make a showing
  Do it now!

—*"Boy Wanted"* by NIXON WATERMAN (Forbes & Company)

Production

5066. To contrive is nothing! To construct is something! To produce is everything.

—CAPTAIN EDWARD RICKENBACKER

5067. The best hope of raising our own standards lies in the progressive expansion of production both here and abroad and making sure that the gains of increased productivity are, in fact, applied to social advance.

—CARTER GOODRICH

5068. Needed more than ever is a better understanding of incentives to production. When the price control officials take due account of the need for preserving incentives—and when the Congress also takes this into consideration in the making of tax rates—there will be a better chance to restrain all groups and curb inflationary trends.

—DAVID LAWRENCE

5069. There is no single magic formula for efficient production. There is no patented system that will solve everything. There are certain basic principles that have been proved by time; and it is these principles, faithfully adhered to, which in combination with each other affect good plant operation. There is nothing new about them. They include sound production control, inventory control, labor control and quality control. Modern manufacturing methods applied to a properly engineered product, good plant layout and material handling, and that's about all.

—R. C. Trundle

5069a. One of the most deeply rooted fallacies in the mind of the working man is the idea that to produce less per hour will benefit him, because it will make his work last longer. This is a complete misconception of the fundamental truth that the source of all wealth lies in increased production. The worker fails to understand that the raises in wages, the better job, the continued employment he wants, and the high standard of living he enjoys, all depend upon increasing the rate of production.

—Fred C. Crawford

Profanity

5070. A preacher was asked if a man who learned to play a cornet on Sunday would go to heaven. The preacher's cryptic reply was: "I don't see why he shouldn't . . . but . . ." after a pause, "I doubt whether the man next door will."

5071. "Johnny," said a minister to one of his small parishioners, "every time I hear you swear, a cold chill runs down my back."

"Gee!" said Johnny. "If you had been at our house the other day when Dad caught his finger in the door, you'd have frozen to death."

5072. When I was about twelve years old, I reached the place where I felt that profanity would add a manly flavor to my conversation. My father, with an insight which would have done credit to Solomon, did not scold or threaten but said something which has kept me from using profanity ever since.

"When you feel that some particular bit of profanity would pep up your conversation," he said, "mentally substitute an ordinary word such as 'chair' or 'house' in the sentence and see how ridiculous it sounds. That is precisely how profanity sounds to someone else."

To this day, when I say to myself, "Chair, chair, it's better than house," the words I planned to use stay unsaid.

—Robert C. Hickle

Profession—Professions

5073. A debt collector's job is no profession—it's a pursuit.

5074. There are . . . at least three dimensions to a profession. The width, the height, and the depth of that which may be called a profession can be described. The three D's of a profession may be said to be Dedication, Development and Discipline.

—TED WILSON BOOKER

Professional Fees

5075. A doctor's bill—Curing husband until he died . . . $25.00.

5076. The only thing the modern obstetrician has in common with the stork is the size of his bill.

Profit—Profits

5077. Today's profits are yesterday's good will ripened.

—EUGENE P. BERTIN

5078. Profit is the ignition system of our economic engine.

—CHARLES SAWYER

5079. Business without profit is not business any more than a pickle is candy.

—CHARLES F. ABBOTT

5080. Most of the money a businessman calls profits is merely money that has not been wasted.

—A. V. BURDINE

5081. Profit is the product of labor plus capital multiplied by management. You can hire the first two. The last must be inspired.

5082. It may almost be held that the hope of commercial gain has done nearly as much for the cause of truth, as even the love of truth itself.

—CHRISTIAN NEVELL BOVEE

5083. To put pressure upon the destitute for the sake of gain and to make a profit out of the need of another is condemned by all laws, human or divine.

—POPE LEO XIII

5084. Profit is a must. There can be no security for any employe in any business that doesn't make money. There can be no growth for that business. There can be no opportunity for the individual to achieve his personal ambitions unless his company makes money.

—DUNCAN C. MENZIES

5085. The successful producer of an article sells it for more than it cost him to make, and that's his profit. But the customer buys it only because it is worth *more* to him than he pays for it, and that's his profit. No one can long make a profit *producing* anything unless the customer makes a profit *using* it.

—SAMUEL B. PETTENGILL

5086. In transactions of trade it is not to be supposed that, as in gaming, what one party gains the other must necessarily lose. The gain to each may be equal. If A. has more corn that he can consume, but wants cattle; and B. has more cattle, but wants corn; exchange is gain to each; thereby the common stock of comforts in life is increased.

—BENJAMIN FRANKLIN

5087. Unless a business can stay in the black over the long term, averaging the bad years with good, it cannot sustain itself. A manager may have laudable social intentions of providing security for his employees, better products at lower prices for his customers. But if he cannot keep the business going in realizing these intentions he is defeated before he begins.

—PAUL GARRETT

5088. In Waller, Texas, is a retail store where customers wait on themselves and set their own prices. There are no prices on the merchandise—merely a tag on every item indicating what that particular article cost the store. The customer selects an article, wraps it himself, and pays whatever he thinks the owner's profit should be. The store has been operating on this same principle—and at a profit—for nearly half a century.

5089. In business the earning of profit is something more than an incident of success. It is an essential condition of success; because the continued absence of profit itself spells failure. But while loss spells failure, large profits do not connote success. Success must be sought in business also in excellence of performance; and in business, excellence of performance manifests itself, among other things, in the advancing of methods and processes; in the improvement of products; in more perfect organization, eliminating friction as well as waste; in bettering the condition of the workingmen, developing their faculties and promoting their happiness; and in the establishment of right relations with customers and with the community.

—JUSTICE LOUIS D. BRANDEIS

Progress

5090. I will go anywhere—provided it be forward.

—DAVID LIVINGSTONE

5091. What is now proved was once only imagined.

—WILLIAM BLAKE

5092. Restlessness and discontent are the first necessities of progress.

—THOMAS A. EDISON

5093. All change is not growth; as all movement is not forward.

—ELLEN GLASGOW

5094. Self-denial is simply a method by which man arrests progress.

—OSCAR WILDE

5095. The "silly question" is the first intimation of some totally new development.

—ALFRED NORTH WHITEHEAD

5096. She used to call him "Pilgrim" because every day he made a little progress.

5097. A static hero is a public liability. Progress grows out of motion.

—RICHARD E. BYRD

5098. You can't sit on the lid of progress. If you do, you will be blown to pieces.

—HENRY J. KAISER

5099. Progress consists largely of learning to apply laws and truths that have always existed.

—JOHN ALLAN MAY

5100. Every step forward is made at the cost of mental and physical pain to someone.

—FRIEDRICH WILHELM NIETZSCHE

5101. It is not enough to make progress; we must make it in the right direction.

5102. Anything that interferes with individual progress ultimately will retard group progress.

—George H. Houston

5103. The art of progress is to preserve order amid change and to preserve change amid order.

—Alfred N. Whitehead

5104. You can't say civilization don't advance, however, for in every war they kill you a new way.

—Will Rogers

5105. It is the impulsiveness of the young, tempered with the experience of the old, that makes for progress.

—Justice Oliver Wendell Holmes

5106. Little progress can be made by merely attempting to repress what is evil; our great hope lies in developing what is good.

—Calvin Coolidge

5107. In thousands of years there has been no advance in public morals, in philosophy, in religion or in politics, but the advance in business has been the greatest miracle the world has ever known.

—W. E. Howe

5108. Keeping a little ahead of conditions is one of the secrets of business; the trailer seldom goes far.

—Charles M. Schwab

5109. We are too much inclined to measure progress by the billions spent rather than by the work completed.

5110. Progress is always the product of fresh thinking, and much of it thinking which to practical men bears the semblance of dreaming.

—Robert Gordon Sprout

5111. Progress in industry depends very largely on the enterprise of deep-thinking men, who are ahead of the times in their ideas.

—Sir William Ellis

5112. Because something has been done in a particular way for fifteen or twenty years is a pretty certain sign that it is being done in the *wrong* way.

5113. Progress in every age results only from the fact that there are some men and women who refuse to believe that what they know to be right cannot be done properly.

—Russell W. Davenport

5114. Our only concern should be to do better today than we did yesterday. Step by step is the law of growth. God does not expect the acorn to be a mighty oak before it has been a sapling.

—George E. Carpenter

5115. Progress begins when men begin to doubt conventional methods or standards and to launch out for themselves. Pushed far enough, doubt leads to deeper and broader convictions.

5116. Behind every advance of the human race is a germ of creation growing in the mind of some lone individual. An individual whose dreams waken him in the night while others lie contendedly asleep.

—Crawford H. Greenwalt

5117. We should so live and labor in our time that what came to us as seed may go to the next generation as blossom, and that what came to us as blossom may go to them as fruit. This is what we mean by progress.

—Henry Ward Beecher

5118. Very much of what we call the progress of today consists in getting rid of false ideas, false conceptions of things, and in taking a point of view that enables us to see the principles, ideas and things in right relation to each other.

—W. D. Hoard

5119. What, after all, is really worth doing in this life? If our object be merely to keep things going as they are, then, truly, all the activities of mankind become virtually nothing more than housekeeping on a world-wide scale.

—T. B. Roberton

5120. Every gain made by individuals or societies is almost instantly taken for granted. The luminous ceiling toward which we raise our longing eyes becomes, when we have climbed to the next floor, a stretch of disregarded linoleum beneath our feet.

—Aldous Huxley

5121. Unprogressiveness . . . is usually a function of wrong thinking rather than age. Inflexibility of mind and resistance to "new ideas" crop up among the young as well as the old. To progress, one must be mentally alert and striving for self-improvement.

—Albert Johnson

5122. It isn't the incompetent who destroy the organization. The incompetent never get in a position to destroy it. It is those who have achieved something and want to rest upon their achievements who are forever clogging things up.

—Charles Sorenson

5123. Progress depends upon what we are, rather than upon what we may encounter. One man is stopped by a sapling lying across the road; another, passing that way, picks up the hindrance and converts it into a help in crossing the brook just ahead.

—Jonathan Trumbull

5124. One aftermath, if not result, of World War II has been the greatest upsurge in world literacy yet experienced. We shall not suggest that war is a better teacher than teachers, but it remains a truism that social upheaval and change precede, indeed necessitate progress.

5125. Great steps in human progress are made by things that don't work the way philosophy thought they should. If things always worked the way they should, you could write the history of the world from now on. But they don't, and it is those deviations from the normal that make human progress.

—Charles F. Kettering

5126. Our forefathers did without sugar until the 13th century, without coal fires until the 14th century, without buttered bread until the 15th century, without coffee and tea and soap until the 17th century, without pudding until the 18th century, without gas and matches and electricity until the 19th century, and without canned goods until the 20th century.

5127. There is no law of progress. Our future is in our own hands, to make or to mar. It will be an uphill fight to the end, and would we have it otherwise? Let no one suppose that evolution will ever exempt us from struggles. "You forget," said the Devil, with a chuckle, "that I have been evolving too."

—DEAN WILLIAM RALPH INGE

5128. A young soldier carried the flag far ahead of the rest of the regiment and placed it near the enemy lines. The captain cried: "Bring back that flag, you fool!" But the soldier said: "Never! You bring up the regiment!" When the regiment of soldiers finally arrived at the place where he was under heavy shell fire, they found him dead, but the flag was flying triumphantly in the breeze.

5129. I don't know anything better calculated to keep us humble than a visit to a museum. When we see the household utensils, farming implements, and the clothing that our predecessors used, we wonder how on earth they got along. We wonder, until we remember these crude and clumsy things were once considered very modern. The people of that time considered them "the last word." . . . Each generation starts to build where the previous one left off, and 500 years from now perhaps our cars and planes, and hundreds of other things we think are smart, will be shown in museums to the amusement of our descendants.

—ARCHER WALLACE

5130. On the road to Chicago, a firm has placed a bill-board display which reads in letters three feet high: "Organized in 1866! Need more be said?" What egotistical tommyrot! How many people believe that age is the final proof of worth?

Don't expect me to buy from you simply because you are old. Oldsters often resist change and new ideas; they don't want to be jarred out of their grooves. But how young are your business arteries? Have you kept abreast of the times? I respect your traditions and recognize the value of your experience, but I want to know what these things mean to me in terms of quality and up-to-dateness.

—CHESTER A. JAQUE

Prominence

5131. The highest and most lofty trees have the most reason to dread the thunder.

—CHARLES ROLLIN

5132. If you want a place in the sun, you've got to expect a few blisters.

5133. There are two ways to achieve public awareness: (1) be very much in the public eye; or (2) get in the public's hair.

Promise—Promises

5134. A promise against law or duty is void in its own nature.
—*Old Proverb*

5135. When a man repeats a promise again and again he means to fail you.

—*Ancient Proverb*

5136. Advancement is to be won by qualifying for advancement, not by seeking it.

—Sir Herbert Louis Samuel

5137. It's well to remember that the more you are promised the less you may expect.

5138. When O. Henry was the popular short story writer of the early years of this century, he made a contract with a publisher to supply a story every week. Even O. Henry, genius that he was, sometimes ran into a dry spell and a story just would not be written on time. After he failed his editor two weeks in a row, he got this note:

"My dear O. Henry: If I do not receive that story from you by noon tomorrow, I'm going to put on my heaviest-soled shoes, come down to your rooms, and kick you downstairs. I always keep my promises."

Immediately, O. Henry wrote a characteristic reply: "Dear Sir: I, too, would always keep my promises if I could fulfill them with my feet."

Promotion

5139. A young fellow soon loses his job when he does it too well—he gets promoted to a better one.

5140. Plenty of men can do good work for a spurt and with immediate promotion in mind, but for promotion you want a man in whom good work has become a habit.

—Henry L. Doherty

5141. Many people have the ambition to succeed; they may even have special aptitude for their job. And yet they do not move ahead.

Why? Perhaps they think that since they can master the job, there is no need to master themselves.

—John Stevenson

Promptness. See also Punctuality

5142. Promptness is the soul of business.

—Lord Chesterfield

5143. During a very busy life I have often been asked, "How did you manage to do it all?" The answer is very simple: It is because I did everything *promptly*.

—Sir Richard Tangye

Proof

5144. The less a thing can be proved, the angrier we get when we argue about it.

5145. When one's proofs are aptly chosen four are as valid as four dozen.

—Matthew Prior

5146. To prove yourself in the right is to show that another is in the wrong.

5147. A very wise man has said that "short of the multiplication table there is no truth and no fact which must not be proved over again as if it had never been proven, from time to time."

—Elihu Root

Propaganda

5148. Propaganda is baloney disguised as food for thought.

5149. Propaganda is pervasive in our time. There has always been some propaganda, but in the modern age it is organized, intentional and relatively more effective. Moreover, modern propaganda emphasizes distortion and derationalizes the popular opinion process. It usually does not help the individual to come to a rational understanding of public issues but rather attempts to induce him to follow nonrational emotional drives. All fields of human activity in which special interest groups exist, and there are constantly more of them, are the areas in which the propagandist operates.

—WILLIAM ALIG

Property

5150. He who feeds the hen ought to have the egg.

—*Danish Proverb*

5151. No man acquires property without acquiring with it a little arithmetic also.

—RALPH WALDO EMERSON

5152. Property is the fruit of labor; property is desirable; it is a positive good in the world. That some should be rich shows that others may become rich, and hence is just encouragement to industry and enterprise. Let him who is houseless not pull down the house of another, but let him work diligently and build one for himself, thus by example assuring that his own shall be safe from violence when built.

—ABRAHAM LINCOLN

Prosperity

5153. Few of us can stand prosperity. Another man's, I mean.

—MARK TWAIN

5154. Never before in our history has American's horn of plenty had such a toot.

5155. In the periods of prosperity, most people make more money than they earn and spend more than they make.

5156. To have national prosperity we must spend; but to have individual prosperity we must save—which clears up everything.

5157. You cannot create prosperity by law. Sustained thrift, industry, application, intelligence, are the only things that ever do, or ever will, create prosperity. But you can very easily destroy prosperity by law.

—THEODORE ROOSEVELT

5158. The old thought that one cannot be rich except at the expense of his neighbor, must pass away. True prosperity adds to the richness of the whole world, such as that of the man who makes two trees grow where only one grew before. The parasitical belief in prosperity as coming by the sacrifice of others has no place in the mind that thinks true. "My benefit is your benefit, your success is my success," should be the basis of all our wealth.

—Anne Rix Miltz

Proverb—Proverbs

5159. The proverb answers where the sermon fails.

—William Gilmore Simms

5160. A proverb is much light condensed in one flash.

—Charles Simmons

5161. Proverbs are short sentences drawn from long experience.

—Miguel de Cervantes

5162. Proverbs may be called the literature of the illiterate.

—Frederick S. Cozzens

5163. Small profits and often, are better than large profits and seldom.

—*German Proverb*

5164. Almost every wise saying has an opposite one, no less wise, to balance it.

—George Santayana

5165. Solomon made a book of proverbs, but a book of proverbs never made a Solomon.

5166. Proverbs, like the sacred books of each nation, are the sanctuary of the institutions.

—Ralph Waldo Emerson

5167. There are but few proverbial sayings that are not true, for they are drawn from experience itself, which is the mother of all sciences.

—Miguel de Cervantes

5168. Proverbs are in the world of thought what gold coin is in the world of business—great value in small compass, and equally current among all people. Sometimes the proverb may be false, the coin counterfeit, but in both cases the false proves the value of the true.

—Daniel March

5169. The wisdom of nations lies in their proverbs, which are brief and pithy. Collect and learn them; they are notable measures and directions for human life; you have much in little; they save time in speaking, and upon occasion may be the fullest and safest answers.

—William Penn

5170. Too many ancient proverbs, masquerading as wisdom, have achieved a moral authority greater than that of the Ten Commandments. Take the adage "Whatever is worth doing is worth doing well." Nonsense. There are 100 things that are worth doing, provided you don't bother about doing them well. If you try for perfection, you lose your amateur standing—a priceless boon—and become a tiresome professional.

A man gave up golf because some ancient fool said, "Whatever is worth doing at all is worth doing well." He should have stood on his rights and pointed out the undebatable truth that the man who doesn't play golf well gets twice as much fun and exercise as the man who plays very well: he hits the ball twice as many times.

—*Author Unknown*

Psychiatry

5171. A psychiatrist gets paid for asking a man the same questions his wife asks for nothing.

5172. It is possible for a psychiatrist to become so famous that all the world will beat a psycopath to his door.

5173. Psychiatrist: a guy who tells you all the things you should do to get better and then takes all your dough so you can't afford to.

5174. Love is the touchstone of psychiatric treatment. Psychiatrists believe, with almost religious fervor, that love can be fostered, extended, and used to subjugate hate, and thus cure illness.

—Dr. Karl Menninger

5175.

One thing for sure,
A psychiatrist is no quack,
He guarantees a cure
Or your mania back.

—Don Tanner

5176. We psychiatrists talk about "conflict" and "guilt feelings"—the bases of most emotional disorders. Ministers talk about "sin." But psychologically, perhaps we mean pretty much the same thing. What is sin but failure to do what is known to be right? What are guilt feelings but the realization that wrong has been done? And what is conflict but anxiety about a decision already made that may not have been the moral one?

—Dr. Jacob H. Conn

5177. For psychiatrists and others who plumb the psychic depths, the affinity of women for any fur is a phenomenon at least as absorbing as hysterical paralysis.

"Typically," says Dr. Myron J. Helfgott, a social psychologist, "a woman does not buy her own fur. Therefore, its possession means that she is highly prized by some male. When she is no longer a sexual symbol to him, he buys her a vacuum cleaner or a washing machine. The more expensive the fur, the more highly she is prized, the more desirable her status."

5178. Psychiatrists explain a truth wise men have known for thousands of years: *Every man is the sum total of his thoughts!* What a help if psychiatrists could give their major attention to *producing* happiness, not curing unhappiness. People turn out to be *happy* people because of the kind of thinking they have been doing over the years—*the thoughts they plant are the thoughts they harvest!* Could any parent do his child a greater service than to make sure the *right* seeds are planted during the planting season? Self-confidence, self-respect, faith, confidence in others, kindness, humility, courage, honesty, love, unselfishness, tolerance, sincerity—are seed-thoughts that will choke out weeds and blossom in their time.

5179. Dr. Smiley Blanton, an eminent psychiatrist, once stated to me that in his opinion the wisest psychiatric statement ever made was the words from Ephesians, "Having done all, stand." These words were uttered many generations ago by one of the most astute minds history has ever produced, a man named St. Paul. Dr. Blanton said that he has read practically everything in the field of psychiatry and that there is nothing to equal the wisdom and insight contained in these few words, "Having done all, stand."

The psychiatric, curative value of St. Paul's statement is based on the simple process—do the best you can. Do all you can. Give a proposition or a problem or a situation all the energy both physical and mental of which you are capable. Leave no stone unturned. Exercise all your ingenuity and efficiency, then realize there is nothing further that you can do about it; therefore, there is no use fretting, worrying, or engaging in mental postmortems; no use rehashing or going over the situation. You have done all you can do, therefore *stand;* that is, do not allow yourself to be upset; trust God and trust what you have done. It will come out the way it ought to come out if you will just leave it alone.

—Norman Vincent Peale

Psychology

5180. When Balzac, the French novelist, first visited Vienna, he was unfamiliar with the language and the currency. Whenever he took a cab he did not know how much fare to pay, nor could he understand the driver.

Experience had taught Balzac, however, that money speaks a universal language. Upon arriving at his destination, he would hand the taxi driver a single coin. If the man kept his hand outstretched, he would add another coin. Slowly adding one coin after another, Balzac would carefully watch the driver's face.

The moment a smile appeared there, Balzac knew he had given one coin too many. He would take back the last coin and leave the cab.

5181. Needing a new secretary, the firm's president decided to have applicants judged by a psychologist. Three girls were interviewed together.

"What do two and two make?" the psychologist asked the first.

"Four," was the prompt answer. To the same question the second girl replied: "It might be 22." The third girl answered: "It might be 22 and it might be four."

When the girls had left the room, the psychologist turned triumphantly to the president. "There," he said, "that's what psychology does. The first girl said the obvious thing. The second smelled a rat. The third was going to have it both ways. Now, which girl will you have?"

The president did not hesitate. "I'll have the blonde with the blue eyes," he said.

5182. Benjamin Franklin was a superb psychologist, although the word was not then known. Even as a very young man he knew how to influence those whom he needed on his side. Shortly after his re-election as clerk of the Pennsylvania Assembly he went to work on a "gentleman of fortune and education with talents that were likely to give him great influence in the House which, indeed, afterward happened."

The gentleman, a new member, had, before the election, made an unexpected speech against young Ben. And when the House convened, he brushed past the Assembly Clerk without speaking. Benjamin's approach was not to pay him servile respect. Rather, knowing that the man's splendid library held a very scarce and curious book, he penned a polite note, asking if it would be possible for him to peruse it. He would deem it a great favor if the gentleman would lend it to him for a few days . . .

A messenger delivered the volume to Franklin almost immediately, and a week later, with a gracious letter of gratitude, Ben returned it. The result, in Franklin's own words, was "When next we met in the House, he spoke to me (which he had never done before) and with great civility; and he ever afterward manifested a readiness to serve me on all occasions, so that we became great friends and our friendship continued to his death."

—Mary Alkus

Publicity

5183. Keep too much in the limelight and somebody will discover your long ears.

5184. A telescope will magnify a star a thousand times, but a good press agent can do even better.

5185. I have often wondered if newspaper publicity would not have had thirteen original colonies fighting among themselves if we had been present at their conference at the time of the Revolution.

—William Hard

Public Office

5186. Unless good citizens hold office, bad citizens will.

—Calvin Coolidge

5187. The most powerful men are not public men. The public man is responsible, and a responsible man is a slave.

—Benjamin Disraeli

Public Opinion

5188. I do not regret having braved public opinion, when I knew it was wrong and was sure it would be merciless.

—Horace Greeley

5189. Public opinion is no more than this:
What people think that other people think.

—Alfred Austin

5190. As individuals find crime to be a one-way street, so communities and nations are subject to the same psychology. The moral side of public opinion is traditionally lazy, but there is an indefinable point at which it can be and is aroused.

—Allen E. Claxton

5191. Public opinion is a mysterious, invisible power, which nothing can resist. Nothing is more changeable, more intangible, or stronger. And yet, capricious as it is, it is, nevertheless, right, reasonable, and just, much oftener than we are disposed to think it is.

—Napoleon I

Public Relations

5192. Public relations doesn't mean treating the public like relations.

—Ronald C. Henderson

5193. An egotist talks about himself, but the man with enterprise hires a publicity agent.

—Dan Bennett

5194. A person or persons may decide to go into business, but the public decides whether or not a business stays in business.

—E. J. Corio

5195. Businessmen have learned that public business is their business, and unless it is attended to their business will suffer.

—Chauncey M. Depew

5196. Public relations work is generally considered to be a relatively new development. Actually, the principles involved are as old as the ages. The 9th verse of the 14th Chapter of First Corinthians reads: "Except ye utter by the tongue words easy to be understood, how shall it be known what is spoken? For ye shall speak into the air." With the Bible as our authority, how can we public relations people fail?

—Clifford B. Reeves

5197. Each day it becomes more and more apparent that all questions in this country must be settled at the bar of public opinion. If our laws regulating large business concerns provide for proper and complete publicity—so that the labor of a concern will know what it is doing, so that the stockholders will know what is being done, and the public will have as much information as either—many of our present difficulties will disappear. In place of publicity being an element of weakness to a business concern, it will be an element of strength.

—GEORGE W. PERKINS

Public Service

5198. Courtesy is a duty public servants owe to the humblest member of the public.

—EDWARD ROBERT BULWER-LYTTON

5199. No personal consideration should stand in the way of performing a public duty.

—ULYSSES S. GRANT

5200. What is needed for public service is strong nerves, backbone, the instinct for combat, the hide of a rhinoceros and a willingness to work like a dog for an occasional rain-washed bone.

—ROBERT MOSES

5201. Public money ought to be touched with the most scrupulous conscientiousness of honor. It is not the produce of riches only, but of the hard earnings of labor and poverty. It is drawn even from the bitterness of want and misery. Not a beggar passes, or perishes in the streets, whose mite is not in that mass.

—THOMAS PAINE

Public Speaking

5202. Poets are born but orators are made.

—*Old Adage*

5203. A mediocre speech can never be too short.

—MME. DE LAMBERT

5204. Most banquets turn out to be full discourse dinners.

—ED WHITTAKER

5205. The first rule for speaking well is to think well.

—MME. DE LAMBERT

5206. I have the gift of oratory, but I haven't it with me.

5207. An orator without judgment is a horse without a bridle.

—THEOPHRASTUS

5208. *Advice to public speakers:* Be brief, be sincere, be seated!

5209. Most of us know how to say nothing—few of us know when.

5210. If the speaker won't boil it down, the audience must sweat it out.

—RAYMOND DUNCAN

5211. No man not inspired can make a good speech without preparation.

—DANIEL WEBSTER

5212. *Speaker's lament:* "I feel like an Egyptian mummy—pressed for time."

5213. Most impromptu speeches are not worth the paper they are written on.

—LORD JUSTICE BIRKETT

5214. In the days of Balaam it was considered a miracle when an ass spoke. Things have changed.

5215. Never rise to speak till you have something to say; and when you have said it, cease.

—JOHN WITHERSPOON

5216. Why should he talk, whose presence lends a
grace
To every table where he shows his face!

—DR. OLIVER WENDELL HOLMES

5217. It's not a toastmaster's job to bore you so I will now introduce many who will.

5218. Commencement speakers usually frighten the graduates by telling them the world is theirs.

5219. Nature blunders too—she often gives the biggest mouths to those who have the least to say.

5220. A speaker once concluded his speech as follows: "Be careful driving home—my wife has the car out!"

5221. Many speakers confuse the seating capacity of the hall with the sitting capacity of the audience.

5222. If ever a woman feels proud of her lover, it is when she sees him as a successful public speaker.

—Nathaniel Hawthorne

5223. It isn't the first-hand information that makes the best speech, but second-hand timing.

—Hal Chadwick

5224. Sometimes the difference between a good speaker and a poor speaker is a comfortable nap.

—O. A. Battista

5225. One of the most important ingredients in a recipe for speech-making is plenty of shortening.

5226. As a vessel is known by the sound, whether it be cracked or not; so men are proved, by their speeches, whether they be wise or foolish.

—Demosthenes

5227. The fault with many speakers is that you can't hear what they're saying. The trouble with others is that you can.

5228. You can make an audience laugh anywhere in the world simply by walking on the stage and saying, "I am a married man."

—Charles Curran

5229. Most speeches to an hour-glass do some resemblance show; because the longer time they run the shallower they grow.

5230. The chairman of a meeting is like an official at a bullfight. His main function is to open and close the gates to let the bull in and out.

5231. The longest word in the English language is the one following the phrase: "And now a word from our guest of honor."

5232. Samson was a piker; he killed only a thousand men with the jawbone of an ass. Every hour in the day ten thousand sales are killed with the same weapon.

—G. Stewart

5233. Talking is like playing on the harp. There is as much in laying the hands on the strings to stop their vibrations as in twanging them to bring out their music.

—Oliver Wendell Holmes

5234. Applause before a speaker begins his talk is an act of faith. Applause during the speech is an act of hope. Applause after he has concluded is an act of charity.

5235. Every man is born with the faculty of reason and the faculty of speech, but why should he be able to speak before he has anything to say?

—Benjamin Whichcote

5236. A speech, being a matter of adaptation, and having to win opinions, should contain a little for the few, and a great deal for the many.

—Augustus Hare

5237. Speakers should be careful to sound the letter "h." There was once a chairman who introduced a lecturer as a profound tinker.

5238. Wouldn't it be fine if the fellow who says I'm not used to making a speech would leave it at that instead of going on to prove it?

5239. *Master of ceremonies at banquet:* "Let's have a round of applause for the wonderful job the program committee did in not being able to obtain a speaker."

5240. "Each of us here," the speaker began, "has a job to do in this hour. Mine is to talk and yours is to listen. My hope is that you will not finish your job before I finish mine."

—Chaplain Carl W. McGeehon

5241. I always dislike using a manuscript in making a speech. It's like courting a girl through a picket fence. Everything that is said can be heard, but there isn't much contact.

—Eugene Smith

5242. Any man who makes a speech more than six times a year is bound to repeat himself, not because he has little to say, but because he wants applause and the old stuff gets it.

—William Feather

5243. *Response to a flattering introduction:* "I'm sorry my mother isn't here. She would have believed all the nice things the chairman said about me in his introduction."

5244. A now-famous speech-maker has been relating his past timidity before audiences by confessing that before he took a course in public speaking he couldn't even lead a group in silent prayer.

5245.

I love a finished speaker,
I really, truly do.
I don't mean one who's polished,
I just mean one who's through.

—Richard Armour

5246. The toastmaster is the connecting link between the speeches. It is his duty, first, to put the audience in a receptive, expectant mood. It is his duty to maintain order—to provide an attentive audience.

5247.

My sympathies lie with the speaker
Whose knees grow suddenly weaker,
When his introducer's lengthy patter
Turns out to be *his* subject matter!

—Ray C. Bandy

5248. The audience expects a speaker to be interesting. There is one sure way to be interesting, and that is to be *interested.* If a man is interested in his subject, and in his audience, the reaction will be in his favor.

5249. As soon as you move one step up from the bottom, your effectiveness depends on your ability to reach others through the spoken or written word. This ability to express oneself is perhaps the most important of all skills a man can possess.

—Peter Bruckner

5250. Oratory has a wholesome function: to chronicle great events and pay memorable tribute to those whose deeds empowered them. But when it is offered as a blueprint for action, oratory can be as ill-timed and untrustworthy as a rich dessert served before a meal.

—ARSENE CHATELET

5251. Former White House Press Secretary James Hagerty discovered a bartender in Paris who can determine the nationality of any customer after two double martinis. The bartender explained:

"A Frenchman will want to make love; a Spaniard will dance; a German will boast; an Italian will sing; an Irishman will fight, and an American will want to make a speech."

5252. The best phrased speaking invitation of the season urged that I come a day before the meeting, or stay a day after, to have time to visit with people. I did just that and enjoyed a wonderful time. The way they put it was this: "We don't want you just to blow in, blow off and blow out!"

—WHEELER MCMILLEN

5253. One day while lecturing to his Shakespeare class, Harvard's famed George Lyman Kittredge accidentally stepped off the platform and fell to the floor. Scrambling to his feet, he observed: "In 40 years of teaching, this is the first time I have ever descended to the level of my audience."

5254. When Dr. Edith Sitwell and her brother, Sir Osbert Sitwell, were in Hollywood, they gave a reading of their poems. Sir Osbert suddenly turned to the audience and asked: "Can you hear me?"

One man answered: "No."

Sir Osbert replied: "Then pay a little more attention."

5255. There is a tendency today to make after-dinner speaking a mere string of anecdotes, most of which may have little to do with the subject or with one another. Even the best stories lose their charm when they are dragged in by the head and shoulders, having no connection with the allotted theme. Relevance as well as brevity is the soul of wit.

—JAMES BRYCE

5256. Boys flying kites haul in their white-wing'd birds:
You can't do that way when you're flying words

"Careful with fire," is good advice we know;
"Careful with words," is ten times doubly
so.
Thoughts unexpressed may sometimes fall
back dead,
But God Himself can't kill them once
they're said!

—WILL CARLETON

5257. An anecdote must never be told for its own sake. Its application to the point in hand must be instantly evident. For that reason, it should generally follow instead of precede the truth it is to enforce. It is a skylight, not a foundation stone. It must be tersely told, leaving as much as possible for the audience to guess, giving only the relevant points.

—*Speaking in Public,* by ARTHUR STEVENS PHELPS (Baker Book House)

5258. A popular speaker once confessed that he never told a funny story to an audience unless he felt sure that the majority of them had heard it before. He said that familiar stories are best for two reasons. First, those who have already heard them feel an inner satisfaction over knowing the "latest" jokes. Second, they feel more comfortable during the telling because they are ready to prove their own sophistication by knowing just when to burst out laughing.

5259. He had delivered the master oration of the conference. When finally the applause had subsided, a cocky young doctor of divinity strolled up to him. "That was a masterful address you delivered, and extemporaneous, too. Yet you must have had some preparation to have done it so well. How long did it take you to prepare it?"

The older man looked gently at the younger man for some time before he replied: "Sixty years, young man, sixty years!"

5260. After the dinner is over,
After the waiters have gone,
After the coffee and mint-drops,
After the very last song;
Then come the speeches and laughter,
And we settle ourselves for a smoke,

In the hope that one of the speakers
Will tell us a really good joke.

—*Anonymous*

5261. Bertrand Russell suffered the tortures of the damned each time he was called upon for a speech until one day he said to himself, "What difference does it really make in the scheme of things if Bertrand Russell makes a good or a poor speech?" It would be of no world-shaking importance. History would go on unchanged. And he says that when he overcame his egotistical concern about being humiliated, his fears left him, and he began to enjoy making speeches—and they were better speeches!

—JOHN DAVIS

5262. A successful businessman took a course in public speaking because he thought it could help rid himself of fear. When he had completed the course, he was disappointed. The old ogre Fear was still with him. He complained to his instructor. "Why, of course your fear has not disappeared!" he said. "And you should be thankful it has not. Don't worry about that. The time to worry is when all fear disappears and you become complacent. It is the complacent speaker that bores his audience."

—ALDEN C. PALMER

5263. If they dare to come out in the open and defend the gold standard as a good thing, we will fight them to the uttermost. Having behind us the producing masses of this nation and the world, supported by the commercial interests, the laboring interests, and the toilers everywhere, we will answer their demand for a gold standard by saying to them: "You will not press down upon the brow of labor this crown of thorns, you shall not crucify mankind upon a cross of gold."

—WILLIAM JENNINGS BRYAN at National Convention of the Democratic Party held in the Coliseum at Chicago, Illinois in July, 1896

Publisher—Publishers—Publishing

5264. Though an angel should write, still 'tis devils must print.
—THOMAS MOORE

5265. Learning hath gained most by those books by which the printers have lost.

—THOMAS FULLER

Punctuality

5266. Punctuality is a fine thing. Particularly if you want to avoid people.

5267. Happy is the man who is always early—if he can stand the loneliness.

5268. The trouble with being punctual is that there's nobody there to appreciate it.

5269. Offbeat timing for starting meetings does wonders for insuring punctuality. A meeting scheduled for 10:04 got off to an earlier start than one scheduled for 10 o'clock. A person who is customarily 15 minutes late for a 3 o'clock appointment usually manages to be on time for a 3:08 appointment.

Punctuation

5270. Woman! Without her, man would be uncivilized.
Woman, without her man, would be uncivilized.

5271. The delegates to the National Conference of Teacher Education and Professional Standards were once asked to punctuate this sentence. See how you make out:

That that is is that that is not is not but that that is not is not that that is nor is that that is that that is not.

Solution: That, that is, is; that, that is not, is not; but that, that is not, is not that that is; nor is that, that is, that that is not.

Well, a lot of teachers had trouble with it, too!

Punishment. See also Crime—Punishment

5272. Man punishes the action, but God the intention.

—*Ancient Proverb*

5273. This, it seems to me, is the most severe punishment—finding out you are wrong!

—WALTER WINCHELL

5274. Society does not punish those who sin, but those who sin and conceal not wisely.

—ELBERT HUBBARD

5275. Every jail is a monument on which is writ in letters of iron that we are still heathens.

—THEODORE PARKER

5276. You improve no man by killing him. A human being without a head or with a broken neck is singularly useless.

—F. TENNYSON JESSE

5277. I would not have children much beaten for their faults, because I would not have them think bodily pain the greatest punishment.

—JOHN LOCKE

5278. Lacking all sense of right and wrong, a child can do nothing which is morally evil, or which merits either punishment or reproof.

—JEAN JACQUES ROUSSEAU

5279. Comedian and former school teacher Sam Levenson has this comment on why parental discipline is ineffective these days: "Today, when a child disobeys his mother, he is sent to his room. When he goes to his room, he has a radio, a television set, a 17-year-old baby sitter—his father didn't have it so good on his honeymoon."

5280. We do not shudder when we think of a man with a broken leg being sent to a hospital, for we know that he will not come out with two broken legs, or, if he has a strained tendon, that he will come out with a compound fracture. Yet that is about what we feel will happen to the morally injured man who is sent to prison.

—THOMAS MOTT OSBORNE

Purpose

5281. Be not simply good—be good for something.

—HENRY DAVID THOREAU

5282. All things come to him who waits—provided he knows what he is waiting for.

—WOODROW WILSON

Quarrel—Quarrels

5283. Quarrels would not last long if the fault was only on one side.

—François de La Rochefoucauld

5284. A quarrel between friends, when made up, adds a new tie to friendship, as experience shows that the callosity formed round a broken bone makes it stronger than before.

—St. Francis de Sales

Quest

5285. The fun is in the search, not the finding. The thrill is in the chase, not the quarry.

5286. To be forever reaching out, to remain unsatisfied, is the key to spiritual progress.

5287. Man's reach is always greater than his grasp, his achievements never equal his aspiration, his successes never equal his attempts, his answers never equal his questions. Such is life. It is true in all fields of organized knowledge.

—Dan C. Shannon

5288. A famous philosopher points out the strange fact that mankind has looked upward in admiration at the stars, forgetting that we are actually living on a star. For this earth of ours is a star. We are standing, walking, riding, sitting, sleeping, with a star underneath us. And that star has all the potentialities of heaven.

—Wilferd A. Peterson

Question—Questions

5289. Judge a man by his questions rather than his answers.

—Voltaire

5290. Just about the time you finally learn all the answers, they change all the questions.

5291. An educated man is one who has finally discovered that there are some questions to which nobody has the answers.

5292. John Randolph evaded difficult questions put to him in Congress by saying, "Sir, that is a question, and I never answer questions."

5293. Man has made some machines that can answer questions provided the facts are previously stored in them, but he will never be able to make a machine that will ask questions. . . . The ability to ask the right question is more than half the battle of finding the right answer.

—Tom Watson, Jr.

Question—Answer

5294. Never answer questions, until you are asked.

5295. The man who is afraid of asking is ashamed of learning.

—*Danish Proverb*

5296. What is more embarrassing than to ask a 30-cent question and have to listen to a 64-dollar answer?

Quota—Quotas

5297. Within us all there are wells of thought and dynamos of energy which are not suspected until emergencies arise. Then oftentimes we find it is comparatively simple to double or treble our former capacities and to amaze ourselves by the results achieved. Quotas, when set up for us by others, are challenges which goad us on to surpass ourselves. The outstanding leaders of every age are those who set up their own quotas and constantly exceed them.

—Thomas J. Watson

Quotation—Quotations

5298. Apt quotations carry conviction.

—William E. Gladstone

5299. Appropriate things are meant to be appropriated.

—Samuel Butler

5300. One must be a wide reader to quote wisely and well.

—A. Bronson Alcott

5301. To be occasionally quoted is the only fame I care for.
—Alexander Smith

5302. By necessity, by proclivity, and by delight, we all quote.
—Ralph Waldo Emerson

5303. I often quote myself. It adds spice to my conversation.
—George Bernard Shaw

5304. Every quotation contributes something to the stability or enlargement of the language.
—Dr. Samuel Johnson

5305. It is the little writer rather than the greater writer who seems never to quote, and the reason is that he is never really doing anything else.
—Havelock Ellis

5306. One couldn't carry on life comfortably without a little blindness to the fact that everything has been said better than we can put it ourselves.
—George Eliot

5307. I have somewhere seen it observed, that we should make the same use of a book that the bee does of a flower; she steals sweets from it, but does not injure it.
—Charles C. Colton

5308. Much of the pleasure derived by the reader from a quotation or allusion is that of recognition—one of the earliest pleasures of which the human mind is susceptible.
—E. E. Kellett

5309. It is generally supposed that where there is no quotation, there will be found most originality. . . . The greater part of our writers, in consequence, have become so original that no one cares to imitate them, and those who never quote, in return are seldom quoted.
—Isaac Disraeli

5310. I believe in the power of important quotations. I always keep a few in my mind to think about. Whenever I need words to cheer me I want the best that can help me. I am never alone. I can always join the best minds of the centuries. In their great thoughts I can find the courage to believe in the best that I can find in myself.
—Elmer G. Letermann

5311. All minds quote. Old and new make the warp and woof of every moment. There is no thread that is not a twist of these two strands. We quote not only books and proverbs, but arts, sciences, religion, customs and laws; nay, we quote temples and houses, tables and chairs, by imitation.

—Ralph Waldo Emerson

5312. Once Coolidge gave the press an "interview"; one after another, reporters asked if he had anything to say about the world situation, prohibition, his coming message to Congress, etc., and one question after another was answered, "No." As the reporters were dismissed, Coolidge warned them: "Don't quote me."

Race Relations

5313. What the Negro wants is what every man has wanted from the beginning of time. It is what the Israelites prayed for in Egypt. It is what brought the Pilgrim Fathers to America. It is what each generation of the Negro leaders have sought. There is nothing mysterious about a person's desire for first class citizenship, nor is it subversive. . . . What the Negro wants far more than to marry a white man's daughter is to live where he chooses, to vote in all elections, to be hired on merit; to join unions, stay in hotels and motels, eat in restaurants, to be admitted to hospitals and clinics, worship in churches, finance new homes and insure his belongings without color restriction. He wants to send his child to the nearest school, playground, park or pool. He wants to drink at a fountain when he is thirsty, to go to the washroom without observing the amenities of race.

—*Ebony Magazine*

5314. In a border state city, desegregating on a grade a year basis, the opening of the fall semester was the fateful day for the second grade. The parents of the one 7-year-old had prepared her for this traumatic experience. With her new notebook, pencils, and lunch-box, she bounced out of the family car that had brought her to school in the crispness of the morning. At 3 o'clock in the warming sun, her mother picked her up. Unwilling to force tension, she chatted about everything else on the ride home. Finally, at the kitchen table with cookies and milk spread out, mother asked the important question: "How did it go in school?"

The answer came sharply: "There was a little Negro girl sitting next to me all day."

The constriction in the mother's throat was like a paralysis. She forced out the next question: "What happened?"

"We were both so scared that we held hands all day."

—LESTER J. WALDMAN

Radio

5315. Medical men say that the radio is useful in certain kinds of deafness. So is deafness in certain kinds of radio.

5316. While the bootblack in the prison barbershop was shining my shoes, I listened to the prison radio grinding out the usual daytime drivel. "How do you like those programs?" I asked.

"You know, sir," said the prisoner, "mosta the time I think they're part of the punishment!"

—RABBI JULIUS A. LEIBERT, *Reader's Digest*

Readiness. See also Preparedness

5317. The day I did not sweep the house there came to it one I did not expect.

—*Old Proverb*

5318. The cat has an acute mind, an inflexible will and a patience almost divine. If the cat wishes to leave the room, he makes no fuss about it, and does not annoy you with vocal importunities; he selects a position near the door.

He knows that opportunities come to those who are ready. He pretends he has dismissed the matter from his mind; but when someone happens to open the door, the cat departs.

—WILLIAM LYON PHELPS

Reading

5319. Few are better than the books they read.

5320. The gossip in a house always decreases as the library increases.

5321. Reading a poor book is an opportunity lost of reading a good one.

5322. To read means to borrow; to create out of one's readings is paying off one's debts.

—GEORG CHRISTOPH LICHTENBERG

5323. If one cannot enjoy reading a book over and over again, there is no use in reading it at all.

—OSCAR WILDE

5324. Nowadays it isn't the little red schoolhouse one comes upon, but the little-read schoolboy.

—CY N. PEACE

5325. The love of reading enables a man to exchange the wearisome hours of life which come to everyone for hours of delight.

—CHARLES DE SECONDAT MONTESQUIEU

5326. You may never read again the books you enjoy, but you are never quite satisfied when you are away from them.

—HOLBROOK JACKSON

5327. "Reading maketh a full man," wrote Bacon, but he should have added that what he reads will determine whether he will be full of wisdom or nonsense.

5328. Whilst you stand deliberating which book your son shall read first, another boy has read both: read anything five hours a day, and you will soon be learned.

—DR. SAMUEL JOHNSON

5329. Reading is magic. It enables us to experience and ponder the past. It helps us to live more happily and wisely in the present. And it permits us to cope with the future.

5330. The intense desire for reading always creates opportunities for reading. The oft-repeated statement, "I simply have no time to read," is an absurdity.

—THOMAS DREIER

5331. To destroy the Western tradition of independent thought it is not necessary to burn the books. All we have to do is to leave them unread for a couple of generations.

—ROBERT M. HUTCHINS

5332. To read solely for information or to know the author's point of view is to miss the point of reading. Read to know yourself. You can only get out of a book what is in yourself.

—Holbrook Jackson

5333. Most men have learned to read to serve a paltry convenience, as they have learned to cipher in order to keep accounts and not be cheated in trade; but of reading as a noble intellectual exercise they know little or nothing.

—Henry David Thoreau

5334. To be well informed, one must read quickly a great number of merely instructive books. To be cultivated, one must read slowly and with a lingering appreciation the comparatively few books that have been written by men who lived, thought, and felt with style.

—Aldous Huxley

5335. As life goes on most people tend to read less fiction. . . . It is only while one is young that one is very curious about oneself, how one is likely to feel in certain circumstances, or how different sorts of people are likely to behave, and it is this kind of curiosity which the novelist chiefly satisfies.

—Desmond MacCarthy

5336. Anthony Trollope, nineteenth century English novelist, believed that the habit of reading lasts when all other pleasures fade. "It will be there to support you when all other resources are gone. It will be present to you when the energies of the body have fallen away from you. It will make your hours pleasant to you as long as you live."

5337. Reading books in one's youth is like looking at the moon through a crevice; reading books in middle age is like looking at the moon in one's courtyard; and reading books in old age is like looking at the moon on an open terrace. This is because the depth of benefits of reading varies in proportion to the depth of one's own experience.

—Chang Ch'ao

5338. There's a story about a wise old college president who, delivering a graduation address, said: "Gentlemen, most of you will marry. Be kind to your wives. Be patient with them. When you are going out together, do not fret if she is not ready on time. Keep a good book handy. Read it while you wait. And, gentlemen, I assure you that you will be astonished at the amount of information you will acquire."

Reason—Reasons

5339. There's a mighty big difference between good, sound reasons and reasons that sound good.

—Burton Hillis

5340. In giving your judgment, give it boldly and with decision, but never give a reason for it; your judgment, nine times out of ten, will be right, because it is founded on experience; but your reason will probably be wrong, being only an afterthought.

—George Whitefield

Recognition

5341. A work of real merit finds favor at last.

—Amos Bronson Alcott

5342. The hardest thing each generation has to do is to recognize the genius of its own day. We accept the work of artists of a previous generation, although the work was often unacceptable at that time.

—Frayn Utley

Recreation

5343. Men tire themselves in pursuit of rest.

—Laurence Sterne

5344. If all the year were playing holidays,
To sport would be as tedious as to work.

—William Shakespeare

5345. As manpower is replaced by other sources of energy the entire conception of recreation shifts. What we do with these new leisure hours will determine the value of our culture.

—Morris L. Ernst

5346. Of all the joys of life which may fairly come under the heading of recreation there is nothing more great, more refreshing, more beneficial in the widest sense of the word than a real love of the beauty of the world.

—Sir Edward Grey

5347. Recreation for any individual should be whatever makes a new man of him, recreates him, takes his mind off the routine job, or broadens his mental or spiritual horizons. Many persons make recreation their chief form of relaxation, but recreation need not be entirely physical. It can be found in music, arts and crafts and even in good conversation.

—Fred V. Hein

5348. The right kind of recreation is almost as essential to success as the right kind of education. It should re-create, rejuvenate and re-invigorate the brain cells as well as the red corpuscles of the blood. Books, walks, music, the theater, athletics, travel, automobiling, gardening, friends, conversation—each and all in their proper place can supply ideal recreation. Recreation need not mean, should not mean, rusting. It should mean renewing one's vital forces, getting a fresh outlook and a fresh hold of life, imbibing fresh knowledge, refilling the wellsprings of joy. Recreation is the salt which gives life its flavor.

—B. C. Forbes

Rectitude

5349. A man must stand erect, not be kept erect by others.

—Marcus Aurelius

5350. Keep true, never be ashamed of doing right; decide on what you think is right, and stick to it.

—George Eliot

Reform—Reforms

5351. A reform is a correction of abuses; a revolution is a transfer of power.

—Edward George Bulwer-Lytton

5352. A reformer is a guy who rides through a sewer in a glass-bottomed boat.

—James J. Walker

5353. In our haste to deal with the things which are wrong, let us not upset the things which are right.

5354. The world is to be cleaned by somebody and you are not called of God if you are ashamed to scour and scrub.

—Henry Ward Beecher

5355. Many modern (so-called) Reformers are just as dangerous as the physician who makes a wrong diagnosis of a disease. They see the trouble from without and prescribe external remedies, while the cause of the trouble is within and needs internal treatment.

—William J. H. Boetcker

Regret

5356. The follies a man regrets most are the ones he didn't commit when he could.

5357. Regret is to human beings what mud is to hogs—it's good only for wallowing in.

—Oren Arnold

5358. Don't be afraid to say you are sorry. Nobody has gotten indigestion yet from eating his words.

5359. Regret is an appalling waste of energy. You can't build on it; it's only good for wallowing in.

—Katherine Mansfield

5360. Do not permit yourself futile regret. "If I had only known!" is the morbid complaint of a weak spirit; "I did not know," is the frank confession of a strong one.

—Alice Wellington Rollins

Relative—Relatives

5361. Success is a wonderul thing. You meet such interesting relatives.

5362. There is nothing more distant than a distant relative who has money.

5363. Everyone could use a rich and generous relative—and those who have them usually do.

5364. Never worry about when your ship will come in; your relatives will be around to let you know in time to help you dock.

—O. A. Battista

5365. Money is responsible for many paradoxes, not the least of which is the wealthy relative who is at once both distant and close.

Relaxation

5366. The mind suffers from want of relaxation as the bow, which is constantly strung, loses its vigor.

5367. It is doing some service to humanity to amuse innocently; and they know very little of society who think we can bear to be always employed, either in duties or meditations, without any relaxation.

—Sir Philip Sidney

5368. While it is wise to concentrate upon getting on in the world in the first half of one's life, it is a tragic mistake not to begin thereafter to indulge in a rational amount of rest and enjoyment. Just as one has to learn how to work successfully, one must learn how to play successfully. Many men do not realize this until too late. Then they find that the leisure to which they had looked forward to for many years fails to yield the pleasure they had expected and brings them nothing but lonesomeness and disillusionment. The best plan is to lighten the daily load as one grows older by delegating responsibility to trained associates, but not to retire completely. Neither does all work and no play nor all play and no work make for a happy ending of one's days.

—B. C. Forbes

Religion

5369. Religion is not an end, but a means.

—Johann Wolfgang von Goethe

5370. God looks to pure hands, not full ones.

—Publilius Syrus

5371. Without religion, educated men become devils.

—*Old Proverb*

5372. Those who use religion as a cloak often catch cold.

5373. A man has no more religion than he acts out in his life.

—Henry Ward Beecher

5374. A man devoid of religion, is like a horse without a bridle.

—*From the Latin*

5375. True religion is the life we live; not the creed we profess.

—J. F. Wright

5376. Religion is meant to be bread for daily use, not cake for special occasions.

5377. The more religion a man has the less he will affect the air of a saint.

5378. Religion belongs to the place of business as well as to the church.

—Henry Ward Beecher

5379. Religion may be learned on Sunday, but it is lived in the weekday's work.

—John Doughty

5380. Too many spend too much time arguing about the religion they don't have.

5381. Art is more God-like than science. Science discovers—Art creates.

—Ovid

5382. There is something lacking in a religion which the summer-time can destroy.

5383. Measure not men by Sundays, without regarding what they do all the week after.

—Thomas Fuller

5384. We can never be the better for our religion if our neighbor is the worse for it.

—William Penn

5385. Science and religion no more contradict one another than light and electricity.

—Rev. William Hiram Foulkes

5386. There is no religion where man does not do something about it. Man must act out his belief.

—George Foot Moore

5387. Amusements will help you forget things; religion will help you surmount things.

5388. Men of sense are really all of one religion. But men of sense never tell what it is.

—ANTHONY A. COOPER (Earl of Shaftesbury)

5389. We have just enough religion to make us hate, but not enough to make us love, one another.

—JONATHAN SWIFT

5390. The torch of religion may be lit in church, but it does its burning in the shop and on the street.

—EUGENE P. BERTIN

5391. A religion that is small enough for our understanding would not be large enough for our needs.

—ARTHUR BALFOUR

5392. The vital point about religion, after all, is not what you think about it, but what you do about it.

—SIR WILFRED GRENFELL

5393. Churches come and go, but there has ever been but one religion. The only religion is conscience in action.

—HENRY DEMAREST LLOYD

5394. A man who feels that his religion is a slavery has not begun to comprehend the real nature of religion.

—J. G. HOLLAND

5395. Religion presents few difficulties to the humble man, many to the proud, insuperable ones to the vain.

—JULIUS AND AUGUSTUS HARE

5396. Religion in its most abstract expression may be defined as the affirmation that all is *not* vanity.

—WILLIAM JAMES

5397. It is erroneous to think that religion consists altogether in contributing to the support of your pastor.

—*Keystones of Thought,* by AUSTIN O'MALLEY (The Devin-Adair Co.)

5398. Religion is not an escape from life. It IS life. It is not an abstraction. It is a career.

5399. Religion is not so much man's attempt to know God as his attempt to know himself.

—Stuart Holroyd

5400. There is but one God—is it Allah or Jehovah? The palm-tree is sometimes called a date-tree, but there is only one tree.

—Benjamin Disraeli

5401. Religion without morality is a tree without fruits; morality without religion is a tree without roots.

—Rev. Harold W. Ruopp

5402. The problem of religion is to induce people to practice in their daily lives what they say in church they believe.

5403. People pay very little attention to what you say about your religion—they're busy watching what you do about it.

5404. The writers against religion, whilst they oppose every system, are wisely careful never to set up any of their own.

—Edmund Burke

5405. Those whom religion separates are not religious; all worships are the radii of a circle whose center is the Eternal One.

5406. It were better to be of no church than to be bitter for any. To be furious in religion is to be irreligiously religious.

—William Penn

5407. Religion cannot pass away. The burning of a little straw may hide the stars of the sky; but the stars are there, and will reappear.

—Thomas Carlyle

5408. Granted that life is tragic to the marrow, it seems the proper function of religion is to make us accept and serve in that tragedy.

—Robert Louis Stevenson

5409. The trouble with some of us is that we have been inoculated with small doses of Christianity which keep us from catching the real thing.

—Dr. Leslie D. Weatherhead

5410. Religion is the first thing and the last thing, and until a man has found God, and been found by God, he begins at no beginning, he works to no end.

—Herbert George Wells

5411. A civil ruler dabbling in religion is as reprehensible as a clergyman dabbling in politics. Both render themselves odious as well as ridiculous.

—James Cardinal Gibbons

5412. The test of our religion is whether it fits us to meet emergencies. A man has no more character than he can command in a time of crisis.

—Ralph W. Sockman

5413. Religion . . . is the forerunner of international law; because it alone can create the international spirit, the international obligation.

—William Ernest Hocking

5414. There is nothing wanting to make all rational and disinterested people in the world of one religion, but that they should talk together every day.

—Alexander Pope

5415. It is the function of religion to store up the living water of the ages of inspiration in order to quench the thirst of later eras of spiritual drought.

—Rabbi Solomon B. Freehof

5416. The real religion of the world comes from women much more than from men—from mothers most of all, who carry the key of our souls in their bosoms.

—Dr. Oliver Wendell Holmes

5417. In some respects the world is in the same situation that it was in after the fall of the Roman empire. There is an even greater need for a religious revival now because paganism has become sophisticated.

—Barbara Ward

5418. Religion is the answer to that cry of reason which nothing can silence; that aspiration of the soul which no created thing can meet; of that want of the heart which all creation cannot supply.

—Isaac Thomas Hecker

5419. There are three modes of bearing the ills of life; by indifference, which is the most common; by philosophy, which is the most ostentatious; and by religion, which is the most effectual.

—Charles C. Colton

5420. The Church alone can bring about the spiritual revival and the moral regeneration this world needs before there can be permanent peace and sound economic recovery, and to this end we do not need new laws, but a new spirit.

—WILLIAM J. H. BOETCKER

5421. Just as two painters painting the same landscape will give dissimilar views of it, so two minds contemplating God will take of Him only what each is fitted to receive. Water poured into differently colored glasses will take on the color of the cup which it fills, even though it be the selfsame water in them all.

—BASIL KING

5422. Business is religion, and religion is business. The man who does not make a business of his religion has a religious life of no force, and the man who does not make a religion of his business has a business life of no character.

—MALTBIE BABCOCK

5423. The word religion means by derivation: restriction or obligation. Obligation to do, obligation to avoid. This is the negative system of some. Scrupulous avoidance of evil, rather than positive and free pursuit of good or excellence.

—FREDERICK WILLIAM ROBERTSON

5424. What the world craves today is a more spiritual and less formal religion. To the man or woman facing death, great conflict, the big problems of human life, the forms of religion are of minor concern, while the spirit of religion is a desperately needed source of inspiration, comfort and strength.

—JOHN D. ROCKEFELLER, JR.

5425. As all who frequent any place of public worship, however they may differ from the doctrines there delivered, are expected to comport themselves with seriousness and gravity, so in religious controversies, ridicule ought never to be resorted to on either side.

—CHARLES C. COLTON

5426. One's religion must be measured by what it enables him to do. There is no other way to judge the value of religion except by the fruit it produces, the character it develops, the attitudes it creates, and the actions it motivates—in short, by what it does. True religion is known by its fruits.

5427. The fact is that religion is not merely a personal relationship with God but also a joint enterprise conducted by human beings and institutionalized over the centuries. . . . The sociology of religion, in short, is not theology, and it does not pretend to be. If everyone would try to get these facts straight, we would all benefit.

—JOSEPH H. FICHTER

5428. Religion is man's quest for assurance that he can live by faith and love while doubt and fear lay siege to his heart. It is his attempt to resolve inward dilemma by organizing his relation with the world in a way that will serve his need for security and fulfillment. It is the search for what is enduring in time and eternity.

—OREN HULING BAKER, *Human Nature Under God* (Association Press)

5429. Human life may be reverently compared to an opera. God is the author of the music, and He gives each person the part he is to take. Religion is simply the drill-master, who enjoins upon us the necessity of strictly following the score, and insists that we cannot make changes in it without injuring the unity of the production.

—GEORGE H. HEPWORTH

5430. What the church should be telling the worker is that the first demand religion makes on him is that he should be a good workman. If he is a carpenter he should be a competent carpenter. Church by all means on Sundays—but what is the use of church if at the very center of life a man defrauds his neighbor and insults God by poor craftsmanship.

—DWIGHT D. EISENHOWER

5431. Religion is intended as a blessing to mankind, a bond between all the creatures of God. They should be as brothers and sisters, not because they have the same human parents, but because they are all children of one Father, of him who is enthroned in the heavens above. Brothers and sisters must love one another, help, strengthen, and support one another.

—RADEN ADJENG KARTINI

5432. Religion holds the solution to all problems of human relationship, whether they are between parents and children or nation and nation. Sooner or later, man has always had to decide whether he worships his own power or the power of God. When threats force him to look at the limitations of his human power, he's often ready to seek his spiritual one. What we need is patience and awe of God's plan in human history!

—*Attributed to* Arnold Toynbee

5433. Religion must be used in furthering great works of justice and reform. It must be used to establish right relations between different groups of men, and thus to make a reality of brotherhood. It must be used to abolish poverty, the breeding ground of all misery and crime, by distributing equably among men the abundance of the soil. And it must be used to get rid of war and to establish enduring peace. Here is the supreme test of the effectiveness of religion.

—John Haynes Holmes

5434. In his 1939 year-end broadcast to the Empire, soon after the outbreak of World War II, King George VI quoted these reassuring words, written by Minnie Louise Haskins back in 1908: "I said to the man who stood at the gate of the year: 'Give me a light that I may tread safely into the unknown.' And he replied: 'Go out into the darkness and put your hand into the hand of God. That shall be to you better than light and safer than a known way.'"

—*Reader's Digest*

5435. Not long ago I met one of our schoolmasters—a veteran in that high service. "Where in your timetable do you teach religion?" I asked him.

We teach it in arithmetic, by accuracy. We teach it in language, by learning to say what we mean. We teach it in history, by humanity. We teach it in geography, by breadth of mind. We teach it in the playground by fair play. We teach it in kindness to animals, by courtesy to servants, by good manners to one another, and by truthfulness in all things. We teach it by showing the children that we, their elders, are their friends, and not their enemies.

—L. P. Jacks

5436. Instead of a hazy notion as to what religion is, we should recognize that . . . it consists in the effort to employ non-physical means to find . . . more ample satisfactions for the drive for nutrition, the drive for reproduction and the drive for significance. . . .

In its expanded form, the drive for nutrition embraces all means of survival, the drive for reproduction embraces all mental creation as well as physical progeny, and the drive for significance embraces all the various forms of expression. . . .

Perfect conduct depends upon a perfect religion . . . Such a perfect religion must define man's proper relation to all other entities in the universe . . . Perfect relationships can only be determined from a complete knowledge of other men and other entities. Such complete knowledge is not at hand, so consequently there can be no such thing as a complete and perfect religon. Perfection is too much to expect because . . . existence demands new adjustments from time to time.

—John Black

Remorse

5437. We lose time by remorse.

—Frederick William Robertson

5438. Repentance is a second innocence.

—Louis Gabriel Ambroise de Bonald

5439. God speaks to our hearts through the voice of remorse.

—François Joachim de Pierre de Bernis

5440. To be left alone, and face to face with my own crime, had been just retribution.

—Henry Wadsworth Longfellow

Repentance

5441. Not to repent of a fault is to justify it.

—*Old Proverb*

5442. Repentance draws us nearer to the Eternal than sin can separate us from Him.

5443. For making a man repent his sins, there's nothing quite as convincing as catching him.

—G. Norman Collie

5444. Our repentance is not so much regret for the evil we have done, as fear of its consequences to us.

—François de La Rochefoucauld

5445. It is a great deal easier to commit a second sin that it was to commit the first, and a great deal harder to repent of a second than it was to repent of the first.

—Benjamin Whichcote

5446. Repentance hath a purifying power, and every tear is of a cleansing virtue; but these penitential clouds must be still kept dropping; one shower will not suffice; for repentance is not one single action, but a course.

—Robert South

5447. Calamity, war, famine, plague, death, adversity, disease, injury do not necessarily produce repentance. We may become better in a calamity but it does not necessarily make us repent until we confront our own self-righteousness with God's righteousness.

—Fulton J. Sheen

5448. In 1812 an English Quaker was disowned for marrying a Unitarian. It is reported that he was readmitted after having made a declaration to the effect that, though he could not—out of courtesy to his wife—say he repented having married her, he could say that he would not do it again.

—Irvin and Ruth Foley

5449. There are two ways of repenting: One carries us just far enough to make us miserable, and leaves us stuck in the mud of our regrets. The other goes deep enough to be cleansing. It opens our lives to a new power, and sends us forward changed, inwardly made over.

Repetition

5450. A thing is never too often repeated which is never sufficiently learned.

—Seneca

5451. Repetition is a good means of making or keeping impressions vivid, and almost the only means of keeping them unchanged.

—George Santayana

Reputation

5452. A good name keeps its lustre in the dark.

—John Ray

5453. Reputation: character minus what you get caught at.

5454. Never forget, a bad dog with a good name is still a dog.

—Harry William King

5455. Many a man inherits a good reputation, but few can keep it.

5456. What people say behind your back is your standing in the community.

—Ed Howe

5457. If I take care of my character, my reputation will take care of itself.

—Dwight L. Moody

5458. How many people live on the reputation of the reputation they might have made!

—Dr. Oliver Wendell Holmes

5459. No man will ever bring out of the Presidency the reputation which carries him into it.

—Thomas Jefferson

5460. Reputation is what men and women think of us; character is what God and the angels know of us.

—Thomas Paine

5461. A great name is like an eternal epitaph engraved by the admiration of men on the road of time.

—Emile Souvestre

5462. Whatever disgrace we have merited, it is almost always in our power to re-establish our reputation.

—François de La Rochefoucauld

5463. *Young lady, acknowledging an introduction:* "Oh, I've heard so much about you. Now I'd like to hear your side."

—Bill Gold

5464. You can leave a will directing how to handle your money but not your reputation. The public will attend to that.

—B. C. Forbes

5465. There are two modes of establishing our reputation: to be praised by honest men, and to be abused by rogues. It is best, however, to secure the former, because it will invariably be accompanied by the latter.

—Charles C. Colton

5466. The two most precious things on this side the grave are our reputation and our life. But it is to be lamented that the most contemptible whisper may deprive us of the one, and the weakest weapon of the other. A wise man, therefore, will be more anxious to deserve a fair name than to possess it, and this will teach him so to live, as not to be afraid to die.

—Charles C. Colton

Research

5467. Research is to see what everybody else has seen, and think what nobody has thought.

—Dr. Albert Szent-Györgyi

5468. Imperfect knowledge is the parent of doubt; thorough and honest research dispels it.

—Tryon Edwards

5469. No research is ever quite complete. It is the glory of a good bit of work that it opens the way for something still better, and this repeatedly leads to its own eclipse.

—Mervin Gordon

5470. There are no permanent changes because change itself is permanent. It behooves the industrialist to research and the investor to be vigilant.

—Ralph L. Woods

5471. Research is a high-hat word that scares a lot of people. It needn't be. It is rather simple. Essentially it is nothing but a state of mind—a friendly welcoming attitude toward change.

—Charles F. Kettering

5472. The best insurance policy for the future of an industry is research, which will help it to foresee future lines of development, to solve its immediate problems, and to improve and cheapen its products.

—Sir Harold Hartley

Resignation

5473. That which cannot be repaired is not to be regretted.

—DR. SAMUEL JOHNSON

5474. Things cannot always go your way. Learn to accept in silence the minor aggravations, cultivate the gift of taciturnity and consume your own smoke with an extra draught of hard work, so that those about you may not be annoyed with the dust and soot of your complaints.

—SIR WILLIAM OSLER

Resolution—Resolutions

5475. The new leaf you turn is usually the same one turned over again.

5476. A little less impatient with those we deem too slow;
A little less of arrogance because of all we know;
A little more humility, seeing our worth is slight;
We are such trivial candles compared to stars at night!

A little more forgiving and swifter to be kind;
A little more desirous the word of praise to find;
The word of praise to utter and make a heart rejoice—
A little bit more careful to speak with gentle voice.

A little more true eagerness to understand each other;
A little more real striving to help a shipwrecked brother;
A little more high courage to each that must be done;
These be our resolutions—and God help every one.

—*Bible Advocate*

Resourcefulness. See also Ingenuity

5477. The most galling problem harassing a suburbanite was to keep dogs from tearing up his patiently-cultivated lawn. His prominent "Keep Off the Grass" sign wasn't taken seriously by any of the dog owners. Seeking a fresh approach, he erected a small sign on a newly-seeded area. It read: "Protect your dog! Lawn specially treated with poison." Not a dog touched a blade.

5478. If you've ever started to board an airplane and been told that your luggage exceeded the weight limit by a few ounces, you know the feeling of frustration that accompanies your search for something to discard.

Recently, a man in Atlanta solved this problem without any real difficulty when he was informed that his luggage was over the limit by eight ounces. He opened his suitcase, extracted a sizable roll of salami, sliced off half a pound, and calmly ate it before he got on the plane!

5479. When an assistant told C. R. Graham of the Louisville Public Library of certain books that were never read because the subject matter was too difficult, Graham brought all those books together and put them in an attractive display up front under a sign: "Warning—These Books Are Difficult to Read and Require Advanced Knowledge."

Every book on the shelf went into immediate circulation.

—John G. Fuller

5480. A North Carolina woman, eager to attend the State Fair several days, was reluctant to pay the high admission charge and parking fee each time. So she went to the city market and bought a large chrysanthemum for 25 cents which she carried to the fairgrounds and entered as an exhibit. As an exhibitor she received a free pass to the fair for the entire week, plus a sticker which allowed her free parking.

And to cap the week, she won a ribbon and $1 prize for her chrysanthemum.

—Sam Ragan

5481. Despite his father's great wealth, the late John D. Rockefeller, Jr. received but a small weekly allowance when he was a boy and was forced to budget himself strictly. On one occasion, he was invited to a friend's birthday party. He asked his father for an advance with which to buy a gift. The elder John D. would not hear of it.

"You must live within your income," he insisted.

A few days later, Rockefeller, Sr. asked: "What did you do about your friend's birthday gift?"

"I took care of that," said John D., Jr., "I picked a fight with him the day before the party and he took back his invitation."

5482. Quite a lot of people dislike Mondays. During my business career I noticed, too, that certain members of my staff were likely to stay away on Mondays. Apparently they couldn't face that terrible day unless they felt absolutely fit. The sneezes they took to the dance or cinema on Saturday evening would keep them from work on Monday.

But I solved all the difficulties—by changing payday to Monday. What a transformation there was: happy, smiling faces, all present and correct and ready for work—with the pay packet in the pocket on Monday morning.

—Cyril Parry

5483. One man got gold from burned paper. Alton Hall Blackington tells in his book, *More Yankee Yarns,* about what happened to the $15,000,000 in gold aboard the *Kronprinzessin Cecilie* when she sought safety at Bar Harbor when World War I started. Paper was laid on the floors of Pullman cars and the bars of gold placed on it about a foot apart. Cashier Russell H. Britton, of the Bar Harbor American Express office, figured that some of the gold might be rubbed off as the cars jounced along to New York. He collected all the paper on which the bars had lain and had it burned. From this $800 was reclaimed.

5484. On a jet liner late at night the stillness was broken by a pretty girl who had the hiccups. Suddenly a man got up from his seat and grasping the girl's arm, said loudly: "Say, where's my wallet?"

"What?" gasped the girl.

"You heard what I said," snapped the man. "When I picked you up in that nightclub and took you back to my hotel room for a drink, you swiped my wallet and I want it."

"But I never saw you before in my life!" exclaimed the girl, close to tears. Then the man smiled, patted her arm and said gently: "Your hiccups are all gone, I see." The girl's hiccups were gone but she had to call the stewardess for a sedative.

5485. Since you cannot refrain from drinking, why not start a saloon in your own home? Be the only customer and you will not have to buy a license. Give your wife $55 to buy a case of whiskey. There are 240 drinks in a case. Buy all your drinks from your wife at 60 cents a drink and in 12 days (when the case is gone) you wife will have $89 to put in the bank and $55 to buy another case. If you live ten years and continue to buy all your whiskey from your wife and then die in your boots, your widow will have $27,085.47 on deposit . . . enough to bring up your children, pay off the mortgage on the house, marry a decent man and forget she ever knew a bum like you.

5486. During the life of P. T. Barnum's famous old museum in New York there was a memorable day when the population of the city took occasion to visit the strange and interesting place in large numbers. Not only were the numbers large but they were bent upon making a day of it—they brought their lunches. When the ticket sale had to be stopped because of the crowd, poor Barnum was up against a possible loss of patronage. But he solved the problem with typical ingenuity. At the rear of the building there was an exit leading to Ann Street through which, according to actual check, three people had passed during the morning. Barnum rushed to the sign painter; had a flaring oilcloth framed up and decorated with the mystic words: TO THE EGRESS. The old exit sign was taken down and the new one put in its place. And before long the crowds began to wend their way through the door, thinking that an "egress" was some new animal they hadn't seen! To their dismay they found themselves on the street and unable to return, without paying another admission fee!

—*2800 Jokes, Toasts and Anecdotes,* by EDWARD J. CLODE (Grosset & Dunlap)

Responsibility

5487. He who lets the goat be laid on his shoulders is soon after forced to carry the cow.

—*Italian Proverb*

5488. In trying to duck responsibility we have to be careful we are not dodging success.

5489. Let us not shrink from the responsibility which comes down upon the age in which we live.

—ORMSBY M. MITCHELL

5490. It is easy to dodge our responsibilities but we cannot dodge the consequences of dodging our responsibilities.

—JOSIAH CHARLES STAMP

5491. Never shirk from doing anything your business calls you to do.—The man who is above his business, may one day find his business above him.

—Samuel Drew

Restlessness

5492. Show me a thoroughly contented person, and I will show you a useless one.

—Henry Wheeler Shaw

5493. The ideal life is in our blood and never will be lost. Sad will be the day for any man when he becomes contented with the thoughts he is thinking and the deeds he is doing—where there is not forever beating at the doors of his soul some great desire to do something larger which he knows that he was meant and made to do.

—Phillips Brooks

Retirement

5494. A man who has no office to go to is a trial of which you can have no conception.

—George Bernard Shaw

5495. Many people have plenty to live on during their retirement, but nothing to live for.

5496. To retire a man when he is still going strong may literally kill him, for hard, interesting work is the closest thing to an elixir of youth that man has yet discovered.

5497. Before people are 50, retirement seems a happy event. In their 50's they change their ideas and begin to dread it. This is especially true of those in higher-paid prestige jobs. One study of a group of doctors past 65 showed more than 70% still practicing.

—Robert J. Havighurst

5498. Not long after Dr. James Moffatt retired from active service on the faculty of Union Theological Seminary, someone commented on his new title of Professor Emeritus.

"You know what that means?" replied Dr. Moffatt. "It comes from the Latin *e* meaning 'out,' and *meritus* which means 'ought to be.' "

—Luther A. Weigle

5499. At the funeral of a friend who had taught school for years, the priest had many fine things to say about her character, ending on the theme that she is probably carrying on her work in heaven.

The teacher sitting next to me leaned over and snorted into my ear, "Good heavens, don't we *ever* get to quit?"

—E. McGrath, *Reader's Digest*

5500. When the good Lord said to mankind that he must earn his bread by the sweat of his brow, He was not pronouncing a curse but bestowing a blessing. Many a man or woman forced into retirement has discovered idleness isn't always heavenly. The happiest people in the world are those who have useful work to do and the health, energy, and ambition to do it.

5501. It is not just a studied use of words that has led experts in the field of gerontology—the study of the later years of life—to substitute for the word "retirement" the words "change of occupation." This recognizes the fact that man is not made for inactivity. Observers who have watched what happens to active men when they "retire" with no new responsibilities or obligations have been appalled at the changes that this produces in men's health, in their attitudes, in their spiritual responses.

—John Park Lee

5502. We men might as well face the fact that our women will survive us. There are 7,600,000 widows in the United States. Many of them are in a precarious financial position. Some experts tell women that the best way to avoid being widowed is to marry a man five or ten years younger. Some women think they will hold on to their husbands longer if they can persuade them to retire earlier. This is a doubtful solution. The shock of retirement often is quite devastating. Retired men die off because they lose their dominant desire to be active and creative.

—Thomas Dreier

5503. Those who face the issue of retirement squarely, and cross the barrier by decisive action that admits of no doubt as to its finality, enter at once into a new and wonderful promised land. Preparation for the full use of the dividend years is . . . a by-product of the intelligent employment of all the years. Just as prudence requires that out of each pay check something be set aside to meet the economic necessities of the senior period, so later contentment requires that in each working year some new talent be developed, some new interest cultivated, that looks to the future for fulfillment.

—Clarence B. Randall

5504. I don't think time is the same for every man. It depends on what he is doing and what he has to offer. I think if a man is retiring because he is tired of his job that he is headed for misery. Man cannot go someplace and not take himself along. If he could retire from himself that would be fine. My advice would be this: Change—don't retire. Change from a position to something else where you may try to express your forces in another line. To retire to achieve self-indulgence doesn't mean anything.

—David Sarnoff

5505. Think of what the world would have missed had a retirement age, even at 70, been universally enforced.

Gladstone was Prime Minister of England at 83; Benjamin Franklin helped frame the Constitution of the United States at 80; Oliver Wendell Holmes retired from the Supreme Court bench at 91; Henry Ford, when past 80, took up the presidency of the Ford Motor Company for the second time after his son's death; and Amos Alonzo Stagg was named the "Football Man of the Year" at 81.

Dr. Lillien J. Martin learned to drive an automobile when she was 76 years old, and at the same age founded the Old Age Center in San Francisco, where she received aged people not as patients but as students. She continued to direct it until her death at 91.

After the late Dr. Milton J. Rosenau had to retire from Harvard Medical School at 67, he went to the University of North Carolina and built one of the greatest schools of public health in America.

—Wingate M. Johnson

5506. ODE TO RETIREMENT

Old age is golden, I've heard it said,
But sometimes I wonder as I get into bed—
With my ears in a drawer, my teeth in a cup,
My eyes on the table until I wake up.

Ere sleep dims my eyes, I say to myself,
"Is there anything else I should lay on the shelf?"
And I'm happy to say as I close my door,
"My friends are the same, only perhaps even more!"

When I was young, my slippers were red—
I could kick my heels right over my head.
When I grew older, my slippers were blue—
But I still could dance the whole night through.
Now I am old, my slippers are black;
I walk to the store—and puff my way back!

The reason I know my youth is all spent?
My get up and go has got up and went.
But I really don't mind when I think, with a grin,
Of all the grand places my get up has been.

Since I have retired from Life's competition,
I busy myself with complete repetition:
I get up each morning and dust off my wits;
Pick up my paper and read the "Obits."
If my name is missing, I know I'm not dead;
So I eat a good breakfast—and go back to bed.

—Len Ingebrigtsen

Reunion, Class

5507. No man is as important as he sounds at his alumni banquet.

5508. How is it that at college reunions you find that your classmates have got so stout and bald they hardly recognize you?

Revenge

5509. Revenge is the only debt which it is wrong to pay.

5510. It costs more to revenge injuries than to bear them.

—Thomas Wilson

5511. The only kind of revenge which a man of sense need take upon a scoundrel is, by a series of worthy behavior, to force him to admire and esteem his enemy and yet irritate his animosity by declining a reconciliation.

—William Shenstone

Revolution—Revolutions

5512. Inferiors revolt in order that they may be equal, and equals that they may be superior. Such is the state of mind which creates revolutions.

—Aristotle

5513. History records all violent changes as revolutions, while orderly changes are usually called progress, yet both fulfill the same purpose in society's cultural evolution.

—Lumir Victor Mika

5514. Before we put down our bets on a revolutionary movement, we have a right to ask that it, like ours, have the broad goals of freedom and human welfare clearly before it . . . lurch toward these goals with . . . popular enthusiasm and support, and . . . place genuine independence at the top of its scale of values.

—Clinton Rossiter

Reward—Rewards

5515. He that plants thorns must never expect to gather roses.

—Pilpay

5516. For everything you have missed you have gained something else.

—Ralph Waldo Emerson

5517. Seems to me that the highest possible reward for any man's labor is not what he gets for it, but what he becomes by it.

—Brock Bell

5518. The great scientists, as all great men, have not been concerned with fame. The joy of achievement that comes from finding something new in the universe is by far their greatest joy. A great research scientist is constantly discovering new things in his field. This is his reward. He knows how to spend long years in preparation and long hours in investigation, with no thought of public honor or reward.

—William P. King

5519. Eugene Field once ran up a bill of $140 at a Kansas City bar. Unable to pay the bill, he stopped coming to the saloon. This distressed the proprietor, since Field's presence had attracted other customers. The proprietor summoned Field one day and presented him with the bill marked "Paid in full." Field folded the bill into his pocket and leaned solemnly across the bar. "Now isn't it customary," he asked quietly, "for the bartender to set 'em up when a man pays his bill?"

—Debs Myers

5520. An impressive story was recounted several years ago by R. Lee Sharpe of Carrolton, Georgia, and published in *Alabama Baptist:*

"I was just a child," related Mr. Sharpe. "One spring day, father called me to go with him to old man Trussell's blacksmith shop. He had left a rake and a hoe to be repaired. And they were ready, fixed like new. Father handed over a silver dollar for the repairing. But Mr. Trussell refused to take it. 'No,' he said, 'there's no charge for that little job.' But father insisted.

"If I live a thousand years," said Mr. Sharpe, "I'll never forget that great blacksmith's reply. 'Sid,' he said to my father, 'can't you let a man do something—just to stretch his soul?'"

Ridicule

5521. Resort is had to ridicule only when reason is against us.

—THOMAS JEFFERSON

5522. One of the most disconcerting things which pioneers in any field must face is ridicule. And the man with a new idea which is contrary to established patterns of thought must have the courage to face the laughter of the wise ones and to proceed in spite of it.

When Christopher Columbus satisfied himself that the world was round instead of flat, he went to King John of Portugal with his project to reach the East by sailing West. King John was sorely tempted to sponsor Columbus because he could see that success would make Portugal the greatest nation of his time. But one thing held him back. If Columbus were wrong and the world was flat, as most geographers and his own learned advisers contended, then he might become the butt of the world's laughter. In every court of Europe they would tell how he, King John of Portugal, was stupid enough to let a Genoese sailor talk him out of ships and men and supplies to sail off the edge of the earth into nowhere. He could imagine how everyone would laugh at him and the prospect chilled his heart. The fear of being ridiculed was stronger than any confidence inspired by the logic of Columbus. He sent the Genoese sailor away.

In the Spanish Court the wise men laughed, too. But Queen Isabella was not afraid of laughter because her faith was stronger than her fears. Spain sponsored the voyage of Columbus and shared the honors and wealth of a great discovery.

The courage to be laughed at by those who are supposed to know better is the courage that spells success in any pioneering venture.

—*Nuggets*

Right

5523. There is no right way to do a wrong thing.

5524. It is not who is right, but what is right, that is of importance.

—THOMAS HUXLEY

5525. If a man is right, he can afford to go ahead full steam. To be "right" means mainly to be in tune with destiny, and willing to carry on. It does not necessarily mean to be agreeable, nor to be agreed with, nor to be popular; but it does mean to be useful in the purpose which destiny is trying to achieve. If a man is right he need not fear about standing alone. He is not alone. If he seems to be, it is only a test of his mettle and sincerity. Every idea that is right has many silent adherents. Raise your voice and you will hear them coming. Destiny is kind; it never asks a human being to do anything alone.

Risk

5526. Contrary to the commonly accepted belief, it is the risk element in our capitalistic system which produces an economy of security. Risk brings out the ingenuity and resourcefulness which insure the success of enough ventures to keep the economy growing and secure.

—Robert Rawls

5527. There is a calculated risk in everything. There has been a calculated risk in every stage of American development. The nation was built by men who took risks—pioneers who were not afraid of the wilderness, businessmen who were not afraid of failure, scientists who were not afraid of the truth, thinkers who were not afraid of progress, dreamers who were not afraid of action.

—Brooks Atkinson

Romance

5528. A college girl may be poor on history, but great on dates.

—Sarah Vaughan

5529. Faint heart never won fair lady—nor escaped one, either.

5530. Give a man too much rope and he may tie you up in knots.

5531. A young man often falls for the same kind of girl who hurried dear old dad.

—Noel Wical

5532. As the dawn precedes the sun, so acquaintance should precede love.

—Charles Francois Du Bose

5533. The first thing a girl learns at her new job is which men around the office are still single.

5534. There will always be romance in the world, so long as there are young hearts in it.

—Christian Nevelle Bovee

5535. When one is in love one begins by deceiving oneself and one ends by deceiving others. That is what the world calls romance.

—Oscar Wilde

5536. The American may not be a materialist but he has certainly hallowed commercialism, and made of it both a romantic and a moral venture.

—Agnes Repplier

5537. There is a story that when Sarah Bernhardt in her later years lived in an apartment high over Paris an old admirer climbed all the stairs and asked her breathlessly. "Why do you live so high up?" "Dear friend," she replied, "it is the only way I can still make the hearts of men beat faster."

Royalty

5538. The modern king has become a vermiform appendix—useless when quiet, when obtrusive in danger of removal.

5539. Royal personages enjoy two notable advantages over their subjects: their health is in the hands of the most illustrious medicos of the day and their likenesses are taken by the most popular portrait painters. While in the former case their chances of survival are far rosier than they were in Victorian times, in the latter they are infinitely worse.

—Osbert Lancaster

Sacrifice

5540. No man is worth his salt who is not ready at all times to risk his body, to risk his well-being, to risk his life, in a great cause.

—Theodore Roosevelt

5541. My experience of life makes me sure of one truth which I do not try to explain—that the sweetest happiness we ever know, the very wine of human life, comes not from love, but from sacrifice, from the effort to forget ourselves so as to make others happy.

—John Boyle O'Reilly

5542. The great temple in Kyoto is to the Japanese what Westminster Abbey is to the British. It cost $10 million to build and took 17 years. A curious thing there is a big coil of rope in the courtyard before the main entrance. It was used to lift the stones, pillars and beams into position and it is made of human hair. When the men and boys were giving labor for the building, the women and girls wanted to have a part. Hearing the workmen needed a strong rope, thousands of them cut off their hair, plaited it into a rope 300 feet long and 3 inches thick, and gave it to the workmen. They solved their problem by sacrificial love.

—REV. WIL R. JOHNSON

Saintliness

5543. The saints are the sinners who keep on trying.

—ROBERT LOUIS STEVENSON

5544. Patience in calamity, mercy in greatness, fortitude in adversity; these are the self-attained perfections of great saints.

—HITOPODESA

Salary. See also Wages

5545. There is a difference between wanting to get a good salary and wanting to earn a good salary.

5546. Many years ago Arthur Frederick Sheldon, seeking the reason why some men are paid high salaries and others never rise above ordinary day wages, found that the value of a man depends upon the amount of supervision he requires. Men who see needs and supply them without being told or bossed are the ones who climb the heights.

Salesmanship

5547. Cash can buy, but it takes enthusiasm to sell.

5548. A sale is not made until the last dollar is paid.

—JOHN H. PATTERSON

5549. Good listeners generally make more sales than good talkers.

—B. C. HOLWICK

5550. Successful salesmanship is 90% preparation and 10% presentation.

—BERTRAND R. CANFIELD

5551. I am the world's worst salesman, therefore I must make it easy for people to buy.

—F. W. Woolworth

5552. Good salesmen, like good cooks, create an appetite when the buyer doesn't seem hungry.

5553. Selling is a little like hog calling—it isn't the noise you make, it's the appeal in your voice.

5554. What the seller often forgets is that he is more needful to the buyer than the buyer is to him.

5555. It may have ruffled his feathers in the armed forces, but a salesman likes to hear it in peace time: "That's an order!"

—T. Harry Thompson

5556. The old "You can lead a horse to water . . ." adage isn't true in the case of a salesman. He leads his prospect through the steps required to make a sale and closes the deal by asking for an order.

5557. A good product and a poor salesman mean disappointing sales; a poor product and a good salesman mean disappointed customers; but a good product and a good salesman mean both satisfying sales and satisfied customers.

5558. Every product has its greatest appeal when presented properly to the customer by a salesman who knows about the product, who knows how to present it, who knows how to romanticize—if you please—to dramatize the story back of it.

—Glen R. Fouche

5559. Creating the desire to buy is one of the most important steps in preserving our prosperity. The productive capacities of our factories, farms and mines are meaningless statistics unless the urge to own is aroused in the hearts of the people.

5560. A sense of order is as much a part of female nature as an urge for bargains. One grocer disarranges displays of items he wants to push, so it looks as if they had fallen. Women automatically reach out to set the cans straight. They look at the merchandise and they buy.

5561. Actually there are only four primary sales appeals to persuade others to action. They are the four S's: Sex (to make a favorable impression on the other sex); Snob (to keep up with the Joneses); Self (to improve one's status in life); Soul (to be at peace with God).

5562. Salesmanship consists of having the goods; being enthusiastic about them; telling your story to the customer or prospect sincerely and in the fewest possible words; feeling deep down inside that you are truly rendering him a service rather than merely being interested only in getting his money.

—Jerry Fleishman

5563. There is a creed that every salesman who succeeds lives up to. It is simple and brief—and it works. Here it is:

Believe first in what you sell.
Believe your prospect will profit by it.
Believe in the firm back of you.

—George J. Barnes

5564. Personal magnetism is a mixture of rugged honesty, pulsating energy, and self-organized intelligence. I believe, absolutely, that truth is the strongest and most powerful weapon a man can use, whether he is fighting for a reform or fighting for a sale.

—Arthur Dunn

5565. The salesman who only had to wait around until customers came in to buy did not learn how to get out and interest prospects who were indifferent about buying. During periods of easy sales, such men do enjoy the prosperity of boom times, but they are spoiled for the time when prospects have to be sought out and sold.

5566. Modern business requires that its salesmen be businessmen in the best sense of the word—men who know the ins and outs of the product or service they are selling . . . men who can make an intelligent and effective presentation . . . and most of all, men who have the modern concept of service to the customer.

—Hugh W. Coburn

5567. In every walk of life there are times when it is best to use few words and be a good listener. Sales people especially would be wise to become sphinx-like whenever a customer shows a disposition to talk. To do otherwise loses a chance to find out what the customer is thinking. Knowing that, the sales person has a better opportunity to qualify the customer. Letting the customer talk is good sales strategy.

5568. To write books is easy; it requires only pen and ink and the ever-patient paper. To print books is a little more difficult, because genius so often rejoices in illegible handwriting. To read books is more difficult still, because of the tendency to go to sleep. But the most difficult task of all that a mortal man can embark upon is to sell a book.

—STANLEY UNWIN (paraphrased from the German of FELIX DAHN), *The Truth About Publishing* (George Allen & Unwin, Ltd., London and Macmillan Co., New York)

5569. A life insurance agent had called on an important businessman time after time without being able to see him. Finally one late afternoon the salesman was admitted. "You ought to feel highly honored," the executive told him. "I never see salesmen. Do you know that today alone, for example, I have refused to see seven insurance agents?"

"I know, sir," replied the salesman brightly. "I was them."

5570. Many of the most successful Japanese businessmen of the last century would trade only with salesmen who first submitted their horoscopes for study to the firm's astrological consultant.

A deal was closed only if the latter approved. If the consultant didn't like the horoscope, no offer of any sort was generous enough to induce the potential purchaser to change his mind.

5571. Once upon a time practically every salesman used to have drilled into him the lesson that successful selling meant pounding away at the customer insistently, continually, and loudly. Smart dealers have decided for themselves that the "Hard Sell" is obsolete. The customer must be convinced rather than pressured. They base their sell on knowledge of their customers' needs and their customer opportunities for productive use of the things they have to offer.

5572. Salesmanship has been spelled out by R. C. Reager, director of speech and debate, Rutgers University. His story:

Say it well, in short sentences, with sincerity and a smile.
Think it through from the audience point of view.
Omit the negative, avoid apologies.
Respect the individual, and use the
Yes technique, say "yes" three times before saying "no" once.

5573. The young sergeant was passing out apricots in small paper dishes to the chow line. He decided to experiment. He asked the next few men as they came by, "You don't want any apricots, do you?" and 90% said, "No." Then he tried a more positive approach: "You *do* want apricots, don't you?" Approximately 50% answered, "Uh . . . yeah, I'll take some." The sergeant decided to test another well-known selling technique, and started asking, "One dish of apricots, or two?" And in spite of the fact that soldiers don't like Army apricots, 40% took two dishes, and 50% took one!

5574. The best sales talk consists of a sequence of ideas organized to accomplish the following essential objectives of the interview:

1. To open wide the prospect's ears—to sell an interview under favorable circumstances;
2. To open wide the prospect's eyes—to fix a problem so clearly that he cannot help but see it;
3. To open the prospect's mouth—to get him talking so that he will furnish the facts without which the problem cannot be fixed;
4. To open up mental roadblocks—to clear away objections;
5. To open up the prospect's check-book—to close the sale.

5575. The salesman's best sale is that one in which he first sold himself. Thereafter it is only a matter of time, or merit, that a sale of the product offered is completed. We always buy our friends. Not in any material sense—we pay in pleasantness, sincerity, warmth of heart or an inspiring personality.

These are things that are not matched in mere money measure. They are of the quality of people—something of finer design and workmanship than the most exquisite spun wool, or even threads of gold!

—George Matthew Adams

5576. Too many salesmen today do not really know their business. You may kid yourself for a while, but when you don't know the answers, dwindling self-confidence and excuse-making start taking over. Then fear gains the upper hand. For example, if a new salesman is afraid to call on a prospect, it is usually for one of two reasons: (1) He lacks understanding of people and their problems, and/or (2) he lacks knowledge of his own product. Such a situation creates the very best kind of opening for a competitor who knows both!

5577. It is rumored that a large corporation has an idea that will go far toward ending whatever business recession we may be going through. It seems that the word "salesmanship" has lost the zip and stature it once had. This corporation has employed a classicist to come up with a new word to replace it. Two leading candidates are said to be "eupriatics," which means good buying, and "eupoletics," which means good selling. Instead of a salesman dawdling around waiting for a customer, a eupoletic will soon go out after a eupriatic. And when enough eupoletics get together with enough eupriatics, business will hum.

—*Nuggets*

5578. Should a salesman pester a prospect? Every salesman is automatically a pest. He calls on prospective customers, he tries hard to sell them something. He puts over answers to all their arguments. He tries to prove how wrong his listeners are.

If the prospect says "No," then the salesman pesters him again and again.

Yes—the salesman is a pest—but he knows how to pester in a polite way. He knows how to force his way into a buyer's office, to make it appear as if he had been specially invited.

Yes—the salesman is a pest. The art of pestering a prospective customer, if properly put over, is profitable salesmanship.

5579. A sale is half made when a customer is greeted with a smile. When prices, quality and a lot of other things are forgotten, people still remember a smile.

The men who figure out psychological reactions tell us the most important part of a sale is the first ten minutes after a customer enters a place of business. He is either well impressed or poorly impressed. If the place impresses him as a refrigerator, he, too, is cold and unresponsive. To a large extent he is guided by the reception given him.

In the employes' rest room of a store I noticed a sign reading, "You are never fully dressed until you wear a smile." There's a lot of truth in that one.

—Don Ross

5580. A professor once said that the trouble with the distribution field is that prices are too high, and that if companies would only step up their mass production, prices would become lower. Then, everybody could buy and business would be good.

Too many people think like the professor—placing the cart before the horse. The fact is that excessive manufacturing capacity will develop only into a sizable management headache.

The salesman, the professional salesman, is the solution to this headache. If conditions get tough, he knows how to intensify his selling. If buyers are on the fence, he knows how to help them climb off without getting caught on the barbs.

5581. His boss sent him to a strange market expecting orders. The boss got no orders. He got alibis. He went in person to find out why, to salvage a promising salesman if he could. And he could when he found the trouble. The salesman hadn't mastered the simple technique of getting the right kind of interviews. He wasn't getting in. So he wasn't having anyone to whom to tell his story. How do you get interviews?

It isn't hard to get interviews. Here are some tricks of the best salesmen. Rely on curiosity as much as you can; do not deceive but don't give your whole story when asking for an interview. Be positive, expect success. Remember it is better to ask for odd-hours interviews rather than on the hour and half hour. This suggests that you are a respecter of time. Practice your story until it sounds plausible.

—Emille Raux

5582. The first job Harvey Firestone had on the road was for a man who manufactured patent medicines and flavoring extracts. The future rubber magnate was sent to sell in small towns in Ohio.

After he had registered rather proudly at the hotel in a place called Apple Creek, he got up courage to call on storekeepers.

He walked around the little town two or three times to steady his nerves. Finally he picked out the smallest store. From there he went from one small store to another without making a sale.

Then, probably because he was a bit angry, he went to the biggest store. It was right there he learned something valuable. It was there he made his first sale.

What he learned was that the proprietors of the little stores hadn't learned how to listen and usually disliked change.

The boss of the big store was on the lookout for anything that would help increase his profits. He listened to salesmen with an open mind.

After that, Mr. Firestone went after the biggest prospects first.

5583. THE SALESMAN

He works alone among outsiders,
yet he belongs to a team.
He produces nothing, yet he greatly
increases production.
He employs no one, yet he
prevents unemployment.

He is not supervised, yet he is
responsible for results.
He influences people over whom
he has no authority.
He does much to raise the
standard of living.
He is a maker of better
balance sheets.
He is the man who sends in orders.
He is the salesman.

—*Anonymous*

5584. A small businessman was in trouble with his sales. He had confidence in his products, was reasonably sure his prices were fair, and he had a large number of salesmen assigned to what should be productive territory. He decided to call in an expert to give him an outsider's viewpoint.

After he had gone over his plans and problems, the businessman took the sales expert to a map on the wall and showed him brightly colored pins struck wherever he had a salesman. Looking at the expert, he asked, "Now for a starter what is the first thing we should do?"

"Well," replied the expert, "the first thing is to take those pins out of the map and stick them in the salesmen."

5585. A WORKABLE SALESMAN'S CREED

I believe in the goods I am selling, in the firm I am working for and in my ability to get "results."

I believe that honest goods can be sold to honest men by honest methods.

I believe in working not waiting, in laughing not weeping, in boosting not knocking, and in the pleasure of selling goods.

I believe that a man gets what he goes after, that one order today is worth two orders tomorrow, and that no man is down-and-out until he has lost faith in himself.

I believe in today and the work I am doing, in tomorrow and the work I hope to do and in the sure reward which the future holds.

I believe in courtesy, in kindness, in generosity, in good cheer, in friendship and honest competition.

I believe there is an order somewhere for every man ready to take one.

I believe I'm ready—right now!

—Edwin Oscood Grover

5586. "DO's AND "DON'Ts" IN ADVERTISING

Don't try to cram all your advertising effort into a few big "blasts." Frequency is usually more important than volume.

Don't let your advertising scream and boast and pound at the prospect. The "soft sell," oft repeated, gets better results.

Don't permit clichés, exaggerated stock expressions and stereotypes.

Don't go in for large areas of black ink in printed ads.

Don't indulge in even a touch of half-truth.

Don't try to say too much.

Do your best to make your advertising good to look at or easy to listen to. This does not necessarily mean fancy art work in printed media. A New York retail men's store is famous for its newspaper advertisements that contain nothing but type.

Do try to make your ads interesting and attention getting.

Do remember that every ad is a selling message. It should contain the same persuasive elements you would use if you were talking to a good prospect in your own establishment. Good ads must influence the prospect; and "influence," by definition, is the act of producing a result without apparent force.

—*Sales Talk*

5587. CREED OF A MODERN SALESMAN

I believe that an ounce of fact is worth a ton of ballyhoo;

I believe that the day of desk-thumping is over and that a big idea is more important than a big fist;

I believe in the abolishment of bunk, hokum and black magic;

I believe that funny stories are passé and that the foundation of every sale is a straightforward presentation of what my product will do for my prospect;

I believe that the Go-Giver will surpass the man who is interested only in Go-Getting;

I believe that quality is a greater selling point than price;

I believe that pleased customers are my greatest asset;

I believe in the constructive force of creative thinking;

I believe that a loud voice is taboo and that low words are charged with sincerity and strength;

I believe that listening is more important than talking;

I believe that when I knock a competitor I block my own progress;

I believe that the confidence of a prospect or customer is a sacred trust that never should be violated;

I believe that I must sell myself before I can sell others;

I believe in the gospel of courage, confidence and good cheer;

I believe in the radiant power of a smile;
I believe in the victorious mental attitude;
I believe in shaves, shoeshines, haircuts and clean shirts;
I believe that salesmen are creators of prosperity, progress and happiness, and I am proud to list my name among those who sell;
I believe in old-fashioned hard work;
I believe in keeping my chin up, my head high and my enthusiasm keen;
I believe that my success is up to me.

—*The Art of Getting Along*, by WILFERD A. PETERSON (Harmony Press)

Santa Claus

5588. Christmas is the time of year when every contract between child and parent has a Santa clause in it.

5589. Santa enters through a hole in the chimney and leaves through a hole in the pocket.

5590. One of these days we expect to see this sign in a department store: "Five Santa Clauses. No Waiting."

5591. Just to prove Santa Clause never lets a fellow down: I know a boy who asked for a soldier suit, and fifteen years later he got it.

5592. A youngster is growing up when he finds that the opinions of the department store Santa Claus do not necessarily reflect those of his parents.

5593. Probably the most superior smile in the world is registered by a small boy who has found out that there is no Santa Claus, and whose little sister hasn't.

—DAN BENNETT

Sarcasm

5594. Sarcasm is an insult in dress suit.

5595. It is better to sacrifice one's love of sarcasm than to indulge it at the expense of a friend.

Satiety

5596. Nothing is enough for the man to whom enough is too little.

—Epicurus

5597. A woman is a well-served table, that one sees with different eyes before and after the meal.

—*French Saying*

Satire

5598. Satire is the soured milk of human kindness.

—Alfred North Whitehead

5599. Men are satirical from vanity more often than from malice.

—François de La Rochefoucauld

5600. Lampoons and satires, that are written with wit and spirit, are like poisoned darts, which not only inflict a wound, but make it incurable.

—Joseph Addison

Saving—Savings. See also Thrift

5601. The reason that so many people find it hard to accumulate money for future needs is that they put aside for tomorrow what little they have left from today's spending. The secret of successful saving is to put aside first what is to be saved and to spend what is left.

5602. There is a difference between *saving* and *hoarding.* Saving is putting aside small amounts of money (or things) at intervals in an effort to accumulate a large enough amount to use purposely. Hoarding is hiding money (or things) out of an unreasonable fear that there may be a shortage sometime in the future. Saving builds prosperity; hoarding destroys it.

Scandal

5603. Scandal and failure make news—only success makes history.

5604. Scandal is a 50–50 proposition—50 per cent of the people take pleasure in inventing it and the other 50 per cent in believing it.

5605. I never listen to calumnies, because if they are untrue, I run the risk of being deceived, and if they are true, of hating persons not worth thinking about.

—CHARLES DE SECONDAT DE MONTESQUIEU

Science

5606. The science of today is the technology of tomorrow.

—EDWARD TELLER

5607. Give a scientist an inch and he will take 2.54 centimeters.

—FRANKLIN P. JONES

5608. Science moves, but slowly, slowly, creeping on from point to point.

—ALFRED LORD TENNYSON

5609. Even in science we can never really know. We must always do.

—JOHANN WOLFGANG VON GOETHE

5610. In science the important thing is to modify and change one's ideas as science advances.

—CLAUDE BERNARD

5611. The truth in science is usually simpler than the theories which precede its demonstration.

—W. E. GYE

5612. Steam is no stronger now than it was a hundred years ago, but it is put to better use.

—RALPH WALDO EMERSON

5613. While science has been able to make an easier world, it cannot by itself make a happier world.

—LUELLA B. COOK

5614. Somebody has described science as an orderly arrangement of what at the moment seem to be facts.

5615. Science has provided so many substitutes recently that it's hard to remember what it was we needed in the first place.

5616. The man of science is unworthy of the name, if he disdains to listen to objections to a favorite theory.

—James Anthony Froude

5617. Science is a first-rate piece of furniture for a man's upper chamber, if he has common sense on the ground floor.

—Oliver Wendell Holmes

5618. Where neither confirmation nor refutation is possible, science is not concerned. Science acts and only acts in the domain of uncompleted experience.

—Ernest Mach

5619. Science is teaching man to know and reverence truth, and to believe that only as far as he knows and loves it can he live worthily on earth and vindicate the dignity of his spirit.

—Moses Harvey

5620. Science can give mankind a better standard of living, better health, and a better mental life, if mankind in turn gives science the sympathy and support so essential to its progress.

—Vannevar Bush

5621. Scientific progress is like mounting a ladder; each step upward is followed by a brief pause while the body regains its balance, and we can no more disregard the steps which have gone before than we could cut away the lower part of the ladder.

—O. G. Sutton

5622. Secrecy in science makes for inefficiency and inbreeding. I think you can safely tell the whole world anything you've done in science up to a year ago. Either your competitor is dimwitted, in which case you don't have to worry about what he'll do with your secrets, or he's not far behind you anyway.

—Sir George Thomson

5623. Great as I think are the values which science has brought and will bring to humanity, I would not wish to leave you with the impression that man can live by science alone, for science does not provide him with the ethical guidance nor the spiritual insights which are needed to realize our ideals of the good life.

—E. U. Condon

5624. We live in an age notable for the extent to which the ordinary affairs of people everywhere are dependent upon the discoveries of science developed and applied by engineering to the use and convenience of man. It is not the fault of the scientist and engineer that those responsible for political and social relationships have caused these same discoveries and developments to be used for man's destruction.

—THORNDIKE SAVILLE

5625. There isn't one single immutable truth in the whole of science and there never will be. A phenomenon is discovered and explained. Time passes, and both the phenomenon and its explanation are continuously shaded and revised, until the original concept proves erroneous and utterly worthless. We claim to build a firm foundation of truth, but our underpinnings rot away as rapidly as we build. Given sufficient time, every single law of present science will become invalid, to be replaced by another set of laws, which in turn, etc. . . .

—T. J. SCHOCH

Science—Religion

5626. Science and religion are partners in man's constant effort to learn the truth about himself and the universe.

—DAVID SARNOFF

5627. The scientist who recognizes God . . . feels that God is in nature, that the orderly ways in which nature works are themselves the manifestations of God's will and purpose. Its laws are His orderly way of working.

—ARTHUR HOLLY COMPTON

5628. Science is entering our lives more and more on all sides. Atomic power, jet propulsion, television, industrial machines, as well as dozens of appliances in the home can be great blessings in our lives. But we should take great care always to be in complete mastery of each and all of them, as God intended, and not gradually become mechanical, depersonalized robots enslaved by the science we helped to create.

5629. The claim that there is an inherent conflict between science and our immortal souls—that science is the natural enemy of the soul—does not stand up under examination. The man in an airplane is not necessarily less devoted to truth, justice, and charity than his forefathers in oxcarts. Virtue does not necessarily go with primitive plumbing, and human dignity can be nurtured in a skyscraper no less than in a log cabin.

—DAVID SARNOFF

5630. Peace and brotherhood can be achieved. Two of the most potent forces in civilization—religion and science—can be used to create *one world* in its truest and greatest sense. Through religion, we can minimize the evils of envy and greed, intolerance, and a lust for power. Through science, we can reduce the physical burdens of mankind, make the earth more fruitful, create plenty in place of scarcity, break down the barriers of ignorance and misunderstanding and make life more meaningful for everyone.

Season—Seasons

5631. The only difference between April and March is that you don't expect it in April.

—Elizabeth Pearson

5632. Just as the soaring flight of the fungo fly is the first sight of spring to untold Americans, so the brisk slap of a baseball into a catcher's mitt is the first lovely sound of it.

—John Ward

Secret—Secrets

5633. Tell nothing to thy friend which thy enemy may not know.

—*Danish Proverb*

5634. None are so fond of secrets as those who do not mean to keep them.

—Charles C. Colton

5635. A woman's idea of keeping a secret is to refuse to tell who told it to her.

5636. The man who has no secrets from his wife either has no secrets or no wife.

5637. The best way for a man to keep a secret from his wife is not to do it in the first place.

—Kathryn Gelander

5638. A woman who can keep a secret sometimes has the bad luck to tell it to a woman who can't.

5639. One of the gravest errors which men daily fall into is that of supposing that their secrets are unknown to others.

—Conte Giacomo Leopardi

5640. Of course a woman can keep a secret. What she can't keep is the secret that she's keeping a secret.

—Frances Rodman

5641. I usually get my stuff from people who promised somebody else that they would keep it a secret.

—Walter Winchell

5642. The wise never tell secrets to the young—new boots creak; nor to the aged—old boots sag at the seams.

—Winifred Gordon

5643. The longer a woman guards a secret, the less importance she attaches to the disclosure of it.

5644. It is safer to be silent than to reveal one's secret to any one, and telling him not to mention it.

—Saadi

5645. Nothing is more annoying than to find everyone already knows the secret you have promised to keep to yourself.

5646. Never confide in a young man—new pails leak. Never tell your secret to the aged—old doors seldom shut closely.

5647. A man can keep another person's secret better than his own; a woman, on the contrary, keeps her secret though she blabs all others.

—Jean de La Bruyère

5648. If a fool knows a secret, he tells it because he is a fool; if a knave knows one, he tells it whenever it is his interest to tell it. But women and young men are very apt to tell what secrets they know, from the vanity of having been trusted.

—Lord Chesterfield

Secretary

5649. A secretary's job isn't complicated if she looks like a woman, thinks like a man, and works like a horse.

5650. The secretary who marries her boss has had exceptional opportunities to form a sensible judgment of the man. She has seen him under the testing conditions of business, when he had a frayed temper, when he was worried and harassed. In spite of all that, she marries him.

Being wise, the secretary knows that a man's troubles are a good woman's opportunity.

Security

5651. There is no security on this earth. There is only opportunity.

—GENERAL DOUGLAS MACARTHUR

5652. An old person without income and unable to work may find financial security by moving in with a son or daughter—but not independence.

5653. Our security may depend less upon priority in exploring outer space than upon our wisdom in managing the space in which we live.

—DR. PAUL B. SEARS

5654. Uncertainty and expectation are joys of life; security is an insipid thing; and the overtaking and possessing of a wish discovers the folly of the chase.

—WILLIAM CONGREVE

5655. It is the risk element which produces an economy of security. Risk brings out the ingenuity and resourcefulness which insure the success of enough ventures to keep the economy growing and secure.

5656. Security is mostly a superstition. It does not exist in nature, nor do the children of men as a whole experience it. Avoiding danger is no safer in the long run than outright exposure. The fearful are caught as often as the bold. Faith alone defends.

—From *The Open Door,* by HELEN KELLER. Copyright © 1957 by HELEN KELLER. Reprinted by permission of *Doubleday & Company, Inc.*

5657. The citizen who calls on government to supply him with security from cradle to grave, thereby encouraging government spending, is a danger to himself and his fellow citizens. If his pleas are successful, he can lose his freedom and gain no security in exchange.

—F. A. TRUSLOW

5658. If the choice is given to us of liberty or security, we must scorn the latter with the proper contempt of free men and the sound judgment of wise men who know that liberty and security are not incompatible in the lives of honest men.

—JAMES A. FARLEY

5659. There is a growing sentiment in America that regular saving should be ignored—that the government will take care of people and give them security when they get beyond a certain age or become old and unable to work, but it must be borne in mind that the people who earn and *do* save, take care of the government! Were it not for the thrifty and the willing workers, the government would be in a bad way.

—GEORGE MATTHEW ADAMS

Self

5660. Staring up to admire your own halo creates a pain in the neck.

—HAROLD COFFIN

5661. The debt that a man owes to himself is generally set up on an easy payment plan.

5662. Our first duty is not to hate ourselves; because to advance we must have faith in ourselves first and then in God. He who has no faith in himself can never have faith in God.

—VIVEKANANDA

5663.

It matters not how straight the gate,
How charged with punishments the scroll,
I am the master of my fate:
I am the captain of my soul.

—WILLIAM E. HENLEY

5664. Man's problem in the last analysis is man himself. A man beset by evil within and from without can mobilize his spiritual resources to conquer that evil. Just so can the human race mobilize its moral and spiritual power to defeat the material power of evil that threatens it.

—RICHARD E. BYRD

5665. It is a nice point in ethics whether it is dishonest to rob one's own money-box. Obviously, each of us consists of two selves—the self that wishes to save and the self that wishes to spend—and one of them differs as much from the other as a man does from his first cousin. Not only this, but each of them distrusts and is hostile to the other.

—ROBERT LYND

5666. I find in life that most affairs that require serious handling are distasteful. For this reason, I have always believed that the successful man has the hardest battle with himself rather than with the other fellow. To bring one's self to a frame of mind and to the proper energy to accomplish things that require plain hard work continuously is the one big battle that everyone has. When this battle is won for all time, then everything is easy.

—Thomas A. Buckner

5667. WHICH AM I?

I watched them tearing a building down
A gang of men in a busy town;
With a ho-heave-ho and a lusty yell
They swung a beam and a side wall fell.
I asked the foreman, "Are these men skilled,
The men you would hire if you had to build?"
He gave me a laugh and said, "No, indeed!
Just common labor is all I need.
I can easily wreck in a day or two,
What builders have taken a year to do."
I thought to myself as I went my way,
Which of these roles have I tried to play?
Am I a builder who works with care,
Measuring life by the rule and square?
Am I shaping my deeds to a well-made plan,
Patiently doing the best I can?
Or am I a wrecker who walks the town
Content with the labor of tearing down?

—*Anonmyous*

5668. MYSELF

I have to live with myself, and so
  I want to be fit for myself to know.
I want to be able, as days go by,
  Always to look myself straight in the eye.
I don't want to stand, with the setting sun,
  And hate myself for the things I've done.
I don't want to keep on a closet shelf
  A lot of secrets about myself,
And fool myself, as I come and go,
  Into thinking that nobody else will know

The kind of man I really am;
  I don't want to dress myself up in sham.
I never can hide myself from me;
  I see what others may never see;
I know what others may never know;
  I never can fool myself, and so
Whatever happens, I want to be
  Self-respecting and conscience free.

—EDGAR A. GUEST

Self-Appraisal

5669. Distrust him who talks much of his honesty.

—DUSSAULX

5670. He who knows his incapacity knows something.

—MARGUERITE DE VALOIS

5671. He is not laughed at that laughs at himself first.

—THOMAS FULLER

5672. The coward calls himself cautious, the miser thrifty.

—PUBLILIUS SYRUS

5673. There's something to laugh at every day—if you shave regularly.

5674. How seldom we weigh our neighbor in the same balance with ourselves!

—THOMAS À KEMPIS

5675. Most of us will admit we're fairly intelligent—we just have a lot of stupid help.

5676. A bear never knows until he is muzzled how many people are not afraid of him.

5677. He who knows others is clever, but he who knows himself is enlightened.

—LAO TZU

5678. When we know how to read our own hearts, we acquire wisdom of the hearts of others.

—DENIS DIDEROT

5679. Our opinion of ourselves, like our shadow, makes us either too big or too little.

5680. The man with insight enough to admit his limitations comes nearest to perfection.

—JOHANN WOLFGANG VON GOETHE

5681. Men who know themselves are no longer fools, they stand on the threshold of the Door of Wisdom.

—HAVELOCK ELLIS

5682. There is no greater fool than he who thinks himself wise; no one wiser than he who suspects himself a fool.

—MARGUERITE DE VALOIS

5683. No institution which does not continually test its ideals, techniques and measure of accomplishment can claim real vitality.

—JOHN MILTON

5684. Public opinion is a weak tyrant, compared with our private opinion. What a man thinks of himself, that it is which determines, or rather indicates, his fate.

—HENRY DAVID THOREAU

5685. If you must criticize someone, criticize yourself. Not only will your criticism be fairer and more constructive, but you can also do something about it.

5686. Do not shelter the mirror which reflects your soul's lack of beauty; rather welcome the truth, and believe that next to the knowledge of God nothing is so precious as the knowledge of self.

—JEAN NICOLAS GROU

5687. The doctrine of human equality reposes on this: that there is no man really clever who has not found that he is stupid. There is no man big who has not felt small. Some men never feel small; but these are the few men who are.

—G. K. CHESTERTON

5688. Your success in handling a crisis depends to a large extent on how you picture and value yourself. If you have an accurate estimation of your intelligence and capabilities, you'll have greater courage. If you know your true worth, you'll be able to work within those bounds and be happy doing so.

—GEORGE S. STEVENSON

5689. Be very slow to believe that you are wiser than all others; it is a fatal but common error. Where one has been saved by a true estimation of another's weakness, thousands have been destroyed by a false appreciation of their own strength.

—Charles C. Colton

5690. Do not imagine yourself to have what you have not; but take full account of the excellencies which you possess, and in gratitude remember how you would hanker after them, if you had them not. At the same time take care that in thus hugging them, you do not get into the habit of prizing them so much that without them you would be perturbed.

—Marcus Aurelius

5691. A woman invited to tea at the Winston Churchill's, took her young grandson upon whom she tried to impress the significance of the occasion. "Today you become a part of history. You are going to meet the greatest man in the world," she told him.

While his grandmother chatted with Lady Churchill, the boy wandered into the garden, where he came upon an elderly gentleman reading a book. "I beg your pardon, sir," the lad said. "Are you Sir Winston Churchill?"

"I am," was the reply.

"My grandmother says you are the greatest man in the world. Is that true, Sir?"

"It is," Churchill calmly assured him.

Self-Assurance

5692. One man's way may be as good as another's, but we all like our own best.

—Jane Austen

5693. A man is little the better for liking himself if nobody else likes him.

—Thomas Fuller

5694. The best evidence that people are easily pleased lies in the fact that so many are pleased with themselves.

5695. A steady assurance, with seeming modesty, is possibly the most useful qualification that a man can have in every part of life.

—Lord Chesterfield

5696. We are inconsolable at being deceived by our enemies and betrayed by our friends; and yet we are often content to be so by ourselves.

—FRANÇOIS DE LA ROCHEFOUCAULD

Self-Blame

5697. Don't condemn yourself by revealing the faults of others.

5698. All censure of a man's self is oblique praise. It is in order to show how much he can spare. It has all the invidiousness of self-praise, and all the reproach of falsehood.

—DR. SAMUEL JOHNSON

Self-Confidence

5699. He who knows little is confident in everything.

—*Ancient Proverb*

5700. It's fine to believe in ourselves, but we mustn't be too easily convinced.

—BURTON HILLIS

5701. Calm self-confidence is as far from conceit as the desire to earn a decent living is remote from greed.

—CHANNING POLLOCK

5702. Have confidence that if you have done a *little* thing well, you can do a *bigger* thing well, too.

—MOORFIELD STOREY

5703. Do not attempt to do a thing unless you are sure of yourself; but do not relinquish it simply because someone else is not sure of you.

—STEWART E. WHITE

5704. To think we are able is almost to be so; to determine upon attainment is frequently attainment itself; earnest resolution has often seemed to have about it almost a savor of omnipotence.

—SAMUEL SMILES

5705. You have powers you never dreamed of. You can do things you never thought you could do. There are no limitations in what you can do except the limitations of your own mind as to what you cannot do. Don't think you cannot. Think that you can.

—DARWIN P. KINGSLEY

5706. Self-confidence is built up by a total pattern of successful experiences. Self-confidence can neither be quickly developed nor quickly destroyed. It deserves to be carefully guarded because it is often the difference between success and failure.

—EUGENE E. JENNINGS

5707. Confidence in oneself is the cornerstone. It is difficult for those who do not believe in themselves to have much faith in anyone else. Self-confidence breeds confidence in others, and the two together build confidence in the whole country.

Self-confidence comes from habits of accomplishment.

5708. An outstanding trait of a successful man is self-confidence. Whatever he may think of others, he believes in himself. He believes he can do anything he sets out to do. He has not only faith but courage. Such self-confidence is not conceit. It is always based upon solid things like knowledge, skill, and the willingness to work. It is not a gift of nature, but one of her awards that anyone can earn.

5709. *Trust thyself:* every heart vibrates to that iron string. Accept the place the divine providence has found for you, the society of your contemporaries, the connection of events. Great men have always done so, and confided themselves childlike to the genius of their age, betraying their perception that the absolutely trustworthy was seated at their heart, working through their hands, predominating in all their being. And we are now men, and must accept in the highest mind the same transcendent destiny; and not minors and invalids in a protected corner, not cowards fleeing before a revolution, but guides, redeemers, and benefactors, obeying the Almighty effort and advancing on Chaos and the Dark.

—RALPH WALDO EMERSON

Self-Consciousness

5710. As valedictorian of her high school class Margaret Lee Runbeck, the author, trembled with self-consciousness when she took her seat on the platform next to the guest speaker.

"I'm supposed to talk wittily to you," she whispered to the guest, "but I haven't a thing to say. I'm scared to death."

"I'm scared, too," the speaker confided. "I've got a speech written down, but I don't think it's much good . . ."

"But *you* don't have to be afraid," the girl interrupted.

"Neither do you," the speaker replied. "I'll tell you a secret; then you'll never need to be troubled again. Everyone on earth is shy and self-conscious. Everybody's timid about meeting strangers. So if you'll just spend the first minute you're with a stranger trying to make *him* feel comfortable, you'll never suffer from self-consciousness again. Try it."

Margaret Runbeck accepted the advice and now, years later, says that it works unfailingly.

—G. Ernest Thomas, *Faith Can Master Fear* (Revell)

Self-Control

5711. Self-control: mind over madder.

5712. The man who loses his head is usually the last one to miss it.

5713. Government of the will is better than increase of knowledge.

—*Old Proverb*

5714. None is deemed to be free who has not perfect self-command.

—Pythagoras

5715. There never has been, and cannot be, a good life without self-control.

—Count Leo Tolstoi

5716. As a sword in the hand of a madman, so likewise is the soul of him that lacks discretion.

—Dandemis

5717. If you wish to succeed in managing and controlling others—Learn to manage and control yourself.

—William J. H. Boetcker

5718. On two occasions you should be careful to keep your mouth shut—when swimming and when angry.

5719. Self-control may be developed in precisely the same manner as we tone up a weak muscle—by little exercises day by day.

—W. G. Jordan

5720. The virtue of all achievement is victory over oneself. Those who know this victory can never know defeat.

—A. J. Cronin

5721. The use of self-control is like the use of brakes on a train. It is useful when you find yourself going in the wrong direction, but merely harmful when the direction is right.

5722. Over time thou hast no power; to redeem a world sunk in dishonesty has not been given thee. Solely over one man in the world thou hast a sovereign and absolute power: redeem him; him make honest!

—THOMAS CARLYLE

5723. Fortunate is the person who has developed the self-control to steer a straight course toward his objective in life, without being swayed from his purpose by either commendation or condemnation.

—NAPOLEON HILL

5724. When man learns to understand and control his own behavior as well as he is learning to understand and control the behavior of crop plants and domestic animals, he may be justified in believing that he has become civilized.

—E. C. STAKMAN

5725.

He who holds back rising anger,
As one might a rolling chariot,
Him, indeed, I call a driver,—
Others only hold the rein!

—DHAMMAPODA

5726. Six greatest words on earth:

Control Thyself—*Cicero*
Know Thyself—*Socrates*
Give Thyself—*Christ*

5727. For want of self-restraint many men are engaged all their lives in fighting with difficulties of their own making, and rendering success impossible by their cross-grained ungentleness; while others, who may be much less gifted, make their way and achieve success by simple patience and self-control.

—SAMUEL SMILES

5728. Much is being said and more is being written about the philosophy of self-expression: let yourself go, obey that impulse, do what you like. But what confronts everyone is the question, "Have you a self worth expressing?" What is needed today is not so much self-expression as self-control.

—JOSEPH R. SIZOO

5729. A man once went up in my esteem under the following circumstances. Speaking of a certain critic, I said that what I objected to in him was that his necktie was always crooked. When I went upstairs before dinner I noticed that my own necktie was conspicuously crooked. My friend had not mentioned the fact, or even hinted at it. He knew that I was bound to discover it myself. An example of masterly self-control.

—Arnold Bennett

5730. It was said that Frederick the Great of Prussia was walking along a road on the outskirts of Berlin one day, when he accidentally brushed against a very old man.

"Who are you?" the king asked out of idle curiosity as the walk came to an abrupt halt.

"I am a king," the old man answered.

"A king? Over what principality do you reign?" asked the amazed Frederick.

"Over myself. I rule myself because I control myself. I am my own subject to command," replied the elderly one proudly.

Self-Deception

5731. No man was ever so much deceived by another as by himself.

—Charles Greville

5732. There are certain tears which often deceive ourselves, after having deceived others.

—François de La Rochefoucauld

5733. The easiest thing of all is to deceive one's self; for what a man wishes he generally believes to be true.

—Demosthenes

Self-Denial

5734. These are difficult times when we have to do without the things our parents never had.

5735. Toward the end of his tragic devoted life, General Robert E. Lee attended the christening of a friend's child. The mother asked him for a word that would guide the child along the long road to manhood.

Lee's answer summed up the creed that had borne him, through struggle and suffering, to a great place in the American legend. "Teach him," he said simply, "to deny himself."

—Bruce Catton

Self-Depreciation

5736. No man can ever be noble who thinks meanly or contemptuously of himself, and no man can ever be noble who thinks first and only of himself.

—W. H. Dollinger

5737. He who blames himself takes a by-road to praise; and, like the rower, turns his back to the place whither he desires to go.

—St. Francis de Sales

5738. A person who doubts himself is like a man who would enlist in the ranks of his enemies and bear arms against himself. He makes his failure certain by himself being the first person to be convinced of it.

—Alexander Dumas

Self-Determination

5739. As we are, so we do; and as we do, so is it done to us; we are the builders of our fortunes.

—Ralph Waldo Emerson

5740. The shape of a man's head, the length of his legs, the color of his eyes are inherited from his ancestors, but he alone is responsible for his attitude toward other men.

—Oliver G. Wilson

5741. Your living is determined not so much by what life brings to you as by the attitude you bring to life; not so much by what happens to you as by the way your mind looks at what happens. Circumstances and situations do color life but you have been given the mind to choose what the color shall be.

—John Homer Miller, *Take a Second Look at Yourself* (Abingdon Press)

Self-Development

5742. He that can compose himself, is wiser than he that composes books.

—Benjamin Franklin

5743. You have to do your own growing up no matter how tall your grandpa was.

5744. There is not a self-made man in the world. The so-called self-made man is the man who has seized his opportunities, and those given him by circumstances, and has made use of them.

—Lucius Tuttle

Self-Discipline

5745. What we do upon some great occasion will probably depend on what we already are; and what we are will be the result of previous years of self-discipline.

—Henry Parry Liddon

5746. I have seen boys on my baseball team go into slumps and never come out of them, and I have seen others snap right out and come back better than ever. I guess more players lick themselves than are ever licked by an opposing team. The first thing any man has to know is how to handle himself. Training counts. You can't win any game unless you are ready to win.

—Connie Mack

5747. Try as we may, none of us can be free of conflict and woe. Even the greatest men have to accept disappointments as their daily bread. . . . The art of living lies less in eliminating our troubles than in growing with them. Man and society must grow together. Each individual's efforts to discipline himself must be matched by society's struggle to enforce the rules of law and of justice under the law.

—Bernard M. Baruch

Self-Education

5748. He that teaches himself has a fool for a master.

—*Ancient Proverb*

5749. Every man has two educations—that which is given to him, and the other, that which he gives to himself. Of the two kinds, the latter is by far the more valuable. Indeed, all that is most worthy in a man, he must work out and conquer for himself. It is that which constitutes our real and best nourishment. What we are merely taught seldom nourishes the mind like that which we teach ourselves.

—Jean Paul Richter

Self-Examination

5750. He who knows himself, knows others.

—Charles C. Colton

5751. Seeing ourselves as others see us wouldn't do much good. We wouldn't believe it.

5752. Far too often most of us find self-congratulation much more agreeable than self-examination.

5753. When you see a good man, think of emulating him; when you see a bad man, examine your own heart.

—Confucius

5754. If things are not going well with you, begin your effort at correcting the situation by carefully examining the service you are rendering, and especially the spirit in which you are rendering it.

—Roger Babson

5755. The next time you walk down the sidewalk of a crowded, busy street and see only fixed stares instead of smiles on approaching faces, stop in front of the first show-window mirror and examine your own countenance. You will most likely discover that it is as frozen and cold as those of the others. They, too, were staring instead of smiling while eagerly searching for a sign of comradeship. When you find yourself thinking or saying: "He, or she, is an unfriendly person," consider well if what you really mean is not this: "I am being an unfriendly person."

—Rabbi Louis Binstock in
The Power of Faith
(Prentice-Hall, Inc.)

5756. Don't shift all the responsibility on to your neighbor, and when you are listening to a sermon or a lecture don't pick out some one you think it may fit, but take it to yourself. How full of faults we all are! Who are you, whom am I, that we should think ourselves more deserving than our fellowmen? How do we know but some one else is suiting that same sermon to us, and thinking we need to follow its teachings? We forget that the faults we fail to see in ourselves are so glaring to others. Therefore, let us examine our own hearts and see that they are right, before we criticize or condemn our neighbors.

—Ida Scott Taylor

Self-Government

5757. Self-government is no less essential to the development, growth, and happiness of the individual than to the nation.

—W. H. Douglas

5758. I know of no safe repository for the ultimate powers of society but the people themselves; and if we think them not enlightened enough to exercise their control with a wholesome discretion, the remedy is not to take it from them, but to increase their discretion by education.

—Thomas Jefferson

Self-Gratification

5759. Man only multiplies his troubles when he gets everything he wants.

5760. The secret of most men's misery is that they are trying to please themselves.

—Frederick D. Maurice

Self-Help

• **5761.** Meeting trouble halfway means poor company the rest of the way.

5762. The man who is his own worst enemy has a mighty one-sided fight on his hands.

5763. There is no use whatever trying to help people who do not help themselves. You cannot push anyone up a ladder unless he be willing to climb himself.

—Andrew Carnegie

5764. God gives every bird its food, but He does not throw it into the nest. He does not unearth the good that the earth contains, but He puts it in our way, and gives us the means of getting it ourselves.

—J. G. Holland

Self-Importance

5765. Nothing is more likely to make you feel big than a little sports car.

5766. No cause more frequently produces bashfulness than too high an opinion of our own importance.

—Dr. Samuel Johnson

5767. Lack of something to feel important about is almost the greatest tragedy a man may have.

—Dr. Arthur E. Morgan

5768. The first lesson of life is to burn our own smoke; that is, not to inflict on outsiders our personal sorrows and petty morbidness, not to keep thinking of ourselves as exceptional cases.

—James Russell Lowell

5769. Sometime, when you're feeling important,
Sometime, when your ego's in bloom,
Sometime when you take it for granted,
You're the best qualified in the room.
Sometime when you feel that your going,
Would leave an unfillable hole,
Just follow this simple instruction,
And see how it humbles your soul.

Take a bucket and fill it with water,
Put your hand in it, up to the wrist,
Pull it out, and the hole that's remaining,
Is a measure of how you'll be missed.
You may splash all you please when you enter,
You can stir up the water galore,
But stop, and you'll find in a minute,
That it looks quite the same as before.

The moral in this quaint example
Is do just the best that you can.
Be proud of yourself, but remember,
There is no indispensable man.

—*Anonymous (based on on ancient French Proverb)*

Self-Improvement

5770. One way you can improve yourself is by writing your biography.

5771. Be at war with your vices, at peace with your neighbor, and let every new year find you a better man.

—Benjamin Franklin

5772. Our business in life is not to get ahead of others, but to get ahead of ourselves—to break our own records, to outstrip our yesterdays by our today, to do our work with more force than ever before.

—Stewart B. Johnson

5773. There's only one corner of the universe you can be certain of improving, and that's your own self. So you have to begin there, not ouside, not on other people. That comes afterward, when you've worked on your own corner.

—Aldous Huxley

5774. The natural effort of every individual to better his own condition is so powerful that it is alone, and without any assistance, not only capable of carrying on the society of wealth and prosperity, but of surmounting a hundred impertinent obstructions with which the folly of human laws too often incumbers its operations.

—Adam Smith

5775. First, always seek to excel yourself. Put yourself in competition with yourself each day. Each morning look back upon your work of yesterday and then try to beat it. Second, I ask you to look upon the whole of life as a vast university—the ideal university of the future whose students will spend a part of the time in learning what to do and how to do it and then a larger part in actually doing the things they learn to do.

—Charles Monroe Sheldon

5776. The greatest satisfaction in life is not in getting ahead of others, but in getting ahead of ourselves. It comes from breaking records, from doing something better today than we were able to do it yesterday. Trying to get ahead of others is a mistake, which often leads to envy from failure or conceit from success. In trying to outdo ourselves we have nothing to lose, and a world of satisfaction to gain.

Self-Interest

5777. If I am not for myself, who will be for me.

—*The Talmud*

5778. The man who is all wrapped up in himself always finds fault with his surroundings.

5779. Self-interest is but the survival of the animal in us. Humanity only begins for man with self-surrender.

—Henri Frèdèric Amiel

5780. 'Tis not contrary to reason to prefer the destruction of the whole world to the scratching of my finger.

—DAVID HUME

5781. The joyless man has his mind centered on himself. The happy, contented man has his mind on others and is interested in their happiness as well as his own.

5782. Officials of a railroad, disturbed because commuters neglected to close doors in winter weather, put up signs that read, "For the comfort of other passengers, please close the doors." The doors stayed open. The poster was changed to read, "Please close the doors for your own comfort." The doors were closed.

—From an article *"Homework: Nouns and Pronouns"* by ROBERT J. CADIGAN in *Presbyterian Life*

5783. Like most older people, I am constantly fighting the temptation to slip into self-absorption. If one loses interest in the people who tie one to life, then it is very easy to lose interest in the world as a whole. This, I think, is the beginning of death. For all of us, as we grow older, perhaps the most important thing is to keep alive our love for others and to believe that our love and interest are as vitally necessary to them as to us.

—ELEANOR ROOSEVELT

Selfishness

5784. No man is more cheated than the selfish man.

—HENRY WARD BEECHER

5785. Selfishness corrodes. Unselfishness ennobles, satisfies.

5786. He who lives but for himself lives but for a little thing.

—BARJAUD

5787. The force of selfishness is as inevitable and as calculable as the force of gravitation.

—GEORGE STILLMAN HILLARD

5788. He is a slave of the greatest slave, who serveth nothing but himself.

5789. The same people who can deny others everything are famous for refusing themselves nothing.

—LEIGH HUNT

5790. Too many people conduct their lives on the cafeteria plan—self-service only.

5791. The man who lives by himself and for himself is apt to be corrupted by the company he keeps.

—*Believe Me,* by Virginia Hutchinson (Comet Press Books)

5792. A man is called selfish, not for pursuing his own good, but for neglecting his neighbor's.

—Richard Whately

5793. The selfish, loving only themselves, are loved by no one: so, selfishness is moral suicide.

—De Gaston

5794. Selfishness is not living as one wishes to live. It is asking others to live as one wishes to live.

—Oscar Wilde

5795. Selfishness is that detestable vice which no one will forgive in others, and no one is without in himself.

—Henry Ward Beecher

5796. Some people think that all the world should share their misfortunes, though they do not share in the sufferings of anyone else.

—Achilles Poincelot

5797. A purely selfish life, even when it is crowned with a kind of success, such as wealth or literary achievement, or fame in any of its shapes, is worth less in the way of general happiness than the life of the humblest artisan who has made the most of his environment and the best of himself.

—George H. Hepworth

5798. A famous Indian chief, Blackfeather, once spoke these words to his tribe: "I have lived long. I have seen many things. What I know I speak. Selfishness is the great enemy of peace. Selfishness walks by itself and no one walks with it. Selfishness never goes unseen. It raises flags and banners as it goes. People are quick to see these signs. They are like the hiss of the rattlesnake that the wise avoid. What I have said is true—selfishness is the enemy of peace."

Self-Knowledge

5799. No man knows himself until he has suffered.

—Alfred de Musset

5800. The first step to self-knowledge is self-distrust. Nor can we attain to any kind of knowledge, except by a like process.

Self-Love

5801. Self-love well understood is philanthropy well practiced.

—Constancio C. Vigil

5802. Know that the love of thyself doth hurt thee more than anything in the world.

—Thomas à Kempis

5803. Some of the greatest love affairs I've known have involved one actor—unassisted.

—Wilson Mizner

5804. Self-love is always the mainspring, more or less concealed, of our actions; it is the wind which swells the sails, without which the ship could not go.

—Mme. du Châtelet

5805. Self-love is the instrument of our preservation; it resembles the provision for the reproduction of mankind: it is necessary, it gives us pleasure, and we must conceal it.

—Voltaire

5806. People fall in love with themselves almost immediately after birth. This is invariably the beginning of a life-long romance. There is no record of infidelity, separation, or divorce between humans and their egos.

—Harry Singer

5807. Maurice Barrymore, the famous actor, was never bothered by the frequent reports of the reckless escapades of his three famous offspring. On one occasion, a friend suggested that he keep an eye on John, who had his eye on a shapely showgirl.

"Don't let him become involved," urged the friend. "You know how quickly these young fellows imagine they are in love."

"Don't worry about that," laughed the elder Barrymore. "A Barrymore falls in love only once in his life. With himself!"

—Harold Metcalf

Self-Mastery

5808. The man who masters himself is free.

—Epictetus

5809. No one is free who is not master of himself.

—William Shakespeare

5810. He conquers twice who conquers himself in victory.

—Publilius Syrus

5811. No man is free who is not master of his soul and controller of his spirit.

—Thomas Crombie

5812. 'Tis easier to suppress the first desire, than to satisfy all that follow it.

—Benjamin Franklin

5813. The first and best victory is to conquer self. To be conquered by self is, of all things, the most shameful and vile.

—Plato

5814. No one is so free as the slave who has achieved freedom. No one is so weary as the man who does nothing. No one is so strong as he who has conquered weakness.

—Elsa Barker

5815. The great scientific discoveries of the past hundred years have been as child's play compared with the titanic forces that will be released when man applies himself to the understanding and mastery of his own nature.

—Melvin J. Evans

5816. Once a Quaker, calm and poised after a volley of bitter abuse, was asked how he conquered his patience. He replied: "Friend, I will tell thee. I was naturally as hot and violent as thou art. Yet, when I observed that men in passion always speak loud, I thought if I could control my voice, I should repress my passion. I have therefore made it a rule never to let my voice rise above a certain key. By careful observance of this rule I have, by the blessing of God, mastered my tongue."

5817. The most precious of all our possessions is power over ourselves; power to withstand trial, to bear suffering, to confront danger; power over pleasure and pain; power to follow our convictions, however resisted by menace and scorn; the power of calm reliance in scenes of darkness and storms. He that has not a mastery over his inclinations; he that knows not how to resist the importunity of present pleasure or pain, for the sake of what reason tells him is fit to be done, wants the true principle of virtue and industry, and is in danger of never being good for anything.

—John Locke

Self-Pity

5818. What poison is to food, self-pity is to life.

—Oliver C. Wilson

5819. Sympathy is never wasted except when you give it to yourself.

—John W. Roper

5820. Self-pity is a bad habit. It is a poisonous habit. It hurts self and it disgusts others. It breeds despair. It saps one's self-reliance. The strong don't indulge in self-pity. They are too busy thinking and working and talking constructively. They are intent on attaining some goal. They are so engrossed in practicing self-help that they have no time to waste on self-pity. They refuse to be cowards. They refuse to wear the white feather. They strive to be men. They become men.

—B. C. Forbes

Self-Praise

5821. Man is Creation's masterpiece. But who says so?—Man!

—Gavarni (Sulpice Guillaume Chevalier)

5822. He is a fool that praises himself and a madman that speaks ill of himself.

—*Danish Proverb*

5823. When you do anything worthy of praise, do not let your joy be to proclaim it; for men do not say: "Behold! He has done it"; what they say is: "See how proud he is of it."

—Dandemis

Self-Preservation

5824. Self-preservation prompts men to move in the line of least resistance.

—Elbert Hubbard

5825. A man who was suing over an automobile accident was being questioned by the defendant's lawyer.

"Did you, or did you not, at the time of the accident when asked if you were hurt, reply that you weren't?"

"I did," said the plaintiff, "but it was like this: I was driving along the road with my old horse and wagon when along comes this fellow and knocks us into the ditch. You never saw such a mess in all your life.

"There I was flat on my back with my legs in the air. And there was my horse on his back, with his legs in the air.

"This motorist gets out of his car and looks at us. He sees my horse has a broken leg. He goes back to his car, gets a gun and shoots him. Then he turns to me still lying there and says, 'Now, what about you? Are *you* hurt?' "

—CLARE JAMISON, *Coronet*

5826. The members of a crew on a submarine were about to take battle stations, and the ship's captain was worried about a young seaman second class whose job it was to close the watertight doors between certain compartments. The boy didn't seem to realize his responsibility and the captain undertook to impress him. He told him that if he failed in his job the ship might be lost, and it had cost around $8 million. Not only that, some of the men aboard were specialists and it cost Uncle Sam thousands to train each of them; they might be drowned.

"So you see how important it is that you do your job. This very expensive ship, these important men—" the captain concluded.

"Yes, sir, and then there's me, too," replied the lad.

The captain stopped worrying.

Self-Reformation

5827. A man who reforms himself has contributed his full share toward the reformation of his neighbor.

—NORMAN DOUGLAS

5828. Be not angry that you cannot make others as you wish them to be since you cannot make yourself as you wish to be.

—THOMAS À KEMPIS

Self-Reliance

5829. Self-reliance can turn a salesman into a merchant; a politician into a statesman; an attorney into a jurist; an unknown youth into a great leader. All are to be tomorrow's big leaders—those who in solitude sit above the clang and dust of time, with the world's secret trembling on their lips.

5830. It is an undeniable fact that people made soft through indolence and misguided charity soon lose their self-respect and self-reliance. Let us recognize the historical truth that anything worthwhile must be earned, and that plenty can be properly appreciated only after experiencing scarcity. Let us make our children strong and self-reliant. They need to be to meet the challenge of communism.

Self-Respect

5831. No one is happy unless he respects himself.

—Jean Jacques Rousseau

5832. Form a good opinion of yourself and then deserve the good opinion of others.

5833. Good sense makes men capable. Self-respect is the breeze which swells the sails and wafts their barks into port.

—Napoleon I

5834. At this critical period of our country, we must have a government of self-respect. As a people, we create that self-respect in our government. However, we must recognize that we are in a conflict which will be with us for at least a generation. Perhaps for fifty years to come. Let us face the simple fact: there is no gadget or device for victory. To think so is to delude ourselves. We cannot buy our way out nor appease our way out. Our moral strength is in ourselves, in our patience, in our courage, in our decision and in our resolution.

—William J. Donovan

Self-Restraint

5835. He is twice a conqueror, who can restrain himself in time of victory.

—*Old Proverb*

5836. The person that always says just what he thinks at last gets just what he deserves.

5837. It is good to be helpful and kindly, but don't give yourself to be melted into candle grease for the benefit of the tallow trade.

—George Eliot

5838. I think the first virtue is to restrain the tongue: he approaches nearest to the gods, who knows how to be silent, even though he is in the right.

—Cato

Self-Sacrifice

5839. Treasures in heaven are laid up only as treasures on earth are laid down.

5840. Self-sacrifice enables us to sacrifice other people without blushing.

—George Bernard Shaw

5841. He who sees farther than others can give the world vision; he who stands steadier than others can give it character; he who forgets himself in doing things for others can give it religion.

—Arthur T. Hadley

Self-Satisfaction

5842. The punishment for self-satisfaction is general contempt.

—Baltasar Gracián

5843. One's self-satisfaction is an untaxed kind of property which it is very unpleasant to find depreciated.

—George Eliot

5844. A man who shows himself too well satisfied with himself, is seldom pleased with others, and they, in return, are little disposed to like him.

—François de La Rochefoucauld

5845. "Mr. Shaw, you look as though you are enjoying yourself at this party."

"If I am," replied the inimitable George Bernard Shaw, "it's the only thing I am enjoying."

Self-Sufficiency

5846. He who thinks he can find in himself the means of doing without others is much mistaken; but he who thinks that others cannot do without him is still more mistaken.

—François de La Rochefoucauld

5847. Those who have resources within themselves, who can dare to live alone, want friends the least, but, at the same time, best know how to prize them the most. But no company is far preferable to bad, because we are more apt to catch the vices of others than their virtues, as disease is far more contagious than health.

—Charles C. Colton

Service

5848. Service makes men competent.

—Lyman Abbott

5849. Doing nothing for others is the undoing of ourselves.

—Horace Mann

5850. There is no service like his that serves because he loves.

—Sir Philip Sidney

5851. It is high time the ideal of success should be replaced with the ideal of service.

—Albert Einstein

5852. You are on the pathway to a successful life when you do more for the community than the community does for you.

5853. To give real service you must add something which cannot be bought or measured with money, and that is sincerity and integrity.

—Donald A. Adams

5854. Have I done anything for society? I have then done more for myself. Let that question and truth be always present to thy mind, and work without cessation.

—William Gilmore Simms

5855. If you would find greater joy in life, attempt to serve and please someone every day. The gift of yourself to someone who needs you will, in return, bring the gift of confidence and serenity to you.

—John H. Crowe

5856. No enterprise can exist for itself alone. It ministers to some great need, it performs some great service, not for itself, but for others; or failing therein, it ceases to be profitable and ceases to exist.

—CALVIN COOLIDGE

5857. The value of all service lies in the spirit in which you serve and not in the importance or magnitude of the service. Even the lowliest task or deed is made holy, joyous, and prosperous when it is filled with love.

—CHARLES FILLMORE

5858. For my own part, when I am employed in serving others, I do not look upon myself as conferring favors, but as paying debts. In my travels and since my settlement I have received much kindness from men and numberless mercies from God. Those kindnesses I can only return to their fellow men; and I can only show my gratitude for these mercies from God by my readiness to help my brethren.

—BENJAMIN FRANKLIN

5859. The need and the desire to serve have always been and always will be a major motivating force of business. Neighbor competes with neighbor, and pretty ruggedly, too, but nearly always to the end of giving the consumer more and better products, superior service, higher value. This is the American tradition. The fact that it has built the highest standard of living the world has ever known is evidence, to me at least, that there is something more than a dream of profits behind the progress we have achieved and hope to achieve in the future.

—JERVIS J. BABB

Sexes, The

5860. In the battle of the sexes, you never meet what you can truly call a conscientious objector.

5861. Men walk from the knee, women from the hip. Men strike matches toward themselves, women away. Men dress to look like other men, women to look unique within the current fashion. Men look at their fingernails by cupping their palms and bending their fingers toward themselves, women extend their fingers palms outward. Men nag their wives for what they do, women nag their husbands for what they don't do.

—KENNETH COLBY

Shame

5862. Not to be ashamed of sin is to sin double.

—*German Proverb*

5863. Shame is a strange thing, it can lift us to heaven or push us down to hell; it gives courage or it makes us cowards. An animal doesn't know shame.

—Margaret Deland

Sharing

5864. When someone shares his fears with you, share your courage with him.

5865. Of no worldly good can the joy be perfect, unless it is shared by a friend.

—*From the Latin*

5866. You must give some time to your fellow man. Even if it is a little thing, do something for those who have need of help, something for which you get no pay but the privilege of doing it.

—Albert Schweitzer

5867. Our most valuable possessions are those which can be shared without lessening—those which, when shared, multiply. Our least valuable possessions, on the other hand, are those which, when divided, are diminished.

—William H. Danforth

5868. Two young hikers were going through a part of the country where water seemed scarce. Upon inquiry, a man led them down a little path where, under overhanging leaves, a clear spring bubbled up. As the boys refreshed themselves, the man told them how he had discovered the spring many years ago. He had scraped away moist leaves to find a little pool of very cold water. He feared to reveal the discovery.

"But my fears were all for nothing," laughed the man. "The more the neighbors used the spring, the more water there was for me. If I were young and starting out like you, I'd never be afraid to share all the good things life gave to me. They yield more for being shared with others."

5869. Sam Walter Foss relates, as follows, how he came to write the poem *The House by the Side of the Road.* "I was tramping in New England one hot and weary day. Had sent my valise ahead twenty-five miles and had walked twenty-four of them. I was tired out and longed for a man with a wagon to come along and take me up. I sat down under a tree. Pretty soon I noticed a sign in the tree: '*There is a spring of good water inside the fence. Drink if you are thirsty.*' I went in and drank, and then I saw another sign on a bench: '*Sit down and rest if you are tired.*' While I was resting there I saw another sign on a basket of apples: '*If you like apples help yourself.*' After a little I looked around and saw an old man, and asked him what those signs meant. 'Well,' he said, 'we had the water going to waste and we thought it would be a good thing if we could get some thirsty travelers to drink a little of it. Then this is a pleasant spot to rest in, and mother reminded me of this old bench that was doing nobody any good in our attic. So I brought it down here. We have more apples than we can eat at this time of the year, and we thought that it would be a satisfaction to us if they could be used somehow. So we put up the signs, and they seem to be doing some little good.' I thanked the old man and pursued my journey, refreshed in body and in mind, for I had learned a great lesson and gained an inspiration. There was no weariness in that last mile, and when it was finished I sat down and wrote those lines, 'Let me live in a house by the side of the road, and be a friend to man.'"

Silence

5870. Silence: wisdom in dead storage.

5871. Men of few words are the best men.

—William Shakespeare

5872. Silence in woman is like speech in man.

—Ben Jonson

5873. Silence is a true friend who never betrays.

—Confucius

5874. Wise men say nothing in dangerous times.

—John Selden

5875. A man is known by the silence he keeps.

—Oliver Herford

5876. Silence may be golden—but oftener it is guilt.

5877. Let thy speech be better than silence, or be silent.

—Dionysius the Elder

5878. The silence of the people is the lesson of kings.
—LOANEN, BISHOP OF SENEZ

5879. What this country needs is more and better mouthtraps.

5880. Silence is the safest course, where a man distrusts himself.
—*Old Proverb*

5881. The college yell of the school of experience is silence.

5882. It often shows a fine command of language to say nothing.

5883. We can refute assertions, but who can refute silence?
—CHARLES DICKENS

5884. He watches chess games in silence . . . What a superior man!
—*Chinese Proverb*

5885. Judicious silence is far preferable to the truth roughly told.
—ST. FRANCIS DE SALES

5886. One minute of keeping your mouth shut is worth an hour of explanation.

5887. I regret often that I have spoken; never that I have been silent.
—PUBLILIUS SYRUS

5888. Beware of a man that does not talk and a dog that does not bark.
—*Portuguese Proverb*

5889. Even women find it difficult to argue with a man who won't talk.

5890. Some men are born great, some achieve greatness, and others just keep still.
—KIN HUBBARD

5891. Silence is not always tact, and it is tact that is golden, not silence.
—SAMUEL BUTLER

5892. I believe in the discipline of silence, and could talk for hours about it.
—GEORGE BERNARD SHAW

5893. Truth is violated by falsehood, and it may be equally outraged by silence.

—AMMIAN

5894. What should not be heard by little ears, should not be said by big mouths.

5895. No one has finer command of language than the person who keeps his mouth shut.

5896. Better that ignorant men remain silent than babble from the lack of argument.

—WILLIAM SCOTT DOWNEY

5897. Nothing so stirs a man's conscience or excites his curiosity as woman's dead silence.

—W. R. GOLDSMITH

5898. Silence is a talent as greatly to be cherished as that other asset, the gift of speech.

5899. It is good to remember that if you can't improve on the silence, it is better to keep still.

5900. He that would live in peace and at ease, must not speak all he knows, nor judge all he sees.

—BENJAMIN FRANKLIN

5901. Think all you speak, but speak not all you think. Thoughts are your own; your words are so no more.

—HENRY DELAUNE

5902. Most of us know how to say nothing. That's true of both women and men. But what is the queer thing about it—so few of us ever learn when.

5903. If you wish to appear agreeable in society you must consent to be taught many things which you already know.

5904. If nobody ever said anything unless he knew what he was talking about, what a ghastly hush would descend upon the earth!

—SIR ALAN HERBERT

5905. A silent person often speaks more impressively than one who talks. We fear and respect what we don't quite understand.

5906. It is better either to be silent or to say things of more value than silence. Sooner throw a pearl at hazard than an idle or useless word; and do not say a little in many words, but a great deal in a few.

—PYTHAGORAS

5907. It doesn't pay to say too much when you are mad enough to choke, for the word that stings the deepest is the word that's never spoke. Let the other fellow wrangle till the storm has blown away, then he'll do a heap of thinking 'bout the things *you* didn't say.

—JAMES WHITCOMB RILEY

5908. Shortly after assuming the burdens of the presidency, Calvin Coolidge was approached by an interviewer, who asked him to outline the political success route which brought him from the farmhouse to the White House.

"It was very simple," replied Silent Cal. "I just listened my way along."

5909. A man may have intelligence enough to excel in a particular thing and lecture on it, and yet not have sense enough to know he ought to be silent on some other subject of which he has but a slight knowledge; if such an illustrious man ventures beyond the bounds of his capacity, he loses his way and talks like a fool.

—JEAN DE LA BRUYÈRE

5910. There are three kinds of silence. Silence from words is good, because inordinate speaking tends to evil. Silence or rest from desires and passions is still better, because it promotes quietness of spirit. But the best of all is silence from unnecessary and wandering thoughts, because that is essential to wandering recollection, and because it lays a foundation for a proper regulation and silence in other respects.

—MIGUEL DE MOLINOS

5911. It had been a rather stormy session of the board and some very harsh things had been said, but one man—always highly respected and unusually wise in his judgments—had said nothing.

Suddenly one of the leaders in the debate turned to him and said: "Brother J——, you have not said a word. I would like to have your opinion in this matter." Whereupon the wise man said, "I have discovered that there are many times when silence is an opinion."

—ROY L. SMITH

Similarity—Similarities

5912. No two people are alike and they are both glad of it.

5913. No two children are alike, especially if one is yours and the other isn't.

5914. The Duke of Wellington and Napoleon Bonaparte were both born in the same year, 1769. Each was born on an island, each became fatherless in early boyhood, each had four brothers and three sisters, each attended military school in France and at the same time. Both became lieutenant-colonels within a day of each other, both excelled at mathematics, both were great soldiers, and each commanded a great army. And both are remembered for what happened at Waterloo, where one became the victor and the other the vanquished!

Simplicity

5915. The supreme excellence is simplicity.

—Henry Wadsworth Longfellow

5916. Finding a way to live simply is today's most complicated problem.

5917. With two wings a man is lifted up above earthly things, that is, with simplicity and purity.

—Thomas à Kempis

5918. *Physics professor:* "Physics is exceedingly simple. Whenever anything comes up which is unusually complicated, I simply call it chemistry."

5919. Possessions, outward success, publicity, luxury—to me these have always been contemptible. I believe that a simple and unassuming manner of life is best for every one, best both for the body and the mind.

—Dr. Albert Einstein

5920. Refined policy has ever been the parent of confusion, and ever will be so, as long as the world endures. Plain good intention, which is as easily discovered at the first view as fraud is surely detected at last, is of no mean force in the government of mankind. Genuine simplicity of heart is a healing and cementing principle.

—Edmund Burke

5921. Much of the corruption, decay and dissolution threatening the English language is due to Americans. The American penchant for using big words is particularly deplorable. If an American had uttered Winston Churchill's famous line, "Give us the tools and we will finish the job," it would have come out, "Donate the implements and we shall finalize the solution of the matter."

—LORD CONESFORD

5922. When Eleanor Roosevelt visited California's Monterey Peninsula a local mother took her youngsters to the airport to see her arrive. Before the plane came in the mother gave them a thorough briefing on just who Mrs. Roosevelt is, and concluded, "She's a *very* great lady."

As the visitor disembarked, one of the children, a little girl, slipped away from her mother and trotted alongside Mrs. Roosevelt to the terminal, looking interestedly up at her face. Returning to her mother, she remarked thoughtfully, "You know, I don't think she knows she's a great lady."

—"PROF. TORO"

5923. A. A mass of concreted earthly material perenially rotating on its axis will not accumulate an accretion of bryophyitic vegetation. (A rolling stone gathers no moss.)

B. A superabundance of talent skilled in the preparation of a gastronomic concoction will impair the quality of a certain potable solution made by immersing a gallinaceous bird in ebullient Adam's ale. (Too many cooks spoil the broth.)

C. Individuals who perforce are constrained to be domiciled in vitreous structures of patent fragibility should on no account employ petrous formations as projectiles. (People who live in glass houses should never throw stones.)

D. That prudent avis which matutinally deserts the coziness of its abode will ensnare a vermiculate creature. (The early bird catches the worm.)

E. Everything that coruscates with effulgence is not ipso facto aurous. (All is not gold that glitters.)

F. He who does not dissipate his competence by hebetudinous prodigality will not subsequently lament an exiguous inadequacy. (Waste not, want not.)

G. An addle-pated beetlehead and his specie divaricate with startling prematurity. (A fool and his money are soon parted.)

H. It can be no other than a maleficent horizontal current of gaseous matter whose portentous advent is not the harbinger of a modicum of beneficence. ('Tis an ill wind that blows no good.)

I. One should hyperesthetically exercise macrography upon that situs which one will eventually tenant if one propels oneself into the ether. (Look before you leap.)

J. Abberation is the hallmark of homo sapiens while longanimous placability is the indicia of supramundane omniscience. (To err is human, to forgive divine.)

Sin—Sins

5924. Without knowledge there is no sin.

5925. You can't put your sins behind you until you face them.

5926. Sins make all equal whom they find together, and they are worst who ought to be best.

—Robert Browning

5927. He that falls into sin is a man; that grieves at it, is a saint; that boasteth of it, is a devil.

—Thomas Fuller

Sincerity

5928. Sincerity is more than lying.

5929. The sincere alone can recognize sincerity.

—Thomas Carlyle

5930. Be sincere. Be simple in words, manners, and gestures. Amuse as well as instruct. If you can make a man laugh, you can make him think and make him like and believe you.

—Alfred E. Smith

5931. Sincerity is like travelling in a plain beaten road, which commonly brings a man sooner to his journey's end than by-ways, in which men often lose themselves.

—John Tillotson

5932. The only conclusive evidence of a man's sincerity is that he gives himself for a principle. Words, money, all things else, are comparatively easy to give away; but when a man makes a gift of his daily life and practice it is plain that in that truth, whatever it may be, he is sincere.

—James Russell Lowell

5933. The first virtue of all really great men is that they are sincere. They eradicate hypocrisy from their hearts. They bravely unveil their weaknesses, their doubts, their defects. They are courageous. They boldly ride a-tilt against prejudices. No civil, moral nor immoral power overawes them. They love their fellowmen profoundly. They are generous. They allow their hearts to expand. They have compassion for all forms of suffering. Pity is the very foundation-stone of genius.

—Anatole France

Skepticism

5934. Skepticism which seeks without cessation, serves truth more acceptably by far than easy belief that takes its breakfast in bed, and lets hearsay speak for truth.

—Henry S. Haskins

5935. Not too many years ago, weird ideas having to do with something called "television," and others promising propellerless planes, were greeted generally with indulgent skepticism. But times have changed. Today imaginative thinking has taken hold. Just tell us that in twenty years we may be taking trips to the moon, and we are ready to buy a reserved seat on the first excursion. The scientists have taught us to accept imaginative thinking, and to lay aside our instinctive reaction that it can't be done.

—Neil McElroy

Slander

5936. He who blackens others does not whiten himself.

—*German Proverb*

5937. Slander is the revenge of a coward, and as often is the result of vanity as of malice.

5938. Slander cannot destroy an honest man . . . when the flood recedes the rock is there.

—*Chinese Proverb*

5939. A single sentence sometimes casts an odium on a man's character that years of integrity will not efface.

—Jean Jacques Rousseau

5940. The slanderer is like one who flings dust at another when the wind is contrary; the dust returns on him who threw it.

—BUDDHA

5941. The worthiest people are frequently attacked by slander, as we generally find that to be the best fruit which the birds have been pecking at.

—JONATHAN SWIFT

5942. What is slander? A verdict of "guilty" pronounced in the absence of the accused, with closed doors, without defense or appeal, by an interested and prejudiced judge.

—JOSEPH ROUX

Sleep

5943. I rise early because no day is long enough for a day's work.

—LOUIS D. BRANDEIS

5944. No civilized person ever goes to bed the same day he gets up.

—RICHARD HARDING DAVIS

5945. The amount of sleep required by individuals varies except that each person needs just five minutes more.

Smallness. See also Little Things

5946. Little boats should keep near shore.

—BENJAMIN FRANKLIN

5947. Small kindnesses, small courtesies, small considerations, habitually practiced in our social intercourse, give a greater charm to the character than the display of great talent and accomplishments.

5948. Small thoughts, small goals, small aims never lead to big accomplishments. The first step toward achievement is to create the big picture in your mind and then work to make it come true. Thoughts are the blueprints by which you build your future. Shanty-size thoughts will not build a skyscraper. To build big you must first think big.

Smile—Smiles

5949. If you can't crown yourself with laurels, you can at least wreathe your face in smiles.

5950. Smile, once in awhile,
'Twill make your heart seem lighter;
Smile, once in awhile,
'Twill make your pathway brighter.
Life's a mirror, if we smile
Smiles come back to greet us;
If we're frowning all the while
Frowns for ever meet us.

—Nixon Waterman

5951. Smiles is the longest word in the world—there is a mile between the first and last letters of the word. He smiled—and his home was a place of happiness. He smiled—and the children ran out of the way to meet and greet him. He smiled—and his co-workers in business worked better than in any other place of employment. He smiled—and his business clients and callers spoke well of him and his business increased. He smiled—and all who entered his office door were pleased to be greeted as friend and equal. He smiled—and followed the smile with a brotherly handclasp; and those who were discouraged and downcast went out and took a new grip on life and their work. He smiled—and while the years rolled on, he grew younger, because—He smiled.

5952. GIVE ME A SMILE

Give me a smile—that gay and joyous gleam,
As when, through clouds, some golden beam
Steals out to warm the day!
A smile; the first sight glimpsed on mother's face
By peering baby eyes!
A smile; the mark of gentle, kindly grace
We learn to love and prize!

Give me a smile—that sign of happiness
Which drives away
Dull thoughts of weariness and stress,
And makes the moments gay!
Within the spirit of a smile there lives
The stirring breath of cheer;
The surety of friendliness that gives
New hope—when skies are drear!

Give me a smile—that flash of hidden gold
Within the heart;

That hint of harmony and good untold,
Of which—we all are part!
A smile—born of a cheerful thought,
A word of hope, a jest;
Is as a thing by angels wrought,
'Tis love—made manifest!

—*Author Unknown*

Smoking

5953. A good cigar is as great a comfort to a man as a good cry to a woman.

—Edward Bulwer-Lytton

5954. Cigars are more jealous than women. If they feel you're losing interest in them, they stop burning!

—Arthur Rubinstein

5955. A boy begins to smoke to show he is a man. After twenty or thirty years he tries to stop with the same objective.

5956. The pipe draws wisdom from the lips of the philosopher, and shuts up the mouths of the foolish; it generates a style of conversation contemplative, thoughtful, benevolent and unaffected.

—William Makepeace Thackeray

5957. Want to quit smoking? Really, it's quite simple. Just stop buying cigarettes. Then, when you feel the urge to smoke, borrow a cigarette from a friend. Soon all of your friends will be helping you to quit smoking . . . if you still have any friends.

5958. I've promised my sons £100 each if they don't smoke until they are twenty-one. If they started at sixteen, I reckon they'd spend that easily in the five years at the present prices of cigarettes.

But if they postpone smoking for five years, science may then have made it safe. Or, indeed, they might not want to start at all. So, however you do it, stop the children from smoking for as long as you can. I'm glad that London County Council has taken a lead in this direction by issuing pamphlets outlining the dangers of smoking to school leavers.

—*Anonymous*

Socialism

5959. Socialism is simply the Golden Rule unlimbered.

—Elbert Hubbard

5960. Socialism is not equal distribution of wealth. It is equal distribution of poverty.

—William Feather

5961. From each according to his abilities, to each according to his needs.

—Karl Marx

5962. It is a socialist idea that making profits is a vice. I consider the real vice is making losses.

—Winston Churchill

5963. Socialism is indeed the great leveler. But the fact that the leveling is always downward seems to escape most theoretical socialists.

—Leonard E. Read

5964. If Karl Marx were alive today, his problem would be to find parking spaces for the American proletariat rather than break their chains of economic slavery.

—G. K. Reddy

5965. Socialism is simply a yearning for no risks. Without risks there is never a gain, and those who are afraid to lose a race have no business entering it. . . . We'd love a world without dolts, where everyone is king, but God planned it otherwise.

5966. When a government takes over a people's economic life it becomes absolute, and when it has become absolute it destroys the arts, the minds, the liberties and the meaning of the people it governs. . . . Men who are fed by their government will soon be driven down to the status of slaves or cattle.

—Maxwell Anderson

5967. The progressive taxation system which puts a penalty on success by draining off as high as 91% of individual income, is not an "American" system. It was first advocated by Karl Marx in the *Communist Manifesto,* as a device to destroy the capitalist system and bring on socialism.

Solitude

5968. A wise man is never less alone than when he is alone.

—Jonathan Swift

5969. One can acquire everything in solitude—except character.

—Henri de Stendahl

5970. I love to be alone. I never found the companion that was so companionable as solitude.

—Henry David Thoreau

5971. Solitude is as needful to the imagination as society is wholesome for the character.

—James Russell Lowell

5972. I would rather sit on a pumpkin and have it all to myself than be crowded on a velvet cushion.

—Henry David Thoreau

5973. The great man is he who, in the midst of the crowd, keeps with perfect sweetness the independence of solitude.

—Ralph Waldo Emerson

5974. That which happens to the soil when it ceases to be cultivated, happens to man himself when he foolishly forsakes society for solitude; the brambles grow up in his desert heart.

—Antoine Rivaroli

5975. It would do the world good if every man in it would compel himself occasionally to be absolutely alone. Most of the world's progress has come out of such loneliness.

—Bruce Barton

5976. Solitude is one of the highest enjoyments of which our nature is susceptible. Solitude is also, when too long continued, capable of being made the most severe, indescribable, unendurable source of anguish.

5977. It is often said that a man's personal religion grows out of the uses to which he puts his moments of solitude. A sure mark of an irreligious person is one who hates to ever be alone, who must be constantly amused by radio, television, bridge and canasta or idle companionship.

—Gilbert N. Holloway

5978. Solitude is a blessed state. It is twice blessed. First, in what it gives to those who really welcome it and take it home; second, in what they, or some of them, may by great luck be able to give back to life through profitable use of its beneficence.

To have an appetite for silence is not necessarily to be smug. It is not smug to like to stand back and think things over, to be meditative rather than intuitive. The average selfish solitary may know—indeed has profitably learned by experience—that it is only by indulging his own detachment that he is likely to be of any use at all to life and his fellows.

What the solitary learns is to see the wood as well as the trees, a thing which it is practically impossible to learn in the fuss or frivolity of communal life.

—Kate O'Brien

Sorrow

5979. Sorrow is the child of too much joy.

—*Chinese Proverb*

5980. Silence is the ultimate eloquence of sorrow.

—William Winter

5981. When the heart is full, the lips are silent.

5982. The soul would have no rainbow had the eyes no tears.

—John Vance Cheney

5983. The display of sorrow is sometimes a subtle form of vanity.

5984. Sorrow is the mere rust of the soul. Activity will cleanse and brighten it.

—Dr. Samuel Johnson

5985. Sorrow cannot be fought and overcome; it cannot be evaded or escaped; it must be lived with.

—Janet Gray

5986.

Grief may be joy misunderstood
Only the good discerns the good.

—Elizabeth Barrett Browning

5987. A great sorrow is a great repose, and you will come out from your grief stronger than when you entered it.

—Alexandre Dumas

5988. An excess of sorrow is as foolish as profuse laughter; while, on the other hand, not to mourn at all is insensibility.

—SENECA

5989. Sorrows may take from life its delights but, thank God! they can never take its duties. At the lowest ebb of dejection we still have much to do.

—FREDERICK D. MAURICE

5990. Sorrow for the death of a father lasts six months; sorrow for a mother, a year; sorrow for a wife, until another wife; sorrow for a son, for ever.

—*Sanskrit Proverb*

5991. There is something totally wrong with the blood of a man who reveals the same unhealed wound year after year. For it is the impulse of a healthful nature to heal wounds. So is there something radically wrong in the makeup of the person who shows you the same cankering sorrow year after year, for it is also the wish and purpose of progressive nature that we should outgrow our griefs. He who does not has a right to our pity.

Space Age

5992. Anyone who still thinks the sky is the limit has no imagination.

5993. Perhaps the reason that life on other planets is extinct is that their scientists were a little more advanced than ours.

5994. According to a scientist, first space travelers will know they are nearing the moon when they see this sign: "Song writers go home."

5995. I really think that it is monstrous that having so mismanaged our own planet we should attempt management of any other planet in space.

—SIR ROBERT WATSON-WATT

5996. Science has put man in his place; one among the millions of kinds of living things crawling around on . . . a minor planet circling a trivial star. We can't really face the implications of this. . . . A billion years into the past and a billion light-years into space remain abstractions that we can handle glibly, but hardly realize.

—MARSTON BATES

5997. There is beauty in space, and it is orderly. There is no weather, and there is regularity. It is predictable. . . . Everything in space obeys the laws of physics. If you know these laws, and obey them, space will treat you kindly. And don't tell me man doesn't belong out there. Man belongs wherever he wants to go.

—WERNHER VON BRAUN

5998. It is related by a peasant that he had persuaded himself that beyond his fields there were no others, and when he happened to lose a cow and was compelled to go in search of her, he was astonished at the great number of fields beyond his own few acres. This must also be the case of many theorists who have persuaded themselves that beyond this field or little globe of earth there lie no other worlds—simply because he has not seen them.

—BARUCH SPINOZA

Space, Outer. See Outer Space

Speaker, Introduction of. See Introduction of Speaker

Specialization

5999. Specialization has reached such a state today that patients have to learn to diagnose themselves before they know which specialist to call.

—FULTON J. SHEEN

6000. One of the principal challenges of our world to the individual is that he must not only achieve a fairly high degree of specialization to make him a useful member of society, but at the same time achieve enough general knowledge to enable him to look with sympathy and understanding on what is going on about him.

—OLIVER J. CALDWELL

Speculation

6001. A speculator is a man who observes the future and acts before it occurs.

—BERNARD BARUCH

6002. There are two times in a man's life when he should not speculate; when he can't afford it and when he can.

—MARK TWAIN

6003. A man cannot administer great corporations which employ armies of men and serve large communities if his judgment is diluted and distracted by huge speculative transactions. . . . A man cannot be a good doctor and keep telephoning to his broker between visits to his patients, nor a good lawyer with one eye on the ticker.

—Walter Lippmann

Speech

6004. The true use of speech is not so much to express our wants as to conceal them.

—Oliver Goldsmith

6005. It is a great misfortune not to have enough wit to speak well, or not enough judgment to keep silent.

—Jean de La Bruyère

6006. A dog is not considered a good dog because he is a good barker. A man is not considered a good man because he is a good talker.

—Chuang Tzu

6007. As a vessel is known by the sound, whether it be cracked or not; so men are proved, by their speeches, whether they be wise or foolish.

—Demosthenes

6008. God, that all-powerful Creator of nature and Architect of the world, has impressed man with no character so proper to distinguish him from other animals, as by the faculty of speech.

—Quintilian

6009. The first duty of a man is to speak; that is his chief business in this world; and talk, which is the harmonious speech of two or more, is by far the most accessible of pleasures. It costs nothing; it is all profit; it completes our education; it founds and fosters our friendships; and it is by talk alone that we learn our period and ourselves.

—Robert Louis Stevenson

6010. Speech is not merely the dress, as it is often called but the very body of thought. It is to the intellect what the muscles are to the principle of physical life. The mind acts and strengthens itself through words. It is a chaos, till defined, organized by language. The attempt to give clear precise utterance to thought is one of the most effectual processes of mental discipline. It is, therefore, no doubtful sign of the growing intelligence of a people, when the power of expression is cultivated extensively for the purpose of acting on multitudes.

—WILLIAM ELLERY CHANNING

Spelling

6011. An ambitious office boy should learn how to spell—some day he may have a secretary.

6012. Many an office worker knows that if you are poor at spelling it helps a lot if your handwriting is terrible, too.

6013. As our alphabet now stands, the bad spelling, or what is called so, is generally the best, as conforming to the sound of the letters and of the words.

—BENJAMIN FRANKLIN

6014. A curious reversal has taken place in modern education. We now teach some students the rudiments of research in the fifth grade while we teach others how to spell in college.

Sportsmanship

6015. Nobody with gumption is what you would call a good loser. But I try to be gracious.

—TERRY BRENNAN

6016. Win if you can, lose if you must, but learn to take your whippings without whimper.

—WALTER CAMP

6017. Always play fair, and think fair; and if you win don't crow about it; and if you lose don't fret.

—EDEN PHILLPOTTS

Stability

6018. Make keeping your feet on the ground a habit and you'll never have far to fall.

6019. It is great to have your feet on the ground, but keep them moving.

6020. One way to keep a man's feet on the ground is to put a heavy responsibility on his shoulders.

Stagnation

6021. He who is silent is forgotten; he who abstains is taken at his word; he who does not advance falls back; he who stops is overwhelmed, distanced, crushed; he who ceases to grow greater becomes smaller; he who leaves off, gives up; the stationary condition is the beginning of the end.

—Henri Frederic Amiel

6022. Life does not stand still. Where there is no progress there is disintegration. Today a thousand doors of enterprise are open to you, inviting you to useful work. To live at this time is an inestimable privilege, and a sacred obligation devolves upon you to make right use of your opportunities. Today is the day in which to attempt and achieve something worth while.

—Grenville Kleiser

Statesmanship

6023. The heart of a statesman should be in his head.

—Napoleon I

6024. The three great ends for a statesman are, security to possessors, facility to acquirers, and liberty and hope for the people.

—Samuel T. Coleridge

6025. A statesman, we are told, should follow public opinion. Doubtless . . . as a coachman follows his horses; having firm hold on the reins, and guiding them.

—Thomas Hare

Statistics

6026. Statisticians collect facts and draw their own confusions.

6027. Statistics is the art of drawing a crooked line from an unproved assumption to a foregone conclusion.

—Emil Frankel

6028. Before we all get so shaken up about statistical warnings that such-and-such percentage of all people who die of this-and-that disease were those who followed this-or-that common personal habit—someone should point out that upwards of 80% of those who go insane are coffee, tea or beer drinkers, at least 98% of those who commit suicide are people who sleep indoors, and darned near 100% of those injured in traffic accidents are people who move from one place to another.

Stature

6029. A man never adds to his stature by treading on others' toes.

6030. Little minds are concerned principally with methods, opinions, and precedents. Men with big minds go from the natural heart within them direct to the problem to solve it in a fundamental way.

—Lowell Fillmore

Status Quo

6031. Never disturb the waters in which you intend to fish.

6032. We win half the battle when we make up our minds to take the world as we find it, including the thorns.

—Orison S. Marden

Stinginess

6033. A stingy man is always poor.

—*French Proverb*

6034. He that spareth in everything is an inexcusable niggard. He that spareth in nothing is an inexcusable madman. The mean is to spare in what is least necessary, and to lay out more liberally in what is most required.

—Lord Halifax

6035. All children are born stingy. A child comes into the world with concern only for himself. If an adult is covetous and stingy, it is not a habit he has acquired. Rather, it is infantile behavior he has not been able to overcome.

—Adeline Dutton Whitney

Stock Market

6036. Financial statistics tend to prove that the best time to buy any given stocks or bonds is a year ago.

6037. Keith Funston, President, New York Stock Exchange, tells of a lady visitor to the exchange who stood, bewildered and fascinated by symbols and quotations on the gigantic ticker tape. Finally, above the tape, she spied a large clock, flashing the time at intervals—10:31, 10:32, 10:33. Grabbing the sleeve of the nearest exchange employe, she said urgently: "Quick! I want to buy that stock. It seems to be going up a point every time I look at it!"

Strength

6038. Nothing is so strong as gentleness; nothing so gentle as real strength.

—St. Francis de Sales

6039. You become strong by defying defeat, and by turning loss to gain and failure to success.

6040. You know any fool can stay up all night, but it takes a strong man to get up in the morning.

6041. It is excellent to have a giant's strength,
But it is tyrannous to use it like a giant.

—William Shakespeare

6042. Many times it takes real courage to stand up and be counted, but to keep on standing up after being counted is the real test of strength.

—J. T. Rutherford

Stubbornness

6043. It is pretty hard to talk horse sense to a mule.

—Dan Bennett

6044. Those who never retract their opinions love themselves more than they love truth.

—Joseph Joubert

Subjugation

6045. So long as you keep a person down, there must be some part of you down there to keep him down.

—Marian Anderson

6046. Man is a creature who has to argue down another man's opinion before he can believe in his own.

Subterfuge

6047. In one of the southern states, where a literacy test is required before one is permitted to vote, a colored citizen successfully baffled all the examiner's attempts to disqualify him on these grounds. Finally, the examiner said: "Very well, what does eeny-meeny, miny, mo mean?" "I guess," said the applicant, dejectedly "it means you gentlemen just don't want to give me the right to vote."

6048. A motorist traveling toward a backwoods area stopped at a filling station to fill up his tank and to ask about the roads ahead. The service-station man thought a bit and then answered, "They say the roads in the next county are fine, but you got to watch the detours. They're bad."

The motorist drove on and suddenly realized he had gotten off the road somewhere and was now on a detour. The filling-station man was right. It was bad. Passing a farmer plowing near the fence, he stopped the car and shouted, "How do I get off this detour and on one of those fine roads you're supposed to have in this county?"

The farmer stopped plowing and shouted back, "You won't never get off the detour. Our folks just won't stand for bad roads in this county, so they just took down all the road signs and marked 'em 'Detour.' "

Success

6049. Success is good management in action.

—William E. Holler

6050. Success covers a multitude of blunders.

—George Bernard Shaw

6051. Success comes in cans; failure in can'ts.

6052. Success tip: start at the bottom and wake up.

6053. Success is a series of failures—put to flight.

6054. The secret of success is constancy of purpose.

—BENJAMIN DISRAELI

6055. If you itch for success, keep on scratching.

6056. If at first you don't succeed, you have plenty of company.

—ELDON PEDERSEN

6057. You may have success if you do not demand victory.

—JOHN BUCHAN

6058. Success is only a matter of luck—ask any man who fails.

6059. There aren't any rules for success that work unless you do.

6060. The success that turns a man's head sometimes wrings his neck.

6061. About the best method of climbing higher is to remain on the level.

6062. Success shuns the unworthy, the unwilling, and the unprepared.

6063. To reach the front many a man has to be kicked in the rear.

6064. The only way to get anywhere is to start from where you are.

—WILLIAM LEE

6065. If hard work is the key to success, most people would rather pick the lock.

—MAURICE SEITTER

6066. The road to success runs uphill, so don't expect to break any speed records.

6067. The worst use that can be made of success is to boast of it.

—ARTHUR HELPS

6068. We have only to explain failures; success speaks for itself.

6069. You can't get to the top by dealing from the bottom.

6070. You can't find a path to the top; you have to make one.

6071. Industry is the mother of success—luck a distant relative.

6072. Real success is more of an inward feeling than an outward show.

6073. The glory that attends success gives strength for the labor.

—SEXTUS AURELIUS PROPERTIUS

6074. There's plenty of room at the top, but there's no room to sit down.

6075. To many, the most important ingredient in the recipe for success is crust.

—PHIL H. TUSETH

6076. Making hay isn't so hard today, but stacking it up—that's the problem.

—H. C. DIEFENBACH

6077. Success generally depends upon knowing how long it takes to succeed.

—CHARLES DE SECONDAT MONTESQUIEU

6078. The road to success is never as crowded as the parking space beside it.

6079. Success comes to those who make the greatest profit from the fewest mistakes.

6080. You're on the road to success when you realize that failure is merely a detour.

6081. Success in life is a matter not so much of talent as of concentration and perseverance.

—C. W. WENDTE

6082. The best way to succeed in this world is to act on the advice you give to others.

6083. Someone has defined success as the art of making your mistakes when nobody is looking.

6084. One never mounts so high as when one does not know how high he is going.

—Napoleon I

6085. Behind many a successful man can be found three people—his wife and Mr. and Mrs. Jones.

6086. Some people have ability and some have ambition—those who succeed have both.

6087. The successful man is the one who does what he has to do at the time he hates to do it most.

6088. Success to some men is marrying a girl with money who is too proud to let her husband work.

6089. The kind of success that turns a man's head always leaves him facing in the wrong direction.

6090. The most difficult part of getting to the top of the ladder is getting through the crowd at the bottom.

—Arch Ward

6091. The best way to guard against losing your shirt is to keep your sleeves rolled up.

6092. Many a man lives a rich full life because he knows how to turn his failures into assets.

6093. Despite all the progress of science, the best way to get ahead still is to use the one you've got.

—O. A. Battista

6094. All men want to succeed, but some want to so much that they're willing to work for it.

6095. The secret of success lies in doing well what you can do, and forgetting about the rest.

6096. Let us be thankful for the fools. But for them the rest of us could not succeed.

6097. Some men are successful chiefly because they didn't have the advantages other people had.

6098. It is an unhealthy attitude to think success a trivial incident in life.

6099. The gain which is made at the expense of reputation, should be set down as loss.

—PUBLILIUS SYRUS

6100. You advance in life according to the time you spend that you don't get paid for.

6101. Success: the proper ratio between what one contributes and what one derives from life.

6102. Everybody's a self-made man, but only the successful ones are ever willing to admit it.

6103. It is easy to be a success when conditions are right. "Anyone can hold the helm when the sea is calm," said Publilius Syrus.

6104. Most people would succeed in small things if they were not troubled with great ambitions.

—HENRY WADSWORTH LONGFELLOW

6105. Success is attained not by lying awake at night, but by keeping awake in the daytime.

6106. Success has a great tendency to conceal and throw a veil over the evil deeds of men.

6107. To achieve success not by heritage but by individual effort is the greatest joy in life.

—J. P. MORGAN

6108. When a man blames others for his failures, it's a good idea to credit somebody else with his successes.

6109. Life does not require us to make good; it asks only that we give our best at each new level of experience.

—THE REV. HAROLD W. RUOPP

6110. The secret of success can be stated in nine words: stick to it, stick to it, stick to it.

6111. When a man leaves out the working parts it's hard for him to become a successful self-made man.

6112. You'll be successful if you make hay from the grass that grows under the other fellow's feet.

6113. The man who doesn't give a hoot what people say about him is either at the bottom or the top.

6114. The difference between failure and success is doing a thing nearly right and doing it exactly right.

—EDWARD C. SIMMONS

6115. The superior man makes the difficulty to be overcome his first interest; success comes only later.

—CONFUCIUS

6116. Success or failure in business is caused more by the mental attitude even than by mental capacities.

—WALTER DILL SCOTT

6117. The talent of success is nothing more than doing what you can do well, without a thought of fame.

—HENRY WADSWORTH LONGFELLOW

6118. The man who works for the gold in the job rather than for the money in the pay envelope, is the fellow who gets on.

—JOSEPH FRENCH JOHNSON

6119. The only ladder it is bad luck to walk under is the ladder of success—it's there to climb.

6120. A man cannot expect to make a place in the sun for himself without acquiring some painful blisters.

6121. You don't have to make a lot of money to amount to something in this world. You can inherit it.

—FRANKLIN P. JONES

6122. You are half way up the ladder of success if you are doing the work you like, and making a living at it.

6123. Success does not consist in never making blunders, but in never making the same one the second time.

—Henry Wheeler Shaw

6124. You don't have to climb the highest mountain to succeed. Still around are several molehills which haven't yet been scaled.

6125. When you can think of yesterday without a regret, and of tomorrow without a fear, you are on the road to success.

6126. Success is a fraud after all. By the time you're rich enough to sleep late, you're so old you always wake up early.

6127. It used to be that everyone hoped to climb the ladder of success. Now we look for a fast trip on the express elevator.

6128. The successful man lengthens his stride when he discovers that the signpost has deceived him; the failure looks for a place to sit down.

—J. R. Rogers

6129. When a little success goes to a man's head it usually means he's already reached the top of the ladder.

6130. Many imagine that the higher you go, the easier the climbing. Don't be governed by that theory unless you have a soft place to fall back into.

—J. L. Boggus

6131. The formula for success is putting the right people in the right jobs and then sitting on the sidelines and being a rousing good cheerleader.

—A. Marshall Jones

6132. Probably the biggest advantage of success resides in the fact that you don't have to listen to good advice any more.

6133. There is a *four-word* recipe for success that applies equally well to organizations or individuals—*make yourself more useful.*

6134. The measure of success is not whether you have a tough problem to deal with, but whether it's the same problem you had last year.

6135. Henry Ford was once asked by an ambitious young employee, "How can I make my life a success?" and Mr. Ford's answer was simply, "When you start a thing, finish it."

6136. Success lies, not in achieving what you aim at, but in aiming at what you ought to achieve, and pressing forward, sure of achievement here, or if not here, hereafter.

—R. F. Horton

6137. Starting out to make money is the greatest mistake in life. Do what you feel you have a flair for doing, and if you are good enough at it the money will come.

—Lord Rootes

6138. In everything that we do or mean to do, the first condition of success is that we understand clearly the result which we desire to produce.

—James Anthony Froude

6139. There is one rule for industrialists and that is: Make the best quality of goods possible at the lowest cost possible, paying the highest wages possible.

—Henry Ford

6140. If you wish success in life, make perseverance your bosom friend, experience your wise counsellor, caution your elder brother, and hope your guardian genius.

—Joseph Addison

6141. If there is any one secret of success, it lies in the ability to get the other person's point of view and see things from his angle as well as from your own.

—Henry Ford

6142. Man cannot be satisfied with mere success. He is concerned with the terms upon which success comes to him. And very often the terms seem more important than the success.

—Charles A. Bennett

6143. No legitimate businessman ever got started on the road to permanent success by any other means than that of hard, intelligent work, coupled with an earned credit, plus character.

—F. D. Van Amburgh

6144. How to succeed, if you think it's worth the trouble: Hitch your wagon to a star, put your shoulder to the wheel, keep an ear to the ground and watch the handwriting on the wall.

6145. Success in business implies optimism, mutual confidence, and fair play. A businessman must hold a high opinion of the worth of what he has to sell and he must feel that he is a useful public servant.

—R. H. Cabell

6146. There is but one straight road to success, and that is merit. The man who is successful is the man who is useful. Capacity never lacks opportunity. It cannot remain undiscovered, because it is sought by too many anxious to use it.

—Bourke Cockran

6147. The men whom I have seen succeed best in life have always been cheerful and hopeful men, who went about their business with a smile on their faces, and took the changes and chances of this mortal life like men, facing rough and smooth alike as it came.

—Charles Kingsley

6148. To succeed, a business must occupy a field of public usefulness by producing a good article at the lowest price consistent with fair treatment of all those concerned with its production, distribution and consumption.

—Walter C. Teagle

6149. The minute we say to ourselves that we have succeeded, we have confessed failure. When a man is satisfied that he has succeeded, he means that his striving for success is over, and that marks him as a failure. A man who is doing his best each day is truly alive, but a man who did his best yesterday is starting to die.

—Thomas J. Watson

6150. Vigilance in watching opportunity; tact and daring in seizing upon opportunity; force and persistence in crowding opportunity to its utmost of possible achievement—these are the martial virtues which must command success.

—William Lyon Phelps

6151. One never learns by success. Success is the plateau that one rests upon to take breath and look down from upon the straight and difficult path but one does not climb upon a plateau.

—JOSEPHINE PRESTON PEABODY

6152. There is a major disaster when a person allows some success to become a stopping place rather than a way station on to a larger goal. It often happens that an early success is a greater moral hazard than an early failure.

—HALFORD E. and ROBERT E. LUCCOCK

6153. The man who starts out with the idea of getting rich won't succeed; you must have a larger ambition. There is no mystery in business success. If you do each day's task successfully, stay faithfully within the natural operations of commercial law, and keep your head clear, you will come out all right.

—JOHN D. ROCKEFELLER, SR.

6154. The men whom I have seen succeed best in life, have always been cheerful and hopeful men, who went about their business with a smile on their faces, and took the changes and chances of their mortal life like men facing rough and smooth alike as it came, and so found the truth of the old proverb, that "good times, and bad times, and all times pass over."

—CHARLES KINGSLEY

6155. Successful people rarely consider work as just so much labor; they regard it in the nature of an opportunity for service and feel enjoyment in and derive success from it. The person who makes money his sole object of labor is cheating himself.

6156. The courage to be just; the courage to be honest; the courage to resist temptation; the courage to do one's duty; this is the moral courage that characterizes the highest order of manhood and womanhood—it is the courage without which no great, permanent success is achieved.

—SAMUEL SMILES

6157. We fail most frequently when we seek a goal by someone else's path. We stumble most trying to walk the other fellow's way; we get best results when we do the best we can. "Making the most of what you have" is not the worst definition of success.

—NORMAN C. SCHIDLE

6158. What is the recipe for successful achievement? To my mind there are just four essential ingredients: Choose a career you love. . . . Give it the best there is in you. . . . Seize your opportunities. . . . And be a member of the team. In no country but America, I believe, is it possible to fulfill all four of these requirements.

—BENJAMIN F. FAIRLESS

6159. This is success: To be able to carry money without having it burn a hole in your pocket. To be able to bear an injustice without getting back at somebody. To be able to do one's duty even when one is not watched. To be able to stick with a job until it is finished—on time. To be able to make use of criticism without letting it whip you.

6160. Success lies very largely in our own hands. It means effort, it means having a definite aim and striving earnestly to achieve it; it means wise planning, a knowledge of oneself, of one's circumstances and possibilities; it means the power to judge truly of values.

—GRENVILLE KLEISER

6161. Success is not a matter of position or possessions. It is a frame of mind. It is the satisfying feeling of a life spent in a worthwhile way, and a feeling of service rendered. There have been rich men, important men, whose lives were complete failures. And there have been poor men whom the ages have delighted to honor.

—STEPHEN M. PAULSON

6162. A retired business executive was once asked the secret of his success. He replied it could be summed up in three words—"and then some." "I discovered at an early age," he declared, "that most of the difference between average people and top people could be explained in three words. The top people did what was expected of them —*and then some.*"

—CARL HOLMES

6163. All men seek one goal: success or happiness. The only way to achieve true success is to express yourself completely in service to society. First, have a definite, clear, practical ideal—a goal, an objective. Second, have the necessary means to achieve your ends—wisdom, money, materials and methods. Third, adjust all your means to that end.

—ARISTOTLE

6164. Men do not succeed in business or in life, no matter how intelligent they may be, no matter how sharply their aptitudes are defined, no matter how brilliantly they may be educated unless they are oriented toward the proper goals and have the drive or motivating force to succeed. One has to want something mighty hard and keep on wanting things all his life.

—WALLACE H. WULFECK

6165. To find a career to which you are adapted by nature, and then to work hard at it, is about as near to a formula for success and happiness as the world provides. One of the fortunate aspects of this formula is that, granted the right career has been found, the hard work takes care of itself. Then hard work is not hard work at all.

—MARK SULLIVAN

6166. There are two kinds of success. One is the very rare kind that comes to the man who has the power to do what no one else has the power to do. That is genius. But the average man who wins what we call success is not a genius. He is a man who has merely the ordinary qualities that he shares with his fellows, but who has developed those ordinary qualities to a more than ordinary degree.

—THEODORE ROOSEVELT

6167. The reason most people do not succeed is that they will not do the things that successful people *must* do. The successful scientist must follow a formula. The tourist follows a road map. The builder follows a blueprint. The successful cook follows a recipe. . . . It is not important that you merely want to succeed, unless you want to badly enough that you are willing to do certain things.

6168. Any formula for individual success begins and ends with a man's personal enterprise. The rules are few, but mighty; establish your goal, fire yourself with enthusiasm and positive thinking, and begin and end your career by helping others. Within this pattern each man can carve a statue from his own block of marble. And the finished product, his American success story, will be a tribute to his initiative, ambition, and enterprise.

—HARRY A. BULLIS in
Manifesto for Americans
(McGraw-Hill Book Co.)

6169. Although there have been many "secrets" of success presented and defended, the real secret is very simple. It is interest.

If you are interested enough in anything, you cannot help succeeding with it, but if you are disinterested or apathetic, you can't win. This goes for everything, from your job to the hobby you take up to beguile you.

6170. Success is relative. It does not mean a man has progressed to the limit of his capabilities, but only that he has made remarkable progress. It implies continued improvement—for only those who are improving are a success. Curiously, though, when a person comes to the point in his evolution where he epitomizes success, nobody calls him successful. He represents achievement, which is greater than success.

—Paul P. Wentz

6171. Recipe for success: Be polite, prepare yourself for whatever you are asked to do, keep yourself tidy, be cheerful, don't be envious, be honest with yourself so you will be honest with others, be helpful, interest yourself in your job, don't pity yourself, be quick to praise, be loyal to your friends, avoid prejudices, be independent, interest yourself in politics, and read the newspapers.

—Bernard M. Baruch

6172. There was once a man who was obsessed with the idea that there was a secret known to those who achieved success. To discover this secret he devoted years to study and research.

Philosophy, astrology, psychology, salesmanship, religious beliefs, the various cults that have enjoyed success—all these he studied long and diligently.

Finally, he gave his conclusion, and it came in two short words: "I will."

6173. To achieve what the world calls success a man must attend strictly to business and keep a little in advance of the times. The man who reaches the top is not content with doing just what is required of him. He does more.

Every man should make up his mind that if he expects to succeed, he must give an honest return for the other man's dollar.

Grasp an idea and work it out to a successful conclusion. That is about all there is in life for any of us.

—Edward H. Harriman

6174. When business is not all that it should be there is a temptation to sit back and say, "Well, what's the use! We've done everything possible to stir up a little business and there is nothing doing so what's the use of trying!" There is always a way. There was a way in and there is a way out. And success comes to the man who grits his teeth, squares his jaw, and says, "There is a way for me and, by jingo, I'll find it." The stagnator gathers green scum, finally dries up and leaves an unsightly hallow.

—Clifford Sloan

6175. He has achieved success who has lived well, laughed often and loved much, who has enjoyed the trust of pure women, the respect of intelligent men and the love of little children; who has filled his niche and accomplished his task; who has left the world better than he found it, whether by an improved poppy, a perfect poem, or a rescued soul; who has never lacked appreciation of earth's beauty or failed to express it; who has always looked for the best in others and given them the best he had; whose life was an inspiration; whose memory a benediction.

—Bessie Anderson Stanley

6176. A cartoon published in a great newspaper on Lincoln's birthday some years ago drew considerable attention. In it the artist had depicted a log cabin nestling at the foot of a high, frowning mountain. On the summit stood the White House. A ladder extended from the open door of the log cabin to the handsome structure on the mountaintop. Over the top of the drawing the artist had placed this inscription: *"The ladder is still there."*

A whole volume of inspiration in one short sentence!

—Philip Jerome Cleveland

6177. The successful man has nothing important to say about success, once declared Henry Ford. He did not achieve it by talk but by toiling at his task. Conspicuous successes are comparatively few because most people think of success as acquired; it is more correctly contributed. People who try to break in by the gate of acquisition are knocking at the wrong door. The entrance to success is by the gate of contribution. Everything that is taken out, someone has put in. How much have you put in? Of your own great endowment of life and its powers, how much have you contributed to any service besides your own? It is a good question for checking up one's usefulness.

6178. State of mind is a very important factor in success because you can condition your mind to a point where it enables or prevents you from going forward and doing things. You can poison your own mind and limit your own capacity. Don't admire the fellow that says he has an open mind—it is usually a mind with nothing in it. A man who has a state of mind based on knowledge and wisdom, experience and reason, has won half the battle, and, conversely, the other man has lost the battle. State of mind based on balanced judgment is a precious possession, but being unreasonably optimistic means nothing to me, nor does being excessively worried.

—David Sarnoff

6179. The young man who would succeed must identify his interest with those of his employer and exercise the same diligence in matters entrusted to him as he would in his own affairs. Back of all the gifts the candidate for success may possess must be a willing capacity for hard work. . . . Youth today is not considered a handicap in selecting men for responsible jobs, as it was twenty years ago. In almost any field today in which a youngster has an intelligent interest, the road to the top is open as it never was before. But the one way to the top is by persistent, intelligent, hard work.

—A. T. Mercier

6180. I WILL SUCCEED

If you will keep your faith in me,
Though life be like a stormy sea
And difficult my task may be—
I will succeed.

If you will look with smiling eyes,
Let days be dark with lowering skies
And nights be fraught with weary sighs—
I will succeed.

If you will speak a word of cheer,
Though harassed oft by doubt and fear
And ugly failure hover near—
I will succeed!

—Grenville Kleiser

6181. Let us recognize a basic truth. Success in life is not a destination. It is a journey.

Fortunately, this means that no one is obliged to work toward a single distant goal and be judged successful only if he attains that one objective. As with a traveller, the end of the journey is usually beyond the range of vision, but there is much of interest and beauty along the way to reward each day's steps.

The happiest journey is not made with downcast eyes which see only tired, dusty feet. It is made with uplifted sight to appreciate the visible panorama and with imagination to understand its significance and to picture what may lie beyond.

The stars were made for those who look up and whose imagination knows no limitations.

—Edward B. Newill

6182. The following Andrew Carnegie story is a characteristic one of poverty and pluck.

His father, a Scotch weaver who worked with handlooms, thrown out of employment by improved machinery, came to Pittsburgh when "Andy" was but ten years of age. The boy went to work as a bobbin-boy at $1.20 a week. At thirteen he was appointed to the post of engineer of the factory engine. At fourteen he became telegraph boy, and was promoted at sixteen, for quick intelligence, to the post of telegraph operator at a salary of $300 a year.

About this time his father died, and the support of the family devolved on him. He soon got a dollar a week extra for copying telegrams for the papers, which he called his "first bit of capital." His salary went for household expenses, but the dollar surplus he invested wisely, first in the express business, then in sleeping cars, and, finally, as an outcome of his management of transportation in the Civil War, in a plant to manufacture iron railway bridges.

And so by alertness and economy and untiring energy he came to be the world's most distinguished manufacturer and philanthropist, putting as much talent into giving as he had before put into getting.

6183.

It takes a little courage
  And a little self-control,
And some grim determination,
  If you want to reach the goal.
It takes a deal of striving
  And a firm and stern-set chin,
No matter what the battle,
  If you're really out to win.

There's no easy path to glory,
  There's no rosy road to fame;
Life, however we may view it,
  Is no simple parlor game;
But its prizes call for fighting,
  For endurance and for grit,
For a rugged disposition
  And a "don't-know-when-to-quit."

You must take a blow, or give one,
  You must risk and you must lose,
And expect that in the struggle
  You will suffer from a bruise.

But you mustn't wince or falter
If a fight you once begin.
Be a man and face the battle;
That's the only way to win.

—*Author Unknown*

Suffering

6184. If thou canst suffer—die!

—Alfred de Musset

6185. He who fears to suffer, suffers from fear.

—*French Proverb*

6186. The world is full of suffering, and the world is also full of the overcoming of suffering.

—Adapted from *The Open Door,* by Helen Keller. Copyright © 1957 by Helen Keller. Reprinted by permission of Doubleday & Co., Inc.

6187. Perhaps to suffer is nothing else than to live deeply. Love and sorrow are the conditions of a profound life.

—Alexandre Vinet

6188. It is a crushed grape that gives out the blood red wine; it is the suffering soul that breathes the sweetest melodies.

—Mary Abigail Dodge

6189. Suffering becomes beautiful, when any one bears great calamity with cheerfulness, not through insensibility, but through greatness of mind.

—Aristotle

6190. It is difficult to conceive anything more beautiful than the reply given by one in affliction, when he was asked how he bore it so well. "It lightens the stroke," he said, "to draw near Him who handles the rod."

Superficiality

6191. A whitewashed crow soon shows black again.

—*Chinese Proverb*

6192. The profoundly wise do not declaim against superficial knowledge in others, so much as the profoundly ignorant; on the contrary, they would rather assist it with their advice than overwhelm it with their contempt; for they know that there was a period when even a Bacon or a Newton were superficial, and that he who has a little knowledge is far more likely to get more than he that has none.

—Charles C. Colton

Superiority

6193. What the superior man seeks is in himself, but what the small man seeks is in others.

—Confucius

6194. The superior man is the providence of the inferior. He is eyes for the blind, strength for the weak, and a shield for the defenseless. He stands erect by bending above the fallen. He rises by lifting others.

—Robert H. Ingersoll

6195. It has always been a crime to be above a crowd. That's the real reason why some men in public life are maligned, attacked and slandered, for they are beyond the reach of those who realize in their own heart that the greatness of others shows their own smallness, their own inferiority.

—William J. H. Boetcker

Superstition

6196. I am not superstitious, but I would not sleep thirteen in a bed on a Friday night.

—Chauncey Depew

6197. Claude Terrail, proprietor of the elegant Paris restaurant La Tour d'Argent, had his own explanation for the superstition about having thirteen at the table. "The reason is," he said, "that most people have sets of only twelve knives and forks."

6198. We Americans should not be superstitious about the number 13. In the Great Seal of the United States there are 13 stars; 13 stripes; 13 arrows in the eagle's talons; 13 letters in the motto; 13 laurel leaves; 13 feathers in each of the eagle's wings. On the reverse side of the seal the 13 courses of Masonry are represented in the pyramid, and there are 13 roses in the Glory around the All-Seeing Eye.

6199. There is a prejudice existing, generally, on the pretended danger of being the thirteenth at table. If the probability be required, that out of thirteen persons, of different ages, one of them, at least, shall die within a year, it will be found that the chances are about one to one that one death, at least, will occur. This calculation, by means of a false interpretation, has given rise to the prejudice, no less ridiculous, that the danger will be avoided by inviting a greater number of guests, which can only have the effect of augmenting the probability of the event so much apprehended.

—LAMBERT ADOLPHE JACQUES QUETELET

Surprise

6200. There's not much use for an exclamation point anymore—nobody's surprised at anything these days.

6201. When the cat's away the mice will play, and so it was that a certain young benedict thought to take advantage of his wife's absence for a few days (on a visit to her mother) and have his old pals in for an all-night poker session. That evening, two hours after his wife's departure, bottles, dishes, cigar and cigarette butts, the ashes therefrom, and sundry fragments of pretzels and sandwiches, were scattered profusely throughout the living room.

At the height of the revelry the host was called to the door. Presently he came with a telegram. "Boys," he cried, pale with consternation, "I'm in a spot! You gotta help me out. This wire is from my wife. The car broke down and she will be back home any minute on the bus. Look at this terrible mess! What'll we do?"

There was a minute of stunned silence while all hands pondered the problem. Then one of the guests jumped up. "I've got it!" he shouted. "Let's burn the house down!"

Suspense

6202. It is a miserable thing to live in suspense; it is the life of the spider.

—JONATHAN SWIFT

6203. A man's mind is in suspense when it is balancing the weight of different arguments or considerations, or when it is uncertain respecting facts unknown, or events not in his own power.

—NOAH WEBSTER

Suspicion

6204. Be ever vigilant, but never suspicious.

—*Old Proverb*

6205. Avoid suspicion: when you're walking through
Your neighbor's melon patch, don't tie your
shoe.

—*From the Chinese*

6206. If you suspect him,
Then reject him.
If you select him,
Don't suspect him.

—*From the Chinese*

6207. The trouble with witch-hunting is that eventually the best people, the original hunters of witches, come under suspicion themselves. It becomes impossible, in the final stage, to tell which is witch. The good citizens of Salem discovered that a long time ago.

6208. A man lost an ax and suspected his neighbor's son. Everything that his neighbor's son did looked suspicious to him: the way he walked, the tone of his voice, his countenance and his gestures. But when he recovered his ax in digging a ditch, he could not see anything suspicious in his neighbor's son at all.

—*Chinese Wit & Humor,* by George Kao (Coward-McCann)

Sympathy

6209. Sympathy is two hearts tugging at *one* load.

—Charles H. Parkhurst

6210. The busy world sometimes forgets that we need sympathy in our happiness as well as in our sorrow.

—C. Hanford Henderson

Tact

6211. Tact is the ability to change a porcupine into a possum.

6212. We cannot always oblige, but we can always speak obligingly.

—Voltaire

6213. Tact is not the quality by which you often please, but by which you seldom offend.

—ALICE WELLINGTON ROLLINS

6214. Tact is the ability to remove the sting from a dangerous stinger without getting stung.

—JAMES BRYCE

6215. Tact is the ability to make a person see the lightning without letting him feel the bolt.

—O. A. BATTISTA

6216. Tact is one of the first mental virtues, the absence of which is often fatal to the best of talents; it supplies the place of many talents.

6217. Tact is not merely shown in saying the right thing at the right time and to the right people. It is shown quite as much in the many things left unsaid, and apparently unnoticed.

—WILLIAM EDWARD HARTPOLE LECKY

6218. Tact is merely doing things in the way the other person would like them done, rather than in the way you yourself would do them if you had only yourself to please. Watch your tact—and watch your influence over others rise.

—DR. DONALD A. LAIRD

Talent

6219. A great deal of talent is lost in the world for want of courage.

—SYDNEY SMITH

6220. There are two kinds of female painters; one kind wants to marry, the other also has no talent.

—MAX LIEBERMANN

6221. Talent for talent's sake is a bauble and a show. Talent working with joy in the cause of universal truth lifts the possessor to new power as a benefactor.

—RALPH WALDO EMERSON

6222. The toughest thing about success is that you've got to keep on being a success. Talent is only a starting point in business. You've got to keep working that talent.

—Irving Berlin

6223. If a man has a talent and cannot use it, he has failed. If he has a talent and uses only half of it, he has partly failed. If he has a talent and learns somehow to use the whole of it, he has gloriously succeeded, and won a satisfaction and triumph few men know.

—Thomas Wolfe

Taxation. See also Taxes

6224. Thinking is one thing no one has ever been able to tax.

—Charles F. Kettering

6225. It has reached the point where taxes are a form of capital punishment.

6226. There is only one way to kill capitalism—by taxes, taxes and more taxes.

—Karl Marx

6227. Any government big enough to give you everything you want is big enough to take everything you've got.

6228. I do not believe that the government should ask social legislation in the guise of taxation. If we are to adopt socialism, it should be presented to the people of this country as socialism and not under the guise of a law to collect revenue.

—Calvin Coolidge

6229. TAXES

Now, he's a common, common man,
Tax him! Tax him all you can,
Tax his house and tax his bed,
Tax the bald spot on his head;
Tax his bread, tax his meat,
Tax his shoes clear off his feet.
Tax his pipe and tax his smoke,
Teach him government is no joke.
Tax his "Henry," tax his gas;
Tax the road that he must pass;

Tax the farmer, tax his fowl,
Tax the dog and tax his howl,
Tax his plow, and tax his clothes,
Tax the rags that wipe his nose.
Tax his pig and tax his squeal,
Tax his boots, run down at heel,
Tax his cow, and tax his calf,
Tax him if he dares to laugh;
Tax his barns and tax his lands
Tax the blisters on his hands.
Tax the water, tax the air,
Tax the sunlight, if you dare.
Tax the living, tax the dead,
Tax the unborn before they're fed.
Tax them all and tax them well,
And do your best to make life h--l.

—Author Unknown

Taxes. See also Taxation

6230. You've got to hand it to the Tax Collector. Otherwise he'll come and get it.

6231. I wanted my son to share in the business. But the government beat him to it.

6232. *The Chinese have a word for it.* A Chinese word for taxes is Li-kin, pronounced "lickin."

6233. People are living longer, for it is necessary that they do in order to get their taxes paid.

6234. One thing is sure, the man who says that taxes keep us half-way broke was a bad judge of distance.

6235. This is still a land of opportunity. Where else could a man borrow money at 6% to pay his taxes?

6236. The tax? No wonder men abhor it!
You raise a crop, they fine you for it!

—From the Chinese

6237. Time was when it was only Washington's face that was on our money. Now it's Washington's hands on it as well.

6238. It is a mistake to believe that Uncle Sam can open his pocketbook and let you keep yours closed.

6239. A man pays a luxury tax on a leather billfold, an income tax on the stuff he puts into it, and a sales tax when he takes the stuff out.

6240. Capital punishment is when the government taxes you to get capital, in order to go into business in competition with you, and then taxes the profits on your business in order to pay its losses.

6241. Taxed on the coffin, taxed on the crib,
On the old man's shroud, on the young babe's bib,
To fatten the bigot and pamper the knave,
We are taxed from the cradle, plum into the grave.

—*"If Elected, I Promise . . ."*
by John F. Parker
(Doubleday)

6242. In America today taxes are not a tribute collected to enrich a ruler and his friends. In many parts of the world in the past that was true of taxes. In some parts of the world today it may still be true. But in our country taxes are the means by which people can work together to provide themselves with services which they could not provide as effectively in any other way.

Teacher—Teachers

6243. Good teachers cost more, but poor teachers cost most.

6244. A teacher affects eternity; he can never tell where his influence stops.

—Henry Brooks Adams

6245. The world seldom notices who teachers are; but civilization depends on what they do.

—Lindley J. Stiles

6246. There is no final way to judge the worth of a teacher except in terms of the lives of those he has taught.

6247. One of the teacher's constant tasks is to take a roomful of live wires and see that they are grounded.

6248. I would not for a moment be a teacher . . . if I thought that education had nothing to do with moral power.

—ROBERT F. GOHEEN

6249. The teacher is the real soldier of democracy. Others can defend it, but only he can make it work.

—OMAR BRADLEY

6250. Teachers are prophets who can look into the future and see the world of tomorrow into which the children of today must fit.

—EUGENE P. BERTIN

6251. I put the relation of a fine teacher to a student just below the relation of a mother to her son and I don't think I could say more than this.

—THOMAS WOLFE

6252. To be a schoolmaster is next to being a king. In the opinions of fools it is a humble task, but in fact it is the noblest of occupations.

—ERASMUS

6253. The teacher is a builder who works with the higher and finer values of civilization; a pioneer who is always attempting the impossible and winning out; and a believer who has abiding faith in the improvability of the race. He is a humble instrument in the furtherance of mankind.

—EUGENE P. BERTIN

6254. The best teacher is willing to be forgotten. His only reassurance needs to be the faith that somehow his efforts have increased the amount of mind in a world which can never have too much of that commodity. . . . His final reward is the quality of his life, which teaching has helped to shape.

—MARK VAN DOREN

6255. To a child thrust into a strange world, a teacher is the best thing that can happen.

A teacher is courage with Kleenex in its pocket, sympathy struggling with a snow-suit, and patience with papers to grade.

Teachers spend twelve hours a day searching for truth and the other twelve searching for errors.

A teacher does not really mind sniffles, squirmings, stomach aches and spills. Neither does she disintegrate before tears, fights, futility, excuses, parents who spout, little boys who shout and little girls who pout.

Most of all a teacher is somebody who likes somebody else's children—and has strength left to go to the PTA meeting.

6256. THE TEACHERS SPEAK

We are the women who take your sons,
The brilliant, the charming, the lazy ones.
They come from your care to the firm command
Of women who love them and understand
The problems that shadow their clear young eyes,
Startling innocent, solemnly wise.
Part of our hearts go to each new life;
We are something of a mother, a little of wife,
Prayer for their future is warm on our lips,
For our children on wings, on the earth, and on ships.
God, bring them back safely, these boys now men,
To the women who bore them and taught them. Amen.

—*Author Unknown*

Teacher–Pupil

6257. It is a poor pupil that does not excel his master.

—RAFAEL (Raffaello Santi)

6258. *Johnnie:* "I got the highest mark of any kid who flunked."

6259. I was attending a homecoming celebration in the little midwestern town where I taught high school 27 years ago. In the midst of the festivities a buxom matron came up to me. "Remember me?" she asked. I said that I was sorry, but I could not seem to place her. "Why," she beamed, "you wuz my English teacher."

—GLADYS M. REESE in *Readers' Digest*

Teaching

6260. Who is too old to learn is too old to teach.

—*Old Proverb*

6261. Nothing makes teaching such a satisfying job as an independent income.

—Franklin P. Jones

6262. As long as the public believes that anyone can teach, the public will believe that anyone can criticize teachers.

—Arthur F. Corey

6263. The teacher has the greatest profession, for through the hands of our instructors pass all members of every profession.

—Jesse Stuart

6264. Teaching is not lecturing or telling things. Teaching is devising a sequence of questions which enables kids to become aware of generalizations by themselves.

—Max Beberman

6265. The best teacher is not necessarily the one who possesses the most knowledge but the one who most effectively enables his students to believe in their ability to learn.

—Norman Cousins

6266. Definition of the three "R's," which represent my faith as teacher: *Reverence* for the creative achievements of men of the past, *Respect* for the continued creativity of men of the present, and *Responsibility* for maintaining and improving the conditions of creative achievement for the men of the future.

—Joseph L. Blau

6267. Teaching may be compared to driving an automobile. If the car has plenty of gasoline and a good battery and the mechanism for igniting the gasoline vapor, the engine will purr happily and the automobile will travel under its own process of internal combustion. The driver guides its course according to his own ability and wisdom. But if there is no gasoline, no spark, no internal driving power, the driver has little choice but to push or be towed.

—Verna Walters

6268. As a country schoolteacher, Charles F. Kettering frequently went beyond his schoolbooks. One day Kettering took his pupils to see their first X-ray machine. A local minister objected. "If the Lord had intended people to see through their bodies," said the minister, "He would have given them that kind of eyes. That infernal machine is nothing but the work of the devil, and the young man who took the pupils out of school to see it is not the person to be teaching our young ones."

—THOMAS ALEXANDER BOYD

6269. When I began teaching in a first grade at Foster school I made up my mind that teaching should be a personal matter carried out in an impersonal manner. I convinced myself that a child could never insult a teacher, because the more unruly and unreasonable he was, the more he needed help, and I have always made that my rule. I am going to use it in the same way with the teachers.

—ELLA FLAGG YOUNG when Superintendent of the Chicago Public Schools

6270. Teaching is lighting a lamp and not filling a bucket. That is to say the real teacher is one who inspires the pupil with love of learning or of craftsmanship. The only way to find out whether a person can teach or not is to let him try. If he can awaken enthusiasm and make the child want to learn, he is a good teacher, no matter how ill-informed he may be. If he cannot light the flame of desire for knowledge in the child's spirit, he is a poor teacher, no matter how many college degrees he may possess.

—DR. FRANK CRANE

Teamwork. See also Cooperation

6271. There are few, if any, jobs in which ability alone is sufficient. Needed, also, are loyalty, sincerity, enthusiasm and team play.

—WILLIAM B. GIVEN, JR.

Tears

6272. To weep is not always to suffer.

—MME. DE GENLIS

6273. There is a sacredness in tears. They are not the mark of weakness, but of power. They speak more eloquently than ten thousand tongues. They are the messengers of overwhelming grief, of deep contrition, and of unspeakable love.

—WASHINGTON IRVING

Technique

6274. Technique is really personality. That is why the artist cannot teach it, why the pupil cannot learn it, and why the aesthetic critic can understand it.

—Oscar Wilde

6275. A man who handles the complaint desk at a large Los Angeles public service organization has evolved a devastating technique for squelching unreasonable beefers. When a telephone caller works up to a bitter tirade against the organization, the complaint man waits till the caller reaches the sputtering point, then breaks in with, "Pardon me, madam, I was called away from the phone—would you mind repeating what you just said?"

—Matt Weinstock

Teen Age

6276. Mother Nature is providential. She gives us 12 years to develop a love for our children before turning them into teen-agers.

—William A. Galvin

6277. TEEN-AGE COMMANDMENTS

1. Stop and think before you drink.
2. Don't let your parents down, they brought you up.
3. Be humble enough to obey. You will be giving orders yourself someday.
4. At the first moment turn away from unclean thinking.
5. Don't show off when driving. If you want to race, go to Indianapolis.
6. Choose a date who would make a good mate.
7. Go to church faithfully. The Creator gives you a week. Give Him back at least one hour.
8. Choose your companions carefully. You are what they are.
9. Avoid following the crowd. Be an engine, not a caboose.
10. Recall the original Ten Commandments.

6278.

"What is a teen-ager?"
I was asked one day.
I knew what he was,
But what should I say?

He is noise and confusion.
He is silence that's deep.
He is sunshine and laughter,
Or a cloud that will weep.
He is swift as an arrow.
He's a waster of time.
He wants to be rich,
But can't save a dime.
He is rude and nasty.
He is polite as can be.
He wants Parental guidance,
But fights to be free.
He is aggressive and bossy.
He is timid and shy
He knows all the answers,
But still will ask "Why?"
He is awkward and clumsy.
He is graceful and poised.
He is ever changing,
But don't be annoyed.
"What is a teen-ager?"
I was asked one day.
He is the Future unfolding;
Don't stand in his way.

—ELIZABETH LANGSDALE

Telephone

6279. A woman traded her vacuum cleaner for a telephone claiming she could pick up more dirt that way.

6280. Thomas A. Watson, working with Alexander Graham Bell on experiments that were to lead to the invention of the telephone, accidentally plucked a bit of clock spring that lay near his end of their experimental "telephone" wire. A moment later Bell burst into the room, tense with excitement. "What was that sound?" he cried. He had heard it carried by the wire in the adjoining room. The principle had been verified. Nearly a year of intensive work remained before the first intelligible words were carried over a wire.

—*Almanac for Americans*, by WILLIS THORNTON (Greenberg)

Television

6281. One trouble with television commercials is too much tell and not enough vision.

6282. Why are television's half-baked musicals overdone, while those that are well done are rare?

6283. One reason they say television is educational is it teaches you how much you can put up with.

—Franklin P. Jones

6284. A lot of people dislike television so much that they sit up all night and glare at it.

6285. We admit many characters to our living rooms via the television screen that we would never dream of letting in through the front door.

—Bonardo Forncrook

6286. Another change television has made in a number of homes is that there are now more cockroaches in the living room than in the kitchen.

6287. An intellectual is a fellow who is willing to discuss the preceding night's television programs, but makes it clear he only happened to be watching because the children turned the set on.

6288. When I was a young man, I had an uncle who frequently took me out to dinner. He always accompanied these dinners with minutely detailed stories about himself. But I listened—because he was paying for the dinner. I don't know why I am reminded of this but we are about to have one of our commercials.

—Alfred Hitchcock

Temptation

6289. If we avoid temptation, God will keep us from sinning.

—*Old Proverb*

6290. Everything is a temptation to the man who fears temptation.

—*French Proverb*

6291. The devil never tempted a man whom he found judiciously employed.

—Charles H. Spurgeon

6292. Resist no temptation: a guilty conscience is more honorable than regret.

6293. The number of times the average man says no to temptation is once weakly.

6294. The only trouble with resisting temptation is that a man may not get another chance.

6295. There are several good protections against temptations, but the surest is cowardice.

—Mark Twain

6296. It is one thing to be tempted,
And another thing to fall.

—William Shakespeare

6297. In so far as you approach temptation to a man, you do him an injury; and if he is overcome, you share his guilt.

—Dr. Samuel Johnson

6298. It was said of John Quincy Adams: "The temptation to perform his duty was always strong; and if the duty were a particularly disagreeable one, the temptation became ungovernable."

—William Lyon Phelps

6299. Whoever yields to temptation debases himself with a debasement from which he can never rise. A man can be wronged and live; but the unrestricted, unchecked impulse to do wrong is the first and second death.

—Horace Mann

6300. The difference between those whom the world esteems as good, and those whom it condemns as bad, is in many cases little else than that the former have been better sheltered from temptation.

Thanksgiving Day

6301. 'Twas founded be th' Puritans to give thanks f'r bein' presarved fr'm the Indyans, an' we keep it to give thanks we are presarved fr'm th' Puritans.

—Finley Peter Dunne

6302. If gratitude is due from children to their earthly parents, how much more is the gatitude of the great family of men due to our Father in heaven.

—HOSEA BALLOU

6303. Our harvest being gotten in, our Governor sent foure men on fowling, that so we might after a more speciall manner rejoyce together, after we had gathered the fruit of our labours.

—EDWARD WINSLOW, one of the founders of Plymouth Colony

6304. We can be grateful to a friend for a few acres or a little money; and yet for the freedom and command of the whole earth, for the great benefits of our being, our life, health and reason, we look upon ourselves as under no obligation.

—SENECA

6305. There is one day that is ours. There is one day when all we Americans who are not self-made go back to the old home to eat saleratus biscuits and marvel how much nearer to the porch the old pump looks than it used to . . . Thanksgiving Day . . . is the one day that is purely American.

—O. HENRY

6306.

Thanksgiving-day, I fear,
If one the solemn truth must touch,
Is celebrated, not so much
To thank the Lord for Blessings o'er,
As for the sake of getting more.

—WILL CARLETON

6307. Let us give thanks to God on Thanksgiving Day. Nature is beautiful, and fellowmen are dear, and duty is close beside us, and God is over us and in us. We want to trust him with a fuller trust, and so at last to come to that high life where we shall "be careful for nothing, but in everything, by prayer and supplication, with thanksgiving, let our request be made known unto God;" for that, and that alone, is peace.

—PHILLIPS BROOKS

6308. It is not a good spiritual policy for us . . . to thank God only for the material progress of our times; because these material things will soon give place to something better, and then our prayers and hymns will seem lost, and we who lived for them will seem to perish with them; but if we bless God for the sun that has held us in its arms, and for the autumns that have painted the fields . . . then have we a worship which the future cannot take away from our souls or memories.

—DAVID SWING

6309. WE GIVE OUR THANKS

We give our thanks this year for simple pleasures,
For crusted loaves and fire-shine on the floor;
For cupboards that hold bounty for the sharing
With hungry ones who knock upon our door.

Seedtime and harvest never really perish,
Night brings the stars, hope comes with each new day;
That we have learned to walk hard roads, hearts fearless,
Without the need of drums along the way!

—HELEN WELSHIMER

6310. THANKSGIVING

Give thanks, O heart! for these: A woman's face,
The gift of love, and love's enduring grace;
For man's firm friendship through the marching years,
The comfort of all children; even for tears
Shed in your grief, because these prove that you
Have pity that is beautiful and true.
Give thanks for raiment, and a loaf of bread;
And for a good thatched roof above your head;
But most of all give thanks if you can say,
"Lord, I have courage on my pilgrim's way!"

—CHARLES HANSON TOWNE

6311. The Dutch people also celebrate a thanksgiving day, but unlike our Thanksgiving turkey their main dish is a beef stew called "hotsput."

During the war with Spain in the 16th century, the town of Leyden held out against a Spanish siege for about a year. When the Prince of Orange breeched the dikes in order to raise the siege, the approaching flood made the Spanish positions untenable. As the invaders fled, the half-starved people of Leyden were delighted to find the pots of "hotsput" left by the besiegers in their haste to save themselves. The following year when the grateful people again celebrated their deliverance from Spain, "hotsput" became the traditional dish.

It is even possible that our own Pilgrim Fathers, who spent eleven years in Leyden before sailing for America, were influenced to declare a day of thanksgiving by the example of their Dutch friends.

6312. Ah, on Thanksgiving Day, when from East and from West,
From North and South, come the pilgrim and guest,
When the gray-haired New Englander sees 'round his board
The old broken links of affection restored,
When the care-wearied man seeks his mother once more,
And the worn matron smiles where the girl smiled before.
What moistens the lips and what brightens the eye?
What calls back the past, like the rich pumpkin pie?

—John Greenleaf Whittier

6313. A REAL THANKSGIVING

If I am thankful for my toys,
I must be glad to share.
If I am thankful for my friends,
I'll show them that I care.

If I am thankful for my home,
I'll help to make it gay;
I'll try to like what others like
And not just my own way.

The "thank you's" that come just from lips
God has a right to doubt.
I'm trying this Thanksgivingtime
To act my "thank you's" out.

—Edith May Cunnings

6314. THANKSGIVING DAY

We think of Thanksgiving in harvest time—
In the yielding, gathering golden time;
When the sky is fringed with a hazy mist,
And the blushing maples by frost lip kissed;

When the barns are full with the harvest cheer,
And the crowning, thankful day draws near.

We think of Thanksgiving at resting time—
The circle completed is but a chime
In the song of life, in the lives of men;
We harvest the toils of our years, and then
We wait at the gate of the King's highway,
For the dawn of our soul's Thanksgiving Day.

—Rose Hartwich Thorpe

6315. If our Thanksgiving is only for our country, our friends, loved ones, material things, health and religious faith, then our thanksgiving is a fickle thing, for even a pagan could be thankful for these. If our gratitude depends on outward circumstances, then it does not occupy a permanent place in our lives. When we no longer live on "the sunny side of the street," when the winds of adversity blow, when we are in trouble and need help, it is not the strong person who has never known difficulty who helps us. Rather it is the person who brings his testimony that one can triumph over every obstacle. We give thanks, too, for the assurance that, no matter what our mood says, God has not deserted us. In all the world there is no such thing as a God-forsaken soul.

—Dr. Howard C. Brown

6316. WOULD YOU BE THANKFUL?

Would you be thankful if you had
  Only a cabin of logs for a home,
A crude fireplace for draughty warmth,
  And a candle to light the dreary room?

Would you kneel tonight on a bearskin rug
  Before crawling into your pine-needle bed,
And thank your God with fervent grace
  For the crude bark roof above your head?

Would Thanksgiving be the same to you
  If there weren't a store in a thousand miles,
And all you loved and held so dear
  Were far away in the British Isles?

Would you like to trade with the Pilgrim band?
  They were thankful for liberty.
Look up at the Stars and Stripes tonight,
  And breathe your thanks that you are free.

—*Author Unknown*

6317. FOR THIS—THE LAND

(A Song of Thanksgiving)

For this, the Land in which we live,
In which we hope, and plan, and strive—
For this, the Land, today we give
Our thanks, O Lord, to be alive.

And for the cities teemed with light,
Around which rivers wind and flow . . .
For view of mountain, green and bright,
Or stacked with snow.

And for the mines which hills contain:
For span of forest edged with blue . . .
For wide-flung valleys, rich with grain,
And cattle, too.

And for a Faith, most positive,
In towns where people build and pray,
And dwell in Freedom—Lord, we give
Our thanks, today.

—Mario Speracio

6318. THANKSGIVING

Lord God of Hosts, we render thanks
For all Thy mercies sure;
Thy tender love environs us
And will through life endure.

Teach us to know Thy perfect will
And truly humble be;
May we in gladness praise Thy name
Through all eternity.

Lord God of Hosts, we offer thanks
And call upon Thy name;
A psalm of praise to Thee we sing,
Thy wondrous love proclaim.

Thou art our refuge and our strength,
There is no other power;
If sudden danger threatens us,
We find in Thee a tower.

Lord God of Hosts, we proffer praise,
Direct us on our way;
With grateful hearts we worship Thee
On this Thanksgiving Day.

—GRENVILLE KLEISER

6319. THANKSGIVING PROCLAMATION

As the colors of autumn stream down the wind, scarlet in sumach and maple, spun gold in the birches, a splendor of smoldering fire in the oaks along the hill, and the last leaves flutter away, and dusk falls briefly about the worker bringing in from the field a late load of its fruit, and Arcturus is lost to sight and Orion swings upward that great sun upon his shoulders, we are stirred once more to ponder the Infinite Goodness that has set apart for us, in all this moving mystery of creation, a time of living and a home. In such a spirit I appoint Thursday, the twenty-fourth of November,

A Day of Public Thanksgiving

In such a spirit I call upon the people to acknowledge heartily, in friendly gathering and house of prayer, the increase of the season nearing now its close: the harvest of earth, the yield of patient mind and faithful hand, that have kept us fed and clothed and have made for us a shelter even against the storm. It is right that we whose arc of sky has been darkened by no war hawk, who have been forced by no man to stand and speak when to speak was to choose between death and life, should give thanks also for the further mercies we have enjoyed, beyond desert or any estimation, of justice, freedom, loving kindness, peace—resolving, as we prize them, to let no occasion go without some prompting or some effort worthy in a way however humble of those proudest among men's ideals, which burn, though it may be like candles fitfully in our gusty world, with a light so clear we name its source divine.

—Proclamation by GOVERNOR WILBUR L. CROSS, of Connecticut (1938), rated to be the most beautiful of all Thanksgiving documents

6320. The author of *Mary Had a Little Lamb* gets credit for making Thanksgiving a regular national event. She was Sarah J. Hale, a magazine editor who, 'way back in 1827, began to prod for a yearly Thanksgiving. Until she got her way, poor old Thanksgiving was kicked around the calendar—or, worse, ignored.

The first United States Thanksgiving was called by George Washington in 1789 to celebrate adoption of the Constitution. He was editorially spanked for this by the papers, who said the states, not the President, ought to proclaim Thanksgivings. Unbothered, George called for another Thanksgiving in 1795, this time in February.

From time to time, as governors or Presidents thought of it, there were Thanksgivings. Jefferson was against 'em. He said they smacked of royal practices. Madison declared a day of Thanksgiving in 1815 to mark the end of the War of 1812.

By 1859, Mrs. Hale's editorials had lined up 30 states for Thanksgiving on the last Thursday of November. In 1863 she got Lincoln to declare a national holiday, the first since 1815. From then on, Thanksgiving was a fact every year, always on the last Thursday in November except for four years.

In 1943 Congress, irked by F.D.R.'s attempt to move the day from the fourth to the third Thursday, issued a joint resolution saying that, President or no President, Thanksgiving ought to be the last Thursday in November *every* year.

—Herb Daniels

Theatre

6321. A comedy is like a cigar; if good everyone wants a box; if bad no amount of puffing will make it draw.

—Harry James Byron

6322. The first comedy was acted at Athens, on a scaffold, by Saffarian and Dolon, 562 B.C.; and tragedy was first acted at Athens, in a wagon or cart, 535 B.C.; by Thespis. Melpomene is the presiding muse of tragedy; she is represented by a splendidly attired young woman, with a serious countenance; she wears a buskin, and holds a dagger in one hand and in the other a sceptre and crowns. Thalia is the muse of comedy; she leans on a column, holds a mask in her right hand, and carries a shepherd's crook.

—*Things Not Generally Known*,
by David A. Wells

Thievery

6323. He who buys what he doesn't need steals from himself.

—*Ancient Proverb*

6324. Thieves respect property. They merely wish the property to become their property that they may more perfectly respect it.

—G. K. Chesterton

Thinking

6325. Scientists regard it as a major intellectual virtue, to know what not to think about.

—C. P. Snow

6326. You can't stop people from thinking, but sometimes you can start them—and that is important.

6327. He who can think, and loves to think, will become, if he has a few good books, a wise man; he who knows not how to think, or who hates the toil of doing it, will remain imbecile, though his mind be crowded with the contents of a library.

—Alonzo Potter

6328. A man thinks. He not only thinks, but he lives on thoughts; he is the prisoner of thoughts; ideas, which in words he rejects, tyrannize over him, and dictate or modify every word of his mouth, every act of his hand. There are no walls like the invisible ones of an idea.

Thought—Thoughts

6329. By words we learn thoughts, and by thoughts we learn life.

—Père Girard

6330. Speech is external thought, and thought internal speech.

—Count de Rivarol

6331. Men are not influenced by things, but by their thoughts about things.

—Epictetus

6332. A little reflection makes a skeptic; a lot of reflection makes a believer.

—Louis Pasteur

6333. Thought is supreme, and to think is often better than to do.

—Elbert Hubbard

6334. Hear about the street cleaner who got fired for daydreaming? Couldn't keep his mind in the gutter.

—Mike Connolly

6335. Those who do unlawful acts are no more sinners in the eyes of God than we who think them.

—Elbert Hubbard

6336. Do not think that what your thoughts dwell upon is of no matter. Your thoughts are making you.

—Bishop Steere

6337. The way we are going to think tomorrow depends largely on what we are thinking today.

—David Leslie Brown

6338. In matters of conscience first thoughts are best; in matters of prudence last thoughts are the best.

—Robert Hall

6339. There are two distinct classes of what are called thoughts; those that we produce in ourselves by reflection and the act of thinking and those that bolt into the mind of their own accord.

—Thomas Paine

6340. What you *think* means more than anything else in your life. More than what you earn, more than where you live, more than your social position, and more than what anyone else may think about you.

—George Matthew Adams

6341. Men's thoughts and opinions are in a great degree vassals of him who invents a new phrase or re-applies an old epithet. The thought or feeling a thousand times repeated becomes his at last who utters it best.

—James Russell Lowell

6342. No lions are ever caught in mouse traps. To catch lions you must think in terms of lions, not in terms of mice. Your mind is always creating traps of one kind or another and what you catch depends on the thinking you do. It is your thinking that attracts you to what you receive.

—Thomas Dreier

6343. If America is to be run by the people, it is the people who must think. And we do not need to put on sackcloth and ashes to think. Nor should our minds work like a sundial which records only sunshine. Our thinking must square against some lessons of history, some principles of government and morals, if we would preserve the rights and dignity of men to which this nation is dedicated.

—Herbert Hoover

6344. You can develop nothing that does not exist first of all in your mind. It is your thinking that is your most precious asset. Nothing outside you can possibly affect you and your fortunes as much as what goes on in your mind. What you think affects your actions. Lovable thoughts produce one result. Thoughts of hate produce the opposite result. It is scientifically true: "As a man thinketh in his heart, so is he."

Thoughtfulness

6345. Consideration is not merely a matter of emotional good-will but of intellectual vigor and moral self-sacrifice. Wisdom must combine with sympathy. That is why consideration underlies the phrase "a scholar and a gentleman," which really sums up the ideal of the output of a college education.

—Charles Seymour

6346. What is the secret of being able to get along happily with others? Surely it lies in the one word *consideration.*

If we consider the happiness, comfort, feelings of others, our behavior cannot be of the kind which will create friction and strife. Automatically we shall be helpful, sympathetic, tolerant, and respectful.

These qualities constitute the lubricant which ensures the smooth running of every human contact.

Success in this sphere of human relationships crowns, beautifies and justifies success in every other.

—Robert J. Lumsden

Thrift. See also Economy; Saving

6347. When it comes to saving money, you've got to hand it to the women.

—Charles Ruffing

6348. There can be no economy when there is no efficiency.

—Lord Beaconsfield

6349. When a man begins to think seriously of saving for a rainy day, it's probably a rainy day.

6350. Folks who live within their incomes are just trying to mess up prosperity.

6351. Saving is a very fine thing. Especially when one's parents have done it for one.

—Sir Winston Churchill

6352. Thrift is broader than mere saving. It is to the individual what conservation is to the nation.

—John A. Lapp

6353. When a woman doesn't spend all her husband earns, she's probably saving to buy something.

—Franklin P. Jones

6354. Economy is the art of making the most of life. The love of economy is the root of all virtue.

—George Bernard Shaw

6355. Economy is half the battle of life; it is not so hard to earn money as to spend it well.

—Charles H. Spurgeon

6356. No gain is so certain as that which proceeds from the economical use of what you already have.

—*Latin Proverb*

6357. Economizing for the purpose of being independent is one of the soundest indications of manly character.

—Samuel Smiles

6358. To earn enough to pay bills is labor—to have something left after paying bills is management.

—W. L. Hudson

6359. If youth knew what age would crave,
It would both get and save.

—*Old Proverb*

6360. Economy is a savings-bank into which men drop pennies and get dollars in return.

—Henry Wheeler Shaw

6361. A new kind of Christmas Club started early this year—you save enough money to pay for last year's gifts.

6362. The secret of financial success is to spend what you have left after saving instead of saving what is left after spending.

6363. Thrift: a moss-grown obsession of those primitive men whose accomplishment was to create the United States of America.

6364. Any fool can waste, any fool can muddle, but it takes something of a man to save, and the more he saves the more of a man does it make of him.

—Rudyard Kipling

6365. All men are not equally qualified for getting money but it is in the power of everyone to be thrifty and save.

—Benjamin Franklin

6366. The doctrine of thrift for the poor is dumb and cruel, like advising them to try and lift themselves by their bootstraps.

—Norman M. Thomas

6367. The world abhors closeness, and all but admires extravagance; yet a slack hand shows weakness, a tight hand strength.

—Charles Buxton

6368. Old men are always advising young men to save money. That is bad advice. Invest in yourself. I never saved a dollar until I was 40 years old.

—Henry Ford

6369. The habit of saving is itself an education; it fosters every virtue, teaches self-denial, cultivates the sense of order, trains to forethought, and so broadens the mind.

—T. T. Munger

6370. People who never had enough thrift and forethought to buy and pay for property in the first place seldom have enough to keep property up after they have gained it in some other way.

—Thomas Nixon Carver

6371. Live according to your proper station in life; yet do not spend to the utmost of what you can afford, that your prudence may be a comfort in your old age.

—Dandemis

6372. The secret of making money is saving it. It is not what a man earns—not the amount of his income, but the relation of his expenditures to his receipts, that determines his poverty or wealth.

6373. Sometimes the poor are praised for being thrifty. But to recommend thrift to the poor is both grotesque and insulting. It is like advising a man who is starving to eat less.

—Oscar Wilde

6374. Whatever a person saves from his revenue he adds to his capital, and either employs it himself in maintaining an additional number of productive hands, or enables some person to do so . . . for a share of profits. As the capital of an individual can be increased only by what he saves . . . so the capital of a society can be increased only in the same manner.

—Adam Smith

6375. Individual thrift and responsibility for the future must be preserved if we are to be healthy and prosperous under any social system, whatever it is to be. No social planning can invent a substitute for the general principle of individual self-support. Two irresponsible persons added together do not make a happy home, nor do a thousand individual failures, however organized, make a successful community.

—Ralph W. Sockman

6376. The secret of thrift is knowledge. The more you know the more you can save yourself and that which belongs to you and can do more work with less effort. Knowledge of domestic economy saves income; knowledge of sanitary laws saves health and life; knowledge of the laws of the intellect saves wear and tear of brain, and knowledge of the laws of the spirit—what does it not save?

—Charles Kingsley

Time

6377. By losing present time we lose all time.

—*Old Proverb*

6378. He who knows most, grieves most for wasted time.

—Dante Alighieri

6379. It is what you do with time, not time itself, that is worth money.

6380. Dost thou love life? Then waste not time; for time is the stuff that life is made of.

—Benjamin Franklin

6381. Time is that which the average American never seems to have quite enough of and is nearly always behind.

6382. There are persons who do not know how to waste their time alone, and hence become the scourge of busy people.

—Louis Gabriel Ambroise de Bonald

6383. Time is like a river, in which metals and solid substances are sunk, while chaff and straws swim upon the surface.

—Francis Bacon

6384. Time is a fixed income and, as with any income, the real problem facing most of us is how to live successfully within our daily allotment.

—Margaret B. Johnstone

6385. I wish I could stand on a busy street corner, hat in hand, and beg people to throw me all their wasted hours.

—Bernard Berenson

6386. There is never enough time to say our last word—the last word of our love, of our desire, faith, remorse, submission, revolt.

—Joseph Conrad

6387. Regret for time wasted can become a power for good in the time that remains, if we will only stop the waste and the idle, useless regretting.

—Arthur Brisbane

6388. One realizes the full importance of time only when there is little of it left. Every man's greatest capital asset is his unexpired years of productive time.

—P. W. Litchfield

6389. It's the dentist who tells us that our own teeth won't last ten years who scares us; not the scientist who warns that mankind will lose its teeth in ten centuries.

6390. Time is painted with a lock before, and bald behind, signifying thereby, that we must take time (as we say) by the forelock, for when it is once passed there is no recalling it.

—Jonathan Swift

6391. You must have been warned against letting the golden hours slip by. Yes, but some of them are golden only because we let them slip.

—James M. Barrie

6392. Opinions, theories, and systems pass by turns over the grindstone of time, which at first gives them brilliancy and sharpness, but finally wears them out.

—Antoine Rivaroli

6393. Time has no divisions to mark its passage; there is never a thunderstorm or blare of trumpets to announce the beginning of a new month or year. Even when a new century begins, it is only we mortals who ring bells and fire off pistols.

—THOMAS MANN

6394. Distance is no longer a serious obstacle due to modern means of travel, but time remains unconquerable. It cannot be expanded, accumulated, mortgaged, hastened or retarded. It is the one thing completely beyond man's control.

6395. What is time? The shadow on the dial, the striking of the clock, the running of the sand—day and night, summer and winter, months, years, centuries—these are but arbitrary and outward signs, the measure of time, not time itself. Time is the life of the soul.

—HENRY WADSWORTH LONGFELLOW

6396. There is only one thing which is irreplaceable. That is Time. We cannot waste Time without losing it forever. There is only so much for each of us and no replacement source. Time is something we have to use as it comes, for it waits on no one.

—*Nuggets*

6397.

Time is
Too slow for those who Wait,
Too swift for those who Fear,
Too long for those who Grieve;
Too short for those who Rejoice;
But for those who Love,
Time is Eternity.

—HENRY VAN DYKE

6398. Time enters into efficiency in every activity. The essence of efficiency is economy of energy, space and time.

The well-organized life leaves time for everything, for planning, doing, and following through.

Time does not boss this sort of life like a taskmaster with a whip. Time is not used up in regretting, or in trying to live life retroactively, or in explaining why something needed has not been done.

6399. Man's regard for time is always a good index to his happiness. When he is indifferent to its passing he is likely to be idle, bored and depressed. Men in prison reach the lowest depths of despondency when they no longer count the days and hours. When his days are crowded and each task encroaches on the one to follow, you may be sure a man quaffs copiously of life, even though he complains loudly of being over-pressed for time.

6400. TIME AND YOU

Take time to work, it is the price of success.
Take time to think, it is the source of power.
Take time to play, it is the secret of youth.
Take time to read, it is the foundation of wisdom.
Take time to pray, it is the way to Heaven.
Take time to dream, it is the highway to the stars.
Take time to be friendly, it is the road to happiness.
Take time to laugh, it is the music of the soul.
Take time to look around, it is the short cut to unselfishness.

6401. Time is one of God's greatest gifts, and yet how often men devise ingenious methods to make it pass lightly and quickly and refer to it as "killing time."

The value of time arises from:

1. Its brevity. The time is short. "We all do fade as a leaf."
2. Its uncertainty. "Boast not thyself of tomorrow."
3. The fact that it is irrecoverable. The hand on the dial of time can never be turned back.

Time is given that we may prepare for eternity. The watchword of the moment should be "now."

6402. Artisans of the past devised the sundial to cope with the magic and mystery of time. That's why each sundial offers a thought for remembrance with minutes that pass. Here are some:

An illusionist wrote:

"Time passes only when the sun shines."

A dreamer dreamed:

"So flies time away."

An optimist's inscription:

"I record none but sunny hours."

And the realist:

"It is later than you think."

6403. Time is precious, not because of itself, but for the opportunities for service to our fellowmen, and for further improvement in ourselves against the end of our experience in this world of steadily passing time. . . . What we call time is in fact motion—advancement, progress toward something, and that we are in reality approaching a commencement rather than an ending, the greater usefulness for which we are preparing during this period we measure by the calendar, and which is, after all, but a demonstration of the accurate and unhurried movement of our solar system.

—C. I. McReynolds

6404. THOUGHTS ON TIME

Time wasted is existence; when used, it is life. It is your ability to know what is waste of time that enables you to use it correctly. Dreaming is no waste of time if you strive to make the dream come true.

Playing games is no waste of time if you find in them relaxation and delight. Dancing is no waste of time if you listen to the music and renew the harmony in your soul by keeping the rhythm.

Movie-going is no waste of time if it permits you to escape from yourself. Reading is no waste of time if you choose your literary menu wisely.

Autoing is no waste of time if it allows you to accomplish more or if it takes you to clear, fresh air.

Talking is no waste of time if you think and evaluate before you speak.

Feasting is no waste of time when you do it with joy.

Work is no waste of time if in your work there is an element of art—something to make the world better.

Envy is a waste of time! Revenge is a waste of time! For envy saps your vitality and revenge hinders progress. Envy retards, and revenge weakens.

The great do not envy. And the successful are too busy for revenge.

Time wasted is existence; used, is life!

Time-Saving

6405. To save time is to lengthen life.

—*Old Proverb*

6406. You can't really save time—you can only try to get the most out of every minute available.

Timing

6407. Never put off until tomorrow what you can do today. By then there may be a law against it.

6408. In the grand design of any successful career the element of luck has been a powerful factor. Perhaps it could more accurately be called a sense of timing. Every successful person I have ever known has had it—actor or businessman, writer or politician. It is that instinct or ability to sense and seize the right moment without wavering or playing safe, and without it many gifted people flicker brilliantly and briefly and then fade into oblivion in spite of their undoubted talents.

—Moss Hart

Tit for Tat

6409. If you want people to like you, start liking them.

6410. It is also possible that blondes prefer gentlemen.

6411. For everything you have missed, you have gained something else; and for everything you gain, you lose something.

—Ralph Waldo Emerson

6412. When Admiral Hyman G. Rickover met the Soviet Prime Minister, Khrushchev asked, "Are you the admiral who's always talking about preparing for war with Russia?" To which the admiral replied, "Are you the Mr. Khrushchev who's always talking about attacking the United States?"

—Betty Beale

6413. During a tour of the United States in 1880, Sarah Bernhardt entered a Protestant Church, and there heard a clergyman denounce her as "an imp of darkness, a female demon sent from the Modern Babylon to corrupt the New World." "On returning to her hotel," says Jules Huret, in his *Memoirs of Sarah Bernhardt,* "she wrote and sent to the clergyman this letter: 'My dear Confrère: Why attack me so violently? Actors ought not to be hard on one another. *Sarah Bernhardt.*' "

—*In Lighter Vein,* by John de Morgan (Paul Elder & Co.)

Today. See also Present, The

6414. Today is the only time we can possibly live.

—Dale Carnegie

6415. Don't let yesterday use up too much of today.

6416. You had better live your best and act your best and think your best today; for today is the sure preparation for tomorrow and all the other tomorrows that follow.

—Harriet Martineau

6417. We can easily manage, if we will only take, each day, the burden appointed for it. But the load will be too heavy for us if we carry yesterday's burden over again today, and then add the burden of the morrow to the weight before we are required to bear it.

—John Newton

6418. TODAY

We cannot be sure of tomorrow;
It is better to do it today.
To put a thing off is to borrow
What we may not be able to pay.
We never can tell what the weather,
Or how circumstances may fall,
Or what situation, or whether
We shall be there to do it at all.

We never can know what condition
May come, or what barrier stand
Before us, or what the transition
Of life may fall in our hand.
We cannot imagine what sorrow
And loss may arise from delay.
We cannot be sure of tomorrow.
It is better to do it today.

—Clarence Edward Flynn

Tolerance

6419. Deal with the faults of others as gently as with your own.

—Chinese Proverb

6420. The responsibility of tolerance lies with those who have the wider vision.

—George Eliot

6421. In standing up for your rights, don't step on the other fellow's toes.

6422. He that cannot bear with other people's passions, cannot govern his own.

—Benjamin Franklin

6423. Tolerance comes with age. I see no fault committed that I myself could not have committed at some time or other.

—Johann Wolfgang von Goethe

6424. Goodness and greatness in a man may be difficult to define unless they are associated with a capacity for tolerance.

—Douglas Meador

6425. Men should bear with each other. There lives not the man who may not be cut up, aye, lashed to pieces, on his weakest side.

—John Keats

6426. Whoever kindles the flames of intolerance in America is lighting a fire underneath his own home.

—Harold E. Stassen

6427. Always be tolerant with a person who disagrees with you —after all, he has a right to his ridiculous opinions.

6428. Half the secret of getting along with people is consideration of their views; the other half is tolerance in one's own views.

—Daniel Frohman

6429. Unprincipled intolerance is like the swordfish, all backbone; but unprincipled toleration is like the jelly-fish, no backbone at all.

—Donald Sage Mackay

6430. When there is true brotherliness, friendliness, when there is love in your heart, then you will not talk of tolerance. Only when you feel superior in your certainty, in your position, in your knowledge, only then do you talk of tolerance.

—Jiddu Krishnamurti

6431. I scorn and scout the word "toleration"; it is an insolent term. No man, properly speaking, *tolerates* another. I do not tolerate a Catholic, neither does he tolerate me. We are equal, and acknowledge each other's right; that is the correct statement.

—Wendell Phillips

6432. The word "tolerance" has of late lost much of its original meaning and value. Just to *tolerate* somebody or something is not enough.

We can tolerate while being narrow, smug and even bigoted. In our pride we can look down upon that which we tolerate. All too much of our practice of brotherhood is founded upon this negative aspect of being tolerant. True tolerance . . . has a basis of equality, understanding, and love. It does not condemn, but lifts up. It behaves toward others with respect and helpfulness. It never tries to get the better of those a little more unfortunate. It is even willing to sacrifice that others may rise to higher levels.

—Stanley I. Stuber

Tomorrow. See also Past, The

6433. However powerful one may be, whether one laughs or weeps, none can make thee speak, none can open thy hand before the time, O mute phantom, our shadow! sceptre always masked, ever at our side, called *Tomorrow*!

—Victor Hugo

6434. Finish every day and be done with it. You have done what you could. Some blunders and some absurdities no doubt crept in; forget them as soon as you can. Tomorrow is a new day; begin it well and serenely with too high a spirit to be cumbered with your old nonsense. This day is all that is good and fair. It is too dear, with its hopes and invitations, to waste a moment on the yesterdays.

—Ralph Waldo Emerson

Totality

6435. Better one thorn pluck'd out than all remain.

—Horace

6436. The longer I live and learn experience, the more I am convinced that individual actions prove nothing either for or against a man; the whole life must be taken into account, for there is no other measure of character than the relation of the will to the conscience, or the feeling of right and wrong.

—George Forster

Tradition

6437. It is no good living in the past. But in facing the future we are fortified by traditions. Tradition does not mean that the living are dead—it means that the dead are alive.

—Prime Minister Harold Macmillan

6438. In England, the governors of Oxford University have been debating whether to permit Jewish scholars to teach Hebrew. Since the year 1630, only Church of England clergymen have held this post. The dispute prompted one professor to quip, "They'll be getting Greeks to teach Greek next!"

—Jane Truax

Traffic, Automobile

6439. In traffic tie-ups you meet a very cross section of humanity.
—Maurice Seitter

6440. The careless driver isn't driving his car—he's aiming it.

6441. Automobiles continue to be driven at just two speeds; lawful and awful.

—Frederick C. Russell

6442. Passing on curves is best left to judges of beauty contests.

6443. You have to drive the other fellow's car as well as your own.
—Harry William King

6444. When driving near schools open your eyes and save the pupils.

6445. Mixing alcohol with gasoline helps increase the hearse power.

6446. Reckless drivers cannot expect God to keep them wreck-less.

6447. *Tip to motorists:* Passing on hills and curves is a grave mistake.

6448. Drive so that your driver's license expires before you do.
—*Believe Me,* by Virginia Hutchinson (Comet Press Books)

6449. Men still die with their boots on, but they're usually on the accelerator.

6450. You can't have back-seat drivers in jet planes. They travel faster than sound.

6451. A "Dangerous When Wet" sign should be hung on every driver who drinks.

6452. A woman driver is a woman who drives like a man—and gets blamed for it.

—Tennessee Ernie Ford

6453. We are all entitled to the pursuit of happiness—but not at 90 miles an hour!

—Arnold Glasow

6454. America has more than 50 million motor vehicle missiles, some of them not very well guided.

6455. One arm around the wheel and one around the girl is too few for either operation.

6456. Each year it takes less time to fly around the world and more time to drive to work.

6457. The folks who get up in the world today are the ones who drove carefully last night.

6458. Too many people who have passed their driving tests think they can pass anything.

6459. Speed and progress are two very different things. Ask the ghosts of traffic casualties.

6460. Near its school, a small Ohio town posted this suggestion: "Use your eyes, save the pupils."

6461. The hand that lifts the cup that cheers should not be used to shift the gears.

6462. The automobile may have replaced the horse, but the man who drives should stay on the wagon.

—Maurice Seitter

6463. Highway accidents will diminish only when people use enough brain power to match the horsepower.

6464. Power brakes may stop a car on a dime—but it usually costs about $100 to get the rear end fixed.

—Dan Bennett

6465. One thing to remember while driving on the highways is that other people can be as careless as you are.

6466. Accident: a condition of affairs in which presence of mind is good, but absence of body is better.

6467. Did you hear about the fellow who let his little son drive the car because he was still too young to be treated as a pedestrian?

6468. Many motorists drive as if they owned the road when they've only made a down payment on the car.

6469. There would be fewer accidents if the law required motorists to own their cars before they could drive them.

—O. A. Battista

6470. A pedestrian is one who walks when you are walking. A jay walker is one who walks when you are driving.

—Frances Rodman

6471. There is a line on the ocean where you lose a day when you cross it. There is a line on most highways where you can do even better.

6472. Scientists show us how to sail under the North Pole and fly over the moon, but you're still on your own when you cross the street.

—Harold Coffin

6473. *Japanese road sign:* Please drive carefully. Our children may be disobeying us.

6474. The parents of another era who taught the child to swim by tossing him in the water is succeeded by the kind who gives him a car to teach him to drive.

6475. "Look out, highway, here I come," shouts the lunatic-fringe driver, and he seldom hears the highway's reply: "Goodbye, Life, there you go!"

6476. In Saudi Arabia, any driver who has an accident resulting in a death is executed. When they say, "The life you save may be your own" in Arabic, they aren't kidding.

6477. A group of traffic safety experts, meeting in Washington, came to this conclusion: "The two greatest highway menaces are drivers under 25 going 65 and drivers over 65 going 25."

6478. For years safety experts advised, "If you drink, don't drive." With pedestrian accidents mounting, they are now saying, "If you drink, don't walk." Soon we may expect, "If you drink, don't!"

6479. I do not like the safety slogan, "The life you save may be your own." We're supposed to be a Christian nation. I think "The life you save is someone's loved one" would be much more appropriate.

—VIRGINIA BEARDSLEY

6480. The trouble is, for most of us, when we get behind the wheel of a motor car, five or ten thousand years slip off our shoulders and we are practically back in the Stone Age: no quarter, weakest to the wall, every man for himself.

—G. R. H. NUGENT

6481. If you knew or suspected that someone might put poison in your soup, you would not hesitate to refuse an invitation to his house for dinner. But many people are too polite to refuse to ride with a reckless driver. Does this make sense?

6482. If a Cairo motorist commits a traffic offense, nothing happens—no ticket, no fine. That is, until the end of the year when he goes to renew his license and finds all his mistakes totaled up. He pays—or no car license.

—CLAIRE WALLACE

6483. Warnings to drive carefully are nothing new. In the Old Testament, Nahum 2:5, you will find:

"The chariots shall rage in the streets, they shall jostle one another in the broad ways; they shall seem like torches, they shall run like the lightnings."

—DAN BENNETT

6484. In Turkey the police do not fine a driver if he is found drunk behind the steering wheel of his car. Instead they put him in a patrol car, drive him about 20 miles out of town to a lonely spot in the country and dump him. The police claim that this method has a very sobering effect on the offender.

6485. Two fools had cars they thought perfection;
They met one day at an intersection,
Tooted their horns and made a connection.
A police car came and made an inspection;
An ambulance came and made a collection.
All that is left is a recollection,
And two less votes in the next election.

—*Author Unknown*

6486. A man placed 331 pills in a bottle. Three hundred contained bicarbonate of soda, 30 were composed of a harmless hangover cure, but one contained potassium cyanide. All the pills were mixed together and, when emptied on the table, all looked alike.

"How many here are willing to take a chance and swallow one of these pills?" he asked. Not a man accepted the challenge.

"I guess right now you men aren't in a hurry," he said. "But you might be interested to know that in one out of 331 instances, when a man attempts to beat a traffic light, he is killed."

Tranquility

6487. Great tranquility of heart is his who cares for neither praise nor blame.

—Thomas à Kempis

6488. If you wish to live a life free from sorrow, think of what is going to happen as if it had already happened.

—Epictetus

Translation

6489. Translation is at best an echo.

—George Borrow

6490. Translation is a legitimate form of plagiarism, ever offering the hope of rising to fame on borrowed wings.

—Justin O'Brien

6491. Many thoughts are so dependent upon the language in which they are clothed that they would lose half their beauty if otherwise expressed.

—John Ruskin

6492. At a cocktail party James Thurber once met a young lady who assured him that his books were even funnier in French. "Ah, yes," said Mr. Thurber, "I lose something in the original."

—Jean Kerr

6493. A firm experimenting with an electronic brain designed to translate English into Russian fed it the words: "The spirit is willing but the flesh is weak." The machine responded with a sentence in Russian which meant, a linguist reported, "The whiskey is agreeable but the meat has gone bad."

Travel

6494. To travel hopefully is a better thing than to arrive.

—Robert Louis Stevenson

6495. The trouble with those "all-expense" tours is they usually are.

—Frank J. Goldberg

6496. One of the tragedies of travel is that one must keep moving!

—H. V. Morton

6497. People travel to learn. Most of them before they start should learn to travel.

—George Bernard Shaw

6498. Too often travel, instead of broadening the mind, merely lengthens the conversation.

—Elizabeth Drew

6499. It only takes about half a day at sea to make some tourist look like his passport photo.

6500. To meet an old friend in a distant country is like the delight of rain after a long drought.

—*Chinese Proverb*

6501. Too many people never travel far because they plot their course by lassitude and longitude.

6502. He who would bring home the wealth of the Indies must carry the wealth of the Indies with him.

—*Spanish Proverb*

6503. When through foreign lands you stray,
Smile, and give the first "Good Day!"

—*From the Chinese*

6504. On their vacation trip some people stop trying to balance the budget and begin budgeting the balance.

6505. The whole object of travel is not to set foot on foreign land; it is at last to set foot on one's own country as a foreign land.

—G. K. Chesterton

6506. For the most part travelers who complain loudly on account of lack of luxuries, live on dock-greens and corn bread at home.

—Elbert Hubbard

6507. There are some things one can only achieve by a deliberate leap in the opposite direction. One has to go abroad to find the home one has lost.

—Franz Kafka

6508. The use of travelling is to regulate imagination by reality, and, instead of thinking how things may be, to see them as they are.

—Dr. Samuel Johnson

6509. I have wandered all my life, and I have also traveled; the difference between the two being this, that we wander for distraction, but we travel for fulfillment.

—Hilaire Belloc

6510. It isn't how much you've traveled or where you've been that makes you wise and cultured. It's what you've seen and heard and understood and appreciated.

—Jerry Fleischman

6511. The accepted notion that a traveler to a foreign land must remember everyone with a post card and a present, varying from a tweed coat to a pipe, makes one weary even before leaving home.

6512. A good traveler does not, I think, much mind the uninteresting places. He is there to be inside them, as a thread is inside the necklace it strings. The world, with unknown and unexpected variety, is a part of his own leisure; and this living participation is what separates the traveler and the tourist, who remains separate, as if he were at a theater, and not himself a part of whatever the show may be.

—Freya Stark

6513. A well-known world traveller, noted for his phenomenal memory of things seen and experienced, revealed his secret to a young man about to embark on his first trip abroad:

"When you find yourself looking at one of the wonders of the world, or living through a great moment, close your eyes for a little while and imagine that the experience is long past and you are at home again. Ask yourself what you might have looked at more closely, what you might have done to heighten the experience, how you might have behaved if you had it all to do over again."

Trickery

6514. Trickery and treachery are the practices of fools that have not wits enough to be honest.

—Benjamin Franklin

6515. Some people are so busy learning the tricks of the trade that they don't have time to learn the trade.

Trifle—Trifles. See also Little Things

6516. Little minds are too much hurt by little things; great minds are quite conscious of them, and despise them.

—François de La
Rochefoucauld

6517. One night a man took a little taper out of a drawer and lighted it, and began to ascend a long, winding stair.

"Where are you going?" said the taper.

"Away high up," said the man, "higher than the top of the house where we sleep."

"And what are you going to do there?" said the taper.

"I am going to show the ships out at sea where the harbor is," said the man. "For we stand here at the entrance to the harbor, and some ships far out on the stormy sea may be looking for our light even now."

"Alas, no ship could see my light!" said the little taper. "It is so very small."

"If your light is small," said the man, "keep it burning bright, and leave the rest to me."

Then he climbed the stairs to the top of the lighthouse—for this was a lighthouse they were in—and he took the little taper and lighted the great lamps that stood ready there with their polished reflectors behind them.

You who think your little light of so small account, can you not see what great things it might do?

Trouble—Troubles

6518. You need no collateral to borrow trouble.

—WILLIAM LYON PHELPS

6519. You cannot meet trouble halfway. It travels faster than you can.

6520. Everyone shuns trouble unless it comes disguised as money.

6521. Borrow trouble for yourself, if that's your nature, but don't lend it to your neighbors.

—RUDYARD KIPLING

6522. Trouble is often the lever in God's hands to raise us up to heaven.

6523. People who advertise their troubles never seem to dispose of their stock.

—FRANCES RODMAN

6524. Telling your troubles always helps. The world's indifference makes you mad enough to keep on fighting.

6525. One of the sadder facts of life is that it's quite possible to lend a hand and borrow trouble at the same time.

—FRANCIS O'WALSH

6526. Trouble is the next best thing to enjoyment; there is no fate in the world so horrible as to have no share in either its joy or sorrows.

—HENRY WADSWORTH LONGFELLOW

6527. Trouble is like a stone wall that cannot be moved by worry or wishing; nor will it be moved by self-pity. . . . The only tools that will wear away the stones are faith, hope, cheerfulness and perseverance, used in the hands of an undaunted toiler.

—LUCILLE R. TAYLOR

6528. If you will call your troubles experiences, and remember that every experience develops some latent force within you, you will grow vigorous and happy, however adverse your circumstances seem to be.

6529. Warning! Following are the names of the seven Mischievous Misses who are responsible for most of our troubles: Miss Information, Miss Quotation, Miss Representation, Miss Interpretation, Miss Construction, Miss Conception, Miss Understanding. Don't listen to them! Beware!

—WILLIAM J. H. BOETCKER

6530. The happy and efficient people in this world are those who accept trouble as a normal detail of human life and resolve to capitalize it when it comes along. For trouble is the thing that strong men grow by. Met in the right way it is a sure-fire means of putting iron into the victim's will and making him a tougher man to down forever after.

—H. BERTRAM LEWIS

6531. Mrs. O'Connor was an Irish widow whom the Lord had tried in every possible way. Calamities that hadn't happened to her hadn't happened to anyone, it seemed. Finally, one day, after a thief had entered her house and made off with her pitiful savings, Mrs. O'Connor said sadly: "I know it's not the Lord's plan to send me more trouble than I can bear." She released a great sigh. "But I just wish he didn't have such a powerful good opinion of me."

—THOMAS P. RAMIREZ

Truth. See also Veracity

6532. Truth fears nothing but concealment.

—*From the Latin*

6533. In the mountains of truth you never climb in vain.

—FRIEDRICH WILHELM NIETZSCHE

6534. Truth has only to change hands a few times to become friction.

6535. The pursuit of truth shall set you free—even if you never catch up with it.

—Clarence Darrow

6536. As scarce as truth is, the supply is always greater than the demand.

—Josh Billings

6537. Arguments ensue when two people try to keep the other from finding out the truth.

6538. Truth is as impossible to be soiled by any outward touch as the sunbeam.

—John Milton

6539. There is nothing so strong or safe in an emergency of life as the simple truth.

—Charles Dickens

6540. Without courage there cannot be truth, and without truth there can be no other virtue.

—Sir Walter Scott

6541. Truth has no degrees. The sea has the same level at its greatest depth as that point where it touches the shore.

—Douglas Meador

6542.

A truth that's told with bad intent
Beats all the lies you can invent.

—William Blake

6543. If truth is stranger than fiction, why do so many people stretch the truth to make it more interesting?

6544. Truth is a gem that is found at a great depth; whilst on the surface of the world all things are weighed by the false scale of custom.

—Lord Byron

6545. I have seldom known any one who deserted truth in trifles, that could be trusted in matters of importance.

6546. Some people throw away a bushel of truth because it contains a grain of error, while others swallow a bushel of error because it contains a grain of truth.

6547. The essence of man lies in this, in his marvelous faculty for seeking truth, seeing it, loving it, and sacrificing himself for it.

—GUISEPPE PREZZOLINI

6548. The discovery of truth by slow, progressive meditation is talent. Intuition of the truth, not preceded by perceptible meditation, is genius.

—JOHANN KASPAR LAVATER

6549. I do not think of truth as being made of granite, but rather as resembling a note of music, a note which we instantly recognize as the right one as soon as it is struck.

—IRIS ORIGO

6550. All truth is safe and nothing else is safe; and he who keeps back the truth or withholds it from men, from motives of expediency, is either a coward or a criminal or both.

—MAX MÜLLER

6551. When two truths seem to directly oppose each other, we must not question either, but remember there is a third—God—who reserves to himself the right to harmonize them.

—MME. SOYMONOFF SWETCHINE

6552. It is the calling of great men, not so much to preach new truths, as to rescue from oblivion those old truths which it is our wisdom to remember and our weakness to forget.

—SIDNEY SMITH

6553. The interests of society often render it expedient not to utter the whole truth, the interests of science never: for in this field we have much more to fear from the deficiency of truth than from its abundance.

—CHARLES C. COLTON

6554. To believe is dangerous, to be unbelieving is equally so; the truth, therefore, should be diligently sought after, lest that a foolish opinion should lead you to pronounce an unsound judgment.

—PHAEDRUS

6555. So long as a man is trying to tell the truth, his remarks will contain a margin which other people will regard as mystifying and irritating exaggeration. It is this very margin of controversy that does the work.

—John Jay Chapman

6556. The absolute truth is indestructible. Being indestructible, it is eternal. Being eternal it is self-existent. Being self-existent, it is infinite. Being infinite, it is vast and deep. Being vast and deep, it is transcendental and intelligent.

—Confucius

6557. Without seeking, truth cannot be known at all. It can neither be declared from pulpits, nor set down in articles, nor in any wise prepared and sold in packages ready for use. Truth must be ground for every man by himself out of its husk, with such help as he can get, indeed, but not without stern labor of his own.

—John Ruskin

6558. A young man leaving the penal institution where he had served his term heard these parting words from the warden: "I am not going to preach you a long sermon, just one thing I would recommend you to do—never tell another lie in your life."

The young man went home, looked for a job everywhere but was turned down in each case because of his prison record. Then one day he answered an employment ad, presenting the certificates he had. After reading them the gentleman asked him: "Where have you been the last three years? You don't have any references to show what you have done." "Well," said the young man, "I have been in the penitentiary." "And why do you tell me that so bluntly?" asked the gentleman. The youth eyed him calmly and said, "Because I promised the warden never to tell another lie in my life."

"The job is yours," said his future boss.

Understanding

6559. To know a little less and to understand a little more: that, it seems to me, is our greatest need.

—James Ramsey Ullman

6560. By understanding, I mean that faculty whereby we are enabled to apprehend the objects of knowledge, generals as well as particulars, absent things as well as present, and to judge of their truth or falsehood, good or evil.

—John Wilkins

6561. Great minds comprehend more in a word, a look, a pressure of the hand than ordinary men in long conversations, or the most elaborate correspondence.

—Johann Kaspar Lavater

6562. The realization that there are other points of view is the beginning of wisdom. Understanding what they are is a great step. The final test is understanding why they are held.

—Charles M. Campbell

6563. How much we enjoy what we have is more important than how much we have. Life is full of people who have more than they know what to do with, but who cannot be content. It is the capacity to enjoy life that brings contentment. That capacity is independent of things and something we develop within ourselves.

There are two things needed in these days; first, for rich men to find out how poor men live; and, second, for poor men to know how rich men work.

—E. Atkinson

6564. During a heated discussion at a board meeting of economic conditions, one member sat quietly serene amid the furious argument and table-pounding.

Later, he was told by the chairman, "I want to compliment you. How did you manage to keep so cool in there when everyone else was blowing his top?"

"Well, sir," replied the serene member, "I simply didn't understand what anyone else was talking about."

6565. UNDERSTANDING

Our dreams paint many pleasures
Sometimes the dreams come true,
Our hearts try many treasures
Sometimes retain a few;
But the fairest flowers of living
Bloom for us when we find
The garden that is giving
For love of humankind.

Then wealth is dedication
  Wisdom, the light to lead,
Then power is obligation
  To serve is to succeed;
Then health becomes a holding
  In trust, to spend at will
A fund for the enfolding
  And succor of the ill.

Today, in tones faint-sounding
  From matin to evensong,
"Give of your life abounding!"
  The weak call to the strong;
And they who heed the crying
  Shall but increase their store
They draw on a source undying
  Forever and ever more.

—*Anonymous*

6566. IF WE ONLY UNDERSTOOD

If we knew the cares and trials,
  Knew the efforts all in vain,
And the bitter disappointments,
  Understood the loss and gain—
Would the grim eternal roughness
  Seem—I wonder—just the same?
Should we help where we hinder?
  Should we pity where we blame?
Ah, we judge each other harshly,
  Knowing not life's hidden force;
Knowing not the fount of action
  Is less turbid at its source;
Seeing not amid the evil
  All the golden grains of gold,
And we'd love each other better,
  If we only understood.
Could we judge all deeds by motives
  That surround each other's lives,
See the naked heart and spirit,
  Know what spur the action gives,
Often we should find it better,
  Purer than we judge we would.

We should love each other better,
If we only understood.

—RUDYARD KIPLING

Usefulness

6567. Nothing in this world is so good as usefulness. It binds your fellow creatures to you, and you to them; it tends to the improvement of your own character and gives you a real importance in society, much beyond what any artificial station can bestow.

—BENJAMIN COLLINS BRODIE

6568. When French author Anatole France received the coveted cross of the legion of honor, he was still a poor man, having earned little from the sale of his books. His friends were bitter about the award.

"Why didn't they give you a cash prize?" protested one of them. "This serves no useful purpose."

"Oh, I wouldn't say that," said France, more philosophical. "When I wear the sash, it will cover the stain on my jacket. That's useful."

Vacation

6569. The worst thing about taking your vacation in winter is July.

—JOHN T. MCCUTCHEON, JR.

6570. A good vacation is over when you begin to yearn for your work.

—MORRIS FISHBEIN

6571. *Husband painting house to neighbor washing windows:* "You're lucky only getting a two-week vacation. I get *three*!"

6572. The one drawback to taking vacation movies is that you have to get back home to find out what you saw.

6573. Among the things that never turn out as big as you expected is the welcome the office force gives you when you return from your vacation.

6574. *Worker to colleague:* "I'm taking a honey-dew vacation this year. You know, that's where you stay home and the whole time your wife says, 'Honey, do this' and 'Honey, do that.' "

6575.

VACATION?

Vacation days are here . . . and you
Leave home and friends and comforts rare
To spend your time, and money, too,
On things for which you do not care.

The cool front porch so still at night,
The home-cooked meals, the shady street,
The savory ice-box's cool delight—
Real antidotes for summer heat . . .

All these and others you forego,
Just why you'll never, never know;
Yet off you trek, you know you must
Do what your neighbors do . . . or bust!

—*Author Unknown*

6576.

VACATION TIME

Oh, now that it's vacation time
Where is it you are going?
Along the road with bulky load
Through towns the maps are showing?

And shall you climb a mountain top?
Or seek a sandy shore?
(I'll stay at home myself and find
A woodland to explore.)

Oh, now that it's vacation time
Where is it you will journey
While I am drifting down our creek
With banks all cool and ferny?

Shall you be walking city streets
And visiting the zoo,
And picnicking in city parks?
(Well, I shall picnic, too.)

Vacation is a magic time
For those who love to roam;
But once a sailor said to me,
(Full seven times he'd sailed the sea)
"There's magic, too, at home."

—Rowena Bennett

Value–Values

6577. Most folks pay too much for the things they get for nothing.

6578. We never know the worth of water until the well runs dry.

—*Ancient Saying*

6579. A thing is worth precisely what it can do for you, not what you choose to pay for it.

—John Ruskin

6580. The best things in life aren't really free, because most of us have to spend a lifetime learning they're the best things.

—Harold Coffin

6581. Statistics show that 10,000 people are killed by intoxicating liquor where only one is killed by a mad dog. Yet we shoot the dog and license the liquor. Just what sense is there to this?

—James Kurtz

6582. Values are not rules or habits or mottoes, not skills a parent can teach a child as he teaches him to walk, talk, eat, sleep, and say "Thank you." Rather, values are standards for measuring the intrinsic worth of ideas, ideals, purposes, courses of action and especially human relationships.

—Muriel W. Brown

6583. We cannot buy a quart of goodwill, a pound of love, or a yard of patience. We can only create such values from within ourselves by genuine effort. These are the values that build love and help make homes spiritually satisfying.

—Edgar N. Jackson

6584. A man had posted himself in front of an office building with a tray of shoelaces. One executive made it a daily habit to give the unfortunate a dime, but he never took the laces. One day the peddler, on receiving the dime, tapped his departing benefactor on the back: "I don't like to complain, sir, but the laces are now 15 cents."

—Jack Herbert

6585. One of the great arts of living is to learn the art of accurately appraising values. Everything that we think that we earn, that we have given to us, that in any way touches our consciousness, has its own value. These values are apt to change with the mood, with time, or because of circumstances. We cannot safely tie to any material value. The values of all material possessions change continually, sometimes over night. Nothing of this nature has any permanent set value. The real values are those that stay by you, give you happiness and enrich you. They are the human values.

—George Matthew Adams

Veracity. See also Truth

6586. A half-truth is a whole lie.

—*Yiddish Proverb*

6587. If you want to be thought a liar, always tell the truth.

—L. P. Smith

6588. Beware of the half-truth—it may be the wrong half.

6589. It is twice as hard to crush a half-truth as a whole lie.

6590. The reason we hate a liar is not his immorality, but his gall in thinking we'd believe him.

—Charles P. Curtis

6591. Women are to blame for most of the lying which men do. They insist on asking questions!

6592. The liar's punishment is not in the least that he is not believed, but that he cannot believe anyone else.

6593. I look upon the simple and childish virtues of veracity and honesty as the root of all that is sublime in character.

—Ralph Waldo Emerson

6594. A lie which is half a truth is ever the blackest of lies. A lie which is all a lie may be met and fought with outright; but a lie which is part a truth is a harder matter to fight.

—Alfred Lord Tennyson

6595. The late Clarence Darrow once defended an author in one of those trumped-up plagiarism cases and had occasion to challenge the veracity of a dubious witness. "But," protested the witness, " I am wedded to the truth."

"Ah," nodded Darrow, "and how long have you been a widower?"

6596. There is a wide difference between truthfulness and veracity. Veracity implies a correspondence between words and thoughts; truthfulness, a correspondence between thoughts and realities. To be veracious, it is only necessary that a man give utterance to his convictions; to be true, it is needful that his convictions have affinity with fact.

—FREDERICK W. ROBERTSON

Veteran's Day

6597. May we all live to see the day when disputes between all nations will be decided fairly in an atmosphere of friendship and goodwill.

While that is still only a hope, let Veteran's Day remind us that the strength, the courage, and the will to sacrifice which brought victory in war are needed today to keep the peace in an uneasy world.

6598. In many states Armistice Day became Veteran's Day. This does not mean the end of the hopes inspired by the Armistice of 1918 for a lasting peace. It simply means that after all these years we now know that such hopes depend as much upon strength as upon ideals. Veteran's Day serves to remind us that peace and justice will prevail only when and where we have the strength to defend it.

6599. ARMISTICE DAY

I think I hear them stirring there, today,
Who have lain still
So long, so long, beside the Aisne and Loire,
On Verdun hill.

I think I hear them whispering, today,
The young, the brave,
The gallant and the gay—unmurmuring long,
There in the grave.

I think I hear them sighing there, today—
They sigh for all
The glory and the wonder that was life—
Beyond recall!

I think that their young eyes are wistfully
On us who go
So gayly to our sports, this holiday . . .
I think they know!

I think that they are listening today . . .
  I feel them near!
Our orators declaim—they answer back,
  "Why lie we here?"

Across the fleet, forgetting years it comes,
  Today—their cry,
"O World, O World, if it was all in vain,
  Why did we die?"

Above the earth's enduring hates, they ask
  "Was it—for this?"
I think they are remembering this day
  Of Armistice!

And oh, I think I hear them weeping there
  Who should be sleeping . . .
A plaintive thing—to hear across the world
  The young dead weeping!

—ROSELLE MERCIER MONTGOMERY

Victory

6600. When men are subdued by force, it is only for a while for their hearts are not won; only their strength gives out. When men are subdued by moral conduct their hearts are glad within and their submission is sincere.

—MENCIUS

6601. When we conquer our enemies by kind treatment, and by acts of justice, we are more likely to secure their obedience than by a victory in the field of battle; for in the one case they yield to necessity; in the other, it is their own free choice. Besides, how often is the victory dearly bought, while the conquest of an enemy by affection may be brought about without expense or loss!

—POLYBIUS

Virtue—Virtues

6602. Virtue may be overclouded for a while, but will shine at last.

—*Old Proverb*

6603. The virtue of a man ought to be measured not by his extraordinary exertions, but by his everyday conduct.

—BLAISE PASCAL

6604. To be innocent is to be not guilty; but to be virtuous is to overcome our evil feeling and intentions.

—WILLIAM PENN

6605. To be ambitious of true honor, of the true glory and perfection of our natures, is the very principle and incentive of virtue.

—SIR PHILIP SIDNEY

Vision

6606. Where there is no vision, the people perish.

—*Proverbs, 29:18*

6607. You must have long-range goals to keep you from being frustrated by short-range failures.

—CHARLES C. NOBLE

6608. In order to see it is not sufficient merely to open the eyes. There must be an act of the mind.

—FRANÇOIS MILLET

6609. Vision is always a long view into the future as well as a fresh insight into the facts of the present.

6610. A man to carry on a successful business must have imagination. He must see things as in a vision, a dream of the whole thing.

—CHARLES M. SCHWAB

6611. The vision of things to be done may come a long time before the way of doing them becomes clear, but woe to him who distrusts the vision.

—JENKIN LLOYD JONES

Vote—Votes—Voting

6612. When the vote is unanimous, it usually means that nobody has been listening or cares.

6613. Voting: a process of standing in line for the opportunity to help decide which party will spend your money.

6614. One vote has many times made the difference, even in national elections. Three of our early Presidents were made head of our country by a one-vote margin over their opponents: Thomas Jefferson, John Quincy Adams and Rutherford B. Hayes. . . . One man in history, were he alive today, could tell you what a powerful effect a one-vote margin can have on the neck. King Charles I of England had an appointment with the executioner when the vote to behead him was 67 against and 68 for.

—E. CRENSHAW

War

6615. War means fightin', and fightin' means killin'.

—GEN. NATHAN B. FORREST

6616. War is a proceeding that ruins those who succeed.

6617. In the long run all battles are lost, and so are all wars.

—HENRY L. MENCKEN

6618. The master-secret in fighting is to strike once, but in the right place.

—JOHN C. SNAITH

6619. There's an old diplomatic saying: "If you keep talking, you don't start fighting."

6620. It is the people and the politician who make war and the soldier who makes peace.

—HUGH LENOX SCOTT

6621. There are but two powers in the world, the sword and the mind. In the long run the sword is always beaten by the mind.

—NAPOLEON BONAPARTE

6622. A great war leaves a country with three armies—an army of cripples, an army of mourners, and an army of thieves.

—*German Proverb*

6623. The problem in defense is how far you can go without destroying from within what you're trying to defend from without.

—DWIGHT D. EISENHOWER

6624. Formerly when great fortunes were only made in war, war was a business; but now when great fortunes are only made by business, business is war.

—Christian Nevelle Bovee

6625. As long as war is regarded as wicked it will always have its fascinations. When it is looked upon as vulgar it will cease to be popular.

—Oscar Wilde

6626. Although a soldier by education and profession, I have never felt any fondness for war, and I have never advocated it except as a means of peace.

—Ulysses S. Grant

6627. Outlawing all atomic weapons would be a magnificent gesture. However, it should be remembered that Gettysburg had a local ordinance forbidding the discharge of firearms.

6628. The most unjust war, if supported by the greatest force, always succeeds; hence the most just ones, when supported only by their justice, as often fail.

—St. John de Crevecoeur

6629. It is only necessary to make war with five things: with the maladies of the body, the ignorances of the mind, with the passions of the body, with the seditions of the city, and the discords of families.

—Pythagoras

6630. One thing the war has taught us is, that there is no death. The old distinction between life and death exists no longer. We do not mourn our dead as formerly, because the dead, we know, live on.

—Gertrude Slaughter

6631. Though fraud in all other actions be odious, yet in matters of war it is laudable and glorious, and he who overcomes his enemies by stratagem, is as much to be praised as he who overcomes them by force.

—Niccolo Machiavelli

6632. War has become a Frankenstein to destroy both sides. No longer is it the weapon of adventure whereby a short cut to international power and wealth—a place in the sun—can be gained. If you lose, you are annihilated. If you win, you stand only to lose. No longer does it possess the chance of the winner of a duel—it contains rather the germs of double suicide.

—Gen. Douglas MacArthur

6633. Of all the evils to public liberty, war is perhaps the most to be dreaded, because it comprises and develops every other. War is the parent of armies; from these proceed debts and taxes. And armies, and debts, and taxes, are the known instruments for bringing the many under the dominion of the few. In war, too, the discretionary power of the executive is extended; its influence in dealing out offices, honors, and emoluments is multiplied; and all the means of seducing the minds are added to those of subduing the force of the people! No nation could preserve its freedom in the midst of continual warfare.

—James Madison

War–Peace

6634. If we perspired more in times of peace, we should bleed less in times of war.

—Chiang Kai-shek

6635. The nobility of a people lies, not in its capacity for war, but in its capacity for peace. It is indeed only because the nations are incapable of the one that they plunge so readily into the other.

—G. Lowes Dickinson

Waste

6636. Waste today lamenting tomorrow and you'll waste tomorrow lamenting today.

—Arnold H. Glasow

6637. Waste is worse than loss. The time is coming when every person who lays claim to ability will keep the question of waste before him constantly. The scope of thrift is limitless.

—Thomas A. Edison

6638. Believe me when I tell you that thrift of time will repay you in after life, with a usury of profit beyond your most sanguine dreams; and that waste of it will make you dwindle, alike in intellectual and moral stature, beyond your darkest reckoning.

—William E. Gladstone

6639. Thousands of tons of tobacco-ash are lost in this country every year. This ash has a very high value as a fertilizer, yet no one has ever evolved a satisfactory method for collecting it.

Then take tea. Expended tea-leaves are rich in tannin, chlorophyll and caffeine—all products of considerable value. Could they be gathered, they would be worth nearly a million dollars.

Weakness

6640. Even the feeble can push over what already totters.

—Ovid

6641. Do not show your wounded finger, for everything will knock up against it.

—Baltasar Gracian

6642. People who have no weaknesses are terrible; there is no way of taking advantage of them.

—Anatole France

Wealth

6643. Enough is great riches.

6644. Ill-gotten wealth is never stable.

—Euripides

6645. He is rich who knows when he has had enough.

—Lao Tzu

6646. He is a poor man who has nothing but money.

6647. The luxury of the rich gives bread to the poor.

—*French Proverb*

6648. A man's true wealth is the good he does in this world.

—Mohammed

6649. Wealth is not his that has it, but his that enjoys it.

—Benjamin Franklin

6650. He alone is rich who makes a proper use of his riches.

—Horace

6651. Nothing distributes wealth like taxation and a large family.

6652. A thief passes for a gentleman when stealing has made him rich.

—*Ancient Proverb*

6653. A great fortune in the hands of a fool is a great misfortune.

—*Ancient Proverb*

6654. Few rich men own their own property. The property owns them.

—Robert G. Ingersoll

6655. The greatest evidence of demoralization is the respect paid to wealth.

—*Old French Proverb*

6656. I should not like to be rich. It makes you too forgetful of your Creator.

—B. R. Haydon

6657. He is richest who is content with the least, for content is the wealth of nature.

—Socrates

6658. A man who possesses wealth possesses power, but it is a power to do evil as well as good.

—Azel Stevens Roe

6659. Life is short. The sooner, then, a man begins to enjoy his wealth the better.

—Dr. Samuel Johnson

6660. Every man has the secret of becoming rich who resolves to live within his means.

6661. The futility of riches is taught very plainly, both in the Bible and in the income tax blank.

6662. The world is coming, more and more, to the belief that superfluous wealth is a public trust.

—Mary Elizabeth Hewitt

6663. It is far more easy to acquire a fortune like a knave, than to expend it like a gentleman.

—Charles C. Colton

6664. Knowing how to make money and also how to keep it—either of these gifts might make a man rich.

—Seneca

6665. A little home well filled, a little field well tilled, and a little wife well willed, are great riches.

—BENJAMIN FRANKLIN

6666. If we command our wealth, we shall be rich and free; if our wealth commands us, we are poor indeed.

—EDMUND BURKE

6667. The highest use of capital is not to make more money, but to make money do more for the betterment of life.

—HENRY FORD

6668. The wealth of man is the number of things which he loves and blesses, which he is loved and blessed by.

—THOMAS CARLYLE

6669. To acquire wealth is difficult, to preserve it more difficult, but to spend it wisely most difficult of all.

—EDWARD PARSONS DAY

6670. The darkest hour in any man's life is when he sits down to plan how to get money without earning it.

—HORACE GREELEY

6671. Economic independence doesn't set anyone free. Or it shouldn't, for the higher up you go, the more responsibilities become yours.

—BERNARD F. GIMBEL

6672. Inherited wealth is a big handicap to happiness. It is as certain death to ambition as cocaine is to morality.

—WILLIAM K. VANDERBILT

6673. As riches and favor forsake a man, we discover him to be a fool, but nobody could find it out in his prosperity.

—JEAN DE LA BRUYÈRE

6674. The acquisition of wealth is a work of great labor; its possession, a source of continual fear; its loss, of excessive grief.

—*From the Latin*

6675. A rich man without charity is a rogue; and perhaps it would be no difficult matter to prove that he is also a fool.

—HENRY FIELDING

6676. There is nothing which continues longer than a modest fortune; nothing of which one sees the end sooner than a large fortune.

—Jean de La Bruyère

6677. Surplus wealth is a sacred trust which its possessor is bound to administer in his lifetime for the good of the community.

—Andrew Carnegie

6678. Never respect men merely for their riches; but rather for their philanthropy: we do not value the sun for its height, but for its use.

—Rev. William Scott Downey

6679. He that is proud of riches is a fool. For if he be exalted above his neighbors because he hath more gold, how much inferior is he to a gold mine.

—Jeremy Taylor

6680. The greatest humbug in the world is the idea that money can make a man happy. I never had any satisfaction with mine until I began to do good with it.

6681. Money does not always enlarge a man; on the contrary, it frequently belittles him. It has more than once happened that as a man grew rich he grew small.

—George H. Hepworth

6682. Riches are gotten with pain, kept with care, and lost with grief. The cares of riches lie heavier upon a good man than the inconvenience of an honest poverty.

—Sir Roger L'Estrange

6683. The greatest and the most amiable privilege which the rich enjoy over the poor, is that which they exercise the least—the privilege of making them happy.

—Charles C. Colton

6684. He is a great simpleton who imagines that the chief power of wealth is to supply wants. In ninety-nine cases out of a hundred it creates more wants than it supplies.

6685. It may be discovered that the final outcome and consummation of all wealth is in producing as many as possible bright-eyed, and happy-hearted human creatures.

—John Ruskin

6686. Fortunes are saved, not made. If you spend as much as you get you will never be richer than you are. It is not what a man gets but what he saves that constitutes his wealth.

6687. No man can tell whether he is rich or poor by turning to his ledger. It is the heart that makes a man rich. He is rich according to what he is, not according to what he has.

—Henry Ward Beecher

6688. It takes a great deal of boldness mixed with a vast deal of caution, to acquire a great fortune; but then it takes ten times as much wit to keep it after you have got it as it took to make it.

—Mayer A. Rothschild

6689. If we command our wealth, we shall be rich and free; if our wealth commands us, we are poor indeed. We are bought by the enemy with the treasure in our own coffers.

—Edmund Burke

6690. The greatest luxury of riches is, that they enable you to escape so much good advice. The rich are always advising the poor, but the poor seldom venture to return the compliment.

—Sir Arthur Helps

6691. There is a burden of care in getting riches; fear in keeping them; temptation in using them; guilt in abusing them; sorrow in losing them; and a burden of account at last to be given concerning them.

—Matthew Henry

6692. Worldly wealth is the devil's bait; and those whose minds feed upon riches, recede in general from real happiness, in proportion as their stores increase; as the moon, when she is fullest of light, is farthest from the sun.

—Richard E. Burton

6693. Now the problem to the poor is one of necessity: to earn wherewithal to live, they must find remunerative labor. But the problem to the rich is one of honor; having the wherewithal they must find serviceable labor.

—Robert Louis Stevenson

6694. What a man does with his wealth depends upon his idea of happiness. Those who draw prizes in life are apt to spend tastelessly, if not viciously; not knowing that it requires as much talent to spend as to make.

—Edwin Percy Whipple

6695. Ill fares the land
To hastening ills a prey
When wealth accumulates
But men decay.

—Oliver Goldsmith

6696. The sole aristocracy of today is the aristocracy of wealth; the sole aristocracy of tomorrow will be the eternal divine, beneficent aristocracy of intellect and virtue—at its highest, genius; but that, like everything that descends from God, will rise among the people and labor for the people.

—Guiseppe Mazzini

6697. If thou art rich, then show the greatness of thy fortune—or what is better, the greatness of thy soul, in the meekness of thy conversation; condescend to men of low estate, support the distressed, and patronize the neglected.

—Benjamin Franklin

6698. To acquire wealth is not easy, yet to keep it is even more difficult. . . . It is said that wealth is like a viper which is harmless if a man knows how to take hold of it; but, if he does not, it will twine around his hand and bite him.

—Frank K. Houston

6699. An accession of wealth is a dangerous predicament for a man. At first he is stunned if the accession be sudden, and is very humble and very grateful. Then he begins to speak a little louder, people think him more sensible, and soon he thinks so himself.

—Richard Cecil

6700. Nations, like men, can he healthy and happy, though comparatively poor. . . .

Wealth is a means to an end, not the end itself. As a synonym for health and happiness, it has had fair trial, and failed dismally.

—John Galsworthy

6701. The way to wealth is as plain as the way to market. It depends chiefly on two words, industry and frugality; that is, waste neither time nor money, but make the best use of both. Without industry and frugality, nothing will do; and with them, everything.

—Benjamin Franklin

6702. Those who obtain riches by labor, care, and watching, know their value. Those who impart them to sustain and extend knowledge, virtue, and religion, know their use. Those who lose them by accident or fraud know their vanity. And those who experience the difficulties and dangers of preserving them know their perplexities.

—C. Simmons

6703. The pulpit and the press have many commoplaces denouncing the thirst for wealth; but if men should take these moralists at their word, and leave off aiming to be rich, the moralists would rush to rekindle, at all hazards, this love of power in the people lest civilization should be undone.

—Ralph Waldo Emerson

6704. If thou desire to purchase honor with thy wealth, consider first how that wealth became thine; if thy labor got it, let thy wisdom keep it; if oppression found it, let repentance restore it; if thy parent left it, let thy virtues deserve it; so shall thy honor be safer, better and cheaper.

—Francis Quarles

6705. Men pursue riches under the idea that their possession will set them at ease and above the world. But the law of association often makes those who begin by loving gold as a servant, finish by becoming its slaves; and independence without wealth is at least as common as wealth without independence.

—Charles C. Colton

6706. The contempt of riches among the philosophers was a hidden desire to revenge their merit for the injustice of fortune, by contempt of the very advantages of which she deprived them. It was a secret to secure themselves from the degradation of poverty: it was a by-road to arrive at that consideration which they could not obtain by riches.

—François de La Rochefoucauld

6707. Very few men acquire wealth in such a manner as to receive pleasure from it. As long as there is the enthusiasm of the chase they enjoy it. But when they begin to look around and think of settling down, they find that that part by which joy enters in, is dead in them. They have spent their lives in heaping up colossal piles of treasure, which stand at the end, like the pyramids in the desert, holding only the dust of things.

—Henry Ward Beecher

6708. In discussions of the capitalistic system, those who stress sharing the wealth forget the importance of creating the wealth. You can't share if you have not created. It seems to me, too, that in the preservation of the enterprise system there has recently grown up the philosophy of "survival of the sickest" instead of "survival of the fittest." In the many investigations which take place in our country, it is almost always true that a successful company or a successful enterprise is the subject of suspicion and investigation. I wish they would start investigating the failures instead of the successes. This might result in some very interesting economic information.

—David Sarnoff

6709. THAT'S WEALTH

A calm devotion to one's native sod;
That's Wealth.
A faith implicit in the living God;
That's Wealth
A few choice friends who feel life's real meaning,
Who sense reality, yet prize the dreaming,
Who from the skies see knowledge ever streaming;
That's Wealth.

A body sparkling with the health of youth;
That's Wealth.
A mind serenely poised, restrained by truth;
That's Wealth.
An eye that feeds on flowers and fields and skies,
That sees the heaven in a baby's eyes,
That finds in life the door to Paradise—
That's Wealth.

A home among the trees, the blue above;
That's Wealth.
The perfect goodness of a woman's love;
That's Wealth.
The sense to grin when all the world looks wrong,
To take defeat with gameness and a song,
To smile a mile when worry comes along;
That's Wealth.

—Charles F. Steele

Weather

6710. Bad weather always looks much worse through a window.

6711. Bad weather has its good points. It gives people who have to kick about something, something to kick about.

6712. One nice thing about the change in seasons is that it inspires a change in conversation. People who used to say, "Is it hot enough for you?" now ask, "Is it cold enough for you?"

Widowhood

6713. A buxom widow must be either married, buried, or shut up in a convent.

—*Spanish Proverb*

6714. Many men who were considerate of their wives are extremely unkind to their widows.

Wife–Wives

6715. A wife who has good old-fashioned horse sense never becomes a nag.

6716. There are three kinds of wives: the prize, the surprise, and the consolation.

—*Believe Me,* by VIRGINIA HUTCHINSON (Comet Press Books)

Will Power

6717. Lack of will power has caused more failure than lack of intelligence or ability.

—FLOWER A. NEWHOUSE

6718. A just man is not one who does no ill,
But he, who with the power, has not the will.

—PHILEMON

Wisdom

6719. Knowledge comes but wisdom lingers.

—ALFRED LORD TENNYSON

6720. Knowledge is power, but only wisdom is liberty.
—WILL DURANT

6721. Wisdom is the scar tissue of intelligence.
—GENE GLEASON

6722. Nine-tenths of wisdom is being wise in time.
—THEODORE ROOSEVELT

6723. A man becomes wise by watching what happens to him when he isn't.

6724. He is a fool who cannot be angry: but he is a wise man who will not.

6725. A man remains wise as long as he seeks wisdom. The minute he thinks he has found it, he becomes a fool.

6726. Knowledge comes by taking things apart: analysis. But wisdom comes by putting things together.
—JOHN A. MORRISON

6727. A wise man will desire no more than what he may get justly, use soberly, distribute cheerfully and leave contentedly.
—BENJAMIN FRANKLIN

6728. He alone is wise who can accommodate himself to all the contingencies of life; but the fool contends, and is struggling, like a swimmer, against the stream.
—*From the Latin*

6729. Wisdom does not show itself so much in precept as in life—in firmness of mind and a mastery of appetite. It teaches us to do as well as to talk, and to make our words and actions all of a color.
—SENECA

6730. Facts are the basis of policies but they do not create policies; they are only the stuff of which policies are made. Here is where synthesis comes in to build up the facts into useful knowledge which is wisdom, and it is wisdom that alone gives meaning and direction to life.
—HAROLD W. DODDS

6731. Because I have stirred a few grains of sand on the shore, am I in a position to know the depths of the ocean? Nature is a riddle without a definite solution to satisfy man's curiosity. Truth ever eludes us. To know how not to know might well be the last word of wisdom.

—Henri Fabre

6732. Knowledge and wisdom, far from being one, have oft times no connection. Knowledge dwells in heads replete with thoughts of other men. Wisdom in minds attentive to their own. Knowledge is proud that she has learned so much. Wisdom is humble that she knows no more.

Wit and Humor

6733. When a thing is funny, search it for a hidden truth.

—George Bernard Shaw

6734. Wit in conversation is, in the midwives' phrase, a quick conception and an easy delivery.

—Jonathan Swift

6735. The elements of humor are surprise, unpredictability, playfulness, exaggeration, and understatement.

6736. Puns are good, bad and indifferent, and only those who lack the wit to make them are unaware of the fact.

—Henry Watson Fowler

6737. There is no more dangerous literary symptom than a temptation to write about wit and humor. It indicates the total loss of both.

—George Bernard Shaw

6738. True humor springs not more from the head than from the heart; it is not contempt, its essence is love; it issues not in laughter, but in still smiles, which lie far deeper.

—Thomas Carlyle

6739. Wit laughs at; humor with. Wit is the result of antipathy; humor of sympathy. Wit punishes pungently; humor cherishes cheerfully. Wit is the counterfeit-detector of the issues of life; humor makes even the bogus coin ring merrily. Wit is lightning: it flashes to scathe. Humor is light, and radiates with a pleasing flow.

—Samuel S. Cox

Woman—Women

6740. A truth-telling woman has few friends.

—*Irish Proverb*

6741. No woman holds her own in the battle of tongues.

6742. Nature intended that woman should be her masterpiece.

—GOTTHOLD LESSING

6743. A woman either loves or hates; there is no third course.

—*Latin Proverb*

6744. God forgives, man forgets, but woman remembers forever.

—MINNA THOMAS ANTRIM

6745. The only certain thing about a woman is her uncertainty.

6746. The thing some women dread about their past is its length.

6747. The best man for the job is frequently not a man but a woman.

—PATRICIA THOMAS

6748. A woman who can take "no" for an answer is probably conducting a survey.

6749. It's always the woman who pays—but look at whose money she uses.

6750. Women constitute the only power in the world that constantly wins by surrendering.

6751. Women can make a dollar go farther—they'll drive clear across town to spend it.

—HENRY MORGAN

6752. There are few virtuous women who are not weary of their profession.

—FRANÇOIS DE LA ROCHEFOUCAULD

6753. Women are demons who make us enter hell through the gates of paradise.

6754. The cruelest revenge of a woman is often to remain faithful to a man.

—JACQUES BENIGNE BOSSUET

6755. Nothing so stirs a man's conscience or excites his curiosity as a woman's complete silence.

6756. A woman is like your shadow; follow her, she flies; fly from her, she follows.

—*Old Proverb*

6757. Women are sometimes indecorous, often indecisive, usually indeterminate—always indispensable.

—C. Harold Crump

6758. Women are unpredictable. You never know how they're going to manage to get their own way.

—Beatrice Mann

6759. Woman: the opposition sex; the weeper sex; a species of creature known for untold ages.

6760. A woman is a creature who needs new shoes to go with the dress she has in mind to go with her old shoes.

—Dan Bennett

6761. Women give to men the very gold of their lives. But they invariably want it back in small change.

—Oscar Wilde

6762. Next to God, we are indebted to women; first, for life itself, and then for making it worth having.

6763. A beautiful woman appeals to the eye; a good woman appeals to the heart. One is a jewel, the other a treasure.

—Napoleon I

6764. The resistance of a woman is not always a proof of her virtue, but more frequently of her experience.

—Ninon de Lenclos

6765. Without woman the two extremities of life would be without succor, and the middle without pleasure.

6766. There is a great similarity between girls and cars—a good paint job conceals the years, but the lines tell the story.

6767. Woman's intuition is so keen that she can guess everything except the truth and discover everything except facts.

6768. Women keep yelling for equality but they get mad when you offer them a chance to spade half the flower beds or mow half the lawn.

6769. The only way for a woman to provide for herself decently is for her to be good to some man that can afford to be good to her.

—George Bernard Shaw

6770. The reason a good woman has so little pity for a bad one is that she knows just how hard it is to be good and the privations it often demands.

6771. Women are like thermometers, which on a sudden application of heat sink at first a few degrees, as a preliminary to rising a good many.

—Jean Paul Friedrich Richter

6772. Man cannot degrade woman without himself falling into degradation; he can not elevate her without at the same time elevating himself.

—Alexander Walker

6773. However dull a woman may be, she will understand all there is in love; however intelligent a man may be, he will never know but half of it.

—Madame Fée

6774. Women have more strength in their looks than we have in our laws, and more power by their tears than we have by our arguments.

—Sir Henry Saville

6775. A woman is never displeased if we please several other women, provided she is preferred. It is so many more triumphs for her.

—Ninon de Lenclos

6776. No friendship is so cordial or so delicious as that of girl for girl; no hatred so intense and immovable as that of woman for woman.

—Walter Savage Landor

6777. A pessimist is a woman driver who's afraid she won't be able to squeeze her car into a very small parking space. An optimist is a man who believes she won't try.

6778. A woman who creates and sustains a home, and under whose hands children grow up to be strong and pure men and women, is a creator second only to God.

—Helen Hunt Jackson

6779. Those women who live upon their income, must necessarily be careful; those who live upon the income of others, must be clever; and those who live upon their debts, must be both.

—Minna Thomas Antrim

6780. When women love us, they forgive us everything, even our crimes; when they do not love us, they give us credit for nothing, not even for our virtues.

6781. Most females will forgive a liberty, rather than a slight; and if any woman were to hang a man for stealing her picture, although it were set in gold, it would be a new case in law; but if he carried off the setting, and left the portrait, I would not answer for his safety.

—Charles C. Colton

6782. A woman's life can be divided thus: the age when she dances but does not dare to waltz—it is the spring; the age when she dances and dares to waltz—it is summer; the age when she dances but prefers to waltz—it is autumn; finally, when she dances no longer—it is winter, that rigorous winter of life.

—Mme. de Girardin

6783. Man has not yet reached his best. He never will reach his best until he walks the upward way side by side with woman. Plato was right in his fancy that man and woman are merely halves of humanity, each requiring the qualities of the other in order to attain the highest character. Shakespeare understood it when he made his noblest women strong as men, and his best men tender as women. The hands and breasts that nursed all men to life are scorned as the forgetful brute proclaims his superior strength and plumes himself so he can subjugate the one who made him what he is.

—Eugene V. Debs

Word—Words

6784. The word "engagement" has two meanings: in war, it's a battle; in courtship, it's a surrender.

6785. Words are the soul's ambassadors who go
Abroad upon her errands to and fro.

—James Howell

6786. The word "worship" comes from two old Anglo-Saxon words: "weorthscipe"—worth-shape. In other words, worship is shaping or fashioning our worths or values.

—Anna Laura Gebhard

6787. Although words exist for the most part for the transmission of ideas, there are some which produce such violent disturbance in our feelings that the role they play in the transmission of ideas is lost in the background.

—Albert Einstein

6788. Words happen to be our way of getting to one another. . . . The written word—the word set down—is not only a sword and a trumpet for the present but a link that binds us to all humanity. When we lose touch with the great words of the past—when they seem meaningless to us and we can make no new good words for our own day—then history changes.

—Stephen Vincent Benet

Work

6789. Hard workers are usually honest; industry lifts them above temptation.

—Christian Nevelle Bovee

6790. Nothing is really work unless you would rather be doing something else.

—James M. Barrie

6791. The art of winning in business is in working hard—not taking things too seriously.

—Elbert Hubbard

6792. If the power to do hard work is not talent, it is the best possible substitute for it.

—James A. Garfield

6793. It is better to undertake a large task and get it half done than to undertake nothing and get it all done.

—W. Marshall Craig

6794. It is only those who do not know how to work that do not love it. To those who do, it is better than play—it is religion.

—J. H. Patterson

6795. If you become a parasite, taking and never giving, you'll lose your zest for living. And doing nothing won't be any fun. Work is what makes you able to appreciate rest.

6796. I don't like people who pride themselves on working painfully. If their work was painful, they would better have done something else. The delight one takes in one's work is the sign of its fittingness.

—André Gide

6797. My mother constantly urged my father not to work so hard. She died at 57; but he was a calm person and lived to be 84. Hard mental and physical work does not kill, but stress, strains and tensions can wear a person down.

—Dr. Walter C. Alvarez

6798. If your work is work for you and you don't see beyond that work and see the pleasure in work and the pleasure in service, look out; you are in danger of standing in your present station for a long, long time.

—Milan R. Bump

6799. The secret of the true love of work is the hope of success in that work; not for the money reward, for the time spent, nor for the skill exercised, but for the successful result in the accomplishment of the work itself.

—Sidney A. Weltmer

6800. Men seldom die of hard work; activity is God's medicine. The highest genius is willingness and ability to do hard work. Any other conception of genius makes it a doubtful, if not a dangerous possession.

—R. S. MacArthur

6801. It is not work that kills men; it is worry. Work is healthy, and you can hardly put more upon a man than he can bear; but worry is rust upon the blade. It is not the revolution that destroys machinery, it is the friction.

—Henry Ward Beecher

6802. There isn't any luck that enters into anything, unless it's poker or shooting dice, maybe. There is no luck to merchandising. There is no luck in going out and working from early in the morning to long after dinner. That is not luck, it's work.

—Fred W. Fitch

6803. My suggestion to ambitious young men would be to conserve and develop their physical and mental strength, cram their heads with all the useful knowledge they can, and work, work, work—not simply for their own advancement but to get worthwhile things done.

—Edward G. Seubert

6804. Work is the true elixir of life. The busiest man is the happiest man. Excellence in any art or profession is attained only by hard and persistent work. Never believe that you are perfect. When a man imagines, even after years of striving, that he has attained perfection, his decline begins.

—Sir Theodore Martin

6805. No man is born into the world whose work is not born with him. There is always work, and tools to work with, for those who will, and blessed are the horny hands of toil. The busy world shoves angrily aside the man who stands with arms akimbo until occasion tells him what to do; and he who waits to have his task marked out shall die and leave his errand unfulfilled.

—James Russell Lowell

6806. The superstition that all our hours of work are a minus quantity in the happiness of life, and all the hours of idleness are plus ones, is a most ludicrous and pernicious doctrine, and its greatest support comes from our not taking sufficient trouble, not making a real effort, to make work as near pleasure as possible.

—Lord Balfour

6807. I am wondering what would have happened to me if some fluent talker had converted me to the theory of the eight-hour day and convinced me that it was not fair to my fellow workers to put forth my best efforts in my work. I am glad that the eight-hour day had not been invented when I was a young man. If my life had been made up of eight-hour days I do not believe I could have accomplished a great deal. This country would not amount to as much as it does if the young men of fifty years ago had been afraid that they might earn more than they were paid for.

—Thomas A. Edison

6808. Work was not invented as a punishment for the Garden of Eden episode. Instead it is merely the outward expression of man's ambition, energy, and desire for accomplishment. It is the path over which his desires travel. So work, instead of frowning on this thing we call fun in life, really leads to its threshold. That is why the worker sings at his task, because he is expressing that which is in his heart. The better he works the louder he sings; the more joy he finds in his work, the finer his labors.

World, The

6809. If the world seems cold, make it your business to build fires.

6810. The world is not a playground, it is a schoolroom. Life is not a holiday, but an education. And the one eternal lesson for us all is how better we can love.

—Henry Drummond

6811. It is now evident to all men of spiritual discernment that healing of the world's woes will not come through this or that social or political theory; not through violent changes in government, but in the still small voice that speaks to the conscience and the heart.

—Arthur J. Moore

World Relations

6812. There should be no inferiors and no superiors for true world friendship.

—Carlos P. Romulo

6813. He who thinks that he can find within his own breast that which may enable him to dispense with the whole world is much mistaken; but he who thinks that the world cannot do without him is still more mistaken.

—François de La Rochefoucauld

6814. Interference in the affairs of a nation is like interference in a family quarrel, when the intrusion of an outsider is the only thing that can unite the family.

Worry—Worries

6815. Worry grows lushly in the soil of indecision.

6816. Worry is like a rocking chair—it keeps you busy but it doesn't get you anywhere.

6817. Worry has been defined as a circle of inefficient thoughts whirling about a pivot of fear.

6818. The silent partner says not to worry over the job you do not like—some other fellow will have it soon.

6819. The trouble with getting away from it all is that the people who got there ahead of you brought most of it with them.

6820. Worry is a thin stream of fear trickling through the mind. If encouraged, it cuts a channel into which all other thoughts are drained.

—Arthur Somers Roche

6821. There is no use worrying about things over which you have no control, and if you have control, you can do something about them instead of worrying.

—Stanley C. Allyn

6822. Worry a little bit every day and in a lifetime you will lose a couple of years. If something is wrong, fix it if you can. But train yourself not to worry. Worry never fixes anything.

—Ole Helgerson

6823. Worry is evidence of an ill-controlled brain; it is merely a stupid waste of time in unpleasantness. If men and women practiced mental calisthenics as they do physical calisthenics, they would purge their brains of this foolishness.

—Arnold Bennett

6824.

Some of your griefs you have cured,
And the worst you have survived;
But, think of the pain you have endured
From the evils that never arrived.

—*Author Unknown*

6825. It might help if somebody would invent an "upset pill" to make people worry more about real-life problems that cry for attention and solution. Too many of us tend to be complacent and eager to escape from personal and social problems, when we should be concerned. Anxiety is not always bad; it is often necessary.

—Frederick J. Hacker

6826. It's a difficult or impossible thing to stop worrying completely. The easiest way out is to try to worry about one worry at a time. That way you don't get mixed up and start worrying about the thing you're really not worried about. When you have too many worries on your mind at one time you get confused, and then you've really got something to worry about!

—VINCENT ARGONDEZZI

6827. To try to stop worrying completely is a waste of energy. It is perfectly natural and normal to worry about real dangers or threats; and it is *abnormal* not to be concerned over them. "Most people," says psychiatrist Dr. Judd Marmor, "seem unaware that to be unworried in the face of distressing reality situations may often be a symptom of a serious mental disorder."

—JOHN E. GIBSON

6828. WHY WORRY

Strength for today is all that we need,
As there never will be a tomorrow;
For tomorrow will prove but another day,
With its measure of joy and sorrow.

Then why forecast the trials of life
With such sad and grave persistence,
And wait and watch for a crowd of ills
That as yet have no existence?

—Author Unknown

Youth

6829. Youth is the opportunity to do something and to become somebody.

—T. T. MUNGER

6830. Youth would be an ideal state if it came a little later in life.

—HERBERT HENRY ASQUITH

6831. Youth is the period of happiness, but only age is aware of the fact.

6832. Youth is the wonderful time of life which only the young are strong enough to endure.

6833. The main trouble with the younger generation is that some of us no longer belong to it.

6834. The person who says youth is a state of mind invariably has far more state of mind than youth.

6835. Let's stop criticizing the younger generation. If we can't keep up with them we can at least get behind them.

—MAURICE SEITTER

6836. At twenty he thinks he can save the world; at thirty he begins to wish he could save part of his salary.

6837. People who wonder where the younger generation is headed would do well to consider where it came from.

6838. A boy becomes a man a lot quicker than his parents think but not nearly as quickly as he thinks.

6839. A little boy's mind is like a garden; the seeds you plant therein grow either into weeds or flowers, and both are hard to dig out.

—JOSEPH H. PECK

6840. In this advanced century, a girl of sixteen knows as much as her mother, and enjoys her knowledge much more.

6841. The destiny of any nation, at any given time, depends on the opinions of its young men under five and twenty.

—JOHANN WOLFGANG VON GOETHE

6842. Youth, though it may lack knowledge, is certainly not devoid of intelligence; it sees through shams with sharp and terrible eyes.

—HENRY L. MENCKEN

6843. Young men are fitter to invent than to judge; fitter for execution than for counsel; and fitter for new projects than for settled business.

—FRANCIS BACON

6844. An unspoiled youth of twenty with his mind just waking up and his feeling all fresh and open to good is the most beautiful thing this world produces.

—G. LOWES DICKINSON

6845. Consider what heavy responsibility lies upon you in your youth, to determine, among realities, by what you will be delighted, and, among imaginations, by whose you will be led.

—JOHN RUSKIN

6846. I don't feel the least hostile to young people or bothered about them. I don't understand them, but when I was young, people didn't understand me. It's a perfectly natural process.

—EDWARD MORGAN FORSTER

6847. The best rules to form a young man are: to talk a little, to hear much, to reflect alone on what has passed in company, to distrust one's own opinions, and value others' that deserve it.

—SIR WILLIAM TEMPLE

6848. To keep young, every day read a poem, hear a choice piece of music, view a fine painting, and if possible, do a good action. Man's highest merit always is, as much as possible, to rule external circumstances and as little as possible to let himself be ruled by them.

—JOHANN WOLFGANG VON GOETHE

6849. A boy is a stick of dynamite, a bundle of energy and potential power waiting to be ignited. Guard him zealously from careless sparks that would dissipate his energies or detonate his power for the demolition of society. Guide him carefully to a place where his vigor and strength will be used to build a better world.

6850. Youth has a certain melancholy and sadness, while age is valiantly cheerful. . . . A chief lesson of youth should be to learn to enjoy solitude—a source of peace and happiness. . . . In my years of youth I was delighted when the doorbell rang, for I thought, now it (the great romantic adventure) had come. But in later years my feeling on the same occasion had something rather akin to terror—I thought, there it comes!

—ARTHUR SCHOPENHAUER

Zeal

6851. Zeal is a grand thing, if directed in the right channel. To be zealous in a good cause, with a proper motive, is very desirable. It is well also, to have knowledge, as well as zeal: people who allow their zeal to overbalance their knowledge often make very grievous blunders, and have many things to regret. It is well to weigh a matter before acting upon your first decision—especially a matter of much importance. Take time to consider; allow your judgment and reason to guide you, lest your zeal should lead you into serious error. It may be that one zealous act—where your zeal is utterly devoid of knowledge—may cause you the regret of a lifetime. Use your zeal aright; if wisely directed, it will prove to you a great blessing.

—IDA SCOTT TAYLOR

Toasts

Absence

1. Here's to us that are here, to you that are there, and the rest of us everywhere.

—Rudyard Kipling

2.

Here's to you, my dear,
And to the dear that's not here, my dear.
Were she here, my dear,
I'd not be drinking to you, my dear.

3.

Here's to the friend we love so well,
  To those so far away!
If a drink of cheer would bring them here,
  We would drink the livelong day!

Advice

4.

Advice was made to give away,
  And joy was made to borrow—
Oh, friends, be borrowers today
  And generous tomorrow.

—Theodosia Garrison

Aging. See Old Age

Ambition

5.

Here's a toast to great ambition,
  About which people rant.
It makes one want to do the thing
  That everyone knows one can't.

Anniversary

6. Let anniversaries come and let anniversaries go—but may your happiness continue on forever.

7. May your anniversaries continue until only the recording angel will be able to recall when the first one was celebrated.

Armed Forces

8. Here's to the men in our armed services. Because they are ready to die for our just cause, the rest of us can go on living.

9. Here's to the Army and Navy!
May they never want—and never be wanted!

10. Here's to the soldier who fights and loves—may he never lack for either.

11. Success to our army, success to our fleet;
May our foes be compelled to bow down at our feet!

12. May we always be under the orders of General Peace, General Plenty and General Prosperity.

13. Here's to the girls we've left behind,
Out of sight but never out of mind.

14. Here's to the Army and Navy,
And the battles they have won;
Here's to America's colors—
The colors that never run.

15. Here's to the ships of our Navy and the ladies of our land.
May the former be well rigged and the latter well manned.

16. A health to Uncle Sam's sailors,
God bless them every one,
From the stately gold-laced Admiral
To the man behind the gun.

Army. See Armed Forces

Art—Arts

17. When God conceived the world, that was Poetry; He formed it, and that was Scripture; He colored it, and that was Painting; He peopled it with living beings, and that was the grand, divine, eternal Drama.

—Charlotte Cushman

Author—Authorship

18. Here's to poetry, the eldest sister of all arts, and parent of most.

—William Congreve

19.

Here's to the author, an animal queer;
No other's so odd, it is said;
For while he has features like most other folks,
His tale comes out of his head.

20.

TO A PLAYWRIGHT

If he had written Hamlet, there
Is one thing which we know full well:
He'd have allowed the prince to get
The girl before the curtain fell.

—Nesbit

21.

Then a health to the poets I'll toss,
To Byron and Shelley and Keats,
To Dobson the blithe and Swinburne the lithe,
And the Irish phenomenon Yeats.
Then, pausing a moment on earth,
I'll fill up my glass to the brim,
To the material flow of Miss Phoebe Snow,
And that breakfast food bard, Sunny Jim.

Bachelors—Bachelorhood

22. Here's to Woman—the bitter half of man.

23. May all single men be married and may all married men be happy.

24. Here's to all the Bachelors—they kiss whom they please and please whom they kiss!

25. A pipe, a book, a fire, a friend,
A stein that's always full,
Here's to the joys of a bachelor's life,
A life that is never dull.

26. Here's to the bachelor, so lonely and gay,
It's not his fault, he was born that way.
And here's to the spinster, so lonely and good,
It's not her fault—she's done what she could.

27. Here's to the jolly bachelor,
The man who lives in joy;
Whose cares are few, whose friends are true,
Whose peace holds no alloy,
Who lights his pipe and fills his bowl,
Cries, "Fie to care and strife,
Who takes a sip from every lip
And leads a merry life."

—Richard Stillman Powell

Bankers

28. Here's to the banker—the fine fellow who will gladly lend you an umbrella when the sun is shining and will want it back when it starts to rain.

Beauty

29. Here's to your beauty which is stronger than wine for it intoxicates us both.

Beer. See Wine

Birthday

30. Here's a health to you! If our birthdays treated us half as kindly, we'd celebrate them, too.

31. Another candle in your cake?
Well, that's no cause to spout,
Be glad that you have strength enough
To blow the darn thing out.

Bride and Groom

32. To the Bride and Groom: May their troubles be little ones.

33. To the Bride! May your hours of joy be as numerous as the petals of your bridal bouquet.

34. To ________ and ________: May this be one union that will never go on strike!

—*Here's to It!* Compiled by John M. Koken (A. S. Barnes & Company, Inc.)

35. Laugh and the world laughs with you; snore, and you sleep alone.

36. To the Bride and Groom—may the newness wear off everything but their happiness!

37. To the Bride and Groom—may your wedding days be few and your anniversaries many.

38. Here's to the happy couple—may we all be present at their golden wedding anniversary.

39. Here's to the Bride and Groom—may your courtship be endless and your honeymoon last twice as long!

40. To the Bride and Groom—may your coming anniversaries be outnumbered only by your coming joys and pleasures!

41. Here's to the newly-wedded pair—may their joys be as deep as the ocean and their misfortunes as light as its foam.

42. Here's to marriage—the gate through which the happy lover leaves his enchanted ground and returns from paradise to earth.

43. To the health of the Bride and Groom! You will find that two cannot live as cheaply as one. But, then, it is well worth the difference.

44. Here's to the Bride and Groom—may their happiness through life be as happy and as free as the dancing waves on the deep blue sea.

45. Here's to the Bride and Groom:
"Look down, you gods,
And on this couple drop a blessed crown."
—William Shakespeare, The *Tempest*

46. Here's to the Bride and Groom—may their joys be as bright as the morning, and their sorrows but shadows that fade in the sunlight of love.

47. Here's to the health of the happy pair,
May good luck meet them everywhere,
And may each day of wedded bliss
Be always just as sweet as this.

48. May all your troubles be little ones;
May all your troubles be small;
May all your troubles be light as bubbles;
May you have no troubles at all.
—*Here's to It!* Compiled by John M. Koken (A. S. Barnes & Company, Inc.)

49. Here's to the happy couple
That's just newly wed.
May their lives be ever so long,
And the tears be few they shed.
—*Here's to It!* Compiled by John M. Koken (A. S. Barnes & Company, Inc.)

50. Here's to the bride and bridegroom,
We'll ask their success in our prayers,
And through life's dark shadows and sunshine
That good luck may ever be theirs.

51. Here's a toast to the lovely bride,
And to the husband by her side;
Here's to the home they're going to share;
May love and trust dwell with them there.

52. Let us drink to the health of the bride,
Let us drink to the health of the groom,
Let us drink to the Parson who tied them
And to every guest in this room!

53. Here's to the Bride in her gown of white,
With her flowing veil—what a lovely sight!
Here comes the bride, so fair, so true.
What's that? The Groom? Oh, he's here, too!

54. Here's to my mother-in-law's daughter,
And here's to her father-in-law's son;
And here's to the vows we've just taken,
And the life we have just begun!

55. Here's to the bride that is to be,
Happy and smiling and fair,
And here's to those who would like to be,
And are wondering when and where.

56. Here's a toast to our youthful bridegroom,
All aglow with blissful pride;
Here's a toast to his chosen partner—
To our happy trusting bride.
May love, and joy, and contentment
In their future home abide.

57. Oh, promise me that some day you and I
Will take our love together to some sky,
Where we can be alone and faith renew,
And find the hollows where those flowers grew;
Those first, sweet violets of early spring,
Which come in whispers, thrill us both, and sing
Of love unspeakable that is to be:
Oh, promise me, oh, promise me!

Oh, promise me that you will take my hand,
The most unworthy in this lonely land,
And let me sit beside you, in your eyes
Seeing the vision of our paradise;
Hearing God's message while the organ rolls,
Its mighty music to our very souls,
Of love less perfect than a life with thee;
Oh, promise me, oh, promise me!

Oh, promise me that when with bated breath,
I wait the presence of the angel, Death,

You will be near me, guide my faltering feet,
  And softly breathe these words in accents sweet.
Come sometime to me from that distant shore,
  Caress and comfort as in days of yore,
Triumphant over death our love shall be;
  Oh, promise me, oh, promise me!

—Harry B. Smith

Brotherhood. See Fellowship

Business

58. Here's to our salesmen—the fellows who keep business supplied with its most precious commodity: Customers.

59. TO A REAL ESTATE MAN

He will sell you a lot and build you a house
  And lend you the money. That's right.
But he won't lay the carpets or furnish the meals
  Or sing to the babies at night.

—Nesbit

Cheerfulness

60.

If the world seems cold to you,
  Kindle fires to warm it;
Let their comfort hide from view
  Winters that deform it.
Hearts as frozen as your own
  To that radiance gather;
You will soon forget to moan:
  "Oh, the cheerless weather."

—Lucy Larcom

61.

It's easy enough to be pleasant,
  When life flows by like a song,
    But the man worth while
    Is the one who can smile,
  When everything goes dead wrong.
For the test of the heart is trouble
  And it always comes with the years,

And the smile that is worth
The praises of earth
Is the smile that shines through tears.
—Ella Wheeler Wilcox

Children

62. Here's to babies—the fragile beginnings of a mighty end.
—*Your Health!* by Idelle Phelps (Stanley Paul & Co., London)

63. I drink a toast to Perfection—Bachelor's wives and Old Maid's children.

64.

TO TWINS

Here's to the one
And to the other—
But which one is
The other's brother?
—Nesbit

65.

Here's to the Stork,
A most valuable bird,
That inhabits the residence districts.
He doesn't sing tunes,
Nor yield any plumes,
But he helps out the vital statistics.

Christmas

66.

I wish you a merry Christmas
And a Happy New Year,
A pocketful of money,
And a cellar full of beer,
And a good fat pig
To serve all the year.

Class Reunion. See Reunion, Class

Clergymen

67. Here's to the Ministers who don't preach, and the Preachers who minister.

Companionship

68. Here's to the Have-beens, the Are-nows, and the May-bes!

69.

Here's to you and here's to me
Here's to what we used to be—
Here's to what we might have been
And here's to what we'll be again.

—*Here's to It!* Compiled by JOHN M. KOKEN (A. S. Barnes & Company, Inc.)

70.

We might be better if we would
But it's very lonely being good; and
According to Scripture, you must own,
Man was not built to be alone.

—LAMPTON

71.

If I were I, and you were you, would you?
There are times I would and times I wouldn't,
Times that I could and times I couldn't;
But the times I could and would and I felt game
Are the times I'm with you, dear.
Do you feel the same?

—*Here's to It!* Compiled by JOHN M. KOKEN (A. S. Barnes & Company, Inc.)

Complaints

72. May we never murmur without cause, and never have cause to murmur.

Conceit

73.

Here's to the man who is wisest and best,
Here's to the man who with judgment is blessed.
Here's to the man who's as smart as can be—
I mean the man who agrees with me.

Conscience

74. Here's to Conscience—may it wake up to hear us toast it, and then go to sleep again.

Courage

75. Here's to the man who from morning to night
Has the vim and the will and the courage to fight—
The courage to fight and the courage to live—
The courage to learn, and to love, and forgive.

Creditors

76. Here's to our creditors—may they be endowed with the three virtues—faith, hope, and charity.

Death

77. May we live respected and die regretted.

78. To live in hearts we leave behind,
Is not to die.

—THOMAS CAMPBELL

79. Here's to good food when you're hungry,
Good wine when you're dry,
A pretty girl to love you
And heaven when you die!

—*Here's to It!* Compiled by JOHN M. KOKEN (A. S. Barnes & Co., Inc.)

Discretion

80. Let us always remember that it is much safer to think what we say than to say what we think.

Doctors

81. Here's to the surgeon who bleeds for his fellow men.

82. Fond of doctors, little health,
Fond of lawyers, little wealth.

83. Here's to Medicine: The only profession that labors incessantly to destroy the reason for its own existence!

84. The doctors are our friends, let's please them well,
For they kill but slow they are certain.

—Beaumont and Fletcher

85. The best of all the pill-box crew,
Since ever time began,
Are the doctors who have most to do
With the health of a healthy man.
And so I count them up again,
And praise them as I can:
There's Dr. Diet,
And Dr. Quiet,
And Dr. Merryman!

—W. Duffield

Drinks—Drinking. See also Wine

86. Let us never attempt to lighten care by drowning reason.

87. Drink and be merry, for our time on earth is short, and death lasts forever.

—Amphis

88. The man that isn't jolly after drinking
Is just a driveling idiot, to my thinking.

—Euripides

89. Let us have wine and women, mirth and laugher—
Sermons and soda-water the day after.

—Lord Byron

90. What harm in drinking can there be?
When punch and life so well agree?

—Thomas Blacklock

91. Drink!—and the world drinks with you;
Swear off, and you drink alone!

92. Here's to us, and all of us, and each of us that's here,
And here's to all we each would have a-drinking with us here.

—James Blomfield

93. One drink is plenty;
Two drinks too many,
And three not half enough.

94. Here's to a guy who is never blue,
Here's to a buddy who is ever true,
Here's to a pal, no matter what the load,
Who never declines, just one for the road.

95. Yesterday this day's madness did prepare;
Tomorrow's silence, triumph or despair,
Drink! for you know not whence you came or why;
Drink! for you know not why you go nor where.
—Omar Khayyam

96. I drink to myself and one other
And may that one other be she
Who drinks to herself and one other
And may that one other be me.

97. Here's to the man who drinks when he's dry,
And drinks till his humor is mellow;
And here's to the man who perhaps isn't dry,
But drinks just to be a good fellow.

98. I drink to one, and only one,—
And may that one be he
Who loves but one, and only one,—
And may that one be me!

99. Let schoolmasters puzzle their brain
With grammar and nonsense and learning;
Good liquor, I stoutly maintain,
Gives genius a better discerning.
—Oliver Goldsmith

100. We'll drink tonight, with hearts as light,
To loves as gay and fleeting
As bubbles that swim on the breaker's brim,
And break on the lips while meeting.
—Charles Fenno Hoffman

101. Drink to the girls, and drink to their mothers,
Drink to their fathers and drink to their brothers;
Toast their dear healths as long as you're able,
And dream of their charms while you're under the table.

102. There's many a toast I'd like to say,
If I could only think it.
So fill your glass to anything,
And, thank the Lord, I'll drink it.

103. No chord of music has yet been found
To even equal that sweet sound
Which, to my mind, all else surpasses,—
The clink of ice in crystal glasses.

104. Drink today and drown all sorrow,
You shall perhaps not do't tomorrow;
Best while you have it, use your breath;
There is no drinking after death.

—Beaumont and Fletcher

105. Here's to good old Whiskey
So amber and clear,
'Tis not so sweet as woman's lips
But a damned sight more sincere.

106. There's something I would like to say
But what I cannot think,
So stand up, comrade, anyway—
And drink, confound you, drink!

—Nesbit

107. Here's to the glass, and here's to you,
And here's to the cork you pull—
May the glass do its duty the evening through
And be empty when you are full!

108. Glorious! Glorious!
One keg of beer for the four of us
Glory be to God there are no more of us
For one of us could drink it all alone!

109. Then fill the cup, fill high! fill high!
Nor spare the rosy wine,
If death be in the cup, we'll die—
Such death would be divine.

—JAMES RUSSELL LOWELL

110. Drink to me only with thine eyes,
And I will pledge with mine,
For I would have to pawn my watch
If you should drink more wine.

—*With apologies to Ben Johnson*

111. Fill the goblet again; for I never before
Felt the glow which now gladdens my heart to its core.
Let us drink; who would not? since through life's varied round
In the goblet alone no deception is found.

—LORD BYRON

112. It's easy enough to be pleasant
And to sing of joy and good cheer;
But the man worth while
Is the man who can smile
When the doctor cuts out his beer.

113. There was a young man, who said: "Sonny,
I know that you think it is funny
When you see that I keep
Up so long without sleep;
But I can't go to bed—I've got money!"

—OLIVER MARBLE

114. Here's to lying, stealing, swearing, drinking!
If you must lie, lie for a pretty woman.
If you must steal, steal away from bad company.
If you must swear, swear by your friends and they will swear by you; and
If you must drink, drink with me!

115. A Frenchman drinks his native wine,
A German drinks his beer;

An Englishman his 'alf and 'alf,
Because it brings good cheer;
The Scotchman drinks his whiskey straight,
Because it brings on dizziness;
An American has no choice at all,—
He drinks the whole damned business.

116.

Drink to me only with thine eyes,
And I will pledge with mine;
Or leave a kiss but in the cup,
And I'll not look for wine.

The thirst that from the soul doth rise
Doth ask a drink divine;
But might I of Jove's nectar sup,
I would not change for thine.

—Ben Jonson

117.

A toast to the fellow
Who when he drinks deep
Gets royally mellow
And then falls asleep.
But not to the varlet
Who, as he grows tight,
Turns noisy and scarlet
And starts in to fight.

—W. E. S. Fales

118.

Now here's to Addition—
Another pint, pray!
Then here's to Subtraction—
Take th' old one away!
Here's Multiplication—
So double the wine!
And here's to Division—
That's yours, and this mine!

—Wallace Rice

119.

Here's to Maxwelton's braes bonny,
Where early falls the dew,
But without some good Scotch whiskey
The dew would chill you through.
So take a swig or two—
No harm to make it three—

Ere for bonny Annie Laurie
You shall lay you down and dee.

—*Puck*

120. A RULE OF THREE

There is a rule to drink,
I think,
A rule of three
That you'll agree
With me
Cannot be beat
And tends our lives to sweeten:
Drink ere you eat
And while you eat
And after you have eaten!

—WALLACE RICE

Eating

121. Here's a turkey when you're hungry,
Champagne when you are dry,
A pretty girl when you are lonely,
And Heaven when you die!

122. The Lord gave teeth to men, that they might eat,
And then, to use them on, he gave us meat;
And here's a health to that great man who took
And brought the two together—to the Cook!

123. We may live without poetry, music and art,
We may live without conscience and live without heart;
We may live without friends; we may live without books;
But civilized men cannot live without cooks.
We may live without books—what is knowledge but grieving.
We may live without hope—what is hope but deceiving.
We may live without love—what is passion but pining;
But where is the man who can live without dining?

—OWEN MEREDITH

Editors. See Press, The

Employment

124. May the work that you have
Be the play that you love.

Enemies

125. May we always be happy, and our enemies know it.

126. Here's to our enemies—may the Devil cut off all their toes that we may know them by their limping.

127. Here's to those who wish us well,
And those who don't, may go to—Heaven.

—James Keene

128. To our foes—they spur us on to the achievements for which our friends praise us.

—James H. Channon

129. May your loving cup be always brimming full, with never an enemy to jog your elbow and make the cup spill over.

—Edwin O. Grover

130. Drink to our enemies! Here we get even:
They're far away, and we are in Heaven.

131. Here's hoping we may be spared from the greatest danger of them all—not our open enemies but our tainted friends.

132. Here's to those who love us;
Here's to those who don't;
A smile for those who love us.
A tear for those who won't.

133. We'll drink to the friends who wish us well,
So fill to the brim and toast them;
And if there be those who wish us ill,—
Why, now is the time to roast them!

—Grace Luce Irwin

134. Here's a sigh for those who love me,
And a smile for those who hate;
And whatever sky's above me,
Here's a heart for every fate.

—Lord Byron

Evil

135. In men whom men condemn as ill
I find so much of goodness still;
In men whom men pronounce divine
I find so much of sin and blot,
I do not dare to draw a line
Between the two, where God has not.

—Joaquin Miller

Failure

136. Here's to the man who loses
If his loss is another's gain,
For bad luck sharpens ambition
And success often striving heals pain.

137. Who misses or who wins the prize,
Go, lose or conquer as you can;
But if you fail, or if you rise,
Be each, pray God, a gentleman!

Faithfulness

138. Let's be gay while we may,
And seize love with laughter;
I'll be true as long as you,
But not a moment after.

139. You may talk of a woman's constancy,
And the love that can never die;
But here's to a woman's coquetry,
And the pleasure of saying "good-bye."

Family

140. To our Ancestors—we forgive *them;* we trust that they forgive *us.*

141. Here's to our Brothers—hard to please but Oh! so hard to replace.

142. Here's to all our Relatives—may they forget our faults and mend their own!

143. A son is a son till he gets him a wife
But a daughter's a daughter the whole of her life.

144. We've toasted the mother and daughter;
We've toasted the sweetheart and wife;
But somehow we missed her,
Our dear little sister—
The joy of another man's life.

Fathers—Fatherhood

145. Here's to Dad—the kin you love to touch!

146. Here's a toast to Dad—and a vote of thanks to Grandma for giving him to us.

147. With this toast I pay my greatest respects to the man who has so singularly honored me—by being my Father!

148. Here's to Father—may the love and respect we now bestow upon him make up in part for the worry and care we once caused him.

Fellowship

149. Here's to Hell! May we have as good a time there as we had getting there.

150. May we never condemn that in a brother which we would condone in ourselves!

151. Here's to Eternity—may we spend it in as good company as we have here tonight.

152. Here's to the four of us!
Thank God there's no more of us.

153. Happy are we met, Happy have we been,
Happy may we part, and Happy meet again.

154. Let's drink to us three,
To you, love and me,
For we are never a crowd.

—*From the French*

155. A glass is good, and a lass is good,
And a pipe to smoke in cold weather;
The world is good and the people are good,
And we're all good fellows together.

—O'Keefe

156. Here's to you as good as you are,
And here's to me as bad as I am,
And as bad as I am, and as good as you are,
I'm as good as you are, as bad as I am.

157. God give you sympathy and common sense,
And help you home with courage high;
God give you calm and confidence,
And, please—a twinkle in your eye.

—Baron Mountevans
("Evans of the Broke")

158. You may know the fellow who thinks he thinks,
Or the fellow who thinks he knows;
But find the fellow who thinks he thinks,
And you know the fellow who knows.

159. TO A GOOD FELLOW

The gods bestow their gifts on men,
With many a curious twist and whim;
They handed out an armful when
They chose the gifts they gave to him.

—Nesbit

160. We come into this world naked and bare
We go through this world with sorrow and care
We go out of this world, we know not where
But if we're good fellows here, we'll be thorough-
breds there.

161. Here's to "something-or-other" from you—
A nod or a smile, or a clasp of your hand;
Even a kindly thought will do—
So long as it's "something-or-other" from you.

—R. H. Davis

162. Here's to dear old Chicago,
The home of the ham what 'am,
Where everyone speaks to his neighbor,
And nobody gives a damn.

163. Here's to the best in this generous land;
The faults of our brothers we write in the sand:
Their virtues on tablets of love we engrave;
Their good name unsullied we try always to save.

—William Ferguson

164. If sometimes we forget a while
That life is short and man is vile,
We do so, be it understood,
Because salvation's in a smile
And godliness in Brotherhood.

—Nesbit

165. Here's to you and me
And a bottle and bird,
A heart that's free
And a kindly word;
For we assert
It is not absurd
That no one is hurt
By what he's not heard.

166. Here's to—
The wonderful love of a beautiful maid—
The love of a staunch, true man—
The love of a baby unafraid—
Have existed since life began.
But the greatest love—the love of loves—
Even greater than that of a mother—
Is the passionate, tender, and infinite love,
Of one drunken bum for another.

167. May you have enough happiness to keep you sweet; enough trials to keep you strong; enough sorrow to keep you human; enough hope to keep you happy; enough failure to keep you humble; enough success to keep you eager; enough friends to give you comfort; enough faith and courage in yourself, your business, and your country to banish depression; enough wealth to meet your needs; enough determination to make each day a better day than yesterday.

168. Knock and the world knocks with you,
Boost and you boost alone.
The bad old earth is a foe to mirth,
And has a hammer as large as your own.
Buy and the gang will answer,
Sponge and they stand and sneer;
The revelers joined to a joyous sound
And shout from refusing beer.

Be rich and the men will seek you,
Poor, and they turn and go—
You're a mighty good fellow when you are mellow,
And your pockets are lined with dough.
Be flush and your friends are many,
Go broke and you lose them all.
You're a dandy old sport at $10.00 a quart,
But not if you chance to fall.

Praise and the cheers are many,
Beef and the world goes by,
Be smooth and slick and the gang will stick
As close as a hungry fly.
There is always a crowd to help you
A copious draught to drain,
When the gang is gone you must bear alone
The harrowing stroke of pain.

Fishing—Fishermen

169. Here's to the fish that I may catch;
So large that even I,
When talking of it afterwards,
Will never need to lie.

170. Here's to our fisherman bold;
  Here's to the fish he caught;
Here's to the ones that got away,
  And here's to the ones he bought.

171. TO A FISHERMAN

A fisherman, 'twixt you and I
  Will very seldom tell a lie—
Except when it is needed to
  Describe the fish that left his view.

—NESBIT

Folly

172. Who loves not women, wine, and song,
Remains a fool his whole life long.

—JOHN HENRY VOSS

Food. See Eating

Forgiveness

173. May we ever remember that to err is human and to forgive divine.

174. His heart was as great as the world, but there was no room in it to hold the memory of wrong.

—RALPH WALDO EMERSON

Fortune. See Luck

Friends—Friendship

175. Here's to Friendship—Love without his wings.

—LORD BYRON

176. May the hinges of friendship never grow rusty.

177. May our house always be too small to hold all our friends.

—MYRTLE REED

178. May friendship propose the toast, and sincerity drink it.

179. May you live to be a hundred—and may your shadow never grow less.

180. May we have more and more friends and need them less and less.

181. May we ever be able to serve a friend and noble enough to conceal it.

182. May we have a few real friends rather than a thousand acquaintances.

183. Here's to Friendship—as rare as is true Love, true Friendship is rarer.

184. When we go up the hill of fortune may we never meet a friend coming down.

185. Here's to my Friend—the one who knows I'm no good and is able to forget it.

186. To our friends, who know the worst about us but refuse to believe it.

187. Here's to Friendship—the wine of life
Let's drink of it and to it.

188. Here's to real Friendship—may its lamp ever be supplied by the oil of truth and fidelity.

189. Here's to you, my friend—may your soul be in glory long before the devil knows you're dead.

190. Here's to all of you, my friends. I greet you. And may I never cease to greet you as "my friends."

191. To our friends! May Fortune be as generous with them as she has been with us in giving us such friends.

192. May our wants be so few as to enable us to relieve the wants of our friends.

193. The friends thou hast, and their adoption tried
Grapple them to thy soul with hooks of steel.
—William Shakespeare

194. Here's to our friends—may they always be in our hearts whether they be remembered in wine or water.

195. Here's to you, my friend, and to friendship
For the only way to have a friend is to be one.

196. Here's to our absent friends—although out of sight, we recognize them with our glasses. Let's drink!!!

197. May friendship, like wine, improve as time advances, and may we always have old wine, old friends, and young cares.

198. Here's to the tears of friendship. May they crystallize as they fall and be worn as jewels by those we love.

199. May we never have friends who, like shadows, keep close to us in the sunshine, only to desert us on a cloudy day or in the night.

200. My friend, with thee to love alone,
Methinks were better than to own
A crown, a sceptre, and a throne.

201. Here's to Friendship—
"Of what shall a man be proud, if he is not proud of his friends?"
—Robert Louis Stevenson

202. Here's a toast for you and me:
And may we never disagree;
But, if we do, then to heck with you.
So here's a toast to me!

203. May you live in bliss, from sorrow away,
Have plenty laid up for a rainy day;
And when you are ready to settle in life,
May you be a good husband, and wed a good wife.

204. Though both friends and wine you value,
As you've every right to do,
It's our wish, our dear old pal, you
Keep the love and roses, too!

205. Don't ask me to give you a toast from my head,
For straightway its warmth will depart;
But here's to our friendship—I pledge you instead,
'Tis a toast that was made in my heart.

—Flanders

206. You may prate of the virtues of memory,
Of the days and joys that are past,
But here's to a good forgettery,
And a friendship that cannot last.

207. We may repair and fix again
A shatter'd or a broken pane,
Not friendship: it is beyond
Man's wit to piece the diamond.

208. Old friends are scarce,
New friends are few;
Here's hoping I've found
One of each in you.

209. Let this on Time's eternal scroll
Of him be largely penned:
He never sought to harm a soul
And thousands called him friend.

—Nesbit

210. A little health, a little wealth,
A little house and freedom,
With some few friends for certain ends,
But little cause to need 'em.

211. The world is mine to wander in
And dreams are mine to choose.
But life would never be the same
If a friend like you I'd lose.

212. Let's not fret about the future;
Let's not grieve about the past;
But instead, let's toast the present,
And the friendship that will last.

213. Here's to the fellow who makes us laugh;
Who makes us forget our sorrow,
May he have a good, big bank account,
And friends who never borrow.

—Felix Agnus

214. You are my friends, for you have smiled with me,
My help and hope in fair and stormy weather;
I like you for the joys you have whiled with me,
I love you for the griefs we've wept together.

—Nixon Waterman

215. Now I, friend, drink to you, friend, as my friend drank to me, and I, friend, charge you, friend, as my friend charged me, that you, friend, drink to your friend as my friend drank to me; and the more we drink together the better friends we'll be.

216. Here's a health to you and yours who have done such things for us and ours; and when we and ours have it in our power to do for you and yours what you and yours have done for us and ours, then we and ours *will* do for you and yours what you and yours have done for us and ours.

217. Here's to the heart of friendship tried and true,
That smiles with us when joys our pathways strew,
And kneels with us when sorrow like a pall
Enshrouds our stricken souls, and holds through all
The midnight gloom with human truth and faith.

218. Here's a toast to the future,
A toast to the past,
And a toast to our friends, far and near.
May the future be pleasant;
The past, a bright dream;
May our friends remain faithful and dear.

219. Here's to the friends that I love best,
To those who have always stood the test;
To the friends I love who are tried and true,
Friends that are old, and those that are new.
Life at its best to most is a trial,
'Tis friendship that makes life really worth while.

—E. K. Orr

220. If you have a friend worth loving,
Love him, yes, and let him know
That you love him ere Life's evening
Tinge his brow with sunset glow.
Why should good words ne'er be said
Of a friend until he's dead?

221. A health to you,
And wealth to you,
And the best that life can give to you.
May Fortune still be kind to you,
And Happiness be true to you,
And Life be long and good to you,
Is the toast of all your friends to you!

222. More than silver, more than gold
Are the good friends, new and old;
Giving freely from their store
So that I may have the more.
Sorrow for my troubles voicing,
Yet in my success rejoicing.
New friends, old friends tried and true
Here's a toast from me to you.

223. There are no friends like the old friends
And none so good and true;
We greet them when we meet them,
As roses greet the dew;
No other friends are dearer,
Though born of kindred mold;
We love, we trust the new ones—
We treasure most the old.

—David Banks Sickles

224.

Here's to the hand of friendship,
  Sincere, twice-tried and true,
That smiles in the hour of triumph
  And laughs at its joy with you,
Yet stands in the night of sorrow
  Close by when the shadows fall,
And never turns the picture
  Of an old friend to the wall.

225.

A toast to us, my good, fat friends,
  To bless the things we eat;
For it has been full many a year,
  Since we have seen our feet.

Yet who would lose a precious pound,
  By trading sweets for sours?
It takes a mighty girth indeed,
  To hold such hearts as ours!

226.

Give me a friend with whom to spend
  Life's golden hours in gladness,
A comrade who remaineth true
  Alike in joy or sadness.
A little bread, a roof, bed,
  And each new morn a blessing,
Is all I ask from week to week:
  These wants I am confessing.

—Francis Chambers

227.

When you go away, my friend,
  When you say your last good-by,
Then the summer time will end,
  And the winter will be nigh.

Though the green grass decks the heather
  And the birds sing all the day,
There will be no summer weather
  After you have gone away.

—Ella Wheeler Wilcox

228.

Here's to my friend,
  May you live one thousand years,
To sort'er keep things lively
  In this vale of human tears.

And here's that I may live
  One thousand years too;
Did I say one thousand years?
  No, a thousand less a day,
For I should hate to live on earth
  And know you had passed away.

229. Here's to the joys of friendship,
And here's to the friend who has the bad taste
    to leave us.
May our good wishes follow him wherever he goes,
May fortune lie in wait for him,
May happiness dog his footsteps,
May success pursue and overtake him,
May he be doomed to a long life and a merry one,
And if he ever goes to a warmer place than the one
    he holds in our hearts tonight—
God help him!

—Edwin L. Shuman

230. Farewell to days and pleasant ways
  Of happy auld lang syne;
To friends so true and good times, too,
  That were so fair and fine!
The years roll on. Old times are gone;
  Supplanted by the new.
And when I see the change, ah me,
  It makes me feel quite blue!
And yet 'tis true the friends we knew;
  So dear to you and me;
Though far away; shall live for aye
  In golden memory!
'Tis sweet to know, as on we go,
  This truth, which is divine;
We'll ne'er forget the friends we've met
  In days of auld lang syne!

—*The Optimist*

231. Here's to the kindly hearts of Earth
  That makes this good old world worth while;
Here's to the lips with tender words,
  That bring the caressing smile;

And, I ask my soul this question,
  When my goodly gifts I see:
Am I a friend to as many friends
  As have been good friends to me?

When friends speak a word of praise,
  My wavering will to aid,
I ask, if ever their long, long ways,
  My words, their pathways have brighter made;
Then to my heart I speak again,
  This eager, earnest plea—
Make me a friend to as many friends
  As have been good friends to me.

Fulfillment

232. A WISH FOR YOU

When fulfillment has crowned every wish you could wish;
When full to the brim and o'erflowing the dish
Held out for your joys; when your every prayer
Has brought in reply all that you asked—and to spare;
When the world has done all the kind things that it could
  to you,
May it then have but barely begun to be good to you!

—STRICKLAND W. GILLIAN

Future, The

233. Let's drink to the Future, "lighted for us with the radiant colors of hope!"

—JOHN FISKE

234. May the best day we have seen be worse than the worst that is to come.

235. The world would be dismal and lonely
  And barren of friendship and laughter
If people forever thought only
  Of the dawn of the gray morning after.

—S. E. KISER

236. Here's to the times we might have had,
Here's to the girls we might have won.
Here's that we do the thing next time,
That last time we should have done.

237. Here's to the world, the merry old world
To its days both bright and blue;
Here's to our future, be it what it may,
And here's to my best—that's you!

238. May life be full of hope and praise,
All smiles, without a tear or sorrow;
And may our best of yesterdays
Be bettered by our worst tomorrow.

—Frank M. Morris

239. Here's to your future,
Your present and your past;
May each new day
Be happier than the last.

Girls

240. Here's to the girls—the young ones,
But not too young, for the good die young,
And who wants a dead one.

Here's to the girls—the old ones too,
But not too old, for the old dye too,
And who wants a dyed one.

Good Cheer

241. Let us pay tribute and do honor to our great musicians, our great physicians and our great philosophers. They have brightened our lives, lightened our ills, and heightened our understanding. Yet let us not forget that there is no music like to love, no physician like to laughter, and no better philosophy than the philosophy of good cheer.

—James Elliott Defebaugh

Good Fellowship. See Fellowship

Graduation

242. A toast to the Graduate—may he always remain in a class by himself.

243. Here's to the Sweet Girl Graduate—may she become even more beautiful by degrees!

Greatness

244. May our great men ever be good, and our good men ever be great.

Guest. See Host and Guest

Happiness—Joy

245. I wish you all the joy you can wish.

—William Shakespeare

246. May the sunshine of comfort dispel the clouds of despair.

247. May we never envy those that are happy, but strive to imitate them.

248. May we never abandon present happiness by looking back on past circumstances.

249. May you always be happy
In sunshine and strife,
As we have been happy as husband and wife.

250. Then fill the glass—away with gloom,
Our joys shall always last;
For hope will brighten days to come,
And memory gild the past.

—Moore

251. Happy are we met,
Happy have we been,
Happy may we part,
And happy meet again!

252. Here's to the gladness of her gladness when she's glad!
Here's to the sadness of her sadness when she's sad!
But the gladness of her gladness
And the sadness of her sadness
Are not in it with her madness when she's mad!

Health—Happiness—Prosperity

253. May our feast days be many and our fast days be few.

—Mary L. Booth

254. Here's to your health! You make Age curious, Time furious, and all of us envious!

255. Here's to Money—you can't take it with you but you can send it on ahead.

256. Here's to the health of everybody, lest somebody should feel himself slighted.

257. When you go up the hill of Prosperity
May you never meet any friend coming down.

258. Here's to health, happiness, prosperity, peace;
As the years follow, may they also increase!

259. Here's health and happiness to you. May you always possess the former and find the latter.

260. Here's your health in water, wishing it were wine;
Here's a health to your true love, not forgetting mine.

261. Here's to our Good Fortune—may we leave more when we die and spend more while we live than we inherited when we were born.

262. While there's life on the lip, while there's warmth in the wine,
One deep health I'll pledge, and that health shall be thine!

—Owen Meredith

263. I wish you health; I wish you wealth,
And a happy home with freedom;
And may you always have true friends,
But never have cause to need 'em.

264. Let's drink confusion to that old delusion
That poverty isn't a crime.
Let's drink a health to good old wealth,
For she gets there every time.

265. Here's a health and boundless wealth
To the man who knows how to use it—
Little strife and a real long life
To the man with the courage to lose it.

266. Here's long life and prosperity
To all of our posterity;
And those that don't drink with sincerity
May be damned to eternity.

Home

267. Here's to Home—the place where you are treated best and grumble most.

268. Here's to the Home—a man's kingdom, a child's paradise, and a woman's world.

269. May we never need look away from home to find that which may be gained at home!

270. Here's to our Home—the only spot on earth where the faults and failings of fallen humanity are hidden under a mantle of charity.

Hope

271. May the sunshine of hope dispel the clouds of calamity.

272. Here's to your eyes and mine
Here's to your lips and mine
Our eyes have met, our lips not yet
Here's hoping.

273. Man wants but little here below,
Nor wants that little long;
'Tis not with me exactly so
But 'tis so in my song.
My wants are many, and if told
Would muster many a score;
And were each wish a mint of gold
I still would want for more.

Host and Guest

274. To our Guests—who could have guessed they could be so lucky?

275. Here's a thanks for your welcome which was cordial,
And for your cordial, which is welcome.

276. We've had toasts to our hosts, now one to our guests, without whom it wouldn't be much of a party.

277. By the bread and salt, by the water and wine,
You are welcome, friend, at this table of mine.
—*From the French*

278. Here's a toast to the hostess, toast to the host,
May we all meet again, e'er we give up the ghost.

279. Let's drink a health to our Hostess. If wishes were invitations we would all be your guests every evening.

280. Here's a toast to the host who carved the roast:
And a toast to the hostess—with the mostest!

281. I offer a toast to this wonderful dinner which makes me wish I was a camel—happy animal; it has several stomachs.

282. To our Host—may he make the course of Life in par and have Good Luck as his Caddie and Good Health his constant partner!

283. Here's to the host and hostess;
We're honored to be here tonight.
May they both live long and prosper,
May their hearts be ever light.

284. Bread—to feed our friendship,
Salt—to keep it true,
Water—that's for welcome,
Wine—to drink to you!

—*From the French*

285. Here's a toast to all who are here,
No matter where you're from
May the best day you have seen
Be worse than your worst to come.

286. Here's to our host, may his fortune soar;
May the Gods each venture bless;
May each day bring him friends the more,
And need of them the less.

287. Come in the evening, or come in the morning,
Come when you're looked for, or come without warning;
A thousand welcomes you'll find here before you,
And the oftener you come here the more I'll adore you!

—DAVIS

288. Here's to the hostess who has worried all day,
And trembled lest everything go the wrong way;
May the graces of contentment possess her at once,
May her guests—and her servants—all do the right stunts.

—FRANCIS WILSON

289. Here's a health to thee and thine
From the hearts of me and mine;
And when thee and thine
Come to see me and mine,
May me and mine make thee and thine
As welcome as thee and thine
Have ever made me and mine.

290. You ask me to propose a toast
Before these guests assembled
You wouldn't do it if you only knew
How bad my knees have trembled.
But I'll do my best for host and guest
By wishing one and all
A life of joy and happiness
And may you rise from every fall.

Household

291. May we never allow any servants to become our masters.

Husband—Husbands

292. To the model husband—always some other woman's!

293. To my husband—may he never be tight; but tight or sober, my husband.

International

294. America and England. May they never have any division but the Atlantic between them.

295. TO AN IRISHMAN

If every man could make himself
An Irishman, each one would do it.
But since that can't be done, 'tis well
To try to be the next thing to it.

—Nesbit

Joy. See Happiness

Judgment

296. Here's to sound thinking; may our Imagination never run away with our Judgment.

Justice. See Law—Lawyers

Kindness

297. When we and ours have it in our power to do for you and yours what you and yours have done for us and ours, then we and ours will do for you and yours what you and yours have done for us and ours.

298.

A little kindness shown each day
To help make glad some heart;
A little patience at mistakes
Where anger's apt to start;
A little smile for those who plod,
'Neath loads, up life's steep hill—
If these won't win a little pass
To Heaven, nothing will.

—BIDE DUDLEY

Kisses—Kissing

299. Here's to the only true language of love: a kiss.

—ALFRED DE MUSSET

300. Here's to the lips that are curved with pain and here's to the kisses that will bring them to smiles again.

301.

Here's to the lying lips we meet
For truthful lips are bores.
And lying lips are very sweet,
When lying close to yours.

302.

Here's to our friends in Heaven,
Here's to our friends in Hell!
And damned be the man who kisses a girl
And will then go around and tell!

303.

They say there's microbes in a kiss,
This rumor is most rife,
Come, lady dear, and make of me
An invalid for life.

304.

To the men I've loved
To the men I've kissed
My heartfelt apologies
To the men I've missed!

305. Here's to the lasses we've loved, my lad;
Here's to the lips we've pressed;
For kisses and lasses, like liquor in glasses,
The last is always the best.

306. Here's to the girl who's bound to win
Her share at least of blisses,
Who knows enough not to go in
Whenever it's raining kisses.

307. Here's to the girl with eyes of brown,
If you ask for a kiss she will call you down;
Here's to the girl with eyes of blue,
If you ask for one—she'll say, yes, take two.

308. Drink to me only with thine eyes,
And I will pledge with mine;
Or, leave a kiss within the cup—
I'll wash it down with wine.

—With Apologies to Ben Johnson

309. The kiss that's stolen now is kissed
And gone forever; however,
The kiss that's kissed is seldom missed
So much as the kiss that's never.

310. Here's to the man who kisses his sweetheart
And kisses his sweetheart alone,
For many a man kisses another man's sweetheart
When he thinks he's kissing his own.

311. Here's to my true love's parting kiss—
The lingering one at the door;
It makes no difference how long it is,
I only wish there were more.

312. Yesterday's yesterday while today's here,
Today is today till tomorrow appear,
Tomorrow's tomorrow until today's past,
And kisses are kisses as long as they last.

313. Let us drink to the thought that where'er a man roves
He is sure to find something blissful and dear,
And that when he is far from the lips that he loves,
He can always make love to the lips that are near.

314. Kisses warm, kisses cold,
Kisses timid, kisses bold,
Kisses joyful, kisses sad,
Kisses good, kisses bad.
Here's to kisses, new and old
Pass the bowl ere I go mad.

—Abby Drummond

315. If I were a raindrop, and you a leaf,
I would burst from the cloud above you,
And lie on your breast in a rapture of rest,
And love you—love you—love you!

If I were a brown bee, and you were a rose,
I would fly to you love nor miss you;
I would sip and sip from your nectared lip,
And kiss you—kiss you—kiss you!

—Ella Wheeler Wilcox
Three Women

316. Though a kiss be a-miss
She who misses the kisses,
As Miss without kiss
May miss being Mrs.
And he who a-miss
Thinks both Misses and kisses
Will miss Miss and kiss
And the kisses of Mrs.

—*Puck*

Laughter

317. Some take their gold in minted mold,
And some in harps hereafter;
But give me mine in tresses fine,
And keep the change in laughter.

318.

Laugh at all things,
Great and small things,
Sick or well, at sea or shore;
While we're quaffing,
Let's have laughing,
Who the devil cares for more?

Law—Lawyers

319. The Law: It has honored us; may we honor it!

—Daniel Webster

320. Here's to Justice—may she ever be swayed by the hand of mercy.

321. Here's to the Law—may it ever be a synonym for Justice.

—Orrin N. Carter

322. May the depth of our potations never cause us to let our judgment go by default.

323.

And do as adversaries do in law,—
Strive mightily, but eat and drink as friends!

—William Shakespeare

324.

Here's to the fee simple and the simple fee
And all the fees entail,
They're nothing when compared with thee,
Thou best of fees—female.

325.

When a festive occasion our spirit unbends
We should never forget the profession's best friends.
So we'll pass round the wine
And a light bumper fill
To the jolly testator who makes his own will.

326.

Who taught me first to litigate,
My neighbor and my brother hate,
And my own rights overrate?
It was my lawyer.

Who lied to me about his case,
And said we'd have an easy race,
And did it all with solemn face?
It was my client.

327. You can always tell a barber
By the way he parts his hair;
You can always tell a dentist
When you're in the dentist's chair;
And even a musician—
You can tell him by his touch;
You can always tell a lawyer,
But you cannot tell him much.

Life

328. May you live all the days of your life.

—Jonathan Swift

329. Here's to all of us! While we live, let us live!

330. It is better to smoke here than hereafter.

331. Here's to Life's blessings: Wife, children, and friends!

332. Here's to those who live on because—they have died.

—Anna Morgan

333. May you live as long as you wish and not a minute longer.

334. The good die young; here's hoping you may live to a ripe old age.

335. May you live as long as you want and never want as long as you live.

336. Here's to long life and happiness—for your long life will indeed be my happiness.

337. Here's to Life: entered with a protest—endured on compulsion—and left with a sigh.

338. So live that when your life shall end all men may say, "I've lost a friend."

—TUDOR JENKS

339. Life is a jest, and all things show it—
I *thought* so once, but now I *know* it.

340. May you live as long as you like,
And have what you like as long as you live.

341. To the old, long life and treasure;
To the young, all health and pleasure.

—BEN JONSON

342. While we live let's live in clover
For when we're dead we're dead all over.

343. Here's to Life! The first half is ruined by our parents and the second half by our children!

344. Here's to ______
May you continue to be a good girl—but not too good, for the good die young.

345. Though life is made up of mere bubbles,
'Tis better than many aver,
For while we've a whole lot of troubles,
The most of them never occur.

—From *Boy Wanted* by
NIXON WATERMAN
(Forbes & Co.)

346. God grant you many and happy years,
Till, when the last has crowned you,
The dawn of endless days appears,
And heaven is shining 'round you!

—OLIVER WENDELL HOLMES

347. Here's that you may live a hundred happy years,
And I may live a hundred less one day,
For I don't care to live any longer,
When you good fellows have all passed away.

—RICHARD CARLE

Liquor, Alcoholic. See Wine

Long Life. See Old Age

Love

348. May we have those in our arms that we love in our hearts.

349. Here's to love that begins with a fever and ends with a yawn.

350. Here's to the love we give away for it's the only love we keep.

351. May the sparks of love burst into flames that no adversity can extinguish.

352. Here's to Love—the only fire against which there is no insurance.

353. Here's to love and unity,
Dark corners and opportunity!

354. May nothing divert us from our love, and may our love never divert us from our duty.

355. Here's to the Love that lies in Woman's eyes
And lies—and lies—and lies!

356. Here's to those who love us well,
Those who don't may go to H——.

357. Here's to the memory of a great love for it can never die out of the heart.

358. Here's to Love—but an episode in the life of man and the entire story in the life of a woman.

359. Here's to Love which makes time pass and
Here's to time which makes Love pass.

360. May those who love truly be always believed;
And those who deceive us be always deceived.

361. To the two choicest blessings that come from above;
To the love of Liberty and the liberty of Love.

362. Let those love now who never loved before,
And those who always loved—now love the more!

—Thomas Parnell

363. I have known many,
Liked a few,
Loved one—
Here's to you!

364. Let's be gay while we may,
And seize love with laughter.
I'll be true as long as you,
And not a minute after.

365. Here's to those who'd love us
If we only cared.
Here's to those we'd love
If we only dared.

366. Here's a sigh to those who love me,
And a smile to those who hate;
And, whatever sky's above me,
Here's a heart for every fate.

—Lord Byron

367. I tried to love you lightly, without success;
I tried to like you little, never to excess.
I tried to love you wisely, this I cannot do;
For all my vows are broken each time I look at you.

368. I hold it true, whate'er befall,
I feel it when I sorrow most;
'Tis better to have loved and lost,
Than never to have loved at all.

—Alfred Lord Tennyson

369.

The world is filled with flowers,
The flowers are filled with dew.
The dew is filled with love,
For you and you and you.

370.

Here's to those who love us,
And here's to those who don't,
A smile for those who are willing to,
And a tear for those who won't.

371.

Here's to Love, a thing so divine;
Description makes it but the less.
'Tis what we feel but cannot define,
'Tis what we know but cannot express.

372.

Because I love you truly,
Because you love me, too,
My very greatest happiness
Is sharing life with you.

373.

I drink to Love for:
A mighty pain to love it is,
And 'tis a pain that pain to miss;
But, of all pains, the greatest pain,
Is to love, but love in vain.

—Abraham Cowley

374.

Here's to the love in her heart
And the rainbows in her eyes,
Which cover with gorgeous hues
The blackness of my skies.

—Badé

375.

Here's to the girl I love,
And here's to the girl that loves me,
And here's to all those that love her that I love,
And to those that love her that love me.

376.

Here's to the love that I hold for thee;
May it day by day grow stronger:
May it last as long as your love for me—
And not one second longer.

377. Here's to the girl I love the best,
It ought not to be hard to guess it;
For I raise my glass and gaze at one
Who loves me but won't confess it.

378. All love may be blindness—but where are love's eyes?
All love may be folly—love seldom is wise.
All love may be madness—was love ever sane?
All love must be sorrow, for all love is pain.

379. Here 're lovers two to the maiden true,
And four to the maid caressing;
But the wayward girl, with lips that curl,
Keeps twenty lovers guessing.

380. Here's to this cocktail, wishing it were wine,
Here's to your sweetheart, not forgetting mine,
Here's to my sweetheart, for of course you don't love me,
Here's to your sweetheart, whoever he or she may be.

381. There's a bliss beyond all that the minstrel has told,
When two, that are linked in one heavenly tie,
With heart never changing and brow never cold
Love on thro' all ills, and love on till they die.

382. Here's to the tears of affection,
May they crystallize as they fall
And become pearls, so in after years
They may be worn in memory of those whom we have loved.

383. Here's to the land which gave me birth,
Here's to the flag she flies,
Here's to her sons—the best on earth,
Here's to her smiling skies,
Here's to a heart which beats for me,
True as the stars above,
Here's to the day when mine she'll be,
Here's to the girl I love.

384. Thou art not my first love;
  I had loved before we met,
And the memories of that first love
  Are dear to me yet.

But thou art my last love,
  The dearest and the best,
And my heart would shed its outer leaves
  And give to you the rest.

385. Here's to the man who can bravely say,
  "I have loved her, all my life—
Since I took her hand on our wedding day
  I have only loved my wife."

Would we not praise him long and well
  With the warmest praise that is,
The man who could boldly, firmly tell,
  And stick to—a lie like this?

386. Here's health to the future,
  A sigh for the past,
We can love and remember,
  And hope to the last;
And for all the base lies
  That the almanacs hold,
While there's love in the heart
  We can never grow old.

387. I love your lips when they're wet with wine,
  And warm with a wild desire;
I love your eyes when their light divine
  Is lost in a passionate fire;
I love your arms when their white, hot flesh
  Burns me in close embrace;
I love your hair when its strands enmesh
  My kisses against your face.

Not for me the cold, calm kiss,
  Or a virgin's bloodless love;
Not for me the saint's white bliss,
  The spotless breast of a dove;

Not for me the love that lives
  For a sinless, soulful aim,
But the love that its riches freely gives,
  And laughs though the whole world blame.

So kiss me sweet with your warm, wet mouth,
  Still fragrant with rosy wine;
Say with the fervor that's born in the South,
  Your body and soul are mine;
Clasp me close till the break of day,
  While the pale stars smile above,
And we'll laugh our long, wild lives away
  In the joy of a living love.

Loyalty

388. Here's to Loyalty—
"the noblest word in the catalog of social virtues."
—John Ruskin

389. Franklin was dining with a small party of distinguished gentlemen, when one of them said: "Here are three nationalities represented. I am French, and my friend here is English, and Mr. Franklin is an American. Let each one propose a toast."

It was agreed to, and the Englishman's turn came first. He arose, and, in the tone of a Briton bold, said, "Here's to Great Britain, the sun that gives light to all nations of the earth."

The Frenchman was rather taken aback at this; but he proposed, "Here's to France, the moon whose magic rays move the tides of the world."

Franklin then arose, with an air of quaint modesty, and said, "Here's to our beloved George Washington, the Joshua of America, who commanded the sun and moon to stand still—and they obeyed."

—*Benjamin Franklin Birthday Book* (George W. Jacobs & Co.)

Luck

390. May misfortune follow you all the days of your life and never overtake you.

391. May Dame Fortune ever smile on you
But never her daughter—Miss Fortune.

392. Here's to Miss Fortune—may we always miss her,
Here's to Dame Fortune—may we meet and kiss
her.

—J. E. McCann

393. A health to you, good friends of mine,
A plenty to you all;
May each one be at his own house
When Fortune makes her call!

Man—Men

394. Here's to the best and dearest gift to man—a gentle and lovely woman.

395. Here's to the man whose best girl is his mother, and whose sweetheart is his wife.

396. Here's to man, who, by his life alone,
Gracious and sweet, the better way has shown.

—John Greenleaf Whittier

397. Here's to man: he can afford anything he can get; here's to woman: she can afford anything she can get a man to get for her.

—George Ade

398. Here's to Man—he is like a kerosene lamp: not especially bright, often turned down, generally smokes, and frequently goes out at night.

399. Here's to Man who was built after all other things had been made and pronounced good. If not, he would have insisted on giving his orders as to the rest of the job.

400. Here's to man:
Something a beautiful woman fascinates,
A clever woman interests, and
A sympathetic woman gets!

401. Here's to the men! God bless them!
Worst of my sins, I confess them!
In loving them all; be they great or small,
So here's to the boys! God bless them!

402. Oh, here's to the good, and the bad men, too,
For without them saints would have nothing to do!
Oh, I love them both, and I love them well,
But which I love better, I never can tell!

403. Here's to the man who is wisest and best,
Here's to the man who with judgment is blessed,
Here's to the man who's as smart as can be—
I mean the man who agrees with me.

404. Here's to that most provoking man,
The man of wisdom deep,
Who never talks when he takes his rest,
But only smiles in his sleep.

405. There's a beautiful toast,
To a feminine host,
There's a swing to the "Ladies, God bless 'em!"
But the women should cry,
With their glasses on high,
A toast to the men who dress 'em!

406. Here's to the men
When I meet 'em, I like 'em,
When I like 'em, I kiss 'em,
When I kiss 'em, I love 'em,
When I love 'em, I let 'em,
When I let 'em, I lose 'em,
Gol-darn 'em!

—Vic Fredericks in *Jest Married* (Frederick Fell, Inc.)

407. Here's to man!
Before he's married, he's a dude; after marriage he's subdued.
Before marriage, he has no buttons on his shirt; after marriage, he has no shirt.
Before marriage, he swears he would not marry the best woman in the world; after marriage, he finds that he hasn't.

Marriage

408. Here's to the single, the married and the happily married!

409. May those who enter the rosy paths of matrimony never meet with thorns.

410. Here's to matrimony—the high seas for which no compass has yet been invented.

—H. HEINE

411. Here's to Love, the wine of life, and to Marriage, which is the morning after.

412. Here's Health, Happiness and Harmony to every state in the *Union*—especially the married state.

413. Here's to the gal who sits down to wait for a husband.
And here's to the wife who sits up to wait for one.

414. 'Tis better to have loved and lost
Than to marry and be bossed.

415. Here's to marriage—a ceremony in which rings are put on the finger of the lady and through the nose of the gentleman.

—HERBERT SPENCER

416. Here's to the halo that crowned her head,
When at her feet I tarried,
And here's to the hats she wears instead,
Since she and I were married.

417. You may write it on his tombstone,
You may cut it on his card,
That a young man married
Is a young man marred.

—RUDYARD KIPLING

418. What is there in the vale of life
Half so delightful as a wife,
When friendship, love and peace combine,
To stamp the marriage bond divine?

Matrimony. See Marriage

Medical Profession. See Doctors

Military. See Armed Forces

Ministers. See Clergymen

Mothers—Motherhood

419. Here's to Home—the golden setting in which the brightest jewel is "Mother."

420. Here's to Mother—may the love and appreciation of these later days overshadow the worries we caused her in our childhood.

421. Here's to the happiest days of my life
That I spent in the arms of another man's wife,—
My mother, God bless her!

422. Here's to the noblest woman that God ever made
He never made one such another
Here's to my Mother!

423. Here's to the woman whose words never tire, whose advice never fails, whose love never falters, whose unselfishness never slackens and whose power never weakens—Mother.

424. To the one who loves when future's bright,
But more when the sky's o'er-cast;
Whose heart reveals, yet more conceals,
Our Mother! First and last.

425. You can multiply all the relations of life,
Have more than one sister or brother,
In the course of events have more than one wife,
But you can never have but one Mother.

426. Here's to Mother who'll love me as long as I live,
Should I prosper or go to the deuce;
Who knows that I'm human, knows how to forgive,
And that a slipper has more than one use.

427. Now, boys, just a moment! You've all had your say,
While enjoying yourselves in so pleasant a way.
We've toasted our sweethearts, our friends and our wives,
We've toasted each other, wishing all merry lives;
'Tis one in a million, and outshines the rest,—
Don't frown when I tell you this toast beats all others,
But drink one more toast, boys, a toast to "Our Mothers!"

428. When'er you find a happy home,
With smiling faces in it,
Where loving hearts and busy hands
Are speeding every minute;
Where every one is quite content,
With one thing or another,
You'll know there lives within that home,
A wise and loving Mother.

429. Here's to my dear Mother,
For she's old and her hair is gray;
But that I love her best of all,
I'm not ashamed to say.

You may talk of your girls of beauty
And girls of countless wealth,
But your Mother loves you best of all,
And here's to my Mother's health.

430. To My Mother!—
I've gone about for years, I find,
With eyes half blind,
Squandering golden hours
In search of flowers
That do not grow, it seems,
Except in dreams;
But in my wanderings
From place to place
I've found more fair no face—
No eyes more true than thine,
Oh, mother mine!

—Edward S. Field

Mother-in-Law

431. Here's to our dear old mother-in-law,
With all her freaks and capers,
For were it not for dear old ma,
What would become of the comic papers?

432. A mother-in-law has the name and repute
Of whims and of temper and a love for dispute;
She is roundly abused and maliciously slandered,
An innocent victim, most unjustly bantered.
This is all wrong, and defying objection,
I hold she's a woman of heart and affection,
So here's to the mother of our husband and wife—
God bless her and give her good health and long life!

Music

433. Like the teakettle—though up to your neck in hot water, may you continue to sing!

434. Here's to a return of Prohibition days—it will at least reduce the number of men who think they can sing.

435. Here's to Music
Joy of joys!
One man's music's
Another man's noise.

436. Music! oh, how faint, how weak
Language fades before thy spell!
Why should Language ever speak
When thou canst breathe her soul so well?

—Tom Moore

437. TO A MUSICIAN

If music is the food of love
This may in truth be said:
He aids a lot, day after day,
In keeping love well fed.

—Nesbit

Navy. See Armed Forces

New Year

438. May all your troubles during the coming year be as short-lived as your New Year's resolutions.

439.

Here's to the bright New Year
And a fond farewell to the old;
Here's to the things that are yet to come
And the memories that we hold.

440.

A song for the old, while its knell is tolled,
And its parting moments fly!
But a song and a cheer for the glad New Year,
While we watch the old year die!

—George Cooper

441.

Ring out the old, ring in the new,
Ring, happy bells, across the snow:
The year is going, let him go;
Ring out the false, ring in the true.

—Alfred Lord Tennyson

442.

PROSIT NEUJAHR

Be the New Year sweet and short,
As the days of girl and boy are
Full of friendship, full of sport—
Prosit Neujahr!

Be it beautiful and great
As the days of grief and joy are
Full of wonder and of fate—
Prosit Neujahr!

—George Santayana

443. On the occasion of this New Year's eve, let us resolve to be thankful for each hour of living and to remember that the destinies of the world are not entirely in the hands of the great leaders—political, religious, and military—great inventors, scientists and industrialists. History is shaped not only by great events, invasions, revolutions, treaties and statutes, but by the cumulative, inevitable effect of the thought, work and behavior of each ordinary individual every ordinary day.

—Greer Garson

Old Age

444. Only the good die young—Here's hoping that you live to a ripe old age.

445. Here's that we may live to eat the hen
That scratches on our grave.

446. Here's to the man who can smile through his tears,
And laugh in the midst of a sigh,
Who can mingle his youth with advancing years
And be happy to live or die.

Old Maid. See Spinsters—Spinsterhood

Opportunity

447. Here's to it and to it again!
If you get to it and don't do it,
You may never get a chance to do it again.

Optimism

448. May the sunshine of plenty dispel the clouds of care.

449. Let us drink to Optimism, that indefinable something which in our moments of adversity and sorrow enables us to view the yesterdays and today through glasses tinted with the dawn of the morrow and its luring promise of what may be.

—Watterson R. Rothacker

450. Some men are born to sadly frown,
Some men to praise and some to scoff;
But whether he is up or down
He wears the smile that won't come off.

451. Then fill the cup, fill high! fill high!
Let Joy our goblets crown;
We'll bring Misfortune's scowling eye,
And knock Foreboding down.

—James Russell Lowell

452.

Here's to the fellow that smiles
When life rolls along like a song,
And here's to the chap who can smile
When everything goes dead wrong.

453.

Eat, drink and be merry;
Tomorrow you'll find
The world will be brighter,
The people more kind.

Eat, drink and be merry;
Then pass it along;
'Twill make others happy—
Your money and song.

454.

Laugh, and the World laughs with you;
Weep, and you weep alone;
For the sad old earth
Must borrow its mirth,
It has trouble enough of its own.

Sing, and the hills will answer;
Sigh, it is lost on the air;
The echoes bound
To a joyful sound,
But are slow to voice your care.

Rejoice, and men will seek you;
Grieve, and they turn and go;
They want full measure
Of all your pleasure,
But they do not want your woe.

Be glad, and your friends are many;
Be sad, and you lose them all;
There are none to decline
Your nectared wine,
But alone you must drink life's gall.

Feast, and your halls are crowded;
Fast, and the world goes by;
Succeed and give
And it helps you live,
But no man can help you die.

There is room in the halls of pleasure
For a large and lordly train;
But one by one
We must all file on
Through the narrow aisles of pain.

—Ella Wheeler Wilcox

Parent—Child

455. There are little eyes upon you, and they're watching night and day;
There are little ears that quickly take in every word you say;
There are little hands all eager to do everything you do.
And a little boy that's dreaming of the day he'll be like you.

You're the little fellow's idol, you're the wisest of the wise;
In his little mind about you no suspicions ever rise;
He believes in you devoutly, holds that all you say and do
He will say and do in your way when he's grown up just like you.

Oh, it sometimes makes me shudder when I hear my boy repeat
Some careless phrase I've uttered in the language of the street;
And it sets my heart to grieving when some little fault I see
And I know beyond all doubting that he picked it up from me.

There's a wide-eyed little fellow who believes you're always right,
And his ears are always open and he watches day and night.
You are setting an example every day in all you do
For the little boy who's waiting to grow up to be like you.

—*Anonymous*

Parting

456. As we meet upon the level, may we part upon the square.

457. To all, to each, a fair good-night,
And pleasant dreams and slumbers light!
—Sir Walter Scott

Patriotism

458. Here's to our native land! May we live for it and die in it.

459. May every American be a good citizen in peace and a valiant soldier in war.

460. Here's to our Flag—may it protect only those who honor it!

461. Here's to our Country! When right to be kept right; when wrong to be put right.
—Carl Schurz

462. Here's to our Country! May its prestige never suffer by the actions of its sons.

463. Here's to the land we love and
Here's to the "love" we "land."

464. Our Country! In her intercourse with foreign nations may she always be in the right; but our country, right or wrong.
—Stephen Decatur

465. To the United States of America—may it always be free from oppression; free from bigotry; free from tryranny; a land that is free for all.

466. To the United States of America:
One flag, one land, one heart, one hand,
One nation evermore!
—Oliver Wendell Holmes

467. A toast to the flag of our country,
So old and yet ever so new;
The symbol of safety and freedom—
A toast to the Red, White and Blue!

468. Our hearts where they rocked our cradle,
Our love where we spent our toil,
And our faith, and our hope and our honor,
We pledge to our native soil.

—RUDYARD KIPLING

469. Our Country:
To her we drink, for her we pray,
Our voices silent never;
For her we'll fight, come what may,
The stars and stripes forever!

—STEPHEN DECATUR

470. The wine-cup, the wine-cup bring hither—
A Toast! Glasses full to the brim!
May the wreaths they have on never wither,
Nor the star of their glory grow dim;
May our soldiers and sailors ne'er sever,
United 'neath colors so true:
The Army and Navy forever!
Three cheers for the Red, White and Blue.

—*Anonymous*

471. AMERICA:
My native land! I turn to you,
With blessing and with prayer;
Where man is brave and woman true,
And free as mountain air.
Long may our flag in triumph wave,
Against the world combined,
And friends a welcome—foes a grave,
Within our borders find.

—MORRIS

472. A Health to Old Glory! For page upon page
We may read all the story of glorious age,
We may hear in the rustling of its sweeping folds
The wonderful promise it held and still holds,
The faith that makes strong, and the hope that makes true—
The strength of the red and the white and the blue
We may hear it, and know it, and feel it, and see
All the pride of the past and the glory to be,

The red growing redder, the blue growing bluer,
The stars flashing clearer, and dearer each day,
And the red and the white and the blue all truer—
A health to Old Glory—the flag of today!

473. To the Flag of the United States of America:

Here's to the red of it
  Every red thread of it
Dipped in the blood
  Of our sons brave and true.

Here's to the white of it
  Courage and might of it
Pure as the lily
  Sprinkled with dew.

Here's to the blue of it
  What we would do for it
Little the world ever
  Dreamed or knew.

Here's to the whole of it
  Stars, bars and soul of it
Glorious flag
  The red, white, and blue.

474.

A TOAST TO THE FLAG

Here's to the red of it—
There's not a thread of it,
No, nor a shred of it
In all the spread of it
  From foot to head,
But heroes bled for it,
Faced steel and lead for it,
Precious blood shed for it,
  Bathing it red!

Here's to the white of it—
Thrilled by the sight of it
Who knows the right of it
But feels the might of it
  Through day and night?
Womanhood's care of it
Made manhood dare for it,

Purity's care for it
  Keeps it so white!

Here's to the blue of it—
Beauteous view of it,
Heavenly hue of it,
Star-spangled dew of it
  Constant and true.
Diadems gleam for it,
States stand supreme for it,
Liberty's beam for it
  Brightens the blue!

Here's to the whole of it—
Stars, stripes, and pole of it,
Body and soul of it,
Oh, and the roll of it
  Sun shining through,
Hearts in accord for it,
Swear by the sword for it,
Thanking the Lord for it,
  Red, white, and blue.

—John J. Daly

Peace

475.

Here's to the Dove of Peace!
  May she find a mate some day,
And may her tribe increase
  As fast as she can lay!

476.

Here's to the freedom in our land,
  To peace with one another;
Here's to the day when no man's hand
  Is raised against his brother.

477.

Here's to the cup in the bony clutch
  Of the unseen hand of Death,
Whose nectar no man's lips may touch,
  Except with his last faint breath;
And here's to the hope, that when at last
  I drink to my soul's release,
And the dregs from the cup my lips have past,
  It will bring eternal peace.

Pleasures

478. May we always look forward with pleasure and backward without regret.

479. Here's to the days of our Youth—may the pleasures we now enjoy never bring us pain in old age.

480. Here's to hell!
May the stay there
Be as much fun as the way there!

Poets—Poetry

481. Here's to old Omar Khayyam,
I'm stuck on that old beggar, I am!
His women and wine are something divine;
For his verses I don't give a damn!

Politics

482. Here's to the honest Politician—the man who when bought stays bought.

Praise

483. If with pleasure you are viewing
Any work a man is doing
And you like him, or you love him, say it now!
Don't withhold your approbation
Till the parson makes oration
And he lies with snowy lilies o'er his brow.
For no matter how you shout it
He won't really care about it
He won't know how many tear drops you have shed.
If you think some praise is due him
Now's the time to hand it to him
For he cannot read his tombstone when he's dead!

More than fame and more than money
Is the comment, kind and sunny
And the hearty warm approval of a friend;

Oh! it gives to life a savor
  And strengthens those who waver
And gives one heart and courage to the end.
If one earns your praise—bestow it!
If you like him—let him know it!
  Let the words of true encouragement be said!
Let's not wait 'till life is over,
  And he lies beneath the clover
For he cannot read his tombstone when he's dead!

Preacher. See Clergymen

Present, The

484. I drink to the days that are.

—MORRIS

485. Here's to today! The tomorrow you
Worried about yesterday.

486. Let us wipe out the past, trust in the future and rejoice in the glorious Now.

487. Drink to-day, and drown all sorrow;
You shall perhaps not do't to-morrow.

—FLETCHER

488. Eat, drink, be merry, seize the present hour;
Deem not the future holds a fairer flower.

489. Let's drink to this golden moment
Our hopes with our glasses raise
That today will live on tomorrow
As the best of our yesterdays.

490. Here's to the man who speaks me fair,
  Who'll stoop to give me a little "hot air."
Who does not wait till I've shuffled off care,
  And gone to the whichness of the where.

491.

Fill the bowl with rosy wine,
Around our temples roses twine,
And let us cheerfully awhile,
Like the wine and roses, smile.
To-day is ours; what do we fear?
To-day is ours; we have it here!
Let's banish business, banish sorrow,
To the gods belongs to-morrow.

—ABRAHAM COWLEY

Press, The

492. Here's to the Press, the Pulpit, and the Petticoat, the three ruling powers of the day. The first spreads the knowledge; the second spreads morals; and the third spreads considerably.

493. Drink to the Press, but do not press to drink
The gentlemen whose task is "slinging ink";
They're equally men of sober views,
And ne'er should be full—of aught but news.

Professions

494. Here's to the director of the orchestra—one of our leading citizens.

495. To the Doctors!—may they never become too friendly with the undertakers.

496. Here's to our friend the Carpenter—may we always meet with him on the *level* and part upon the *square.*

497.

Let us drink to the Publisher!
May his virtue be shown
In the Good Works of others
If not in his own.

498.

Here's to the teachers,
Continually yearning
To meet one small boy
Not allergic to learning.

499.

Here's to the Steno!
  Health to her type!
Whether blonde or brunette,
  Budding or ripe.
If she be the right type,
  Be she buxom or slight,
When she doesn't type wrong
  She is sure to typewrite.

Prosperity. See Health–Happiness–Prosperity

Psychiatrists–Psychiatry

500. Here's to Psychiatry—the profession that finds you cracked and leaves you broke!

Religion

501. May Justice and Truth on the forecastle stand,
And Religion dictate the word of command.

502. There is no better religion than to be happy. Here's to Happiness! The way to be happy is to make others happy.

Reunion, Class

503. Here's a health in homely rhyme,
  To our oldest classmate, Father Time;
May our last survivor live to be
  As bald and as wise and as tough as he.

—Oliver Wendell Holmes

Romance

504. Drink to the man who keeps his head, though he loses his heart.

505.

Here's to the chaperone!
  May she learn from Cupid
Just enough blindness
  To be sweetly stupid!

—Oliver Herford

506.

Here's to the girl that's good and sweet,
Here's to the girl that's true;
Here's to the girl that rules my heart,
In other words, here's to you.

507.

Here's to this water,
Wishing it were wine,
Here's to you, my darling,
Wishing you were mine.

508.

To every lovely lady bright,
I wish a gallant faithful knight;
To every faithful lover, too,
I wish a trusting lady true.

—SIR WALTER SCOTT

509.

Here's to the maid who is thrifty,
And knows it is folly to yearn,
And picks out a lover of fifty,
Because he has money to burn.

510.

Here's to the rose and here's to my heart;
They died on the self-same day.
Here's to the woman who owned them both,
And tossed them both away.

511.

Here's to the girls that have jilted me;
I drink their healths, because
It is better to be a "Has been"
Than to be a "Never was."

512.

Here's to the prettiest,
Here's to the wittiest;
Here's to the truest of all who are true.
Here's to the neatest one,
Here's to the sweetest one;
Here's to them all in one—here's to you!

513.

Before I drink, my love, to thee
I kiss the cup,
Then leave my soul therein,
That when thy dear mouth

Drinks to me
My soul may enter heaven
Without sin.

—*From the French*

514. In a world of ceaseless changes,
Where all things fade and pine,
Where love, like fancy ranges
Down many a tangled line,
There are just two hearts worth knowing:
Just two, whose constant glowing
No sign of change is showing,—
Your heart, sweetheart, and mine.

—John McNaught

Self

515. Hail to the conquering hero;
Hail to the strongest of men;
Raise the glass high in my honor;
I've given up smoking—again.

516. Here's to the health of those we love best—
Our noble selves—God bless us;
None better and many a darn sight worse,
Drink today and drown all sorrow;
You shall, perhaps, not do it tomorrow.

—Beaumont and Fletcher

Self-Appraisal

517. May our eyes be no keener when we look upon the faults of others than when we survey our own.

Spinsters—Spinsterhood

518. Here's to the Rose that buds and grows—
Pluck it and call it your own;
For the rose may fade, and so will the maid,
If she lives too long alone.

519. Here's to the poor old maid;
May she know in heaven the bliss
She missed here, because afraid
To be awakened with a kiss.

—J. E. McCann

Sports

520. Here's to our football team—the only group of men on earth not intolerant of interference.

Sportsmanship

521. Here's to the Winning Team—may all its future victories be as skillfully earned and as well deserved!

522. Here's to the Losing Team—sportsmen to the end—who can lose as gracefully as they can win!

Success

523. Let us toast the fools; but for them the rest of us could not succeed.

—Mark Twain

524. To success, which can strike its roots deep only through soil enriched by countless failures!

Sweetheart

525. A toast to our sweethearts, our friends and our wives;
May good fortune smile on them the rest of their lives.

526. Here's to my Sweetheart!
For she is such a smart little craft,
Such a neat little, sweet little craft—
Such a bright little,
Tight little,
Slight little,
Light little,
Trim little, slim little craft.

—Lord Byron

Temptation

527. May we trust those we love, but never tempt them by neglect.

528. Here's to Temptation!
Oh! Lord, give us strength and grace
Against her bewitching smile, to set our face.

Thanksgiving Day

529. Here's to Abundance and Plenty, and may we always remember the Source from which our benefits come.

530. Here's to the Turkey and the Eagle; two great American birds—may we have them where we love them best, the Turkeys on our table and the Eagles in our pockets.

531. For the hay and the corn and wheat that is reaped,
For the labor well done, and the barns that are heaped,
For the sun and the dew and the sweet honeycomb,
For the rose and the song, and the harvest brought home—
Thanksgiving! Thanksgiving!

For the homes that with purest affection are blest,
For the season of plenty and well-deserved rest,
For our country extending from sea unto sea,
The land that is known as the "Land of the Free"—
Thanksgiving! Thanksgiving!

—*The Book of Holidays,* by J. WALKER MCSPADDEN (Crowell)

Time

532. With wine and flowers we chase the hours
In one eternal spring!
No moon, no light to cheer the night,
Thyself that ray must bring.

—PSI SUNG-LING

533. Fill a glass with golden wine,
And the while your lips are wet,
Set their perfume upon mine and forget
Every kiss we take or give
Leaves us less of life to live.

—HENLEY

Toasting

534. When called upon thus suddenly
For sentiments or toasts
The few ideas that I possess,
Flit instantly—like ghosts.

The only thing I think of now—
That seems at all worth saying
Is—Here's to you! May you soon receive
The gifts for which you're praying!

—CHARLES FREDERIC GOSS

Tolerance

535. Here's to freedom—may the shackles of prejudice never fetter the mind.

Trades. See Professions

Wealth. See also Health—Happiness—Prosperity

536. May you have a head to earn and a heart to spend.

537. May our purses always be heavy, and our hearts always light.

538. Money to him who has spirit to use it,
And life to him who has courage to lose it!

Weather

539. Here's to the Cold Weather without and the Warm Hearts within.

Whiskey. See Wine

Widows–Widowhood

540. Here's health to the maiden and health to the dame,
And health to the gay little widow, the same;
May the maid become dame, the dame widow, and then
May the widow be made to get married again!

Wife–Wives

541. To our sweethearts and wives. May they never meet!

542. Here's a toast to those who make toasts worth while—Our Wives!

543. Thy wife is a constellation of virtues; she's the moon, and thou are the man in the moon.

—William Congreve

544. Here's to our better halves,
Who reconcile us to our poorer quarters!

545. Here's to our wives and sweethearts! May our sweethearts become our wives, and our wives ever remain our sweethearts!

546. Here's to the man who loves his wife,
And loves his wife alone.
For many a man loves another man's wife,
When he ought to be loving his own.

547. Till we are built like angels, with hammer, and chisel and pen,
We will work for ourselves and a woman, forever and ever, Amen!

—Rudyard Kipling

548. Here's to our wives, who fill our lives
With little bees and honey!
They break life's shocks, they mend our socks,—
But don't they spend the money!

549. Now, with wine as is due, let the honors be paid,
Whilst I give my hand, heart and hand;
Here's to her, the fond mother, dear partner, kind maid,
Who first taught me to love, woo and wed.

—Thomas Hood

550. Here's to Solomon and David
And their merry, merry, lives,
With their many, many, lady friends
And many, many, wives.
But when old age came creeping with
Its many, many qualms,
Solomon wrote the Proverbs
And David wrote the Psalms

551. There are no times like the old times—they shall never be forgot;
There is no place like the old place—keep green the dear old spot!

There are no friends like old friends—may heaven prolong their lives!
There are no loves like old loves,—God bless our loving wives!

—Oliver Wendell Holmes

Wine. See also Drinks–Drinking

552. In woman I'll take youth, and seek for age in wine.

553. Here's to the heart that fills as the bottle empties.

554. Here's to good old whiskey—may those who use it never abuse it.

555. Old wood to burn, old wine to drink, old friends to trust, and old authors to read.

—Francis Bacon

556. Here's to Champagne which, like Love, when it ceases to bubble becomes stale and flat.

557. He who loves not wine, woman, or song
Remains a fool his whole life long.

558. To you, and yours, and theirs, and mine,
I pledge with you, their health in wine.

—Minna Thomas Antrim

559. If wine tells truth, and so have said the wise;
It makes me laugh to think how brandy lies.

—Oliver Wendell Holmes

560. Here's to you that makes me wear old clothes;
Here's to you that turns my friends to foes,—
But seeing you're so near,—here goes!

561. Little drops of water,
That we used to think
Were only made for chasers,
Are now the whole darn drink.

562. Here's to a temperance supper,
With water in glasses tall,
And coffee and tea to end with—
And me not there at all.

563. Here's to champagne, the drink divine,
That makes us forget our troubles;
It's made of a dollar's worth of wine
And three dollars' worth of bubbles.

564. Here's to wine, wit and wisdom—wine
Enough to sharpen wit; wit enough to
Give zest to wine and wisdom enough
To know when I've had enough.

565. If with water you fill up your glasses
You'll never write anything wise,
For wine's the true horse of Parnassus
Which carries a bard to the skies!

—Tom Moore

566.

Though a sinner ye call me,
I say it the same,—
Wine is nectar delicious,
To scorn it a shame.

—BODENSTEDT

567.

God made man frail as a bubble;
God made Love, Love made Trouble.
God made the Vine; was it a sin
That Man made Wine to drown Trouble in?

568.

Man, being reasonable, must get drunk;
The best of life is but intoxication,—
Glory, the grape, love, gold—in these are sunk
The hopes of all men, and every nation.

—LORD BYRON

569.

With an honest, old friend, and a merry old song,
And a flask of old Port, let me sit the night long,
And laugh at the malice of those who repine,
That they must drink porter whilst I can drink wine.

—HENRY CAREY

570.

Who'd care to be a bee and sip
Sweet honey from a flower's lip,
When he might be a fly and steer
Head first into a can of beer?

571.

'Twas ever thus from childhood's hour,
I've seen my fond hopes disappear;
I've always had a champagne thirst,
But have to be content with beer.

572.

Your doctors may boast of their lotions,
And ladies may talk of their tea;
But I envy them none of their potions,
A glass of good whiskey for me.

573.

Here's to a World rounder than this
A Country better than this;
A City finer than this;
A Wine sweeter than this;
But, tell me, where can you find them?

574.
Wine is good,
Love is good,
And all is good if understood;
The sin is not in doing,
But in overdoing.

575.
Say, why did Time
His glass sublime
Fill up with sands unsightly,
When wine he knew
Runs brisker through
And sparkles far more brightly?
—Thomas Moore

576.
Sparkling and bright in liquid light,
Does the wine our goblets gleam in,
With hue as red as the rosy bed
Which a bee would choose to dream in.

Then fill tonight, with hearts as light,
To loves as gay and fleeting
As bubbles that swim on the beaker's brim,
And break on the lips while meeting.
—Charles Fenno Hoffman

Woman–Women

577. Here's to women and wine—both sweet poison!

578. Here's to earth's noblest thing—a woman perfected.
—James Russell Lowell

579. Here's to Woman—once our superior, now our equal.

580. Here's to Woman—she needs no eulogy; she speaks for herself.

581. Here's to Woman—who generally speaking is generally speaking.

582. Here's to Woman—indestructible, delectable and—so deductible!

583. Here's to the first woman—who, if the legend be true, was only a side issue.

584. Here's to the most fascinating woman, the widow of some other man!

—Carolus Ager

585. Here's to Woman—who came after Man, and who has been after him ever since!

586. Here's to Woman—when she is neither too young to be wise, nor too old to be careful.

587. Here's to Woman—when she's pretty, when she is witty, and when she is not too wise.

588. Here's to Woman—the conundrum of the age. We can't guess her, but we'll never give her up.

589. Here's to the Ladies—may they always be entitled to life, liberty, and the pursuit of man.

590. Here's to Woman who is as old as she looks; and here's to Man who is old when he stops looking.

591. Here's to Woman—they give themselves to God when the Devil wants nothing more to do with them.

592. Here's to Woman—ah, that we could fall into her arms without falling into her hands.

—Ambrose Bierce

593. Here's to Woman—gentle, patient, self-denying; without her, man would be a savage and the earth a desert.

594. Here's to Women who are the poetry of the world in the same sense as the stars are the poetry of heaven.

595. Here's to Woman—the only sex which attaches more importance to what's on its head than to what's in it.

596. I drink to Woman—for each of them who makes a fool out of a man, there is another who makes a man out of a fool.

597. Here's to Woman—the fairest of the Great Author. The edition is large, and no man should be without a copy.

598. Here's to Woman—without her the two extremities of life would be destitute of succor, and the middle devoid of pleasure.

599. Here's to Man—he can afford anything he can get. Here's to woman—she can afford anything she can get a man to get for her.

—George Ade

600. Who loves not woman, wine and song
Remains a fool his whole life long.

601. Here's to woman and wine, both make man's lot smart
Wine makes his head ache, and woman his heart.

602. The toast of any sensible woman whose escort must drive her home from too lively a party should be: "Drink to me only with thine eyes."

603. To the Ladies—the only endurable aristocracy, who rule without laws; judge without jury; decide without appeal; and are never in the wrong.

604. Here's to ________
A perfect woman, nobly planned,
To warm, to comfort and command.

605. Here's to Woman, for
What's a table richly spread
Without a Woman at its head?

606. Here's to Woman, whom we admire for her beauty, respect for her intelligence, adore for her virtue, and love because we can't help it.

607. When women love us, they forgive everything, even our crimes; when they do not love us, they do not credit even our virtues.

—Honoré de Balzac

608. They say that nothing in this world is more beautiful than woman, therefore it is true that nothing in this world is perfect.

—C. E. Kremer

609. Before marriage, a woman thinks a man is better than he is. After marriage, she thinks him worse than he is. So, here's to woman, whatever she thinks about man, whatever he is.

—ALBERT BIGELOW PAINE

610. Here's to Woman, a mistress of arts, who robs a bachelor of his degree, and sometimes even forces him to study philosophy by means of—curtain lectures.

611. At a banquet of firemen, recently, the chief proposed this toast: "The Ladies! Their eyes kindle the only flame which we cannot extinguish, and against which there is no insurance."

612. Here's to the woman who has a smile for every joy, a tear for every sorrow, a consolation for every grief, an excuse for every fault, a prayer for every misfortune, and encouragement for every hope!

—SAINTE-FOIX

613.

Here's to God's first thought, Man!
Here's to God's second thought, Woman!
Second thoughts are always best,
So here's to Woman!

614.

God made the world—and rested,
God made man—and rested,
Then God made woman;
Since then neither God nor man has rested.

615.

Here's to the woman whose heart and whose soul
Are the light and life of each spell we pursue;
Whether sunned at the tropics or chilled at the poles,
If woman be there, there is happiness too.

616.

The woods are full of fairies,
The sea is full of fish;
But the thing I want is a woman,—
And one that's a manly dish.

617.

If to loveliness I could build a shrine
Where all the world might bend the knee,
I'd but lend to it a charm divine
By making it a throne for thee!

—I. H. KEMPNER

618. We may do without song, we may do without wine
And bravely contrive to be human,
But, though she may blight your whole future and mine,
What good would life be without woman?
—S. E. Kiser

619. Here's to the woman of thirty-and-five:
She's as sweet as the Queen Bee throned in her hive.
She's worth all the maidens of "bashful fifteen"
That ever were thought of, heard of, or seen!

620. As unto the bow the cord is,
So unto man is woman;
Though she bends him, she obeys him,
Though she draws him, yet she follows,
Useless each without the other.

621. Here's to woman! born first to believe us,
Yea, also born first to forget;
Born first to betray and deceive us,
Yet first to repent and forget.

622. Here's to woman, the sweetheart, the wife,
The delight of our firesides by night and by day,
Who never does anything wrong in her life,
Except when permitted to have her own way.
—Fitz-Greene Halleck

623. Here's to the woman with face so fair,
Framed in a wreath of beautiful hair;
Pretty red lips as soft as a rose—
How many have kissed them God only knows.

624. Here's to woman, source of every curse,
And every comfort man endures;
You bring relief as well as grief;
What one has caused another cures.
—Cy Warman

625. Here's to her who's good as a saint,
Whose words and good deeds plainly show it,
And here's to the fair little charmer who aint
Though she never permits you to know it.

—S. E. Kiser

626. Here's to the girl that's strictly in it,
Who doesn't lose her head, for even a minute.
She plays the game well and knowing the limit,
Gets all the fun one's able to find in it.

627. Then let us drink and let us love,
While yet our hearts are gay,
Women and wine we all approve,
As blessings night and day.

628. Here's to ______
Her eyes, her lips, her cheeks, her shape, her features,
Seem to be drawn by love's own hand; by love himself in love.

—John Dryden

629. Here's to the Woman
Who, in her hours of ease,
Uncertain, coy, and hard to please,
But, seen too oft, familiar thy face,
First we pity, then endure, and then embrace.

630. Honored be woman! she beams on the sight,
Graceful and fair, like a being of light,
Scatters around her wherever she strays,
Roses of bliss on our thorn-covered ways—
Roses of paradise fresh from above,
To be gathered and twined in a garland of love.

—Thomas Hood

631. Brisk wine and lovely women are
The source of all our joys;
A good drink softens all our care
And beauty never cloys.
Then let us drink and let us love
While yet our hearts are gay;
Women and wine we all approve
As blessing night and day.

632. Here's to the Woman who is glad in her gladness;
And the Woman who is sad in her sadness;
Here's to the Woman who is mad in her madness.
But the Woman who is glad,
And the Woman who is sad,
And the Woman who is mad,
Isn't in it with the Woman
Who is bad in her badness.

633. They talk about a woman's sphere as though it had a limit;
There's not a place on earth or heaven,
There's not a task to mankind given,
There's not a blessing or a woe,
There's not a whispered yes or no,
There's not a life or birth,
That has a feather's worth of worth—
Without a woman in it.

—*Anonymous*

634. Here's to women all over the earth,
Women of beauty and women of worth,
Women with missions and women with fads,
Women with figures and women with pads;
Blondes, brunettes, and all other shades,
Wives and widows and prim old maids;
Savage and heathen, Christian and Jew,
From faraway Tokyo and Kalamazoo;
The plump, the lean, the short, the tall—
Bless their dear hearts, I love them all.

635. Here's to the Garden of Eden
Which Adam was always a-weedin',
Till Eve by mistake
Got bit by a snake
Who on the ripe pippins was feedin'.

Then a longin' it seemed to possess her,
For clothing sufficient to dress her;
And ever since then
It's been up to us men
To pay for her dresses—God bless her!

636. I fill this cup to one made up
  Of loveliness alone,
A woman of her gentler sex
  The seeming paragon;

To whom the better elements
  And kindly stars have given
A form so fair that, like the air,
  'Tis less of earth than heaven.

Her health! And would on earth there stood
  Some more of such a frame,
That life might be all poetry,
  And weariness a name.

—Pinkney

637. Here's to Woman—the source of all our joys The mother, the sister, the wife, the true, sympathetic friend! Without her the first man found the Garden of Eden but a desert; for her kings have given up their thrones, generals have left their armies, and the course of empire has turned aside. When she ceases to exist, the human race will no longer survive. She is to man "the rainbow in his storms of life, the evening beam that smiles the clouds away, and tinges the morrow with prophetic ray!"

—James A. Cooper

638. The Ladies, God bless them—that time-honored
  toast,
The one to be drunk and applauded the most,
The Ladies, God bless them, don't drink it in jest,
For I am toasting tonight the one you love best.

The mother that bore you, now withered and old,
But dearer by far than all the earth's gold.
The sister that followed your footsteps in life,
But what is still dearer, your brave-hearted wife.

The Ladies, God bless them, God bless every one,
May the eye of the Father and the love of the Son
Watch o'er and protect them—keep them holy
  and pure,
With life to sustain and health to endure.
The Ladies, God bless them!

639. Here's to the maiden of bashful fifteen;
Now to the widow of fifty;
Here's to the flaunting extravagant quean,
And here's to the housewife that's thrifty.
Let the toast pass,
Drink to the lass,
I'll warrant she'll prove
An excuse for the glass.

Here's to the charmer whose dimples we prize,
Now to the damsel with none, Sir,
Here's to the girl with a pair of blue eyes,
And now to the nymph with but one, Sir.

Here's to the maid with a bosom of snow,
Now to her that's as brown as a berry,
Here's to the wife with a face full of woe,
And now to the damsel that's merry.

For let her be clumsy, or let her be slim,
Young or ancient, I care not a feather,
So fill up a bumper, nay, fill to the brim,
And let us e'en toast 'em together.
Let the toast pass,
Drink to the lass,
I'll warrant she'll prove
An excuse for the glass.

—R. B. Sheridan

World, The

640. Here's to the whole world, for fear some fool will be sore because he's left out!

641. Here's to this little world of ours, which is not growing worse and here's to the men and women who are doing their best to make it better.

642. Here's to this merry old world,
And its days be they bright or blue.
Here's to the Fates, let them bring what they may—
But the best of them all—that's you!

643. This world is what we make it, and
They say we're a long time dead,
But here's to the man who makes the best
Of the things before him spread.

—Elbridge Hanecy

644. Here's to the world we're a-livin' in
It's mighty hard to beat,
For you get a thorn with every rose—
But ain't the roses sweet!

645. 'Tis not so bad a world,
As some would like to make it;
But whether good or whether bad,
Depends on how you take it.

646. 'Tis a very good world we live in,
To spend or to lend or to give in;
But to borrow, or beg, or to get what's one's own.
It's the very worst that ever was known.

647. This is an old world,
And it is getting older;
This is a cold world
And it is getting colder—
Save when such folk as you
Help make it younger,
And by your friendly faith
Help make it warmer;
So here's to you and to the world—
May you have all of it that is good for you.

Youth

648. Here's to Youth—only possessed fully by those who have passed beyond it.

649. To the Boys and Girls of this great country! They are the Hope of yesterday; the Joy of today and the Guarantee of a better tomorrow.

650. Oh, talk not to me of a name great in story,
The days of our youth are the days of our glory!
And the myrtle and ivy of sweet one-and-twenty
Are worth all your laurels, though ever so plenty!

—BYRON

651. Here's to that gay youth, the spender
Who esteems it a pleasure to pay,
And who'd rather have said
"There's a live one that's dead"
Than be a dead one and living today.

—WATTERSON R. ROTHACKER

Definitions

A

Ability: a poor man's worth.

Ability, Executive: See **Executive ability.**

Abstainer: a weak person who yields to the temptation of denying himself a pleasure.

Absurdity: a statement of belief manifestly inconsistent with one's own opinion.

Accident: **1.** a condition of affairs in which presence of mind is good, but absence of body is better. **2.** a head-on collision between two stationary cars parked on their own sides of the road. **3.** an event frequently descended from a long line of advice not listened to.

Accordion: an instrument invented by the man who couldn't decide how big the one was that got away.

Accordionist: one who can successfully play both ends against the middle.

Accordion music: noise that comes from playing both ends against the middle.

Accountant: a party hired by a successful person to explain to the government how he did it.

Acquaintance: **1.** a degree of friendship called slight when its object is poor or obscure, and intimate when he is rich or famous. **2.** a person we know who falls short of being a friend, either because he isn't well-to-do enough, or because he won't let us borrow from him. **3.** a person whom we know well enough to borrow from, but not well enough to lend to.

Acquaintance, Casual: See **Casual acquaintance.**

Acrimony: what a man gives his divorced wife.

Actor: **1.** a guy who, if you ain't talking about him, he ain't listening. **2.** a man who tries to be everything but himself. **3.** a man with an infinite capacity for taking praise. **4.** a person who makes $50,000 a year some weeks. **5.** one who pays more attention to the bill-board than the board-bill. **6.** a sculptor who carves in snow.

Actor's agent: a guy who sometimes bites the ham who feeds him.

Actor, TV Western: See **TV Western actor.**

Actress, Straight: See **Straight actress.**

Adder: a mathematically-minded serpent.

Adherent: a follower who has not yet obtained all that he expects to get.

Admiration: our polite recognition of another's resemblance to ourselves.

Adolescence: **1.** an independent state, highly taxing yet often insolvent; located just beyond comprehension. **2.** a period in which girls try to make little boys stop asking questions, and big boys begin. **3.** a period in which children begin to question the answers. **4.** that period when a boy refuses to believe that some day he'll be as dumb as his father. **5.** that period when children feel their parents should be told the facts of life. **6.** the period in which the young suddenly begin to feel a great responsibility about answering the telephone. **7.** the period when a girl begins to powder and a boy begins to puff. **8.** when a boy has reached the state when he knows why a strapless gown must be held up, but doesn't understand how. **9.** when boys begin to notice that girls notice boys who notice girls. **10.** when children start bringing up their parents. **11.** when a boy goes from a Mickey Mouse watch to a Marilyn Monroe calendar. **12.** the age at which children stop asking questions because they know all the answers. **13.** that time between pigtails and cocktails. **14.** that period in a child's life when his parents become more difficult. **15.** that wonderful time when you can work up an appetite by opening a refrigerator door.

Adolescent: **1.** a person old enough to stay up for the late programs on TV and young enough to enjoy them. **2.** a teen-ager who acts like a baby when you don't treat him like an adult.

Adore: to venerate expectantly.

Adult: one who has stopped growing except in the middle.

Adult education: what goes on in a household containing teen-age children.

Adultery: democracy applied to love.

Adult western: **1.** one in which the star is smarter than the horse. **2.** one in which the lady who runs the gambling joint invariably shows the goodness and location of her heart. **3.** one in which the hero is an hombre who totes Geiger counters. **4.** when the hero wears a .45 colt and the heroine a 38 sweater. **5.** one in which the plot is more than 20 years old.

Adversity: **1.** the only diet that will reduce a fat head. **2.** the state in which a man most easily becomes acquainted with himself, being especially free from admirers then. **3.** a medicine which people recommend as being good for neighbors.

Advertising: that which makes you think you've longed all your life for something you never even heard of.

Advertising agency: eighty-five percent confusion and fifteen percent commission.

Advertising man: yessir, nosir, ulcer.

Advice: **1.** something which we give by the bushel but take by the grain. **2.** that which the wise don't need and fools won't take. **3.** the one thing which it is "more blessed to give than receive." **4.** the worst vice. **5.** you never know whether it's good or not until you no longer need it. **6.** the approval sought for doing something one has decided to do. **7.** what the old give the young when they can no longer set them a bad example.

After-dinner car: V-8.

After-dinner mint: what you need when the waiter brings the check.

After-dinner speaker: **1.** a fellow who rises to the occasion—and then stands too long. **2.** a man who knows exactly what not to say, but not when to quit saying it. **3.** a person who only has a few words to say, but seldom stops when he has said them. **4.** the guy who starts the bull rolling. **5.** one who knows how to dilute a two-minute idea into a two-hour speech.

After-dinner speaking: an occupation monopolized by men only because women can't wait that long.

After-dinner speeches: though boresome they give us the low-down on a lot of people we used to consider bright.

Age: that which makes wine worth more and women less.

Age, Awkward: See **Awkward age.**

Age, High school: See **High school age.**

Age, Middle: See **Middle age.**

Age, Modern: See **Modern age.**

Agency, Advertising: See **Advertising agency.**

Agent, Actor's: See **Actor's agent.**

Agent, Literary: See **Literary agent.**

Agent, Press: See **Press agent.**

Age, Old: See **Old age.**

Aging: a process in which man loses his hair, his illusions, and what little patience he may have had.

Agriculturist: **1.** a farmer whose son has been to the state college. **2.** a farmer with a station wagon.

Aid, Federal: See **Federal aid.**

Airflow: condition of a car created by putting the wife in the back seat.

Airplanes: one of those things that's of no earthly use.

Air travel: seeing less and less of more and more.

Alarm clock: **1.** that which scares the daylights out of you. **2.** a small device used to wake up people who have no children.

Alas: early Victorian for—oh, hell.

Albums, Photographic: See **Photographic albums.**

Alcatraz: a pen with a lifetime guarantee.

Alcohol: **1.** a liquid good for preserving almost everything except secrets. **2.** something which often puts the wreck in recreation. **3.** the only known substance that will make a woman beautiful when taken internally—by her escort.

Alcoholic: **1.** a man who has worked his way from bottoms up. **2.** a drinker who drinks between drinks. **3.** one who can empty a bottle as quick as a flask. **4.** a guy you do not like who drinks as much as you do.

Alcoholism: the Bourbon spirit.

Alibi: **1.** slip cover. **2.** proof that you were at the office working, where you weren't, instead of at the club playing poker, where you were.

Alimony: **1.** a man's cash surrender value. **2.** another war debt a lot of husbands would like to see canceled. **3.** a one-man war debt. **4.** a splitting headache. **5.** bounty on the mutiny. **6.** giving comfort to the enemy. **7.** man's best proof that you have to pay for your mistakes. **8.** one more form of the guaranteed annual wage. **9.** the high cost of leaving. **10.** the high cost of loving. **11.** the method some women use for taking the drudgery out of housework. **12.** the stuff that makes separations look like reparations. **13.** when a bride continues to get wedding gifts after the divorce. **14.** severance pay. **15.** a matter of wife and debt. **16.** paying for a subscription to a magazine that isn't being published any more. **17.** matrimonial insurance for women paid by men for having poor judgment. **18.** when two people make a mistake and one continues to pay for it. **19.** a return on a bad investment. **20.** a divorce on the "bye now—pay later plan." **21.** just another form of "Go now, pay later." **22.** the billing without the cooing. **23.** a situation analagous to paying off the installments on the car after the wreck. **24.** a grass widow's pension. **25.** feeding oats to a dead horse.

Allergy: See **Virus.**

Alley, Bowling: See **Bowling alley.**

Alliance: in international politics, the union of two thieves who have their hands so deeply inserted in each other's pocket that they cannot separately plunder a third.

Allowance: what you pay your children to live with you.

Amateur boxer: apprentice mortician.

Amateur gardener: one who learns by trowel and error.

Amateur photographer: a person who takes a dim view of things.

Ambassador: an honest man sent abroad to lie for the good of his country.

Ambiguity: telling the truth when you don't mean to.

Ambition: **1.** a boy's future; a man's past. **2.** an itching sensation caused from inflammation of the wishbone. **3.** the last refuge of the failure. **4.** get-ahead ache. **5.** avarice on stilts and masked.

Ambitious wife: the power behind the drone.

Ambush: what age does to a man trying to recapture his youth.

America: **1.** a nation that conceives many odd inventions for getting somewhere but can think of nothing to do when it gets there. **2.** a place where they lock up juries and let defendants out. **3.** a land of untold wealth. **4.** the country where you buy a lifetime supply of aspirin for one dollar, and use it up in two weeks. **5.** the land where in one generation a family can rise from a plain cabin to a cabin plane. **6.** the wonderful land where it's trashy to sit on the back stoop in your undershirt but gracious living if you've got nothing on but your shorts. **7.** a land where, in the middle of winter women buy spring clothes for summer romances with fall guys. **8.** the country that developed hybrid seed and the soil bank. **9.** the land where a citizen will cross the ocean to fight for democracy and yet won't cross the street to vote in a national election.

American: **1.** a person who isn't afraid to bawl out the President, but who is always polite to a politician. **2.** a person who yells for the government to balance the budget and borrows five dollars 'till payday. **3.** one who doesn't know the words to "The Star Spangled Banner."

American, Great: See **Great American.**

American history: the replacement of the red Indian by red tape.

American idealism: being willing to make any sacrifice that won't hurt business.

Americanism: **1.** trying to make hotels more like homes; trying to make homes more like hotels. **2.** voting to set the speed limit at 45 and demanding a car which will do 90.

American, Patriotic: See **Patriotic American.**

Americans: **1.** those who think they are as good as anybody, and those who think they are better. **2.** people who wish we would go back to letting Atlas support the world.

American Way, The: going for broke on the installment way.

Amusement: the happiness of those who can't think.

Anatomy: something that everyone has but it looks better on a girl.

Ancestral pride: going forward by backing up.

Ancient diplomacy: the art of giving a hand without a handout.

Anger: **1.** barbed ire. **2.** a condition where the tongue works faster than the mind.

Angler: a man who spends rainy days sitting around on the muddy banks of rivers doing nothing because his wife won't let him do it at home.

Announcer, Radio: See **Radio announcer.**

Announcer, Train: See **Train announcer.**

Ant: a small insect that, though always at work, still finds time to go to picnics.

Anthologist: a lazy fellow who likes to spend a quiet evening at home "raiding a good book."

Antique: **1.** an object that has made a round trip to the attic. **2.** something no one would be seen with if there were more of them. **3.** something too old to be anything but too expensive. **4.** something nobody liked well enough to wear out. **5.** a piece of furniture that is fully paid for. **6.** something that makes you wonder whether your ancestors had children. **7.** a fugitive from the junkyard with a price on its head. **8.** a six months' old statistic.

Antique furniture: furnishings found in the homes of the rich as well as in homes with many children.

Antique, Rare: See **Rare antique.**

Antique store: a sophisticated junk shop.

Any business man: one who could have made more money with less trouble in an easier way.

Apology: **1.** egotism wrong side out. **2.** laying the foundation for a future offense. **3.** politeness too late. **4.** the attempt to escape puishment for a mistake.

Apparel, Swearing: See **Swearing apparel.**

Appeal: the way in which one court is asked to show its contempt for another court.

Appeaser: one who feeds a crocodile—hoping it will eat him last.

Appendicitis: a modern pain, costing about $200 more than the old-fashioned stomachache.

Appendix girl: the kind that gets taken out.

Appreciation: envy in sheep's clothing.

Appropriation: a tax disguised with a fancy name.

April: **1.** the month when the green returns to the lawn, the lilac and the Internal Revenue Service. **2.** the time of the year when the taxpayer discovers what a good loser he is.

April 15: the day when many a patriotic American feels bled-white and blue.

Archaeology: a science that proves you can't keep a good man down.

Archbishop: a Christian ecclesiastic of a rank superior to that attained by Christ.

Arch criminal: one who robs shoe stores.

Architects: people who now have to measure their patrons for the breakfast nook.

Argument: 1. where two people are trying to get the last word in first. 2. the lowest form of conversation.

Argument, Domestic: See **Domestic argument.**

Aristocrat, Hollywood: See **Hollywood aristocrat.**

Army captain: a uniform with two chips on each shoulder.

Army haircut: hair raid.

Arrogance: the privilege of little people.

Arson: fire caused by friction between the insurance policy and the mortgage.

Art: 1. the demonstration that the ordinary is extraordinary. 2. a collaboration between God and the artist, and the less the artist does the better.

Arthritis: twinges in the hinges.

Artichoke: 1. strip tease with mayonnaise. 2. the only vegetable you have more of when you finish eating it, than you had when you started.

Artist: a dreamer consenting to dream of the actual world.

Artistic temperament: seldom recognized until it's too old to spank.

Artist's model: 1. a girl unsuited for her work. 2. a girl who barely makes a living.

Art, Modern: See **Modern art.**

Art school: a place for young girls to pass the time between high school and marriage.

Ash tray: something for a cigarette butt when there is no floor.

Asleep at the switch: a phrase used to describe a man who owns an electric blanket.

Assassination: the extreme form of censorship.

Assistant: a fellow that can't get off.

Associate producer: the only guy in Hollywood who will associate with a producer.

Atheism: a disease of the mind caused by eating underdone philosophy.

Atheist: **1.** a man who doesn't care who wins the Notre Dame-S.M.U. football game. **2.** a man who has no invisible means of support. **3.** a man who looks through a telescope and tries to explain all that he can't see. **4.** one who prays when he can think of no other way out of his trouble. **5.** a disbeliever who prefers to raise his children in a Christian community.

Athlete: a dignified bunch of muscles, unable to split wood or sift ashes.

Atmosphere: what the quaint little eating place uses instead of fresh air.

Atomic war: a time when all men will be cremated equal.

Auction: a place where, if you aren't careful, you'll get something for nodding.

Auctioneer: the man who proclaims with a hammer that he has picked a pocket with his tongue.

August: **1.** the month you can't open the bus window which you couldn't close in December. **2.** the month when the collapsible wading pool purchased in June finally does.

Author: **1.** a fool who, not content with having bored those who have lived with him, insists on boring future generations. **2.** one who would rather write than be President.

Autobiography: **1.** fiction written by someone who knows the facts. **2.** an unrivaled vehicle for telling the truth about other people.

Autobus: a kiss en route.

Auto driver: a person who speeds up to get in front of you so he can slow down.

Autograph hunters: people who always have stars in their eyes.

Automation: the science of doing it with machines at the plant so that men can have more time to do it themselves at home.

Automobile: **1.** a guided missile. **2.** a vehicle which is rapidly dividing mankind into two classes, the quick and the dead. **3.** a machine with four wheels, a motor, and not quite enough seats, which enables people to get about with great rapidity and ease to places they never bothered going to before and where they'd just as soon not be now, because now that they're there, there's no place to park. **4.** a large iron and rubber contrivance for converting gasoline into speed, luxury, excitement and obituaries. It consists of a handsome upholstered carriage body mounted on fat rubber-tired wheels and contains a gizzard full of machinery suffering from various complications and ailments and can transport people from the porch to the police station, to the bankruptcy courts, or to the golden gate, in less time than any other method.

Average husband: one who isn't as good as she thought he was before she married him, nor as bad as she thinks he is afterward.

Average man: **1.** a person who doesn't want much and usually gets a little less than that. **2.** one who thinks he isn't. **3.** the fellow who gets mad when you refer to him as the average man.

Average person: one who thinks someone else is the average person.

Aviator's goggles: fly specs.

Awkward age: **1.** when girls are too old to count on their fingers and too young to count on their legs. **2.** too old for income tax exemption and too young to claim old age pension. **3.** when a child is too old to have a baby sitter and is too young to be one. **4.** when a girl is too old to count on her fingers and too young to count on her figure.

Axiom: a thing that is so visible that it is not necessary to see it.

B

Babble: a feminine noise somewhat resembling the sound of a brook but with less meaning.

Babies: **1.** angels whose wings grow shorter as their legs grow longer. **2.** little rivets in the bonds of matrimony.

Baby: **1.** alimentary canal with a loud voice at one end and no responsibility at the other. **2.** an inhabitant of Lapland. **3.** a nocturnal animal to which everyone in a sleeping car is eager to give a wide berth. **4.** a tiny feather from the wing of love dropped into the sacred lap of motherhood. **5.** morning caller, noonday crawler, midnight brawler. **6.** something that gets you down in the daytime and up at night. **7.** an angel whose wings decrease as his legs increase.

Baby, New: See **New baby.**

Baby sitter: **1.** one who accepts hush money. **2.** what too many women in slacks definitely don't have. **3.** a modern mother's idea of a labor-saving device.

Baby sitters: girls you hire to watch your television sets.

Bachelor: **1.** a chap who believes it's much better to have loved and lost than to have to get up for the 2 A.M. feeding. **2.** a fellow who hasn't anyone to share the troubles he doesn't have. **3.** a fellow who has only himself to blame. **4.** a fellow who usually wants one single thing in life—himself. **5.** a guy with just a single thought: staying that way. **6.** a guy who is footloose and fiancee-free. **7.** a man who can be miss-led only so far. **8.** a man who can get out of bed from either side. **9.** a man who can have a girl on his knees without having her on his hands. **10.** a man who can keep both a checking account and a savings account. **11.** a man who can pull on his socks from either end. **12.** a man who can take a nap on top of the bedspread. **13.** a man who does not want to play troth or consequences. **14.** a man who'd rather have a woman on his mind than on his neck. **15.** a man who hasn't yet come face to face with a feminine roadblock. **16.** a man who hasn't made the same mistake once. **17.** a man who looks, but does not leap. **18.** a man who plays the field without ever fielding the play. **19.** a man who refuses to run the risk of obtaining a master's degree. **20.** a man who tries to avoid the issue. **21.** a man who, when he accomplishes something, gets all the credit himself. **22.** a man who will get married as soon as he can find a girl who will love him as much as he does. **23.** a man who wouldn't take yes for an answer. **24.** a man who would rather cook his own goose. **25.** a man who would rather wash a pair of socks than a sink full of dishes. **26.** a man with enough confidence in his judgment of women to act upon it. **27.** an eligible mass of obstinacy entirely surrounded by suspicion. **28.** an unmarried man who has been singularly lucky in his love affairs. **29.** a selfish, callous, undeserving man who has cheated some worthy woman out of a divorce. **30.** a guy who didn't have a car when he was young. **31.** one who knows when he receives a Christmas present he won't have to pay for it later.

32. the most miss-informed man in town. **33.** the only species of big game for which the license is taken out after the safari. **34.** a man who knows enough not to go around asking questions. **35.** a man who has faults he doesn't know about. **36.** a man who takes marriage seriously. **37.** a man who has a leaning towards women . . . but does not fall! **38.** a fellow with a lot of girl friends who never Mrs. a single one. **39.** one who never quite gets over the idea that he is a thing of beauty and a boy forever. **40.** a free male. **41.** a man who leans toward women, but not far enough to altar his stance. **42.** a guy who wouldn't change his quarters for a better half. **43.** one who thinks one can live as cheap as two. **44.** a rolling stone that gathers no boss. **45.** a chap who doesn't have to worry about how much of his take-home pay reaches there. **46.** a guy who has to leave a tip after each meal. **47.** a man who is crazy to marry—but realizes it in time. **48.** a chap who isn't fit to be tied. **49.** a guy who'd rather have full ash trays than empty pockets. **50.** a man who has been lucky in his flirtations. **51.** a fellow who comes to work every morning from a different direction. **52.** a man who believes only the brave deserve the fair but is still glad he's a coward. **53.** a man who has taken advantage of the fact that marriage is not compulsory. **54.** a man who has to buy a new pair of socks if he wants to try on a new pair of shoes. **55.** a person who starts a wastebasket in the fireplace and vice versa. **56.** a souvenir of some woman who found a better one at the last minute. **57.** one who enjoys the chase but does not eat the game. **58.** a guy who made a right turn in lover's lane. **59.** a fellow who wonders, whenever he looks in the mirror, if he shouldn't have gotten married and divided the blame.

Bachelor, Confirmed: See **Confirmed bachelor.**

Bachelor girl: a girl who is still looking for a bachelor.

Bachelor party: where a prospective bridegroom has the kind of wonderful time he could have every night if he weren't getting married.

Bachelor, Professional: See **Professional bachelor.**

Bachelors: married men may have better halves but bachelors have better quarters.

Bachelor's life: just one undarned thing after another.

Backward nation: one that hasn't tried to borrow money from the U.S.A.

Bacteria: the only culture to which many children are exposed.

Bad girl: nothing but a good girl found out.

Bad husband: the only thing that beats a good wife.

Bad luck: to have thirteen people seated at the table when you're paying for the drinks.

Bad memory: not one that forgets, but one that remembers the wrong things.

Bad times: a period when people worry about the business outlook instead of being on the lookout for business.

Bagdad: what mother did when she met father.

Bagel: a hole entirely surrounded by concrete.

Balanced budget: when the days of the month and your money run out at the same time.

Balanced diet: what you eat at buffet suppers.

Bald-headed man: **1.** one who when expecting callers has only to straighten his necktie. **2.** one who came out on top and still lost.

Baldness: hair today and gone tomorrow.

Ballet teacher: one who criticizes her pupils in order to keep them on their toes.

Baloney: flattery laid on so thick it cannot be true; blarney: flattery laid on so thin we like it.

Bank: **1.** an institution that has a hard time getting all its vice-presidents to attend a directors' meeting without giving the public the impression of a run on the bank. **2.** an institution that will gladly lend you money provided you can prove you are already so well off that you really don't need it. **3.** a place where you keep the government's money until the tax man asks for it. **4.** an institution that urges you to save part of what you earn, and lends you money so that you can spend more than you earn.

Banker: a man who offers you an umbrella when the sun is shining, then wants it back when it starts to rain.

Bankruptcy: **1.** a legal proceeding in which you put your money in your pants pocket and give your coat to your creditors. **2.** a closed corporation.

Banks, Piggy: **See Piggy banks.**

Banquet: 1. a fifty-cent dinner served in sufficient number to enable a caterer to charge five dollars for it. 2. an affair where you eat a lot of food you don't want before talking about something you don't understand to a crowd of people who don't want to hear you. 3. a plate of cold chicken and anaemic green peas completely surrounded by dreary speakers and appeals for donations.

Barbecue: an incinerator with a press agent.

Barber: a brilliant conversationalist, who occasionally shaves and cuts hair.

Bargain: 1. a disease common to women, caught in the Sunday papers and developed in department stores on Mondays. 2. a transaction in which each party thinks he has cheated the other. 3. something you can't use at a price you can't resist. 4. anything you have enough money to buy (Depression definition). 5. something you have to find use for, once you've bought it.

Bargain hunter: one who is often led astray by false profits.

Bargain sale: where a woman can ruin one dress while she buys another.

Bargain shopper: a woman who will buy everything on which she thinks the shop is losing money.

Barometer: an ingenious instrument which indicates what kind of weather we are having.

Baron, Beer: See **Beer baron.**

Bartender: 1. a guy in a white suit who brings you into contact with the spirit world. 2. a psychiatrist with vertical patients.

Baseball: 1. a game in which the young man who bravely strikes out for himself receives no praise for it. 2. a game many enjoy more than football because they don't need a college education to get tickets. 3. a game played by eighteen men who don't need exercise, watched by thousands who do.

Baseball fan: a spectator sitting 500 feet from the plate who can see better than an umpire standing five feet away.

Bathing beauty: 1. a girl who has a lovely profile all the way down. 2. a girl who is worth wading for.

Bathing suit: **1.** a garment with no hooks but plenty of eyes on it. **2.** the little bit that isn't bare. **3.** something that either shows you off or shows you up. **4.** a device to help people from bathing; it lets the water in, but doesn't let the dirt out.

Bathing suit, Bikini: See **Bikini bathing suit.**

Bathing suit, Modern: two bandannas and a worried look.

Bathroom scale: something you stand on and it makes you mad.

Beach: a place where people lie upon the sand about how rich they are in town.

Beard: a thing you need to wear with gift neckties.

Beatnik: one who figures he's real gone when he's only half there.

Beauty: a pretty, effective substitute for brains.

Beauty, Bathing: See **Bathing beauty.**

Beauty contest: lass roundup.

Beauty parlor: **1.** a place where women can let their hair down while it's being put up. **2.** where the talk alone is enough to curl your hair.

Beauty, Raving: See **Raving beauty.**

Beauty shop: where men are rare and women well done.

Bedbugs: undercover agents.

Bedfellows, Political: See **Political bedfellows.**

Beer baron: a malty millionaire.

Beggar: one who lives from handout to mouth.

Belt, Safety: See **Safety belt.**

Benefactor: one who makes two smiles grow where one grew before.

Berth, Upper: See **Upper berth.**

Best orator: one who can make men see with their ears.

Best people: the ones your wife knew before she married you.

Bigamist: **1.** a man who keeps two himself. **2.** a man who makes the same mistake twice. **3.** a person who took one too many. **4.** one who marries twice in a wifetime. **5.** a man who leads two wives.

Bigamy: **1.** a fellow who loves not wisely—but two well. **2.** having one husband too many and monogamy is frequently the same thing. **3.** when one loves not wisely, but too well. **4.** two rites that make a wrong. **5.** when a man marries a beautiful girl and a good housewife.

Big gun: frequently an individual of small caliber and immense bore.

Bigot: **1.** one who is obstinately and zealously attached to an opinion that you do not entertain. **2.** a person who, under an atheist king, would be an atheist. **3.** a person who thinks he is broad-minded but who is merely thick-headed.

Big party: mixed crowd; mixed drinks; mixed up.

Big shots: only little shots who keep shooting.

Big spender: a man who's tip-heavy.

Bikini bathing suit: something that begins nowhere and ends all at once.

Bilious: the nauseated feeling you get when you open the mail the first of the month.

Bill collector: **1.** a man who doesn't believe in putting off until to-morrow what can be dunned today. **2.** a man whom few care to see but many ask to call again.

Biography: **1.** a region bounded on the north by history, on the south by fiction, on the east by obituary, and on the west by tedium. **2.** posterity's revenge.

Bi-plane: a pilot's farewell on bailing out.

Bird-watcher: a gardener whose neighbors have chickens.

Birth control: evasion of the issue.

Birthday: **1.** anniversary of one's birth—observed only by men and children. **2.** an occasion when a woman wants her past forgotten and her present remembered.

Blarney: See **Baloney.**

Blind date: when you expect to meet a vision and she turns out to be a sight.

Blonde: **1.** an established bleachhead. **2.** a cross between a brunette and a drug store.

Blonde, Suicide: See **Suicide blonde.**

Blotter: something you spend time looking for while the ink is drying.

Blunderbuss: kissing the wrong girl in the dark.

Blunt person: one who says what he thinks without thinking.

Bohemians: people who sit on the floor and drink black coffee when all the while there are chairs and cream in the room.

Bonds of matrimony: worthless unless the interest is kept up.

Book censor: a person who reads so much he gets asterisks in front of his eyes.

Book ends: the part of a book many girls read first.

Bookie: a pickpocket who lets you use your own hands.

Book jacket: fable of contents.

Books, Comic: See **Comic books.**

Bookworm: a person who would rather read than eat, or a worm that would rather eat than read.

Booth, Telephone: See **Telephone booth.**

Bore: **1.** a fellow who can change the subject to his topic of conversation faster than you can change it back to yours. **2.** a fellow who opens his mouth and puts his feats in it. **3.** a guy who is here today and here tomorrow. **4.** a guy who keeps the conversation ho-humming. **5.** a guy with a one crack mind. **6.** a man who deprives you of solitude without providing you with company. **7.** a person who has flat feats. **8.** a person who knows the same stories you do. **9.** one who insists upon talking about himself when you want to talk about yourself. **10.** one who is interesting to a point—the point of departure. **11.** one whose shortcoming is his long-staying. **12.** the kind of man who, when you ask him how he is, tells you. **13.** the one on your invitation list who never has a previous engagement. **14.** a fellow who never mentions you once in his conversation. **15.** a person who sees to it that your company leaves at a reasonable hour. **16.** a person who can be read like a book, but not shut up so easily. **17.** a guy who wraps up a two-minute idea in a two-hour vocabulary. **18.** a fellow who has nothing to say and insists upon saying it. **19.** a person who arrives dragging his tale behind him. **20.** a fellow who tells you all about a disease that you've had. **21.** somebody who's always talking when you're interrupting.

Boredom: an emptiness filled with insistence.

Borrower: 1. a man who tries to live within your means. **2.** one who exchanges hot air for cold cash.

Boss: the man who is early when you are late, and late when you are early.

Boss of the family: whoever can spend ten dollars without thinking it necessary to say anything about it.

Boss' son: the young man who is willing to start at the bottom for a few days.

Bostonian: an American, broadly speaking.

Botanist: a man who knows all about flowers; Florist, a man who knows how much people will pay for them.

Bowling alley: a quiet place of amusement where you can hear a pin drop.

Boxer, Amateur: See **Amateur boxer.**

Boy: 1. a noise with some dirt on it. **2.** a pain in the neck when he is around; a pain in the heart when he isn't. **3.** a piece of skin stretched over an appetite.

Boy, College: See **College boy.**

Boy, Lovesick: See **Lovesick boy.**

Braggart: 1. a person who starts out telling white lies and soon grows color blind. **2.** a person who enters a conversation feat first.

Brain: the apparatus with which we think we think.

Brain, Human: See **Human brain.**

Brains: 1. what a man looks for in a wife, after not using any in selecting one. **2.** what a man looks for in a woman after he's looked at everything else.

Brat: a child who displays his pest manners.

Breach of promise: 1. where a man proposes and a girl discloses. **2.** a form of legal action in which a man discovers his real value.

Breeding: the quality that enables a person to wait in well-mannered silence while the loudmouth gets the service.

Brevity: **1.** words that cover more ground than they occupy. **2.** next best thing to silence.

Bride: **1.** a former bridesmaid who was promoted from catcher to pitcher. **2.** a girl who discovered that where there's smoke there's toast.

Bridegroom: **1.** a wolf who paid too much for his whistle. **2.** a man who spends a lot of money on a new suit that no one notices. **3.** a wolf whose whistle got stuck. **4.** a guy who began by handing out a line and ended up walking it. **5.** something they use at weddings.

Bride, Smart: See **Smart bride.**

Bridge: **1.** a card game in which a good deal depends on a good deal. **2.** a game which gives women something to try to think about while they are talking. **3.** a game in which a wife is always eager to do her husband's bidding. **4.** a friendly game invented by a man with a grudge against three other people.

Bridge lamp, Perfect: See **Perfect bridge lamp.**

Bridge partner: a person who is undesirable if he has a one-trick mind.

Bridge player: one who learns to take it on the shin.

Brief case: eleven bottles.

Brilliant conversation: what you said in response to somebody else's conversation.

Brilliant epigram: a solemn platitude gone to a masquerade ball.

Broadcloth: lingerie.

Broad-mindedness: **1.** the ability to smile when you suddenly discover that your roommate and your girl are both missing from the dance floor. **2.** high-mindedness which has been flattened by experience.

Broadway: **1.** America's hardened artery. **2.** a place where people spend money they haven't earned to buy things they don't need to impress people they don't like.

Broadway pal: someone you can always depend on to depend on you.

Broker: what you are more than last year.

Buccaneer: the price of corn in a night club.

Budget: **1.** a bunch of figures that prove you shouldn't have gotten married in the first place. **2.** a mathematical confirmation of our suspicions. **3.** a method of worrying before you spend instead of afterward. **4.** an attempt to live below your yearnings. **5.** an orderly system of living beyond your means. **6.** telling your money where to go instead of wondering where it went. **7.** what you can't do to a woman's mind once it's made up. **8.** a plan that enables you to pay as you go—if you don't go anywhere. **9.** planned worrying. **10.** a system in which the outcome of the income depends on the outgo for the upkeep. **11.** a family quarrel. **12.** a system of reminding yourself that you can't afford the kind of life you've grown accustomed to.

Budget, Balanced: See **Balanced budget.**

Budgeting: **1.** the most orderly way of going into debt. **2.** the science of distributing dissatisfaction uniformly.

Buffet: **1.** French for making a pig of yourself. **2.** French for slug it out yourselves—or starve.

Buffet dinner: a situation where the hostess doesn't have enough chairs for everybody.

Bulldozing: going to sleep during a political speech.

Bum: **1.** a chap who is jugged by the company he keeps. **2.** a man who has lived down to his own ideals.

Bureaucracy: a seat of government that gets too big for its britches.

Bureaucrat: a person who proceeds in a straight line from an unknown assumption to a foregone conclusion.

Bureau, Government: See **Government bureau.**

Burlesque: where the shock is in the corn.

Burlesque censor: a guy who always has a grind to ax.

Burlesque theatre: a place where they have many acts to grind.

Bus: **1.** a vehicle that has empty seats when going in the opposite direction. **2.** where a man will stand for anything but a woman.

Business: the only thing which can be dead and still have a chance to revive.

Business executive, Successful: See **Successful business executive.**

Business genius: a man who does not have ulcers but whose competitors do.

Business, Hush hush: See **Hush hush business.**

Business man: 1. one who talks golf all morning at the office and business all afternoon on the links. **2.** a man who spends time making money and then spends money killing time. **3.** one who is judged by the company he keeps solvent. **4.** one who, when given enough rope, will be tied up at the office. **5.** one whose friends don't believe he makes as much as he says he does, and the government doesn't believe he makes as little.

Business recession: the time when people get their clothes out of mothballs instead of department stores.

Business sense: when you take a chance and it turns out all right.

Business, Small: See **Small business.**

Bustle: a deceitful seatful.

Busy body: 1. one born with an interferiority complex. **2.** that which is usually occupied with an idle mind. **3.** a sunburned nudist with the hives falling into an ant hill.

Butcher: a man who takes a short cut to wealth.

Bystander, Innocent: See **Innocent bystander.**

C

Cabinet, Filing: See **Filing cabinet.**

Cabinet, Medicine: See **Medicine cabinet.**

Caddie: 1. a boy who stands behind a golfer and who didn't see where it went either. **2.** a golfing expert who loses balls for you in one round, so that he can find them for himself in the next. **3.** a small boy, employed at a liberal stipend to lose balls for others and find them for himself. **4.** one of those little things that count.

Calamity: a more than commonly plain and unmistakable reminder that the affairs of this life are not of our own ordering. Calamities are of two kinds: misfortune to ourselves and good fortune to others.

Calculated risk: when you give every hope and assurance that a plan will be successful, but if it doesn't work, then of course you knew all the time that it wouldn't, and said so.

Calendar: something that goes in one year and out the other.

California: 1. a state that's washed by the Pacific on one side and cleaned by Las Vegas on the other. 2. a state where any man who can afford a Ford buys a Cadillac.

California patriot: a man who derives a certain amount of satisfaction from getting almost killed by a Florida hurricane.

Camel: an animal that looks as though it had been put together by a committee.

Camp: where parents spend $1000 for eight weeks to teach their son to make a 25-cent ash tray.

Campaign, Political: See **Political campaign.**

Camps, Summer: See **Summer camps.**

Canapés: a sandwich cut into 24 pieces.

Candidate: one who talks about public opinion until he's defeated, then about herd ignorance.

Candle maker: one who works only on wick ends.

Cannibal: a guy who goes into a restaurant and orders a waiter.

Cannibal chief: one who gets fed up with people.

Cannibal waiter: one who serves his fellow men.

Canon law: rules exercised by force of arms.

Capital: the money the other fellow has; labor: getting it away from him.

Capitalism: the system by which one lives on the wealth of brains—his father's or his own.

Capitalist: one who thinks he must choose between being held up by native labor or being blown up by imported labor.

Capital punishment: 1. most Washington cocktail parties. 2. the income tax. 3. what a woman gets for marrying a congressman. 4. spending the summer in Washington, D. C. 5. when the government taxes you to get capital, in order to go into business in competition with you, and then taxes the profits on your business in order to pay its losses. 6. the beating your paycheck takes.

Captain, Army: See **Army captain.**

Cardiac: a poker or bridge fiend.

Career girl: **1.** one who gets a man's pay by working for it. **2.** one who is more interested in plots and plans than in pots and pans. **3.** one who can watch a group of children playing in the mud without thinking of a washing machine. **4.** one who'd rather bring home the bacon than fry it.

Career woman: one who goes out and earns a man's salary instead of sitting at home and taking it away from him.

Careful driver: **1.** one who has just seen the man ahead get a traffic summons. **2.** one who looks in both directions when he runs a red light. **3.** a motorist on the way to court to pay a speeding ticket.

Careless driver: a man who gambles on a hearse.

Caricature: the tribute that mediocrity pays to genius.

Carpenter, Good: See **Good carpenter.**

Carpet: a floor-covering that is bought by the yard and worn by the foot.

Car sickness: that feeling you get every month when the payment falls due.

Car, Used: See **Used car.**

Cash: the poor man's credit card.

Casserole: a method used by ingenious cooks to get rid of leftover leftovers.

Castrophobia: a person in Cuba during the revolution who felt things closing in on him.

Casual acquaintance: someone you know well enough to talk about but not to.

Catwalk: the path from the door of one gossip to another.

Cauliflower: a cabbage with a college education.

Cavity: empty space ready to be stuffed with dentist's bills.

Celebrity: **1.** a man who works all his life to become famous enough to be recognized—then goes around in dark glasses so no one will know who he is. **2.** a person who is very much in the public's eye and often gets in the public's hair. 3. a person whose name is in everything but the telephone book. **4.** one who is known to many persons he is glad he doesn't know.

Celebrity, TV: See **TV celebrity.**

Cement: the stuff that won't set until a dog or small boy runs through the middle of it.

Cemetery: a place where a lot of careless drivers stop.

Censor: 1. a man who knows more than he thinks you ought to know. **2.** one who sticks his nose into other people's business. **3.** a man who has never gotten over the initial embarrassment of having been born in bed with a lady.

Censor, Book: See **Book censor.**

Censor, Burlesque: See **Burlesque censor.**

Censure: the tax a man pays to the public for being eminent.

Census taker: a man who goes from house to house increasing the population.

Centaur: a man with a horse where his pants ought to be.

Central America: where presidents expire before their terms do.

Ceremony: the invention of wise men to keep fools at a distance.

Chafing dish: 1. a girl who rubs one the wrong way. **2.** the girl who got one instead of the diamond ring she asked for.

Chain smoker: one who can shave without getting lather on his cigarette.

Chairmaning: the art of being one up on the lecturer.

Chamber of Commerce executive: a man who will never admit he has seen better days.

Champagne: a beverage that makes you see double and feel single.

Chance: a pseudonym that God uses when He doesn't want to seem responsible.

Chance remark: anything a man chances to say when two women are talking.

Change: something which is often identified with progress, like a woman moving furniture around or an office manager shifting offices.

Chaos: three women discussing the two sides of an issue.

Chaperone: 1. one who is too old to get into the game, but still tries to intercept the passes. 2. one too old to play the game, but young enough to keep score.

Character: 1. that which one is called if one doesn't have any. 2. what a man is in the dark. 3. what you have left when you've lost everything you can lose. 4. the courage to say no when it would be easier to say yes, and the will to say yes when it would be selfish to say no. 5. to have the same ailment the other person is describing—and not mention it.

Charge acount: what a woman uses to keep her husband from becoming too independent.

Charitable trust: one that puts all its begs into one askit.

Charity: 1. the sterilized milk of human kindness. 2. a thing that begins at home—and usually stays there.

Charm: 1. that indefinable something possessed by girls with stunning figures. 2. the ability to make someone else think that both of you are pretty wonderful. 3. what one is told he has until he begins to rely on it.

Charm school: a place where you pay someone to tell you what is wrong with you, which your "friends" would do free of charge.

Chauffeur: a man who is smart enough to operate an automobile, but clever enough not to own one.

Cheap skate: one who doesn't cut much ice.

Check book: 1. a book with an unhappy ending. 2. the one book that can tell you where to spend your vacation.

Checking account, Joint: See **Joint checking account.**

Checkmate: the gal you marry for her money.

Checkmated man: a husband who lets his wife write the checks.

Check stubs: a convenient record of how you managed to overdraw your account.

Cheesecake: a magazine with a beautiful girl on the cover—and no cover on the girl.

Chef: a man with a big enough vocabulary to give the soup a different name every day.

Chemical warfare: the eternal conflict between blondes and brunettes.

Cherchez la femme: a French phrase meaning "A chicken in every plot."

Chestnut: a guy who's nuts about chests.

Chief, Cannibal: See **Cannibal chief.**

Child: 1. a thing that stands halfway between an adult and a television set. **2.** a growing object that is both fresh and spoiled at the same time.

Childhood: 1. a happy period when nightmares occur only during sleep. **2.** that wonderful time when all you need do to lose weight is bathe. **3.** the grime of life.

Childish games: those at which your wife beats you.

Child, Modern: See **Modern child.**

Child, Overprivileged: See **Overprivileged child.**

Child psychologist: one who knows how to get the best of his father and mother.

Child psychology: 1. the art of applying a soft pedal instead of a hard paddle. **2.** what parents use in letting their boys and girls have their own way.

Children: 1. small people who are not permitted to act as their parents did at their age. **2.** unreasonable facsimiles. **3.** interest on the bonds of matrimony.

Children, Delinquent: See **Delinquent children.**

Chiropodist: 1. a man who makes money hand over foot. **2.** a man who is always eager to start off on the wrong foot. **3.** a fellow who raises himself by your bootstraps.

Chiropractor: a slipped-disc jockey.

Chiseler: a guy who follows you into a revolving door and comes out first.

Chivalry: 1. a man's inclination to defend a woman against every man but himself. **2.** the attitude of a man toward somebody else's wife. **3.** the attitude of a man toward a strange woman.

Chopped steak: the credit card's hamburger.

Chorus girl: 1. one who never worries about getting ahead because she doesn't need one. **2.** one who reaches success by attireless effort.

Chow line: the men behind the men . . . behind the men . . . behind the men.

Christmas: 1. a time for exchanging a lot of things you can't afford for a lot of things you don't want. 2. a widely observed holiday on which neither the past nor the future is of so much interest as the present. 3. the season when we get the children something for their father to play with. 4. when the radios keep you awake till three in the morning playing "Silent Night." 5. a give and take proposition.

Christmas gifts: those that are sure to add to the family ties.

Chronic grumbler: one who, when opportunity knocks, complains about the noise.

Church: 1. an institution supported by the husbands of the members. 2. a place in which gentlemen who have never been to Heaven brag about it to persons who will never get there. 3. the place where we encounter nodding acquaintances.

Church collection: a function in which many people take only a passing interest.

Churches: soulariums.

Cigarette lighter: where the spirit is willing but the flash is weak.

Cinder: one of the first things to catch your eye in traveling.

Cinemascope: a wider scope of sin.

Cinerama: a new movie process that will make Katherine Hepburn look like Jane Russell.

Circus: a group that carries on where Congress leaves off.

Citizen: one who demands better roads, bigger schools, a new postoffice and lower taxes.

Citizen, Good: See **Good citizen.**

City, Honest: See **Honest city.**

City life: millions of people being lonesome together.

City paving: something always on the up and up.

Civic pride: when you toss an empty cigarette pack on your neighbor's lawn instead of in the street.

Civilization: **1.** a process whereby one generation finds the questions to the previous generation's answers. **2.** a scheme devised by women to get men to work for them. **3.** a system under which a man pays a quarter to park his car so he won't be fined a dollar while eating a fifteen cent meal. **4.** just a slow process of getting rid of our prejudices. **5.** the advancement from shoeless toes to toeless shoes. **6.** a state of society in which the only people who speak about the future with any confidence are the fortunetellers. **7.** a condition in which one generation pays the debts of the last generation by issuing bonds for the next generation to pay. **8.** a slow process of adopting the ideas of minorities. **9.** a process of creating more needs than means to supply. **10.** that state of affairs in which money is collected from women who make up their faces and tint their nails, in order to send missionaries abroad to teach savages not to do the same. **11.** a state of human development that moves a man to pay the laundry for destroying his shirts and collars. **12.** a state of society in which a person who is over ninety has a hope of missing the next war.

Civilized nation: one selling reducing aids while the rest of the world is starving.

Civil service: a commodity formerly obtainable in restaurants.

Civil War golfer: out in 61 and back in 65.

Clarification: to fill in the background with so many details that the fore ground goes underground.

Class hatred: the reason school kids play hookey.

Classic: **1.** a book everyone wants to have read, but no one wants to read. **2.** a book which people praise but don't read.

Classical music: when a piece threatens every minute to be a tune and always disappoints you.

Classmate, Old college: See **Old college classmate.**

Class reunion: a gathering where you come to the conclusion that most of the people your own age are a lot older than you are.

Claustrophobia: an Alaskan in Texas.

Clergyman: **1.** a man who undertakes the management of our spiritual affairs as a method of bettering his temporal ones. **2.** a ticket speculator outside the gates of Heaven.

Clever investment: the one you failed to make.

Clever man: one who can so convincingly agree with his wife that she immediately changes her mind.

Clever person: one who puts his problems away for a brainy day.

Clichés: fixtures of speech.

Climate: weather approved by the Chamber of Commerce.

Clock, Alarm: See **Alarm clock.**

Clothes, Women's: See **Women's clothes.**

Clouds: the traveling mountains of the sky.

Cloverleaf: crossroads puzzle.

Club, Exclusive: See **Exclusive club.**

Club, Night: See **Night club.**

Club, Woman's: See **Woman's club.**

Clue: something the detective finds when he can't find the criminal.

Coach: a fellow who will gladly lay down your life for the school.

Cocktail: an ice cube with an alcohol rub.

Cocktail glasses: hic cups.

Cocktail lounge: a half-lit roomfull of half-lit people.

Cocktail party: **1.** a gathering where you spear olives and stab friends. **2.** a place where they serve whiskey on the knocks. **3.** a place where you meet a lot of old friends you never saw before. **4.** where a handful gather a snootful and earful. **5.** where they cut sandwiches and friends into little pieces. **6.** where two and two make a bore. **7.** an affair which pits the finish of the furniture against that of the guests. **8.** a cheap and convenient means of mixing drinks and bores. **9.** sort of a subway rush hour with martinis.

Cocktail, Reno: See **Reno cocktail.**

Coed: **1.** a girl who also goes to college. **2.** a girl who didn't get her man in high school. **3.** a moron with less on.

Coeducational college: a match factory.

Coffee break: **1.** about the only break some workers feel they get. **2.** anytime you can get a cup of coffee for a nickel. **3.** the only fifteen minutes in the morning when the help stops doing nothing.

Coiffure: a French word meaning "you'll keep coming to us because you'll never be able to do it this way yourself."

Cold cash: something no one can keep long enough to warm up.

Cold shoulder: the unkindest cut of all.

Cold war: nations flexing their missiles.

Colleague: someone who is called in at the last moment to share the blame.

Collection: a church function in which many take but a passing interest.

Collection, Church: See **Church collection.**

Collector: a man whom few care to see but many ask to call again.

Collector, Bill: See **Bill collector.**

Collector, Tax: See **Tax collector.**

College: **1.** a fountain of knowledge where students gather to drink. **2.** just a place to keep warm between high school and early marriage. **3.** an institution which some attend to pass examinations, others to pass time, and still others to pass footballs.

College boy: **1.** a young man who likes to be treated with kindness by his parents, but not with unremitting kindness. **2.** one who gets up at five every day all summer to carry milk but can't make an eight o'clock class all winter.

College bred: **1.** a four-year loaf requiring a fearful amount of dough and seldom self-raising. **2.** something that's made from the flower of youth and the dough of old age.

College classmate, Old: See **Old college classmate.**

College, Coeducational: See **Coeducational college.**

College dean: a man who doesn't know enough to be a professor but who is too smart to be a president.

College education: **1.** a four-year plan for confusing a young mind methodically. **2.** something that enables you to work for someone who hasn't any education at all.

College, Electoral: See **Electoral College.**

College graduate: a person who had a chance to get an education.

College professor: a guy who's paid to study the sleeping habits of students.

Colleges: institutions which sometimes lower entrance requirements with an end in view—not to mention promising tackles and backs.

College years: the only vacation a boy gets between his mother and his wife.

Color, Compatible: See **Compatible color.**

Columnist, Gossip: See **Gossip columnist.**

Columnist, Successful gossip: See **Successful gossip columnist.**

Comeback, Smart: See **Smart comeback.**

Comedian: **1.** a fellow who finds other comedians too humorous to mention. **2.** a man who knows a good gag when he steals one.

Comedian, Successful: See **Successful comedian.**

Comedy, Musical: See **Musical comedy.**

Comic books: illiterature.

Comic relief: when the life of the party goes home.

Comic strip: an eight-column diagram of an old joke.

Commercial: the din you love to shush.

Commercial, Radio: See **Radio commercial.**

Committee: **1.** a body that keeps minutes and wastes hours. **2.** a group of the unfit, appointed by the unwilling to do the unnecessary. **3.** a group which succeeds in getting something done only when it consists of three members, one of whom happens to be sick and the other absent. **4.** a noun of multitude, signifying many, but not signifying much. **5.** a group of people who singly can do nothing and who together decide that nothing can be done. **6.** something which takes a week to do what one good man can do in an hour.

Committee meeting: where someone talks while no one listens.

Committee-of-five: consists of a man who does all the work, three others to pat him on the back, and one to bring in a minority report.

Common gossip: a symptom of an empty mind and a carrion loving heart.

Common sense: seeing things as they are, and doing things as they should be done.

Communist: 1. a fellow who has given up all hope of ever becoming a capitalist. **2.** a fellow who will gladly divide his hunger and thirst with you if you'll divide your beer and salami with him. **3.** a guy who borrows your pot to cook your goose. **4.** a guy who says everything is perfect in Russia but stays here because he likes to rough it. **5.** one who has yearnings for equal division of unequal earnings. **6.** a Socialist in a violent hurry.

Community chest: an organization that puts all its begs in one ask it.

Commuter: a traveling man who pays short visits to his home and office.

Company, Finance: See **Finance company.**

Company, Holding: See **Holding company.**

Company, Mixed: See **Mixed company.**

Compatible color: when the red smear on a man's handkerchief matches the color of his wife's lipstick.

Compliment: 1. something which you say to another which he and you know is not true. **2.** the applause that refreshes.

Composer, Modern: See **Modern composer.**

Compromise: 1. a deal in which two people get what neither of them wanted. **2.** the art of dividing a cake in such a way that everyone believes that he has got the biggest piece. **3.** such an adjustment of conflicting interests as gives each adversary the satisfaction of thinking he has got what he ought not to have, and is deprived of nothing except what was justly his due.

Conceit: 1. a disease that makes everyone sick but the one who has it. **2.** a form of I-strain. **3.** God's gift to little men. **4.** what makes a woman think that her face is her fortune when it's only her beautician's. **5.** nature's compensation for inferiority. **6.** what makes a little squirt think that he is a fountain of knowledge.

Conceited girl: one who never gets married because she can't find a man who loves her as much as she does.

Concentration, True: See **True concentration.**

Conclusion: the only thing a lazy mind will jump at.

Concrete opinions: those that are thoroughly mixed and permanently set.

Condescension: the counterfeit coin that often passes for tolerance.

Cones: ice cream you can walk with.

Coney Island: where the surf is one-third water and two-thirds people.

Conference: **1.** a big business term for swapping stories in somebody's private office. **2.** a group of men who individually can do nothing, but as a group can meet and decide that nothing can be done. **3.** a meeting at which people talk about what they should already be doing. **4.** a place where conversation is substituted for the dreariness of labor and the loneliness of thought. **5.** an organized way of postponing a decision. **6.** coffee-break with real napkins. **7.** the confusion of the loudest talking character multiplied by the number present. **8.** a meeting of the bored.

Conference, Press: See **Press conference.**

Confidence: **1.** the cocky feeling you have just before you know better. **2.** a feeling largely confined to freshmen. **3.** the feeling that makes one believe a man, even when one knows that one would lie in his place. **4.** a trait displayed by a woman who spends more than her husband earns.

Confirmed bachelor: **1.** one who thinks that the only thoroughly justified marriage was the one that produced him. **2.** one who believes that what God has put asunder, no man should join together.

Confusion: one woman plus one left turn; excitement: two women plus one secret; bedlam: three women plus one bargain; chaos: four women plus one luncheon check.

Congress: a place where operations are directed by bloc heads.

Congressman: a man who votes for all appropriations and against all taxes.

Conscience: **1.** a device that doesn't keep you from doing anything; just keeps you from enjoying it. **2.** a guilt-edged knife. **3.** an inner voice that warns us somebody is looking. **4.** a walkie-talkie set by which God speaks to us. **5.** something that feels terrible when everything else feels swell. **6.** that sixth sense that comes to our aid when we are doing wrong and tells us that we are about to get caught. **7.** the still small voice that makes you feel still smaller. **8.** the voice that tells you not to do something after you have done it. **9.** what makes you tell your wife before someone else does. **10.** the small inner voice that tells you the Internal Revenue Service might check your return. **11.** that which tells you that instinct is wrong. **12.** the still small voice that says, "Aha, you've been found out." **13.** God's vice-regent on earth. **14.** that small inner voice that doesn't speak your language. **15.** a playback of the small voice that told you not to do it in the first place. **16.** a thinking man's filter. **17.** that impediment which so often rudely interrupts while money is talking. **18.** a small, still voice that makes minority reports.

Conscientious woman: one who never breaks a confidence without first imposing the strictest secrecy.

Conservatism: radicalism in its dotage.

Conservative: **1.** a man who acts impulsively after thinking for a long time. **2.** a man who is too cowardly to fight and too fat to run. **3.** a man who just sits and thinks, mostly sits. **4.** a statesman who is enamored of existing evils, as distinguished from the liberal who wishes to replace them with others. **5.** one who does not think that anything should be done for the first time. **6.** one who wants you to keep your hand out of his pocket. **7.** one who believes in the things forced on the world yesterday by radicals. **8.** a man with two perfectly good legs who, however, has never learned to walk. **9.** a man who will not look at the new moon out of respect for that ancient and honorable institution, the old one.

Consideration: when a woman shoots her husband with a bow and arrow so that she won't awaken the children.

Consult: to seek another's approval of a course already decided upon.

Consultant: **1.** a colleague who is called in at the last moment to share the blame. **2.** a man who knows less about your business than you do and gets more for telling you how to run it than you could possibly make out of it even if you ran it right instead of the way he tells you. **3.** an executive who can't find another job.

Contact man, Hollywood: See **Hollywood contact man.**

Contempt: **1.** the feeling of a prudent man for an enemy who is too formidable safely to be opposed. **2.** egotism in ill humor.

Contented married woman: one who can't think of a better man she could have married.

Contentment: **1.** that rare state acquired by a person who schools himself to be satisfied with what he has. **2.** the power to get out of any situation all there is in it.

Contest, Beauty: See **Beauty contest.**

Contortionist: a guy who can still make both ends meet these days.

Convalescent: a patient who is still alive.

Convention: **1.** an excuse for doing the unconventional. **2.** where people pass a lot of resolutions but few bars. **3.** what hotels put back their revolving doors after.

Conventional: not necessarily the way a man acts at a convention.

Convention, Political: See **Political convention.**

Conventions: what the road to Hell is paved with.

Conversation: **1.** a form of communication in which some men never stop to think and many women never think to stop. **2.** the slowest form of human communication. **3.** an art in which a man has all mankind for his competitor.

Conversationalist, Intelligent: See **Intelligent conversationalist.**

Conversation, Brilliant: See **Brilliant conversation.**

Convict: **1.** the only person who likes to be stopped in the middle of a sentence. **2.** a felon who needs a friend.

Convictions: what an employe has after he knows what the boss thinks.

Convincing talker: a man who can keep both hands in his pockets while describing the one that got away.

Cook book: a convenience used by an old-fashioned housekeeper for filing her own recipes.

Cooking, Home: See **Home cooking.**

Cookout, Successful: See **Successful cookout.**

Cooperation: three helping one another bear the burden of six.

Coordinator: **1.** a man who brings organized chaos out of regimented confusion. **2.** a man who has a desk between two expediters.

Coquette: a woman without a heart, who makes a fool of a man who has no head.

Co-respondent: the right man in the wrong place.

Corkscrew: an implement used for opening bottles as well as conversation.

Corn-on-the-cob: the stuff you eat like you play a mouth organ.

Corporal: as high as you can go and still have friends.

Corporate image: *what* you think of a company *when* you think of that company.

Corporation: an ingenious device for obtaining individual profit without individual responsibility.

Corpse: a human been.

Corset: like love: something which binds us together and makes us better than we are by nature.

Cosmetics: a woman's way of keeping a man from reading between the lines.

Cost of living: the difference between your net income and your gross habits.

Cough: something you yourself can't help, but everybody else does on purpose to torment you.

Counter-attraction: a pretty salesgirl.

Counterbalance: when a woman buys a new dress and doesn't tell her husband until she has made him buy a new suit.

Counterfeiter: a guy who gets into trouble by following a good example.

Counter-irritant: the woman who shops all day and buys nothing.

Counter, Perfume: See **Perfume counter.**

Country, Foreign: See **Foreign country.**

Country, Free: See **Free country.**

Country, Modern: See **Modern country.**

Country, Primitive: See **Primitive country.**

Couple, Married: See **Married couple.**

Courage: fear that has said its prayers.

Courtesy: the quality that keeps a woman smiling when a departing guest stands at the open screen door and lets the flies in.

Courtship: **1.** a man pursuing a woman until she catches him. **2.** a period during which a girl decides whether or not she can do better. **3.** the period during which a man spends so much on his girl friend that he finally marries her for his money. **4.** when a fellow and a girl are always trying to show how smart he is. **5.** when a fellow gets so wrapped up in a girl that it's easy to tie the knot. **6.** the short interlude between lipstick and mopstick.

Coward: one who in a perilous emergency thinks with his legs.

Crackerjack: fireworks money.

Credit: **1.** a commodity that becomes better the less it is used. **2.** a person who can't pay, gets another person who can't pay, to guarantee that he can pay.

Creditor: **1.** a man who has a better memory than a debtor. **2.** a person who won't let you breathe easily.

Crew cut: furry with a singe on top.

Cribbage: infancy.

Criminal: **1.** one who gets caught. **2.** one who does by illegal means what all the rest of us do legally.

Criminal, Arch: See **Arch criminal.**

Critic: **1.** a legless man who teaches running. **2.** a wet blanket that soaks everything it touches. **3.** one quick-on-the-flaw. **4.** one who finds a little bad in the best of things. **5.** a man who expects miracles. **6.** one who would have you write it, sing it, play it, paint it, or carve it as he would—if he could. **7.** an unmerciful faultfinder, two steps above a fool, and a great many below a wise man. **8.** a gentleman who reports his prejudices and his preferences in such English as he is equipped with. **9.** a wet blanket with a tongue. **10.** one who tells of the adventures of the soul among masterpieces. **11.** a venemous serpent that delights in hissing. **12.** a man who writes about things he doesn't like.

Critic, Drama: See **Drama critic.**

Criticism: **1.** a study by which men grow important and formidable at very little expense. **2.** something you can avoid by saying nothing, doing nothing and being nothing. **3.** the disapproval of people, not for having faults, but for having faults different from yours. **4.** the art wherewith a critic tries to guess himself into a share of the author's fame.

Critic, Literary: See **Literary critic.**

Critics: **1.** people who go places and boo things. **2.** the stupid who discuss the wise.

Crooning: a continuous hollow sound, as of cattle in pain.

Crossing, Grade: See **Grade crossing.**

Cube: a square that went to college.

Cupid: one who when he hits the mark usually Mrs. it.

Current literature: light reading.

Curve: something which may wreck your car . . . if you hug it at the wrong time.

Curved line: the loveliest distance between two points.

Cynic: **1.** a blackguard whose faulty vision sees things as they are, not as they ought to be. **2.** a man who knows the price of everything and the value of nothing; a sentimentalist is one who values everything and knows the price of nothing. **3.** a man who looks at the world with a monocle in his mind's eye. **4.** a man who looks both ways before crossing a one-way street. **5.** a man who, when he smells flowers, looks around for a coffin. **6.** one who looks down on those above him. **7.** one who has sized himself up—and got sore about it. **8.** a man who regards getting engaged as the first step towards divorce. **9.** one who thinks the world never changes, only short changes. **10.** a person who knows everything and believes nothing. **11.** a man who found out when he was about 10 that there wasn't any Santa Claus, and is still upset about it. **12.** one who is married to his first love. **13.** a man who makes carbon copies of his love letters. **14.** a person who thinks the only footprints on the sands of time are heels.

Cynicism: **1.** the form in which base souls approach what they call honesty. **2.** intellectual dandyism. 3. a small brass fieldpiece that eventually breaks and kills the cannoneer.

D

Dachshund: 1. a dog who wags his tail by remote control. **2.** an animal which is half a dog high by a dog and a half long.

Dance, Formal: See **Formal dance.**

Dancer, Hula: See **Hula dancer.**

Dancing: the art of pulling your feet away faster than your partner can step on them.

Dandelion: one of those things which, if given an inch, will take a yard.

Dandruff: chips off the old block.

Dane, Great: See **Great Dane.**

Dark Ages: Knight time.

Dark glasses: a device to make the obscure feel important.

Dark horse: the candidate who keeps his availability well curried and groomed.

Date, Blind: See **Blind date.**

Dead giveaway: a canceled quiz show.

Dean, College: See **College dean.**

Death: 1. Patrick Henry's second choice. **2.** to stop sinning suddenly.

Debt: 1. a trap which a man sets and baits himself, and then deliberately gets into. **2.** the only thing that expands in proportion as it is contracted. **3.** what you get into if you spend as much as you tell your friends you earn. **4.** what some people are head over deals in.

Debts: the certain outcome of an uncertain income.

Debutante: 1. a bareback with greenbacks. **2.** a young girl with bride ideas. **3.** girl who goes out a vision and comes in a sight. **4.** one who comes out at eighteen and gets up at twelve. **5.** one who lives a date-to-date existence. **6.** a girl whose life is one mad whirl of activity . . . day in and night out.

Decency: indecency's conspiracy of silence.

Decision: what a man makes when he can't find anybody to serve on a committee.

Decorator, Interior: See **Interior decorator.**

Delegate-at-large: a man at a convention whose wife didn't accompany him.

Delinquency, Juvenile: See **Juvenile delinquency.**

Delinquent children: those who have reached the age where they want to do what mama and papa are doing.

Delinquent, Juvenile: See **Juvenile delinquent.**

Delta: a river with its mouth full of mud.

Demagogue: a man who can rock the boat himself and persuade everybody else that there is a terrible storm at sea.

Democracy: **1.** a country where you can say what you think without thinking. **2.** a form of religion: the worship of jackals by jackasses. **3.** a land where you are free to choose your own form of government—blonde, brunette or redhead. **4.** a place where you can say what you please, but don't have to listen unless you want to. **5.** a small hard core of common agreement, surrounded by a rich variety of individual difference. **6.** a state of mind in which every man is as good as every other man, provided he really is. **7.** a system whereby the person who never votes can cuss out the man the other people elected. **8.** that form of society, no matter what its political classification, in which every man has a chance and knows that he has it. **9.** a country in which everyone has an equal right to feel superior to the other fellow. **10.** the art and science of running a circus from the monkey cage. **11.** a system built by those who live to give and destroyed by those who live to get. **12.** a form of government based upon the conviction that there are extraordinary possibilities in ordinary people. **13.** the recurrent suspicion that more than half the people are right more than half the time. **14.** no more than an aristocracy of orators, interrupted sometimes with the temporary monarchy of one orator. **15.** a type of government in which everybody knows how things should be handled except those whom we elect to do the job. **16.** a state of mind by and for the individual. **17.** a form of government in which the majority get at least two guesses as to which minority will rule them next.

Dental parlor: a drawing room.

Dentist: **1.** a collector of old magazines. **2.** a man who lives from hand to mouth. **3.** a man who runs a filling station. **4.** a prestidigitator who, putting metal in your mouth, pulls coins out of your pocket. **5.** a fellow who bores you to tears.

Department store detective: counter spy.

Depression: 1. a period during which we have to get along without the things our grandparents never dreamed of. **2.** a time that tries men's soles.

Depression, Economic: See **Economic depression.**

Desertion: the poor man's method of divorce.

Desire: the thing that is so often nipped in the budget.

Desk: wastebasket with drawers.

Detective, Department store: See **Department store detective.**

Detective, Store: See **Store detective.**

Detour: 1. something that lengthens your mileage, diminishes your gas, and strengthens your vocabulary. **2.** the roughest distance between two points.

Diamond: 1. a bright gem, the sparkle of which sometimes renders a woman stone-blind to the defects of the man proffering it. **2.** a stepping stone in every girl's life. **3.** a woman's idea of a stepping stone to success. **4.** nothing harder except making the payments on one. **5.** a chunk of coal that made good under pressure. **6.** the new-rich descendant of coal.

Diamond cutter: one who mows the grass at the ball park.

Diamonds: chunks of coal that stuck to their job.

Diaphragm: a muscular partition separating disorders of the chest from disorders of the bowels.

Diarist: a person who enjoys telling himself something he already knows.

Dictator: one who thinks he can take it—no matter to whom it belongs.

Dictatorship: 1. a place where public opinion can't even be expressed privately. **2.** a system of government where everything that isn't forbidden is obligatory.

Dictionary: 1. the only place where divorce comes before marriage. **2.** a book in which one word leads to another. **3.** a malevolent literary device for cramping the growth of a language and making it hard and inelastic.

Die-hard: a man who worships the very ground his head's in.

Diet: **1.** a short period of starvation preceding a gain of five pounds. **2.** something to take the starch out of you. **3.** something you keep putting off while you keep putting on.

Diet, Balanced: See **Balanced diet.**

Dieting: **1.** the penalty for exceeding the feed limit. **2.** the triumph of mind over platter. **3.** accepting every loss as a gain. **4.** waiting for hips that never come in.

Difficult: that which can be done immediately; impossible: that which takes a little longer.

Dignity: **1.** something that can't be preserved in alcohol. **2.** the capacity to hold back on the tongue what never should have been on the mind in the first place. **3.** the quality that enables a man who says nothing, does nothing and knows nothing to command a great deal of respect.

Dilemma: a politician trying to save both his faces at once.

Dilettante: a philanderer who seduces the several arts and deserts each in turn for another.

Dime: **1.** a dollar with all the taxes taken out. **2.** a chip off the old buck.

Diner: a chew-chew car.

Dining room: the place where the family eats while painters are doing over the kitchen.

Dinner, Buffet: See **Buffet dinner.**

Diplomacy: **1.** a peaceful substitute for shooting. **2.** cutting the other fellow's throat without using a knife. **3.** lying in state. **4.** the ability to take something and make the other fellow believe he is giving it away. **5.** the art of handling a porcupine without disturbing the quills. **6.** the art of laying down the law gently enough to keep it from being broken. **7.** the art of letting someone else have your own way. **8.** the art of saying "Nice doggie!" until you can find a rock. **9.** the art of skating on thin ice without getting into deep water. **10.** the art of turning a dropped stitch into a loophole. **11.** the art of convincing people you really don't want something you know you can't get. **12.** a synonym for discretion when the other guy is bigger. **13.** to do and say the nastiest things in the nicest way. **14.** the ability to pet a skunk and still smell like a lily. **15.** the art of keeping cool.

Diplomacy, Ancient: See **Ancient diplomacy.**

Diplomat: **1.** a fellow who prefers ironing out his differences to flattening his opponent. **2.** a gent who thinks twice before he says nothing. **3.** a man who convinces his wife that a woman looks stout in a fur coat. **4.** a man who has learned that you can't bend a nail by hitting it squarely on the head. **5.** a man who remembers a woman's birthday but forgets her age. **6.** a man who tries to settle problems created by other diplomats. **7.** a person who can be disarming even though his country isn't. **8.** a person who can juggle a hot potato long enough for it to become a cold issue. **9.** a person who can keep a civil tongue in his cheek. **10.** a person who does not think it necessary to understand things in order to argue about them. **11.** a person who says, "I will take the matter under advisement" instead of "no." **12.** if you have the advantage over someone, and you lead him to think that he has the advantage over you, without giving him the chance to take advantage of you. **13.** one who can bring home the bacon without spilling the beans. **14.** a husband who can convince his wife she wants an umbrella when she thinks she wants a fur coat. **15.** a fellow who has to watch his appease and accuse. **16.** one who can put in his oar without rocking the boat. **17.** a person who uses his head without anyone suspecting it. **18.** an artist who sketches the lines between which he hopes people will read. **19.** one who can tell a man he's open-minded when he means he has a hole in his head. **20.** one who can keep his shirt on while getting something off his chest.

Diplomat, Good: See **Good diplomat.**

Diplomatic blunder: a policy slip.

Director: the one who always faces the music.

Disc jockey: **1.** one who earns his living by putting on airs. **2.** one who lives on spins and needles.

Discount: something often sold in place of goods.

Discouragement: seeing the secretary yawn over one of your snappy salesmanship letters.

Discretion: **1.** a comb that experience hands us after we have lost our hair. **2.** a sense that comes to a man too late to do him any good. **3.** closing your eyes to a situation before someone closes them for you **4.** something that comes to a person after he is too old for it to do him any good.

Discussion: **1.** a method of confirming others in their errors. **2.** an exchange of intelligence as opposed to *Argument* which is an exchange of ignorance.

Dish towel: something that wipes the contented look off a married man's face.

Disillusionment: **1.** finding a corn pad when drinking champagne from a slipper. **2.** a summons to explain your tax return when you expected a generous refund.

Distance: that which lends enchantment to the view, but not when you run out of gas.

Distribution, Poor: See **Poor distribution.**

District of Columbia: a territory bounded on all sides by the United States of America.

Dividend: a certain percentum, per annum, perhaps.

Divorce: **1.** going through a change of wife. **2.** hash made from domestic scraps. **3.** what results when the bonds of matrimony no longer bear interest. **4.** a parting word. **5.** when a woman takes a man for better or worse—but not for long.

Divorcee: **1.** a woman who gets richer by decrees. **2.** one who marries for better or for worse . . . but not for good.

Divorce, Hollywood: See **Hollywood divorce.**

Doctor: **1.** a guy who tells you if you don't cut out something he'll cut something out of you. **2.** a man who keeps telling children to eat more and more and parents to eat less. **3.** a man who suffers from good health. **4.** one who kills you today to prevent you from dying tomorrow. **5.** the only man who hasn't a guaranteed cure for a cold.

Doctor's office: a place where you find the newest in medicine and the oldest in reading material.

Doctor's prescription: something written on a subway train with a post office pen.

Dog: a welcome waggin'.

Dogmatism: puppyism come to its full growth.

Dollar: **1.** the jack of all trades. **2.** a piece of metal or paper that never falls as low as the means some people use to get it.

Dollar sign: an S that's been double-crossed.

Domestic argument: one after which the husband either goes to his club or reaches for it.

Dominant wife: the type who wears a worried look on her husband's face.

Door: what a dog is perpetually on the wrong side of.

Doorman: a genius who can open the door of your car with one hand, help you in with the other, and still have one left for the tip.

Dope: a man who picks up a cute blonde's handkerchief and turns it in to the lost-and-found desk.

Dots: symbols which, in the modern novel, mean proceed at your own risqué.

Double jeopardy: when your doctor calls in a consulting physician.

Double time: something a fellow getting it ought to do.

Down beat: a duck with drooping feathers.

Draft board: where young men are weighed and found wanted.

Drama critic: a person who surprises the playwright by informing him what he meant.

Dramatic critic: one who gives the best jeers of his life to the theater.

Draw: the result of a battle between a dentist and a patient.

Dream: to look at night and see things.

Dreamer: **1.** one who waits for something to turn up—whereas a doer turns up something while waiting. **2.** a guy who can sit around reading travel folders after his vacation is over.

Dream house: one that costs twice as much as you dreamed it would.

Dreams: the free movies of sleep.

Dress, Evening: See **Evening dress.**

Dress, Maternity: See **Maternity dress.**

Drinking: act which does not drown your sorrows—only irrigates them.

Drinking fountain, Office: See **Office drinking fountain.**

Drinking fountain, Park: See **Park drinking fountain.**

Drive-in theatre: **1.** sparking place. **2.** where a guy goes to shut off his ignition so he can try out his clutch.

Driver, Auto: See **Auto driver.**

Driver, Careful: See **Careful driver.**

Driver, Careless: See **Careless driver.**

Driver, Reckless: See **Reckless driver.**

Driver, School-bus: See **School-bus driver.**

Driver, Sunday: See **Sunday driver.**

Driver, Truck: See **Truck driver.**

Driver, Woman: See **Woman driver.**

Druggist: a man who used to sell drugs.

Drug store: **1.** a telephone with a business attached. **2.** the poor man's country club.

Drug, Wonder: See **Wonder drug.**

Drunkard: **1.** a man who knows his capacity but gets drunk before he reaches it. **2.** human prune, the more he is soaked the more he swells. **3.** a fellow who is sot in his ways.

Duck, Lame: See **Lame duck.**

Duel: pistols for two; breakfast for one.

Durable goods: those that last longer than the time payments.

Dutch-treat addict: a split purseonality.

Duty: **1.** that which sternly impels us in the direction of profit, along the line of desire. **2.** what one expects from others, not what one does oneself. **3.** what the normal man looks forward to with distaste, does with reluctance, and boasts about forever after. **4.** a word used to excuse our delight in hurting others.

Dyspeptic: a man that can eat his cake and have it too.

E

Early rising: triumph of mind over mattress.

Earth: a solid substance, much desired by the seasick.

Easter millinery: hatrocities.

Easy chair: the hardest one to find empty.

Easy payments: the ones that are easier said than done.

Eccentric: one who minds his own business.

Echo: **1.** no sooner said than said. **2.** the only thing that can cheat a woman out of the last word.

Economic depression: when the tenth word of a telegram is "please" instead of "love."

Economics: **1.** college professor talk for "What happened to the money in the cookie jar?" **2.** the study of how limited resources can best be made to serve the unlimited wants of human beings.

Economics expert: a man who knows tomorrow why the things he said yesterday didn't happen today.

Economist: **1.** a man who knows more about money than the people who have it now. **2.** a man who tells you what to do with your money after you have done something else with it. **3.** one who takes a lot of unwarranted assumptions and reaches a foregone conclusion. **4.** a financier without any money who wears a Phi Beta Kappa key on one end of a watch chain and no watch on the other. **5.** a fellow with charts to prove that all the confusion about what's going to happen to business isn't mere coincidence.

Economy: **1.** a way to spend money without getting any fun out of it. **2.** denying ourselves a necessity today in order to buy a luxury tomorrow. **3.** living within your means even if you have to borrow money to do so.

Economy, False: See **False economy.**

Economy, Planned: See **Planned economy.**

Economy, Political: See **Political economy.**

Ecstasy: a feeling when you feel you are going to feel a feeling you have never felt before.

Editor: **1.** the fellow who makes a long story short. **2.** a fellow with a little desk and a big waste basket. **3.** a person employed on a newspaper, whose business it is to separate the wheat from the chaff, and see that the chaff is printed.

Educate: to render harmless by cultivation.

Educated man: **1.** one who has finally discovered that there are some questions to which nobody has the answers. **2.** one who knows when to use not only commas and periods, but colons and semicolons as well.

Educated person: **1.** one who voluntarily does more thinking than is necessary for his own survival. **2.** one whose emotions have gone to school.

Education: **1.** a debt due from present to future generations. **2.** forcing abstract ideas into concrete heads. **3.** that mysterious process whereby information passes from the lecture notes of the professor through the fountain pen and onto the notebook. **4.** that which discloses to the wise and disguises from the foolish their lack of understanding. **5.** what a father gets when he sits in on a conversation with a group of teen-agers. **6.** what's left over after you've gotten the facts. **7.** that which remains when we have forgotten all that we have been taught. **8.** the ability to describe a beautiful girl without using your hands. **9.** the ability to quote Shakespeare without crediting it to the Bible. **10.** what enables you to pass out insults and call it repartee. **11.** knowledge that a chorus girl gets by stages and that a college girl gets by degrees. **12.** what a man gets in exchange for alimony. **13.** learning a lot about how little you know.

Education, Adult: See **Adult education.**

Education, College: See **College education.**

Education, Hire: See **Hire education.**

Efficiency: **1.** the ability to do a job well, plus the desire to do it better. **2.** the knack of getting somebody to do a job you don't like. **3.** using instant coffee to dawdle away an hour.

Efficiency expert: **1.** a man smart enough to tell you how to run your business and too smart to start his own. **2.** a man who knows less about your business than you do and gets paid more for telling you how to run it than you could possibly make out of it, even if you ran it right instead of the way he told you to. **3.** a man who walks in his sleep so that he can get his rest and his exercise at the same time. **4.** one who always has to make up a foursome before passing through a revolving door. **5.** a man who kills two birds with one stone and gets the stone back. **6.** a man who spends a whole day getting out of an hour's work. **7.** a fellow who can't stand heaven because it lets the other place get most of the business.

Egghead: **1.** a fellow who thinks about thinking. **2.** a guy who's found something more interesting than women.

Ego: **1.** some spark within us which leads us to believe that we are better than we are, and which is often instrumental in proving it. **2.** the only thing that can keep on growing without nourishment.

Egotism: **1.** an anesthetic that nature gives to a man to deaden the pain of being a darn fool. **2.** self-confidence looking for trouble. **3.** something that enables the man in a rut to think he's in the groove. **4.** usually just a case of mistaken non-entity. **5.** the art of seeing something in yourself which others can't see.

Egotist: **1.** a conceited ass who thinks he knows as much as you do. **2.** a fellow who certainly knows a good thing when he says it. **3.** a man who thinks that a woman will marry him for himself alone. **4.** a person of low taste, more interested in himself than in me. **5.** a person who persists in telling you things about himself that you had planned on telling him about yourself. **6.** one who is always me-deep in conversation. **7.** one who thinks that if he hadn't been born people would wonder why. **8.** one whose eyes look in instead of out. **9.** someone who thinks all the world is a stooge. **10.** man with a practiced I. **11.** a man who thinks he is all the things that you think you are. **12.** a person who is always letting off esteem.

Eiffel Tower: the Empire State Building after taxes.

Eisenhower: the second American president with a Gettysburg address.

Elderly wolf: Jill collector with jack.

Elder statesman: a politician who can't get elected.

Election time: when the air is filled with speeches and the speeches are filled with air.

Electoral College: institute of higher yearning.

Electrician: a man who wires for money.

Elementary teacher: an unmarried den mother.

Elephant: an animal occurring in one of three colors, depending on whether you are on safari, a church committee or a week-end party.

Elephant, Pink. See **Pink elephant.**

Eloquence: logic on fire.

Embarrassment: watching the boss do what you just told him couldn't be done.

Emotions, Mixed: See **Mixed emotions.**

Employer, Modern: See **Modern employer.**

Encore: a greedy theater-goer's desire to get more than his money's worth.

Engagement: **1.** a period in which a girl is placed in solitaire confinement. **2.** a period of urge on the verge of a merge. **3.** the time a girl takes until she finds out if she can do any better. **4.** an option on a life sentence.

Engagement period: a time of solitaire confinement.

Engagement ring: a tourniquet applied to the third finger of a girl's left hand to stop circulation.

Engineer: an approaching train.

Engineer, Practical: See **Practical engineer.**

Enough: what would satisfy us if our neighbors didn't have more.

Enthusiasm: that temper of the mind in which the imagination has got the better of the judgment.

Enthusiast: one who preaches four times as much as he believes and believes four times as much as a sane man ought to.

Epigram: **1.** a half-truth so stated as to irritate the person who believes the other half. **2.** a wise crack that's played in Carnegie Hall. **3.** truth on a "binge."

Epigram, Brilliant: See **Brilliant epigram.**

Epitaph: **1.** a belated advertisement for a line of goods that has been permanently discontinued. **2.** a statement that lies above the one that lies beneath.

Equestrienne: saddlebag.

Escape literature: a book in the jail library with a file in it.

Eskimos: people who, after a few months of work, call it a day.

Estates: acreage in the country owned by people who have "gone to town."

Etc.: a sign to make others believe you know more than you do.

Eternal struggle: keeping your earning capacity up to your wife's yearning capacity.

Etiquette: **1.** a convenient code of conduct which makes lying a virtue and snobbishness a righteous deed. **2.** learning to yawn with your mouth closed. **3.** the noise you don't make when you eat soup. **4.** the test of good manners is to put up pleasantly with bad ones. **5.** knowing which finger to put in your mouth when whistling for a waiter.

Eulogy: praise that's too much and too late.

European trip: a vacation you enjoy after you have rested a month at home.

Eve: the first chicken to ruin a man's garden.

Evening dress: more gone than gown.

Evil: that which one believes of others. It is a sin to believe evil of others, but it is seldom a mistake.

Evolution: a clever trick performed by Darwin, who made a monkey of Adam.

Exaggeration: **1.** to paint a snake and add legs. **2.** a truth that has lost its temper.

Exclamation point: a period that has blown its top.

Exclusive club: a place where you can meet the kind of people you would have black-balled, if you'd have gotten in first.

Executive: **1.** a big gun—that hasn't been fired yet. **2.** a fellow who goes out and finds something that needs to be done; then finds someone willing to pay for it; then hires somebody to do it. **3.** a man who can take two hours for lunch without hindering production. **4.** a man who goes around with a worried look on the face of his assistant. **5.** a man who talks to visitors so the other employes can get their work done. **6.** one who makes an immediate decision and is sometimes right. **7.** a guy who is always annoying the hired help by asking them to do something. **8.** a man of rare persuasion, of vision, power and force, who talks golf in the office and business on the course. **9.** a man who can hand a letter back to a red-headed stenographer for a fourth typing. **10.** a fellow who orders, directs and dictates all day long, and who then goes home and meekly dries the dishes. **11.** a man who travels from his air-conditioned home to his air-conditioned office in an air-conditioned car and from there to his air-conditioned club to take a steam bath. **12.** a man who decides; sometimes he decides right, but always he decides. **13.** a man who shows the other fellow how to put his shoulder to the wheel. **14.** a man who can make a decision and stick to it . . . no matter how wrong he is. **15.** a man who believes in sharing the credit with the person who did the work.

Executive ability: **1.** the art of getting the credit for all the hard work that somebody else does. **2.** deciding quickly and getting somebody else to do the work. **3.** the faculty of earning your bread by the work of other people.

Executive, Chamber of Commerce: See **Chamber of Commerce Executive.**

Executive, Good: See **Good executive.**

Executive, Modern: See **Modern executive.**

Executive, Successful business: See **Successful business executive.**

Experience: **1.** a form of knowledge acquired only two ways—by doing and being done. **2.** a name given to our mistakes. **3.** a revelation in the light of which we renounce our errors of youth for those of age. **4.** the name an older man gives to his mistakes. **5.** not what happens to me, but what a man does with what happens to him. **6.** the mistakes we like to remember. **7.** what you get from being inexperienced. **8.** what you get when you're expecting something else. **9.** what causes a person to make new mistakes instead of the same old ones. **10.** that accumulated body of practical wisdom that enables us to have handy, whenever we are offered an unpleasant task, a completely logical reason for not doing it. **11.** what you have left after you've lost everything else. **12.** a comb which nature gives to men when they are bald. **13.** the best teacher but often late to school. **14.** something one always needs until he's got it, then he's too old for the job. **15.** that which makes a man tell his wife the truth the second time. **16.** the knowledge of the effects that follow acts. **17.** what keeps a man who has made the same mistake twice from admitting it the third time around. **18.** what makes you wonder how it got a reputation for being the best teacher.

Experienced gardener: one who, when he puts out a packet of seeds, knows just what plants to expect—weeds.

Experienced married man: one who can tell when his wife comes to the end of one argument and begins another.

Experienced wife: one who can maintain a cheerful silence while her husband grumbles himself into a good humor.

Experience-Training: See **Training-Experience.**

Expert: 1. a fellow who has made a lot of good guesses. **2.** a man from another city, and the farther away that city is, the greater the expert. **3.** a man wearing a tie and an important look on his face who knows how to complicate simplicity. **4.** a man who avoids the small errors as he sweeps on to the grand fallacy. **5.** a man who is seldom in doubt, but often in error. **6.** an ordinary man away from home. **7.** any person who has tried and failed—and can tell you why. **8.** a person who not only knows all the answers but can think up problems to fit them. **9.** one who can take something you already knew and make it sound confusing. **10.** one who knows more and more about less and less. **11.** one who tells you to do something exactly the way you decided to do it before you asked him. **12.** one who has a good reason for guessing wrong. **13.** a little drip under great pressure.

Expert, Economic: See **Economic expert.**

Expert, Efficiency: See **Efficiency expert.**

Expert, Income tax: See **Income tax expert.**

Expert, Memory: See **Memory expert.**

Expert, Military: See **Military expert.**

Expert, Reducing: See **Reducing expert.**

Expert, Tax: See **Tax expert.**

Explanation: something to give your wife at 4 a.m.

Extravagance: buying whatever is of no earthly value to your wife.

Extravagant girl: one who usually makes a poor mother and a bankrupt father.

Extravagant neighbor: one who lives beyond your means.

F

Face, Straight: See **Straight face.**

Fad: something that goes in one era and out the other.

Failure: 1. the quickest method known for making money. **2.** the line of least persistence. **3.** a man who has blundered and is not able to cash in on the experience.

Fairway (golf): the well-kept and seldom used portion of a golf course.

Faith: **1.** belief without evidence in what is told by one who speaks without knowledge, of things without parallel. **2.** illogical belief in the occurrence of the improbable.

Fall: that glorious time of the year when your neighbor comes by with an invitation for golf just as you have your hands full of storm windows.

Fallen woman: a mother who neglected to pick up some toys.

False economy: using only 30 candles on her 40th birthday cake.

Falsies: **1.** a helpful aid to any girl in acquiring a disappointed husband. **2.** a sort of hope chest.

Falsie salesman: a fuller bust man.

Fame: **1.** chiefly a matter of dying at the right moment. **2.** the advantage of being known to those who do not know us. **3.** the best way to rise to its dizzy heights is to stay on the level. **4.** a pedestal on which the victim is placed in order to give the world a better chance to throw bricks at him.

Family: a unit composed not only of children, but of men, women, an occasional animal and the common cold.

Family, Boss of the: See **Boss of the family.**

Family man: **1.** one who has several mouths to feed . . . and one great big one to listen to. **2.** one who has replaced the currency in his wallet with snapshots.

Family swimming pool: a small body of water completely surrounded by other people's children.

Family tree: **1.** the only tree whose branches seek the shelter of its roots. **2.** a device for trying to trace yourself back to better people than you are.

Fanatic: **1.** one who can't change his opinion and won't change the subject. **2.** one who is highly enthusiastic about something in which you are not even remotely interested. **3.** one who redoubles his efforts after he has forgotten his objectives. **4.** one who will stick to his guns whether they're loaded or not. **5.** a fellow with such a large chip on his shoulder that it makes him lose his balance.

Fanaticism: **1.** enthusiasm of the stupid. **2.** redoubling your effort when you've missed your aim.

Fan, Baseball: See **Baseball fan.**

Fan club: a group that agrees with an actor's opinion of himself.

Fan, Football: See **Football fan.**

Farm: **1.** what a city man dreams of at 5 p.m., never at 5 a.m. **2.** a hunk of land on which, if you get up early enough mornings and work late enough nights, you'll make a fortune—if you strike oil.

Farmer: **1.** a handy man with a sense of humus. **2.** a man who is outstanding in his field.

Farmer, Gentleman: See **Gentleman farmer.**

Farmers: men successful only if they sell their farms to golf clubs.

Farmer, Successful: See **Successful farmer.**

Fashion: **1.** a despot whom the wise ridicule and obey. **2.** something that goes out of style as soon as most people have one. **3.** something that goes in one year and out the other. **4.** that by which the fantastic becomes for a moment universal. **5.** gentility running away from vulgarity and afraid of being overtaken.

Father: **1.** one who gives the lover his daughter's hand and hopes he takes the one she's had in his pocket all this time. **2.** a man who hopes to have enough money on Father's Day to pay the bills from Mother's Day. **3.** a person forced to endure childbirth without the aid of an anaesthetic. **4.** a person who gives a daughter to another man who isn't nearly good enough, so there will be grandchildren who are smarter than anybody's. **5.** a person who growls when he feels good and laughs when he's scared to death. **6.** a banker provided by nature. **7.** a man who exchanges the currency in his billfold for snapshots. **8.** one for whom the Christmas bills toll. **9.** an ambitious man who diligently works his son's way through college.

Father's Day: **1.** the annual day in June set aside so merchants can get rid of their leftover Christmas ties and shaving lotion. **2.** just like Mother's Day only you don't spend so much.

Fat man: 1. one who knows where his cigar ashes are going to land. **2.** one who leans heavily against his belt.

Federal aid: a system of making money taken from the people look like a gift when handed back.

Feed store: the only place in town where you can get a chicken dinner for 10 cents.

Female friends: women mad at the same person.

Feminine psychology: being smart enough to ask your husband's advice but not being dumb enough to take it.

Feminine tact: the ability of a woman to look up to a man shorter than she is.

Feminine wile: keeping a man at arm's length by a hair's breadth.

Fern: a plant that you're supposed to water once a day and when you don't it dies, but if you do it dies anyway, only not so soon.

Fever, Potomac: See **Potomac fever.**

Fever, Spring: See **Spring fever.**

Fiction: something that can't hold a scandal to biography.

Fiddler: a violinist before he becomes the virtuoso who refuses to play a real tune.

Fidelity: a virtue peculiar to those who are about to be betrayed.

Fidelity, High. See **High fidelity.**

Figurehead: an accountant.

Figures, Trim: See **Trim figures.**

Figure, Youthful: See **Youthful figure.**

Filing cabinet: a place where you can lose things systematically.

Film, Silent: See **Silent film.**

Finance companies: loan wolves.

Finance company: an outfit that lives on the flat of the land.

Financial genius: a man who can earn money faster than his family can spend it.

Financial wizard: a husband who can pay the last of last month's bills out of next month's salary.

Financier: a pawnbroker with imagination.

Fine–Tax: a tax you have to pay for doing wrong; **Tax:** a fine you have to pay for doing okay.

Fireproof: being related to the boss.

Firmness: the admirable quality in ourselves that is detestable stubbornness in others.

First grade teacher: one who knows how to make little things count.

First love: a little foolishness and a lot of curiosity.

Fish: **1.** an animal that grows fastest between the time it is caught and the time a fisherman describes it to his friends. **2.** a creature that goes on vacation about the time most fishermen do.

Fisherman: See also **Angler.** a fellow who thinks nothing of spending $10 a pound for fish.

Fishing: **1.** a delusion entirely surrounded by liars in old clothes. **2.** a heroic treatment tried by some laymen to avoid falling to sleep in church on Sunday.

Fishing hole: an inhabited body of water surrounded by liars in old clothes.

Flashlight: a case in which to carry dead batteries.

Flatterer: **1.** one who says things to your face that he wouldn't say behind your back. **2.** one who has water in one hand and fire in the other.

Flattery: **1.** a commodity that makes everybody sick except those who swallow it. **2.** a sort of verbal peroxide that turns a woman's head. **3.** a cologne water, to be smelled of but not swallowed. **4.** soft soap; and soft soap is 90% lye. **5.** the art of pretending you like the girl more than you like the kiss. **6.** an insult wrapped as a gift. **7.** something you hear about yourself that you wish were true. **8.** the art of telling your husband what he thinks of himself.

Flirt: **1.** a girl who got the boy you wanted. **2.** a woman who believes it's every man for herself.

Flirtation: **1.** a spoon with nothing in it. **2.** paying attention without intention. **3.** wishful winking.

Flood: a river too big for its bridges.

Florist: See **Botanist.**

Fly paper: stationery they use in airplanes.

Fog: stuff that is dangerous to drive in—especially if it's mental.

Folder, Travel: See **Travel folder.**

Fool: **1.** one whom bigger fools believe to be a man of merit. **2.** a fellow who introduces his best girl to his best friend.

Fool, Learned: See **Learned fool.**

Football: **1.** a clever subterfuge for carrying on prize fights under the guise of a reputable game. **2.** a game played on Saturdays by 22 men before 50,000 or more spectators, most of whom never really went to college either.

Football fan: one who knows the nationality of every man on the All-American team.

Football game: a place where the spectators have four quarters in which to finish a fifth.

Football season: **1.** the only time of the year when a man can walk down the street with a blonde on one arm and a blanket on the other without encountering raised eyebrows. **2.** the time of the year when girls whistle at men in sweaters. **3.** when you watch the numbers on sweaters instead of in 'em. **4.** the short warm-up period between spring practice and the winter bowl games.

Forceful action: doing something which should have been done a long time ago.

Forecaster: a person skilled in the art of drawing useful conclusions from inadequate premises.

Forecaster, Weather: See **Weather forecaster.**

Foreign country: where people tell us Americans to go home and leave them a loan.

Foreign land: a place where peasants try to array themselves as Americans would dress, if Americans weren't so busy adapting the colorful costumes of the peasants.

Foreign policy: a synthesis of conflicting interests played by ear.

Forest, Virgin: See **Virgin forest.**

Forger: **1.** a man who made a name for himself. **2.** the fellow who gives a check a bad name. **3.** one who writes a wrong. **4.** a fellow who writes things you can't bank on.

Forgiveness: the fragrance the violet sheds on the heel that has crushed it.

Formal dance: a place where a woman who hasn't a thing to wear wears it.

Forms, Income tax: See **Income tax forms.**

Forty: the age when a woman stops patting herself on the back and begins under the chin.

Fox: a wolf that sends flowers.

Frankage: the only known method of sending hot air through the mails.

Freckles: a nice sun tan—if they'd only get together.

Free country: one in which there is no particular individual to blame for the existing tyranny.

Freedom: being able to do what you please without considering anyone but the wife, police, boss, life insurance company, state, federal and city authorities, and the neighbors.

Freedom train: the one that runs from New York to Reno.

Free speech: the right to argue about issues you don't understand.

Free verse: the triumph of mind over meter.

Friction, Science: See **Science friction.**

Friend: **1.** one before whom one may think aloud. **2.** one who has the same enemies you have. **3.** one who knows all about you and loves you just the same. **4.** anybody who listens instead of argues. **5.** one who is always thinking of *you*, when all others are thinking of themselves. **6.** a person who knocks before he enters, not after he has taken his departure. **7.** one who comes in when the whole world has gone out. **8.** a present you give yourself. **9.** a speaking acquaintance who also listens. **10.** somebody you don't have to talk to. **11.** someone you can count on to count on you. **12.** someone who runs interference for you in your pursuit of happiness. **13.** one, who having gained the top of the ladder, won't forget you if you remain at the bottom. **14.** one who stands up for you in public and sits down on you in private. **15.** one who refuses to sign your note because he wants to remain your friend. **16.** one who helps you take your bitter pill by sugar-coating it for you. **17.** a present you give yourself by being friendly. **18.** one who is your enemy when you need one. **19.** one who handles you with boxing gloves when you are strong, and with silk gloves when you are weak. **20.** one who waits until the morning after to disagree with you. **21.** one who, when he sees you "in the soup," shows you how to swim out.

Friend, Sincere: See **Sincere friend.**

Friend, True: See **True friend.**

Friends: **1.** people who borrow my books and set wet glasses on them. **2.** persons who stick together until debt do them part. **3.** what you think you have oodles of, until you happen to be badly in need of just one.

Friends, Female: See **Female friends.**

Friendship: two women mad at the same person.

Friendship, Platonic: See **Platonic friendship.**

Frustrated woman: the wife who finds a letter she gave to her husband to mail six months ago in the coat that has been home since then, to have a button sewed on.

Fund-raising effort, Single: See **Single fund-raising effort.**

Furniture, Antique: See **Antique furniture.**

Futile remark: the one a man makes for the purpose of changing the subject when the wife complains because he has forgotten their wedding anniversary.

Future: the past come home to roost.

G

Gambling: a way of getting nothing for something.

Game, Football: See **Football game.**

Games, Childhood: See **Childhood games.**

Garden: **1.** a place where some of the bulbs seem to think they're buried instead of planted. **2.** a thing of beauty and a job forever. **3.** something most men prefer to turn over in their minds. **4.** something that dies if you don't water it and rots if you do.

Gardener: someone who thinks that what goes down must come up.

Gardener, Amateur: See **Amateur gardener.**

Gardener, Experienced: See **Experienced gardener.**

Gardener, True: See **True gardener.**

Gardening: 1. a matter of enthusiasm holding up until your back gets used to it. **2.** man's effort to improve his lot. **3.** an early symptom of lumbago.

Gas: something your son can somehow manage to drive the family car into the garage on the last drop of.

Gastric ulcer: something you get mountain-climbing over molehills.

Genealogist: one who traces your family tree as far back as your money will go.

Genealogy: 1. an account of one's descent from an ancestor who did not particularly care to trace his own. **2.** tracing yourself to people better than you are.

Generalities: the substance of most uninteresting conversations.

Generation, Rising: See **Rising generation.**

Generation, Younger: See **Younger generation.**

Genius: 1. a capacity for making somebody else take infinite pains. **2.** a crackpot who made a screwball idea work. **3.** any other woman's husband. **4.** one percent inspiration and ninety-nine percent perspiration. **5.** one who can do almost anything except make a living. **6.** the infinite capacity not only for taking pains but for giving them. **7.** the ability to evade work by doing something right the first time it has to be done. **8.** a man who shoots at something that no one else can see and hits it. **9.** initiative on fire. **10.** the transcendent capacity of taking trouble. **11.** a promontory jutting out into the future. **12.** the ability to light the fire of your own ambition. **13.** a stupid kid with very happy grandparents. **14.** a man who solves a problem you didn't realize you had in a manner you can't understand.

Genius, Business: See **Business genius.**

Genius, Financial: See **Financial genius.**

Genius (in Washington): the infinite capacity for taking trains.

Genius, Manufacturing: See **Manufacturing genius.**

Gentility: eating meat with a silver fork, neither being paid for.

Gentleman: **1.** a gardener who can call a spade a spade without adding any qualifying adjectives. **2.** a man who doesn't pretend to be anything that he isn't. **3.** a man who holds the door open for his wife while she carries in a load of groceries. **4.** a man who is always as nice as he sometimes is. **5.** a man who never makes passes at girls; to him they're overtures. **6.** a man who remembers a girl's birthday but forgets her age. **7.** a man who will step aside for a lady in a crowd, so she can make a pathway for him. **8.** a man with more hay in the bank than in the barn. **9.** any man a girl hasn't been out with yet. **10.** a worn-out wolf. **11.** nothing but a wolf with his ears pinned back. **12.** one who doesn't care whether he is one or not. **13.** one who has never heard the story before. **14.** one who never hurts another's feelings unintentionally. **15.** one who never strikes a woman without provocation. **16.** something made by three generations or one darn good guess on the stock market. **17.** one who does not blow his knows. **18.** one who is nice even to those who can't be of any help to him. **19.** a man who may shake his dog's paw, but not his servant's hand. **20.** a fellow who when his wife drops something kicks it to where she can pick it up more easily. **21.** one who keeps his promises made to those who cannot enforce them. **22.** a man who can hold his head high without sticking up his nose. **23.** a man who can read a woman's thoughts but wouldn't dare to out loud. **24.** a man who leaves the lawn mower where his wife can find it. **25.** a man who can treat a lady as though he wasn't interested in her. **26.** a man who can disagree without being disagreeable.

Gentleman farmer: **1.** one with more hay in the bank than in the barn. **2.** one who tips his hat every time he passes a good looking tomato.

Gentleman, Perfect: See **Perfect gentleman.**

Gentry, Landed: See **Landed gentry.**

Geriatrics: the science which deals with the perpetuation of second childhood.

Getting ahead: a process which implies that one must have one to start with.

Ghost writers: spooksmen.

Gift necktie: the tie that blinds.

Gift shop: a place where you can see all the things you hope your friends won't send you for Christmas.

Gifts, Christmas: See **Christmas gifts.**

Gigolo: one who feels the ladies owe him a loving.

G.I. haircut: a patch of hair with white sidewalls.

Ginger ale: a drink that tastes like your foot feels when it falls asleep.

Girdle: **1.** accessory after the fat. **2.** a device that a woman uses to make a waist out of her waste. **3.** an article which prevents a lot of loose walk. **4.** the difference between fact and figure. **5.** an uncomfortable item that makes women look comfortable. **6.** polite name for a plain old-fashioned pot holder. **7.** a device that begins at the bottom and works its way up. **8.** a holdup in broad daylight. **9.** a device for bringing a girl in on the beam.

Girdle manufacturer: one who lives on the fat of the land.

Girl: **1.** always one of three things: hungry, thirsty, or both. **2.** a person who will scream at a mouse, but smile at a wolf.

Girl, Bachelor: See **Bachelor girl.**

Girl, Bad: See **Bad girl.**

Girl, Career: See **Career girl.**

Girl, Chorus: See **Chorus girl.**

Girl, Conceited: See **Conceited girl.**

Girl, Extravagant: See **Extravagant girl.**

Girl, Glamour: See **Glamour girl.**

Girl, Intelligent: See **Intelligent girl.**

Girl, Modern: See **Modern girl.**

Girl, Old-fashioned: See **Old-fashioned girl.**

Girls: **1.** creatures who are fond of pretty clothes but are not wrapped up in them. **2.** creatures who can make up their faces more easily than their minds.

Girl, Smart: See **Smart girl.**

Girl, Sweater: See **Sweater girl.**

Girl, Working: See **Working girl.**

Gladiator: what the cannibal said after he dined on the lady explorer.

Glamour girl: 1. one who has what it takes to take what you have. **2.** one who may not be able to add but she sure can detract.

Glass, Cocktail: See **Cocktail glass.**

Glasses, Dark. See **Dark glasses.**

Glove: something you use to keep one hand warm while you look for the other.

Glutton: a man who eats dessert before the echo of his soup has stopped.

Goat: a lamb who has kidded himself into believing that he knows Wall Street.

Goblet: a small sailor full of beer.

God: the John Doe of philosophy and religion.

Go-getter: one who gets in behind you in a revolving door and comes out ahead of you.

Goggles, Aviator's: See **Aviator's goggles.**

Goldbrick: a clock-eyed person.

Golddigger: 1. a fund-loving girl. **2.** a girl who breaks dates by going out with them. **3.** a girl who forgets all about the past and the future and simply enjoys the present. **4.** a girl who will date any man that can pass the asset test. **5.** a girl with a gift for grab. **6.** a human gimme pig. **7.** a woman after all. **8.** a young woman who likes to go buy buy. **9.** a gal who doesn't mind whose means she lives beyond. **10.** a girl who defrauds the males by using them. **11.** a girl who mines her own business. **12.** a girl who loves a man for all she's worth for all he's worth.

Gold tooth: flash in the pan.

Golf: 1. a game in which a ball one and a half inches in diameter is placed on a ball 8000 miles in diameter, the object being to hit the small ball but not the large. **2.** a game that is played by a lot of men to keep from falling asleep in church on Sunday mornings. **3.** a game where the ball usually lies poorly and the player well. **4.** just a lot of walking broken up by disappointment and bad arithmetic. **5.** a game in which a man spends a lot of good time having a bad one. **6.** a game for gents too old for romance who still want to get into a trap. **7.** a form of work made expensive enough for rich men to enjoy. **8.** a game that has turned the cows out of the pasture and let the bull in. **9.** a long walk punctuated with disappointments. **10.** a game in which you drive hard to get to the green only to wind up in the hole. **11.** a game that begins with a golf ball and ends with a high ball. **12.** what men do to relax when they are too tired to mow the lawn.

Golf course, Public: See **Public golf course.**

Golfer: **1.** a guy who can walk several miles toting 25 pounds of equipment but who has Junior bring him an ash tray. **2.** a man who hits and tells. **3.** one who yells "fore," takes six, and puts down five.

Golfer, Civil War: See **Civil War golfer.**

Golf fairway: See **Fairway (golf).**

Good breeding: an expedient to make fools and wise men equal.

Good carpenter: one who can keep a straight face while repairing a do-it-yourself project.

Good citizen: one who behaves as if there were no laws.

Good diplomat: someone who can lose all the points and still win the game.

Good executive: **1.** one who never does anything that he can get anybody else to do for him. **2.** a man who isn't afraid to correct a mistake made by his secretary, no matter how pretty she is.

Good husband: **1.** one who feels in his pockets every time he passes a mail box. **2.** one who will wash up when asked and dry up when told.

Good line: the shortest distance between dates.

Good loser: a person who can stick to a reducing diet.

Good memory: one that can remember the day's blessings and forget the day's troubles.

Good neighbor: **1.** a fellow who smiles at you over the back fence, but doesn't climb it. **2.** one who doesn't borrow his garden hose back too often. **3.** one who gives you the benefit of the dirt. **4.** one who is less for getting and more for giving.

Good old days: **1.** what people fifty years hence will be calling the present time. **2.** when a juvenile delinquent was a kid who owed a few cents on an overdue library book. **3.** when a man looked for money in his pockets before having a suit cleaned. **4.** when a teen-ager went into the garage and came out with a lawn mower. **5.** when the prisoner, not the sentence, was suspended. **6.** when you got the landlord to fix anything by just threatening to move. **7.** when policemen didn't hide at the side of a busy road, but took their chances in traffic like anyone else. **8.** when inflation was just something you did to a balloon. **9.** when you rented a house instead of a mortgage.

Good secretary: one who can keep up with her boss when he's dictating and ahead of him when he's not.

Good speech: a beginning and a conclusion placed not too far apart.

Good sport: one who will always let you have your own way.

Good storyteller: a person who has a good memory and hopes other people haven't.

Good talker: one who learns to listen.

Good teacher: **1.** one who makes himself progressively unnecessary. **2.** someone who can understand those not good at explaining and explain it to those not good at understanding.

Good times: **1.** the period when you accumulate those debts that you're unable to pay in bad times. **2.** those in which people who have money contrive to get a little more.

Good traveler: a good traveler is one who does not know where he is going to; a perfect traveler does not know where he came from.

Good wife: one you can propose to on the front porch and then still love in the kitchen.

Goods, Durable: See **Durable goods.**

Gossip: **1.** a newscaster without a sponsor. **2.** anything that goes in one ear and over the back fence. **3.** a person who puts two and two together—whether they are or are not. **4.** a person who will never tell a lie if the truth will do as much damage. **5.** a person who syndicates his conversation. **6.** letting the chat out of the bag. **7.** conversation without thought. **8.** one who pumps to conclusion. **9.** one who takes people at deface value. **10.** one with a keen sense of rumor. **11.** peddling meddling. **12.** sharing deride. **13.** sociologists on a mean and petty scale. **14.** somebody who knows how to add to . . . and to. **15.** something negative that is developed and then enlarged. **16.** talling the story. **17.** the art of saying nothing in a way which leaves nothing unsaid. **18.** when one just can't leave bad enough alone. **19.** when someone puts two and two together and gets whee. **20.** strictly her-say. **21.** a person who gives you the benefit of the dirt. **22.** one who turns an earful into a mouthful. **23.** what no one claims to like but everyone enjoys. **24.** a free circulating library of lurid fiction. **25.** a woman who makes up in suspicion what she lacks in knowledge. **26.** a person who suffers from acute indiscretion. **27.** a person who creates the smoke in which other people assume there's fire. **28.** one who likes to chin and bear it. **29.** a vehicle of speech which runs down more people than an automobile.

Gossip, A true: See **True gossip.**

Gossip columnist: **1.** a guy who finds out things people don't want known, and tells them to others to whom it doesn't make any difference. **2.** one who keeps us posted on how the other half lives it up. **3.** the spies of life.

Gossip columnist, Successful: See **Successful gossip columnist.**

Gossip, Common: See **Common gossip.**

Gossip, Miserable: See **Miserable gossip.**

Gourmet: one who avoids unfashionable restaurants because he doesn't want to gain weight in the wrong places.

Governmental machinery: a marvelous labor-saving device which enables ten men to do the work of one.

Government bureau: where the taxpayer's shirt is kept.

Government official, High: See **High government official.**

Government, Representative: See **Representative government.**

Government, Stable: See **Stable government.**

Gown, Strapless: See **Strapless gown.**

Grade crossing: a place where headlights and light heads meet.

Graduate, College: See **College graduate.**

Graft: a system which ultimately results in compelling a large portion of the populace to apologize constantly for not having money and the remainder to explain how they got it.

Grandfather: a grandchild's press agent.

Grand jury: one that says "not guilty."

Grandmother: an old lady who keeps your mother from spanking you.

Grand opera: See **Opera.**

Grandparents: people who come to your house, spoil your children, and then go home.

Grapefruit: **1.** that to which there is more than meets the eye. **2.** a lemon that had a chance and took advantage of it.

Grass: the green stuff that wilts in the yard and flourishes in the garden.

Grasshopper: a bug that chews tobacco and camps out.

Grass widow: **1.** the angel a man loved, the human being he married, and the devil he divorced. **2.** the wife of a dead vegetarian.

Gratitude: **1.** an idiotic word; it is put in the dictionary, but it does not exist in the human heart where it belongs. **2.** a secret hope of greater favors. **3.** memory of the heart.

Great American: what speakers call a man when they can't think of anything specifically complimentary to say.

Great Dane: the kind of puppy that has the house broken before he is.

Great timesaver: love at first sight.

Greenhorn: the guy who arrived the day after you.

Green light: what a pedestrian uses to get half way across the street.

Gross ignorance: something that is 144 times worse than ordinary ignorance.

Grouch: a man who thinks that the world is against him—and it is.

Grouchy mother-in-law: no laughing mater.

Group medicine: where 25 relatives and friends pitch in with a cure apiece for the cold in your head.

Growing old: a process hard to do gracefully with modern furniture.

Growing pains: an affliction of middle-aged gardeners.

Gruesome: a little bit taller.

Grumbler, Chronic: See **Chronic grumbler.**

Guest: a person for whom you lay out a special towel, which both of you know won't be used.

Guest, Perfect: See **Perfect guest.**

Guest towel: a small square of non-absorbent fabric surrounded by waterproof embroidery.

Gum chewer's mouth: that which goes without saying.

H

Habit: **1.** a chattel mortgage on a man's individuality. **2.** a series of handcuffs closely locked to which the key has been lost.

Habits: **1.** cobwebs that become cables. **2.** trait jackets.

Hairbrush: cure for unruly heir.

Haircut, G.I.: See **G.I. haircut.**

Halfback: what you don't get when you lend your wife fifty cents.

Halter: something grooms get at the altar.

Handicap (golf): a device for "collective bargaining" on the first tee.

Hangover: **1.** something to occupy a head that wasn't used the night before. **2.** the moaning after the night before. **3.** a toot ache. **4.** when the brew of the night meets the cold of the day.

Hangover (champagne): the wrath of grapes.

Happiness: **1.** a delicate balance between what one is and what one has. **2.** a way station between too little and too much. **3.** good health and a poor memory. **4.** perfume you cannot pour on others without getting a few drops on yourself. **5.** that peculiar sensation you acquire when you are too busy to be miserable. **6.** the perpetual possession of being well deceived.

Happy marriage: **1.** a long conversation that always seems too short. **2.** one in which a man kisses his wife at the door when he leaves in the morning as well as when he returns in mid-afternoon. **3.** one that improves a woman's looks and a man's disposition.

Hard times: 1. when all we can pay is compliments. **2.** when hitchhikers are willing to go either way. **3.** a season during which it is very difficult to borrow money to buy things you don't need.

Hard work: an accumulation of easy things you didn't do when you should have.

Harp: a piano in the nude.

Has-been: one who lives on the reputation of his reputation.

Hash: enthusiastic food—the cook puts all she has into it.

Hat: **1.** a woman's clowning glory. **2.** something the average man covers his head with, the beggar passes around, the statesman throws into the ring, and the politician talks through.

Hate: **1.** a luxury no one can afford. **2.** Hell's gift to the primitive mind. **3.** the power of love misused.

Hatred: the coward's revenge for being intimidated.

Hatred, Class: See **Class hatred.**

Haunting tune: just a ghost of resemblance to the original.

Having: See **Play.**

Hay: grass à la mowed.

Head cold: a drip tease.

Health: the thing that makes you feel that now is the best time of the year.

Hearse: a handsome vehicle in which the man who has always been a tail-ender is finally permitted to lead the procession.

Heaven: the Coney Island of the Christian religion.

Heckler: a guy who ribs you the wrong way.

Heels, High: See **High heels.**

Heirloom: some old thing nobody liked well enough to wear out.

Helicopter: an egg beater with ambition.

Helpmate: a wife, or bitter half.

Hen: an egg's way of making another egg.

Henpecked husband: **1.** one who gives his wife the best ears of his life. **2.** one who holds his pay envelope up to the light to see if he got a raise.

Heredity: **1.** the bad traits a child gets from the other side of the family. **2.** when a teen-age boy winds up with his mother's big brown eyes and his father's long yellow convertible. **3.** an omnibus in which all our ancestors ride, and every now and then one of them puts his head out and embarrasses us. **4.** something you believe in when your child's report card is all A's.

Heroism: endurance for one moment more.

Hero, Movie: See **Movie hero.**

Hiccoughs: messages from departed spirits.

Hick: a person who looks both ways before crossing a one-way street.

Hicks: people who come to town at intervals to provide the gay night life of the city.

Hick town: **1.** one where, if you see a girl dining with a man old enough to be her father, he is. **2.** one where there is no place to go where you shouldn't be.

Hi-fi-fan: one who believes that clarity begins at home.

Highboy: a form of greeting.

Highbrow: **1.** a man who has found something more interesting than women. **2.** a person who has the patience to sit through something that would make him a lowbrow if he didn't. **3.** one who likes a thing so long as he's sure you don't like it too. **4.** one whose learning has outstripped his intelligence. **5.** the kind of person who looks at a sausage and thinks of Picasso. **6.** one who can quote from Shakespeare without attributing it to the Bible. **7.** a person who enjoys a thing until it becomes popular.

High fidelity: two drunks swearing eternal allegiance.

High government official: one who has imbibed too freely.

High heels: the invention of a woman who had been kissed on the forehead.

High noon: three martinis before lunch.

High school age: when boys notice that girls notice boys who notice girls.

Highway, Multi-million dollar: See **Multi-million dollar highway.**

Highway robbery: the price of new cars.

Hildegarde: just another name dropper.

Hire education: when an athlete is given financial inducements to attend a certain college.

Historian: a prophet looking backwards.

Historical novel: a fictitious tale covering up a stern reality.

History: **1.** an account mostly false, of events unimportant, which are brought about by rulers mostly knaves, and soldiers mostly fools. **2.** what enables each nation to use the other fellow's past record as an alibi.

History, American: See **American history.**

Hitching-post, Modern: See **Modern hitching-post.**

Hitler: the greatest seizer of them all.

Hobby: **1.** hard work you wouldn't do for a living. **2.** something you do to have fun whether you enjoy it or not. **3.** something you go nuts about to keep from going nuts about something else.

Hobo: **1.** a road's scholar. **2.** a migratory shirker.

Holding company: a thing where you hand an accomplice the goods while the policeman searches you.

Hole-in-one (golf): a stroke of genius.

Holiday: a day off followed by an off day.

Hollywood: **1.** a place where people from Iowa mistake each other for movie stars. **2.** a place where you live happily and get married forever afterward. **3.** the land of bilk and honey. **4.** where, if a guy's wife looks like a new woman, she probably is.

Hollywood aristocrat: anyone who can trace his ancestry back to his father.

Hollywood contact man: all con and no tact.

Hollywood divorce: one in which the wife is asking for custody of the money.

Hollywood gossip: something that goes in one ear—and out of the mouth.

Hollywood marriage: much "I do" about nothing.

Hollywood pal: someone who is always around when he needs you.

Hollywood wedding: one where you take each other for better or worse—but not for long.

Home: **1.** a place in which we are treated the best and grumble the most. **2.** a place where a man is free to say anything he pleases because no one pays any attention to him. **3.** there's no place like it if you haven't got the money to go out. **4.** where part of the family waits until the rest of them bring back the car. **5.** the place where the college student home for vacation isn't. **6.** the place where, when you have to go there, they have to take you in. **7.** a place where children should be helped to learn from their mistakes and not forced to suffer for them. **8.** a place where the great are small and the small are great. **9.** the place where most men go when they're tired of being nice to people. **10.** where a woman puts up with her husband. **11.** where you can scratch any place that itches.

Home cooking: **1.** what more women should be. **2.** something that most modern women are not. **3.** what a man misses when his wife isn't.

Home, Modern: See **Modern home.**

Home movies: the strange view people take of things.

Homeowner: a person who is always on his way to a hardware store.

Home town: where they wonder how you ever got as far as you did.

Homiletics: the study of sanctified salesmanship.

Honest: that which a man gets credit for being when he's merely doing business with folks that never give him a chance to be anything else.

Honest politician: one who when he is bought will stay bought.

Honesty: the fear of getting caught.

Honeymoon: **1.** a short period of doting between dating and debting. **2.** coo-existence. **3.** the period between "I do" and "You'd better." **4.** the thrill of a wifetime. **5.** the time during which the bride believes the bridegroom's word of honor. **6.** the vacation a man takes before starting to work for a new boss. **7.** the morning after the knot before.

Honeymoon sandwich: just lettuce alone.

Hope: **1.** a pathological belief in the occurrence of the impossible. **2.** unwinding a knotted string you suspect won't be long enough anyway.

Hors d'oeuvres: **1.** a ham sandwich cut into forty pieces. **2.** what you eat to appease the appetite while losing it.

Horse-and-buggy days: when you lived until you died and not until you were just run over.

Horsepower: 1. a power which has put the horse out of business. 2. something which was much safer when only the horses had it.

Horse sense: 1. a degree of wisdom that keeps one from betting on the races. 2. stable thinking coupled with the ability to say nay (neigh). 3. that inestimable quality in a horse that keeps it from betting on a man. 4. when a fellow knows enough to stay away from a nag.

Hose, Nylon: See **Nylon hose.**

Hospital: a place where they wake you up to give you a sleeping pill.

Hospitality: the virtue which induces us to feed and lodge certain persons who are not in need of food and lodging.

Hospital, Maternity: See **Maternity hospital.**

Hospital room: a place where friends of the patient go to talk to other friends of the patient.

Hospitals: places where people who are run down wind up.

Hot dog: the only animal that feeds the hand that bites it.

Hotel: 1. a place where you give up good dollars for bad quarters. 2. where you stay when you ain't got no cousins.

Hotel, Luxury: See **Luxury hotel.**

House, Dream: See **Dream house.**

House, Up-to-date: See **Up-to-date house.**

Housewarming: the last call for wedding presents.

Housework: something you do that nobody notices unless you don't do it.

Howling success: the baby that gets picked up.

Hug: 1. a roundabout way of expressing affection. 2. energy gone to waist.

Hula dancer: a shake in the grass.

Human being: 1. an ingenious assembly of portable plumbing. 2. a creature that can't get its toes in its mouth after babyhood, but can put its foot in anytime.

Human brain: like a freight car—guaranteed a certain capacity but always running empty.

Human nature: something that makes you swear at a pedestrian when you are driving and at the driver when you are a pedestrian.

Humidity, Relative: See **Relative humidity.**

Humiliation: an emotion caused by suddenly shrinking to one's normal proportions.

Humility: the ability to make a correct estimate of one's self.

Humor: **1.** emotional chaos remembered in tranquility. **2.** the kindly contemplation of the incongruities of life and the artistic expression thereof.

Humorist: **1.** a writer who shows us the faults of human nature in such a way that we recognize our failings and smile—and our neighbors' and laugh. **2.** a man who feels bad but who feels good about it. **3.** a fellow who realizes, first, that he is no better than anybody else, and second, that nobody else is either.

Humor, Sense of: See **Sense of humor.**

Hunch: what you call an idea that you're afraid is wrong.

Husband: **1.** a gay dog who is spousebroken. **2.** a man who exchanges a bushel of fun for a peck of trouble. **3.** a man who, if given enough rope, will be tied up at the office. **4.** a man who knows that his wife's reasoning is largely sound. **5.** a man who lost his liberty in the pursuit of happiness. **6.** an experienced domestic creature who can guess what his wife is going to say before she repeats it. **7.** a polygamous animal in a monogamous strait-jacket. **8.** one who lays down the law to his wife, and then accepts all her amendments. **9.** one who stands by you in troubles you wouldn't have had if you hadn't married him. **10.** one who thinks twice before saying nothing. **11.** the next thing to a wife. **12.** what's left of a sweetheart after the nerve has been killed. **13.** a domesticated animal capable of being skinned more than once. **14.** a bachelor whose luck finally failed him. **15.** a man who wishes he had as much fun when he is out as his wife thinks he does. **16.** a fellow who expects his wife to be perfect and to understand why he isn't. **17.** a fellow who co-stars at a wedding and from then onwards has a supporting role. **18.** a man who can wait all day for his dinner—but not five minutes more! **19.** a curious mammal who buys his football tickets in June and his wife's Christmas present on December 24. **20.** a bachelor who solicited directions. **21.** a fellow who winked back once too often. **22.** a fellow who believes that his wife's constant talking is just one of life's little earitations. **23.** a man whose playfulness cost him his freedom of speech. **24.** one who knows his wife is always cooking up something, but not necessarily on the stove. **25.** a man who firmly believes he can eat his breakfast, read his newspaper, listen to his wife talk and not miss anything important.

Husband, Average: See **Average husband.**

Husband, Bad: See **Bad husband.**

Husband, Good: See **Good husband.**

Husband, Henpecked: See **Henpecked husband.**

Husband, Model: See **Model husband.**

Husband, Most henpecked: See **Most henpecked husband.**

Husband, Music-minded: See **Music-minded husband.**

Husband, Perfect: See **Perfect husband.**

Husband, Wise: See **Wise husband.**

Hush hush business: baby sitting.

Hypochondria: a disease without a disease.

Hypochondriac: **1.** a person with infinite capacity for faking pains. **2.** one who can't leave well-enough alone. **3.** a person who wants to have his ache and treat it too. **4.** a man who is always on pills and needles. **5.** one who is happy being miserable.

Hypocrisy: the homage which vice pays to virtue.

Hypocrite: **1.** a man who sets good examples when he has an audience. **2.** one who pretends to be burying the hatchet when he's only digging up dirt. **3.** one who talks on principles and acts on interest. **4.** one who prays on his knees on Sundays and on his neighbors the remainder of the week. **5.** a man who hands his pay to his wife with a smile on his face. **6.** a person who preaches by the yard but practices by the inch.

I

Ice: one of the few things that is what it is cracked up to be.

Icicle: a great eaves-dropper.

Idea: the result of careful thought and experience, when you have it; when somebody else has it, it's a lucky hunch.

Idealism, American: See **American idealism.**

Idealist: 1. a person who helps other people to be prosperous. **2.** one who tries to keep politics out of politics. **3.** a man with a dreamlined brain.

Ideals: funny little things that don't work unless you do.

Ideal summer resort: a place where fish bite and mosquitoes don't.

Ideal wife: 1. any woman who has an ideal husband. **2.** one who knows when her husband wants to be forced to do something against his will. **3.** one who helps her husband with the dishes. **4.** one who remains faithful to you but tries to be just as charming as if she weren't.

Idleness: a condition which is most enjoyed when there is plenty of work to do.

Igloo: an icicle built for two.

Ignoramus: a guy who doesn't know the meaning of a word you first learned yesterday.

Ignorance: 1. when you don't know something and somebody finds it out. **2.** the basic cause of a lot of interesting arguments.

Ignorance, Gross: See **Gross ignorance.**

Illegal: a sick bird.

Illegibility: a doctor's prescription written with a post office pen in the rumble seat of a second-hand car.

Image, Corporate: See **Corporate image.**

Imagination: 1. something that sits up with a woman when her husband comes home late. **2.** what makes you think you're having a wonderful time when you're really only spending money.

Imitator: a man who succeeds in being an imitation.

Immorality: the morality of those who are having a better time.

Immortality: the genius to move others long after you yourself have stopped moving.

Impatience (a child's definition): waiting in a hurry.

Impossible: See **Difficult.**

Improbability: finding another tune you wanted on the other side of the record you've just bought.

Income: 1. in these days, something you cannot live without nor within. 2. the sum of money it costs more than to live.

Income tax: 1. a fine imposed for reckless thriving. 2. guaranteed annual rage.

Income tax collector: that infernal revenue man.

Income tax expert: someone whose fee is the amount he saves you in making out your tax return.

Income tax forms: blankety blanks.

Income tax return: something that if you make out honestly you go to the poorhouse; if you make it out dishonestly—you go to jail.

Incompatibility: when a husband loses his income and a wife her pat-ability.

Incongruous: where our laws are made and how they appear.

Inconvenience: only an adventure wrongly considered.

Indian summer: that period between World Series drawings and football pools.

Indigestion: the failure of a round stomach to adjust to a square meal.

Indignation, Moral: See **Moral indignation.**

Indignation, Righteous: See **Righteous indignation.**

Indispensable man: the motorist who whizzes past you just as you spot a motorcycle cop in the rear view mirror.

Infant prodigies: young people with highly imaginative parents.

Infatuation: the feeling a woman has for the hat she wants; love: the feeling a man has for the one he has.

Inflation: 1. a fate worse than debt. 2. a national headache caused by asset indigestion. 3. a period when two can live as steep as one. 4. a state of affairs where you never had it so good, or parted with it so fast. 5. just a drop in the buck. 6. the art of cutting a dollar bill in half without touching the paper. 7. when dollars to doughnuts becomes an even bet. 8. when nobody has enough money because everybody has too much. 9. being broke with a lot of money in your pocket. 10. too little for too many for too much. 11. when you take your money out in a shopping bag and bring home your purchases in your pocket. 12. when something that cost $10 new a few years ago, now costs $15 to repair. **13.** when you pay top prices for something from the bottom of the barrel. **14.** when, after you get the money to buy something, it isn't enough. **15.** something similar to looking at your life's savings through the wrong end of a telescope. **16.** when everybody is so rich that no one can afford anything. **17.** a financial typhoon that sweeps everything before it and leaves nothing behind. **18.** a cockeyed economic condition that makes the prices you get look good, and the prices you pay look awful. **19.** the only thing people are down on that's on the up and up.

Influence: something you think you have until you try to use it.

Informed source: See **Reliable source.**

Ingenuity: man's cleverness in getting out of spots his stupidity got him into.

Initiative: doing the right thing without being told.

Ink: fluid for thought.

In-law: something like an outlaw . . . only more so.

Innocent bystander: a person so simple-minded he doesn't know enough to get out of the way.

Insincerity: a method by which we can multiply our personalities.

Insomnia: **1.** a contagious disease often transmitted from babies to parents. **2.** what a person has when he lies awake all night for an hour. **3.** when you can't sleep, even on the job.

Insomniac: a guy who keeps sheep jumping over a fence all night just because he can't sleep.

Installment buying: **1.** a plan which enables you to enjoy new, modern household appliances while you're paying for the old ones. **2.** dolling up on dollar down.

Installment paying: a condition which makes the month shorter and the years longer.

Instinct: the faculty which tells a woman whether a man needs inducement or encouragement.

Instructor, Swimming: See **Swimming instructor.**

Insurance, Life: See **Life insurance.**

Insurance policy: what they give you on page one and then take away from you on page two.

Integrity: the thing that keeps you from looking ahead to see how the story ends.

Intellectual: **1.** a fellow who is willing to discuss the preceding night's television programs, but makes it clear he only happened to be watching because the children turned the set on. **2.** a man who hears the name of Monroe and thinks of the fifth president. **3.** someone who knows when to quote what some bright fellow once said. **4.** a person who is so smart that he can't understand the obvious.

Intellectual snob: a man who won't speak to a beautiful girl on a train because he doesn't approve of the book she's reading.

Intelligent conversationalist: one who nods his head in agreement while you're talking.

Intelligent girl: **1.** one who knows how to refuse a kiss without being deprived of it. **2.** one who knows less than the man with whom she happens to be talking at the moment.

Intelligent minority: a group which doesn't stay that way after it becomes a majority.

Interest, Public: See **Public interest.**

Interior decorator: a man who does things to your house he wouldn't dream of doing to his own.

Internal Revenue Service: the world's most successful mail order business.

Intoxication: to feel sophisticated and not to be able to pronounce it.

Intuition: **1.** suspicion in skirts. **2.** that which enables a woman to put two and two together and get your number. **3.** the ability women have to read between the lines on a blank page. **4.** the sixth sense that allows a woman five wrong guesses. **5.** the strange instinct that tells a woman she is right whether she is or not. **6.** woman's ability to read between men's lyings. **7.** a woman's ability to read between the lies. **8.** what enables a woman to size up a situation in a flash of misunderstanding. **9.** suspicion which turns out to be true. **10.** what enables a woman to contradict her husband before he says anything.

Invention: daughter of necessity.

Investment, Clever: See **Clever investment.**

Inveterate smoker: one who can shave without getting lather on his cigarette.

I.O.U.: a paper wait.

Irony: giving father a billfold for Christmas.

J

Jack: a thing that lifts a car and also keeps it going.

Jacket, Book: See **Book jacket.**

Jade: a semiprecious stone or a semiprecious woman.

Jailer: a man with a confining job.

Janitor: **1.** the only man who makes a quick clean-up in Wall Street and gets away with it. **2.** floor flusher.

Jaywalker: See also **Pedestrian** and **Joy rider. 1.** a person who bets two legs against four wheels and usually loses.

Jaywalker–Pedestrian: See **Pedestrian–Jaywalker.**

Jaywalking: a kind of exercise that brings on that run-down feeling.

Jealousy: **1.** the friendship one woman has for another. **2.** the theory that some other fellow has just as little taste. **3.** poison envy.

Jeep: **1.** a cocktail shaker with three speeds. **2.** a man's most nearly successful effort to produce a mechanical mule.

Jeopardy, Double: See **Double jeopardy.**

Jet age: breakfast in London, lunch in New York, dinner in San Francisco and baggage in Buenos Aires.

Jewelers: men who ought to keep abreast of the times and rent wedding rings.

Jilted: when the groom buys the bride the wedding gown, then gives her the slip.

Jockey, Disc: See **Disc jockey.**

Joint acount: an account where one person does the depositing and the other the withdrawing—usually husband and wife.

Joint checking account: a device to allow the wife to beat her husband to the draw.

Journalism: organized gossip.

Journalist: a person who works harder than any other lazy person in the world.

Joy of motherhood: what a woman experiences when all the kids are in bed.

Joy rider: one who is riding while we are walking; jay walker: one who is walking while we are riding.

Judge: 1. a law student who marks his own examination papers. 2. a lawyer who once knew a politician. 3. a man in a trying position.

Judge, Traffic: See **Traffic judge.**

Judgment: the switchman who shuttles most of our thoughts on a siding before they generate too much momentum on the main line.

Jukebox: a device for inflicting your musical taste on people who wouldn't give a plugged nickel for it.

Julep, Mint: See **Mint julep.**

June: 1. the month when unmarried girls like to be well-groomed. 2. the month when a girl gets a Lohengrin on her face.

Junk: something you keep ten years and then throw away two weeks before you need it.

Jury: 1. a body of twelve men selected to decide which of the contestants has the better lawyer. 2. a group of twelve people of average ignorance. 3. something that doesn't work right after it's been fixed.

Jury, Grand: See **Grand jury.**

Justice: 1. the insurance which we have on our lives and property; to which may be added, and obedience is the premium which we pay for it. 2. what we get when the decision is in our favor.

Juvenile delinquency. 1. modern term for what we did as kids. 2. the result of parents trying to train children without starting at the bottom. 3. when a youngster stops asking his parents where he came from and starts telling them where to go.

Juvenile delinquent: 1. a youngster who prefers vice to advice. 2. a minor who is a major problem. 3. a troubled boy whose parents are too poor to send him to a boarding school 3000 miles away when he gets into trouble.

Juvenile delinquents: **1.** other people's children. **2.** teen-agers who want what they want when they want it and won't wait to get it.

K

Keepsake: something given us by someone we've forgotten.

Kibitzer: a guy with an interferiority complex.

Kidnapping: the short snatches of rest a parent gets when baby sleeps.

Kindergarten teacher. a woman who makes little things in life count.

Kindness: **1.** something you can't give away since it always comes back. **2.** a language which the deaf can hear and the blind can read.

Kindred: fear that relatives are coming to stay.

Kiss: **1.** a contraction of the mouth due to an enlargement of the heart. **2.** a course of procedure, cunningly devised, for the mutual stoppage of speech at a moment when words are superfluous. **3.** a mutual interchange of salivary bacteria. **4.** an indescribable something that is of no value to anyone but is much prized by the right two. **5.** a noun, though often used as a conjunction it is never declined; it is more common than proper and is used in the plural and agrees with all genders. **6.** nothing divided by two; meaning persecution for the infant, ecstasy for the youth, fidelity for the middle-aged and homage for the old. **7.** the anatomical juxtaposition of two orbicularis oris muscles in a state of contraction. **8.** the shortest distance between two. **9.** two divided by nothing. **10.** what the child gets free, the young man steals and the old man buys. **11.** a pleasant reminder that two heads are better than one.

Kissing: a means of shortening single life.

Kitchen, Modern: See **Modern kitchen.**

Kleptomaniac: **1.** a person who suffers from fits of abstraction. **2.** one who helps himself because he can't help himself. **3.** a person who takes things lying down.

Kleptomaniac, Sick: See **Sick kleptomaniac.**

Knickerbockers: a long name for short pants.

Knitting: an occupation that gives women something to think about while talking.

Knocker: a fellow who gets caught on the losing side.

L

Labor: a group which in working for the five-day week looks longingly toward a five-day week end.

Ladies' sewing circle: where more husbands are darned than socks.

Lady: **1.** a woman who always remembers others, and never forgets herself. **2.** a woman who has enough willpower to resist a man's advances and enough wile power to block his retreat. **3.** a woman who makes it easy for a man to be a gentleman. **4.** one who never shows her underwear unintentionally.

Lady, Perfect: See **Perfect lady.**

Lady, Tarnished: See **Tarnished lady.**

Lame duck: a politician who is in the process of becoming a cooked goose.

Landed gentry: men who are either married or engaged.

Land, Foreign: See **Foreign land.**

Landlord: **1.** a man who often raises a tenant's rent when the tenant himself can't raise it. **2.** a man who would rather sleep than heat.

Laplander: a clumsy person in a bus.

Las Vegas: **1.** just wheels and wails. **2.** the land of the spree and the home of the knave. **3.** a place where you can lose your appetite at the table. **4.** where when you're dead your number isn't up. **5.** where the odds are you won't get even. **6.** where you get aces wild and faces riled.

Laughter: **1.** the sound you hear when you chase your hat down the street. **2.** the sensation of feeling good all over, and showing it principally in one spot.

Laundry: **1.** a business with clothes competition. **2.** a place where clothes are mangled.

Law: the kind of ban that men forget.

Law, Canon: See **Canon law**

Lawsuit: **1.** a machine which you go into as a pig and come out of as a sausage. **2.** generally a matter of expense and suspense. **3.** something which nobody likes to have and nobody likes to lose.

Lawyer: **1.** a fellow who is willing to go out and spend your last cent to prove he's right. **2.** a learned gentleman who rescues your estate from your enemies and keeps it himself. **3.** a man who induces two other men to strip for a fight, and then runs off with their clothes. **4.** a person who helps you get what's coming to him. **5.** he who is summoned when a felon needs a friend. **6.** one who protects us against robbery by taking away temptation. **7.** the only man in whom ignorance of the law is not punished. **8.** a man who hires out his words and anger.

Leader: an ordinary person with extraordinary determination.

Leadership: the art of getting somebody else to do something you want done because he wants to do it.

Learned fool: one who has read everything, and simply remembered it.

Lease: a written contract in which the big print giveth and the small print taketh away.

Lecture: **1.** an entertainment at which it costs but little to look intelligent. **2.** an occasion when you numb one end to benefit the other. **3.** a process by which the notes of the professor become the notes of the student, without passing through the minds of either.

Lecturer: one with his hand in your pocket, his tongue in your ear, and his faith in your patience.

Lecturers: traveling men who express themselves collect.

Legend: a lie that has attained the dignity of age.

Leisure: **1.** the two minutes' rest a man gets while his wife thinks up something for him to do. **2.** the time you spend on jobs you don't get paid for.

Leisure time: the finished product of greater efficiency.

Letter: a form of composition opening with an excuse for not opening sooner and closing with an excuse for not closing later.

Letters, Love: See **Love letters.**

Level-headed person: one who doesn't get dizzy from doing good turns.

Liar: **1.** one who tells an unpleasant truth. **2.** one with no partition between his imagination and his information. **3.** a man who won't lie to a woman and so has very little consideration for her feelings.

Liberal: **1.** a man who is willing to spend somebody else's money. **2.** a man with his mind open at both ends. **3.** one who has both feet firmly planted in the air.

Liberal–Conservative: liberal: a radical with a family; conservative: a liberal with grandchildren.

Liberty: **1.** consists in giving every one full right to mind every one else's business. **2.** preserved in some countries—canned in others. **3.** the privilege of being free from the things we don't like in order to be slaves of things we do like.

Liberty, Personal: See **Personal liberty.**

Library: a place where the dead live.

License, Marriage: See **Marriage license.**

License, Wedding: See **Wedding license.**

Lie: **1.** a very poor substitute for the truth but the only one discovered up to date. **2.** ever-present help in time of trouble. **3.** man's worst liability. **4.** something that fell from the truth in climbing towards it.

Lie (golf): position of a ball; also proclivity of a golfer.

Lieutenant commander: the wife of a lieutenant.

Life: **1.** a hospital in which every patient is possessed by a desire to change his bed. **2.** a predicament which precedes death. **3.** a span of time of which the first half is ruined by our parents and the second half by our children. **4.** living expensively to impress people who live expensively to impress us. **5.** made up of trials, appeals, reversals, but few convictions. **6.** school tablets; aspirin tablets; stone tablets. **7.** the struggle to keep one's earning capacity up to one's yearning capacity. **8.** what happens to us while we are making other plans. **9.** an everlasting struggle to keep money coming in and hair and teeth from coming out.

Life insurance: a contract that keeps you poor all your life so you can die rich.

Life, Married: See **Married life.**

Life, Mother's: See **Mother's life.**

Lighter, Cigarette: See **Cigarette lighter.**

Light, Green: See **Green light.**

Limousine: a car with a glass partition to shut out stupid remarks from the back seat.

Line, Zig-zag: See **Zig-zag line.**

Linguist: a man who masters every tongue but his wife's.

Lipstick: something which merely adds color and flavor to an old pastime.

Lisp: calling a spade a thpade.

Literary agent: someone to help you fight the Indians.

Literary critic: a person who finds meaning in literature that the author didn't know was there.

Literary movement: two authors who live in the same city and hate each other.

Literature: the orchestration of platitudes.

Literature, Current: See **Current literature.**

Literature, Escape: See **Escape literature.**

Loafer: **1.** a person who tries to make both weekends meet. **2.** one who continues to live even though he complains that he can't exist on the wages he turns down.

Lobbyist: a stowaway on the ship of state.

Lobster Newburg: a dish ordered at hotels by those who usually get beans at home.

Local bus: a device that makes mountains out of molehills.

Logic: an organized procedure for going wrong with confidence and certainty.

Logrolling: an aye for an aye.

Loneliness: a prison that can be opened only from inside.

Lorgnette: **1.** a dirty look you can hold in one hand. **2.** sneer on a spear.

Los Angeles: six suburbs in search of a city.

Loser, Good: See **Good loser.**

Lost weekend: the shortest distance between two pints.

Lounge, Cocktail: See **Cocktail lounge.**

Love: **1.** a conflict between reflexes and reflections. **2.** a form of insanity which makes a girl marry her boss and work for him for the rest of her life without salary. **3.** a form of self-government under a two party system. **4.** a lot of dame foolishness. **5.** a man's insane desire to become a woman's meal ticket. **6.** an insane desire on the part of a chump to pay a woman's board-bill for life. **7.** it may be blind but the neighbors are not. **8.** like a cigar—the brighter it burns, the quicker it's ashes. **9.** oceans of emotions surrounded by expanses of expenses. **10.** the delusion that one girl differs from another. **11.** the triumph of imagination over intelligence. **12.** the feeling that makes a woman make a man make a fool of himself. **13.** the only game which two can play and both win. **14.** a game which is never called off on account of darkness. **15.** the thing that enables a woman to sing while she mops up the floor after her husband has walked across it in his barn boots. **16.** a condition of mind at a time when the mind is out of condition. **17.** folly committed by two. **18.** the doorway through which the human soul passes from selfishness to service and from solitude to kinship with all mankind. **19.** an irresistible desire to be irresistibly desired. **20.** emotion in motion. **21.** a state of affairs when the imitation is always more expensive than the real thing. **22.** friendship set to music. **23.** two divided by nothing.

Love, First: See **First love.**

Love letters: jilt-edge securities.

Love, Puppy: See **Puppy love.**

Lover, Platonic: See **Platonic lover.**

Lovesick boy: one whose pretty girl is like a malady.

Love song: a caress set to music.

Lowbrow: a person who can't appreciate something he doesn't like.

Low neckline: something you can approve of and look down on at the same time.

Luck: **1.** the thing that draws us for jury duty, but never for the sweepstakes. **2.** what happens when effort and opportunity meet. **3.** good planning, carefully executed. **4.** what happens when preparation and opportunity meet. **5.** simply the difference between what we expect and what we get. **6.** what happens to a man who marries a girl who will help him with the dishes.

Luck, Bad: See **Bad luck.**

Luxury: 1. a necessity when it is found that you can make the down payment on it. **2.** any bare necessity—with the taxes added. **3.** anything a husband needs. **4.** something you do without until getting it, but by that time it has become a necessity.

Luxury hotel: a place where guests are welcomed with open palms.

Luxury resort: one where a waiter expects a 25-cent tip when he presents a 60-cent bill for serving a 35-cent bottle of beer.

M

Machine, Political: See **Political machine.**

Madam: one for whom the belles toil.

Mad money: the fee charged by a psychiatrist.

Magazine, Movie: See **Movie magazine.**

Majority: a large number of people who have gotten tired thinking for themselves and have decided to accept somebody else's opinion.

Malady: what a lot of music looks and sounds like on television.

Mal de mer: French for "You can't take it with you."

Male, Modern: See **Modern male.**

Man: 1. a creature of superior intelligence who elects creatures of inferior intelligence to govern him. **2.** a creature who is trying to make something for himself rather than something of himself. **3.** a creature whom God made little lower than angels and who has been getting lower ever since. **4.** a large irrational creature who is always looking for home atmosphere in a hotel and hotel service around a home. **5.** one who wishes he were as wise as he thinks his wife thinks he is. **6.** that wonderful creature which goes to the South Pole, climbs Mt. Everest, yearns to visit the moon, but is terrified by the idea of moving to the rear of the bus. **7.** a creature who has to argue down another man's opinion before he can believe in his own. **8.** an ingenious arrangement of portable plumbing.

Man, Indispensable: See **Indispensable man.**

Man, Married: See **Married man.**

Man, Minute: See **Minute man.**

Man, Modern: See **Modern man.**

Man, Patient: See **Patient man.**

Man, Perfect: See **Perfect man.**

Man, Poor: See **Poor man.**

Man, Rich: See **Rich man.**

Man, Second story: See **Second story man.**

Man, Self-made: See **Self-made man.**

Man, Smart: See **Smart man.**

Man, Successful: See **Successful man.**

Man, Well-informed: See **Well-informed man.**

Man, Wise: See **Wise man.**

Mandate: an appointment with the boy friend.

Manicurist: a girl who makes money hand over fist.

Manners: a contrivance of wise men to keep fools at a distance.

Manufacturer, Girdle: See **Girdle manufacturer.**

Manufacturing genius: a guy who makes a thing just strong enough to hold together until the last installment is paid.

Manuscript: something submitted in haste and returned at leisure.

Marriage: 1. a book in which the first chapter is written in poetry and the remaining chapters in prose. **2.** a ceremony in which rings are put on the finger of the lady and through the nose of the gentleman. **3.** a feast where the grace is sometimes better than the dinner. **4.** a hit-or-miss proposition—if you don't make a hit you remain a miss. **5.** a mutual partnership with the husband as the mute. **6.** an arrangement like the block booking of motion pictures, in which a number of less desirable features must be accepted in order to obtain one or two of major attraction. **7.** an institution that changes a woman from an attraction to a distraction. **8.** a process of finding out what sort of guy your wife would have preferred. **9.** a souvenir of love. **10.** a state where a woman is no longer hoping—just expecting. **11.** a woman's hair net tangled in a man's spectacles on top of the bedroom dresser. **12.** before it he talks and she listens; during the honeymoon she talks and he listens; later they both talk and the neighbors listen. **13.** one long conversation, chequered by disputes. **14.** the alliance of two people, one of whom never remembers birthdays and the other never forgets them. **15.** the difference between painting the town and painting the back porch. **16.** the first union to defy management. **17.** the miracle that transforms a kiss from a pleasure into a duty, and a life from a luxury into a necessity. **18.** the only known example of the happy meeting of the immovable object and the irresistible force. **19.** the only life sentence that is suspended by bad behavior. **20.** the state or condition of a community consisting of a master, a mistress, and two slaves, making, in all, two. **21.** when a woman turns an old rake into a lawn mower. **22.** all your money down and the rest of your life to pay. **23.** when a man gets hooked with his own line. **24.** a lottery in which everybody's trying to get even. **25.** the high sea for which no compass has yet been invented. **26.** an indissoluble contract in which one party obtains from the other more than either may ever hope to repay. **27.** a duet or a duel. **28.** a committee of two on ways and means, with authority to add to their number. **29.** a horrible public confession of a strictly private intention. **30.** a life sentence with partial remission for bad conduct. **31.** an institution in which a man loses his bachelor's degree and a woman gets her master's. **32.** a condition where two can live more cheaply than one wants to. **33.** love parsonified. **34.** a lottery in which men stake their liberty and women their happiness. **35.** a legalized method of suppressing freedom of speech. **36.** a dreamy waltz in three-quarter time until one or the other starts to two-time. **37.** where a man gives up privileges he never knew he had. **38.** an attempt to change a night owl into a homing pigeon. **39.** a romance in which the hero dies in the first chapter. **40.** fever in reverse: it starts with heat and ends with cold. **41.** a school in which the pupil learns too late.

Marriage ceremony: a treaty pledging two powers to coo-existence.

Marriage, Happy: See **Happy marriage.**

Marriage, Hollywood: See **Hollywood marriage.**

Marriage license: an I.O.U. for all the promises a man makes when he's courting.

Marriage, Model: See **Model marriage.**

Marriage, Modern: See **Modern marriage.**

Marriage proposal: a speech often made on the purr of the moment.

Marriage, Second: See **Second marriage.**

Marriage, Successful: See **Successful marriage.**

Marriage, Truly happy: See **Truly happy marriage.**

Married couple: 1. two minds without a single thought. **2.** two people who sit in the balcony at a movie because they want to smoke.

Married life: one undarned thing after another.

Married man: 1. a fellow who used to think that being lonesome was man's worst fate. **2.** a guy who drives with both hands. **3.** a bachelor who didn't notice when a girl closed the escape hatch. **4.** a guy who always turns off the motor when his wife calls: "I'll be right out."

Married man, Experienced: See **Experienced married man.**

Married woman: one who gives up the romantic attention of several men for the phlegmatic attention of just one.

Married woman, Contented: See **Contented married woman.**

Martini: an olive with an alcohol rub.

Martyrdom: 1. telling your wife the exact truth and then having her refuse to believe a word of it. **2.** the only way in which a man can become famous without ability.

Mason-Dixon line: a geographical division between "you all" and "youse guys."

Masseur: an expert on fats and figures.

Mass psychology: doing it the herd way.

Maternity dress: a space suit.

Maternity hospital: an heirport.

Maternity ward: the only place in the world where there isn't a chance of dodging the issue.

Mathematics, Modern: See **Modern mathematics.**

Matrimony: 1. a knot tied by a preacher and untied by a lawyer. **2.** an institution of learning in which a man loses his bachelor's degree without acquiring a master's. **3.** it isn't a word, it's a sentence. **4.** like making a call. You go to adore, you ring a belle, you give your name to a maid . . . and then you are taken in. **5.** something that the bachelor misses and the widower escapes. **6.** the only union which permits a woman to work unlimited overtime without extra pay. **7.** that process by which love ripens into vengeance.

Matrimony, Bonds of: See **Bonds of matrimony.**

Maturity: 1. the time of life when, if you had the time, you'd have the time of your life. **2.** the ability to remain equally unruffled when the elevator boy calls you "Pop" and the senior partner calls you "Son."

Maxim: a short rule of conduct made up by the rich to encourage the poor to keep on working.

Me: the objectionable case of I.

Mealtime: when youngsters sit down to continue eating.

Medicine: 1. inside dope. 2. the only profession that labors incessantly to destroy the reason for its own existence.

Medicine cabinet: a thing which looks like a drugstore only there are no sandwiches.

Medicine, Group: See **Group medicine.**

Medicine, Socialized: See **Socialized medicine.**

Meditation: thinking with a view of doing.

Meek: they inherit the earth and it's just as well—no one else would pay the inheritance taxes.

Meeting: 1. a mass mulling by master minds. **2.** something that happens because 30 days have elapsed since the last one.

Meeting, Committee: See **Committee meeting.**

Meetings: places where people go to learn how to do better the things they know how to do anyway, but don't have time to do, because of too many meetings.

Melancholy: the sovereign source of melancholy is repletion. Need and struggle are what excite and inspire us.

Memories: all you have left when the hangover is gone.

Memory: 1. the feeling that steals over one as he listens to a friend's original stories. **2.** what tells a man his wedding anniversary was yesterday. **3.** what enables you to call a man by a name that's vaguely like his. **4.** the power to gather roses in winter. **5.** what makes you wonder what you've forgotten to do. **6.** a storehouse of *old parts* from which one finds *new wholes.* **7.** what keeps telling you that you know the guy without giving you any idea of who he is. **8.** a nursery in which children who have grown old, play with their broken toys.

Memory, Bad: See **Bad memory.**

Memory expert: a woman who has once been told another woman's right age.

Memory, Good: See **Good memory.**

Men: **1.** often in the back yard looking for four-leaf clovers when opportunity knocks at the front door. **2.** some dislike women without any reason and others like them that way.

Menace: a fellow on the dance floor with a rhumba mind and a waltz technique.

Menace, Vacation: See **Vacation menace.**

Mermaid: not enough fish to fry and not enough woman to love.

Meteorologist: a man who can look into a girl's eyes and tell whether.

Meteorology: the science of being up in the air and all at sea.

Meter, Parking: See **Parking meter.**

Metronome: a very small man working on the Paris Underground Railway.

Microphone: some are metal discs and broadcast exactly what you say—others use rouge and lipstick and don't.

Middle age: **1.** a man who remembers when corn-cure ads showed only the toes. **2.** a time of life when our tripping becomes less light and more fantastic. **3.** a time of life when winking at a girl is closing one eye to reality. **4.** a time when you want to look fit as a fiddle, but bulge like a bass. **5.** that period in a man's life when he'd rather not have a good time than have to get over it. **6.** that period in life when you can't decide which there is more of—age or middle. **7.** that period when a man begins to shed his hair, his teeth, and his illusions. **8.** that period when a woman's life appears to be all bleaches and creams. **9.** that time in a man's life when the elasticity lost from his sinews seems to settle in his conscience. **10.** that time in life when we begin to develop scales resistance. **11.** that time of life when you're reduced to reducing. **12.** the time of life that affects us in the middle. **13.** the time of life when a man can get exhausted simply by wrestling with his conscience. **14.** the time when a man is always thinking in a week or two he will feel as good as ever. **15.** the time when you'll do anything to feel better, except give up what's hurting you. **16.** when a man says he is going to begin saving next month. **17.** when a man starts complaining that the cleaners are shrinking his suits. **18.** when a man stops wondering if he can escape temptations and begins to wonder if he's missing any. **19.** when a woman takes her high school annual out of the bookcase and hides it where the children can't find it. **20.** when greener grass is something that just has to be mowed more often. **21.** when many women consider mending their weighs. **22.** when the girl you smile at thinks you are one of her father's friends. **23.** when the girl you whistle at thinks you must be calling a dog. **24.** when you are sitting at home on Saturday night and the telephone rings and you hope it isn't for you. **25.** when you begin to exchange your emotions for symptoms. **26.** when you can do as much as before, but don't. **27.** when you don't care how long you stay out if you're home by 9:00 p.m. **28.** when you go all-out and end up all-in. **29.** when you laugh at pictures that you once prized. **30.** when you look forward to a dull evening. **31.** when you no longer care where your wife wants to go—so long as you don't have to go with her. **32.** when you're as young as ever, but it takes a lot more effort. **33.** when you're grounded for several days after flying high for one night. **34.** when you start eating what is good for you instead of what you like. **35.** when you step on a scale and the balance is no longer in your favor. **36.** when you still have the old spark but it takes more puffing. **37.** when you stop setting-up exercises and start setting over buttons. **38.** when you've met so many people that every new person you meet reminds you of someone else. **39.** when a woman's hair starts turning from gray to black. **40.** that time of life when, if you're not careful, you will attract wide-spread attention from your mirror. **41.** when you want to see how long your car will last instead of how fast it will go. **42.** when your memory is shorter, your experience longer, your stamina lower and your forehead higher. **43.** that point in life when you use all the wrinkles you can find to get rid of the old ones. **44.** when you feel on Saturday night the way you used to feel on Monday morning. **45.** when you're thin on top and not on the bottom. **46.** the time a man starts turning out the light for economical rather than romantic reasons. **47.** that difficult period between juvenile delinquency and senior citizenship when you have to take care of yourself. **48.** when each day makes you feel two days older. **49.** when the air is springy and you are not. **50.** what a person who is on the verge of being elderly thinks he is. **51.** that period in life when your children leave you one by one, only to return two by two. **52.** when you decide that you are thick and tired of it all. **55.** when a daily dozen is followed by several days of daily doesn't.

54. the time of life when your idea of getting ahead is to stay even. **55.** the time of life when the hardest thing to raise in your garden is your knees. **56.** youth gone to waist. **57.** when you start out with a spring in your step, and wind up with a fall in your arch. **58.** when you're old enough to know better, but young enough to keep on doing it. **59.** when you look both ways before crossing a one-way street. **60.** when you get less for your money every time you go to the barber. **61.** later than you think; sooner than you expected. **62.** that time in life when you wish there was some other way of starting the day than by getting up. **63.** when you are impressed not with the fact that the grass is greener on the other side of the fence but rather how difficult the fence looks to get over. **64.** when you'd rather pay the piper than dance. **65.** when you suspect young folks of doing what you yourself did in your youth. **66.** when it's safe for a woman to ask directions from a strange man. **67.** when you realize your get up and go has got up and gone. **68.** when you quit reading self-improvement books, figuring you'll be lucky just to hold your own the rest of the way. **69.** that 20-year gap in a man's life when he is too timid to wear a loud sports coat. **70.** the time in life when women won't admit their age and when men won't act theirs. **71.** when adults like to refer to one another as "boys and girls." **72.** when your narrow waist and broad mind begin to change places. **73.** when you have a choice between two temptations and choose the one that will get you home earlier. **74.** that stage in life when you get to the middle of the stairs and can't decide whether it will be more tiresome to go up than down.

Middleman: anyone who makes a profit before you do.

Military expert: one who tells you what's going to happen tomorrow—then tells you why it didn't.

Military science: that remarkable art in which the lessons learned in winning one war, if strictly followed, lose the next.

Milk: a liquid that has the decency to get sour when it's no longer fit to drink.

Millinery, Easter: See **Easter millinery.**

Millinery secret: one that should be kept under your hat.

Millionaire: **1.** a billionaire after he pays his taxes. **2.** a man who travels between his air-conditioned home and air-conditioned office in an air-conditioned car, then pays $50 to go over to the steam room at the club and sweat. **3.** a man with enough lettuce to choose his own tomatoes.

Mink: fur from money-bearing males.

Minority, Intelligent: See **Intelligent minority.**

Minor operation: one performed on someone else.

Minor sport: one in which the coach makes only slightly more than a full professor.

Mint julep: depth bomb with a southern drawl.

Minute man: one who can make it to refrigerator and back with a sandwich while the commercial is on.

Miracle: 1. an event described by those to whom it was told by men who did not see it. **2.** something that someone does that cannot be done.

Mirage: where the little man who wasn't there keeps his automobile.

Mirror: something some women will consult at any time except when pulling into a parking space.

Miser: 1. one who's perfectly content to let the rest of the world go buy. **2.** a person who gets his money the hoard way. **3.** a person who is always close but whom you cannot touch. **4.** a man who lives poor so that he can die rich. **5.** a dough nut. **6.** one who lives on doughnuts and coffee, so he can save enough money to have doughnuts and coffee for the rest of his life.

Miserable gossip: someone with no troubles to speak of.

Misogynist: a man who sent his picture to a lonely hearts club and got back the reply, "Our members are not that lonely."

Misstep: something that usually starts with a little trip.

Mistake: proof that somebody tried anyhow.

Mixed company: what you are in when you think of a story you can't tell there.

Mixed emotions: to see your mother-in-law go over the cliff in your brand new Cadillac.

Mixed greens: an assortment of fives, tens and twenties.

Model: lassie with a classy chassis.

Model, Artist's: See **Artist's model.**

Model husband: one who thinks his wife's headache is as important as his own rheumatism.

Model marriage: **1.** one where the husband is honest and tells the truth and his wife is tactful and believes him. **2.** one in which the wife is a treasure and the husband a treasury.

Moderate: a man who makes enemies left and right.

Modern age: **1.** when girls wear less on the street than their grandmothers did in bed. **2.** one which is proud of machines that think, and suspicious of any man who tries to.

Modern apartment building: one in which both the landlord and the tenant are always trying to raise the rent.

Modern art: oodles of doodles.

Modern child: one who, on hearing the story of Cinderella for the first time asks, "when the pumpkin turns into a golden coach, is that regarded as straight income or capital gain?"

Modern composer: one who takes something composed by the old masters and decomposes it.

Modern country: one which can ban fireworks and produce H-bombs.

Modern employer: one who is looking for men between the ages of 25 and 30 with 40 years' experience.

Modern executive: a man who talks golf around the office all morning and business around the golf course all afternoon.

Modern girl: **1.** one who believes in marrying a man to find out if she can live without him. **2.** one who'd rather be well formed than well informed. **3.** one who sticks to the spinning wheel—until her chips give out. **4.** one who refuses to study history on the grounds that there is no future in it.

Modern hitching-post: the third finger of a girl's left hand.

Modern home: **1.** one in which a switch regulates everything but the children. **2.** where the dwellers would speedily become bored, idle, cold, hungry, dirty, and unkempt if the electric current were cut off. **3.** one that has half as much room for twice as much money.

Modern kitchen: one where the pot calls the kettle chartreuse.

Modern living: a senseless whirl that has been spelled in three words —hurry, worry, bury.

Modern male: one who will stand for anything but a woman on a streetcar.

Modern man: one who drives a mortgaged car over a bond-financed highway on credit-card gas.

Modern marriage: to love, honor, and have children that disobey.

Modern mathematics: the number of blasts that come from auto horns in a traffic jam is equal to the sum of the squares at the wheels.

Modern mother: one who worries if her daughter gets in too early.

Modern music: the kind that is played so fast you can't tell what classical composer it was stolen from.

Modern parent: one who puts the cat out at night by shutting off the hi-fi.

Modern party: one where there's always rum for one more.

Modern people: a word used to describe something that has no other meaning.

Modern pioneer: the mother who manages to get through a rainy Saturday with the television set out of order.

Modern plays: most of them have to be sin to be appreciated.

Modern: people who meet a crisis face to face, after taking a pill.

Modern sculptor: a man who can take a rough block of stone or wood, work on it for months, and make it look like a rough block of stone or wood.

Modern thrift: when we take care of the down payments and let the installments take care of themselves.

Modern wife: one who knows what her husband's favorite dishes are and the restaurants that serve them.

Modern wisdom: an open mind and a closed mouth.

Modern woman: one who shows the world the stuff she's made of.

Modesty: **1.** the art of encouraging people to find out for themselves how important you are. **2.** the art of imperfectly concealing your talents. **3.** the feeling that others will surely discover in a little while just how wonderful you are. **4.** the gentle art of enhancing your charm by pretending not to be aware of it. **5.** our studied efforts to conceal from others how wonderful we are.

Monday: in Christian countries, the day after the baseball game.

Money: 1. the mint makes it first and it's up to us to make it last. **2.** something that things run into and people run out of. **3.** something that brushes by you on its way to the income tax people. **4.** a commodity that won't buy everything, but which keeps one from being more than moderately sullen and suppressed.

Money-grabber: anybody who grabs more money than you can grab.

Money, Mad: See **Mad money.**

Money, Pin: See **Pin money.**

Money, Tainted: See **Tainted money.**

Monologue: 1. a conversation between a husband and his wife. **2.** a conversation between a traffic cop and an automobile driver.

Monopolist: a guy who keeps an elbow on each arm of his theatre chair.

Monsoon: a typhoon that's going steady with a tornado.

Moon: a heaveny body which sways the tide, and the untied too.

Moose: an animal that has a head and horns on one end and a living-room wall on the other.

Morale: a condition where your hands and feet keep on working when your head says it just can't be done.

Moral indignation: jealousy with a halo.

Morality: the attitude we adopt towards people whom we personally dislike.

Moratorium: 1. that which results when an implacable creditor meets an unpayable debt. **2.** just the highbrow way of admitting that there doesn't seem to be any blood in the turnip.

Morning after: when getting up gets you down.

Moron: 1. something which in the wintertime girls wouldn't have so many colds if they put. **2.** one who wrinkles his brow while reading the comics. **3.** anyone who doesn't laugh at your jokes; also one who does.

Mortgage: a house with a guilty conscience.

Mosquito: **1.** a small insect designed by God to make us think better of flies. **2.** the original skin diver. **3.** one of the few really indestructible objects in this world.

Most henpecked husband: one whose wife makes him wash and iron his own aprons.

Moth: **1.** a perverse creature that spends the summer in a fur coat and the winter in a bathing suit. **2.** an insect that eats modern bathing suits in one gulp.

Mother: **1.** a woman who runs a temperature of 103 every time her child's temperature hits 101. **2.** a person who sees that there are only four pieces of pie for five persons and promptly remarks that she's never cared for pie.

Motherhood: the thrill of a wife-time.

Motherhood, Joy of: See **Joy of motherhood.**

Mother-in-law: **1.** a referee with an interest in one of the fighters. **2.** a talkie that has come to stay. **3.** a woman who is never outspoken.

Mother-in-law, Grouchy: See **Grouchy mother-in-law.**

Mother-in-law sandwich: Cold shoulder and tongue.

Mother, Modern: See **Modern mother.**

Mother's life: one darned stocking after the other.

Motion, Perpetual: See **Perpetual motion.**

Motion-picture preview: a place where four or five men, each making $5000 or $6000 a week, go to watch an adolescent kid write "It smells" on a card.

Motorist: **1.** a person who, after seeing a wreck, drives carefully for several blocks. **2.** a person who forgets that he used to be a pedestrian. **3.** a traveler with a heavy sun tan on the left arm.

Motorists: people in such a hurry to get into the next county that they often get into the next world.

Motorist, Woman: See **Woman motorist.**

Mouth: the grocer's friend, the orator's pride, the fool's trap, the dentist's salvation.

Mouth, Gum chewer's: See **Gum chewer's mouth.**

Movement, Literary: See **Literary movement.**

Movie actor's salary: the haul of fame.

Movie hero: 1. one who sits through the average double bill. **2.** the guy who can pick out a seat and ignore the usher.

Movie magazine: a periodical filled with idol gossip.

Movies, Home: See **Home movies.**

Mugwump: 1. a man who sits on a fence with his mug on one side and his wump on the other. **2.** a person educated beyond his intellect.

Mule: 1. an animal that is stubbornly backward about going forward. **2.** an animal who boasts that his ancestors were horses.

Multi-million dollar highway: a ribbon of concrete that can be snarled up in two minutes by a stalled $100 jalopy in a quarter-inch snow storm.

Mummy: an Egyptian who was pressed for time.

Music: the only language in which you cannot say a mean or sarcastic thing.

Music, Accordion: See **Accordion music.**

Musical comedy: where all good jokes go just before they die.

Music, Classical: See **Classical music.**

Musician, True: See **True musician.**

Music-minded husband: one who goes out fit as a fiddle and comes home tight as a drum.

Music, Modern: See **Modern music.**

N

Nag: a woman with no horse sense.

Nagging: the repetition of unpalatable truths.

Nagging woman: one who keeps a swivel tongue in her head.

Napkin, Paper: See **Paper napkin.**

Nation, Backward: See **Backward nation.**

Nation, Civilized: See **Civilized nation.**

National air, Our: See **Our national air.**

Nature, Human: See **Human nature.**

Necessity: almost any luxury you see in the home of a neighbor.

Neck: something which if you don't stick out you won't get in trouble up to.

Neckline, Low: See **Low neckline.**

Necktie, Gift: See **Gift necktie.**

Needle: formerly hard to find in a haystack; now hard to find in a woman's hand.

Neighbor: 1. one whom we are commanded to love as ourselves, and who does all he can to make us disobedient. **2.** a person who is always doing something you can't afford. **3.** a person who likes to borrow your equipment and to lend you his troubles.

Neighbor, Extravagant: See **Extravagant neighbor.**

Neighbor, Good: See **Good neighbor.**

Nepotism: putting on heirs.

Nerve: that which enables a man seated on a bus to flirt with a woman who is standing.

Nervousness: when you feel in a hurry all over and can't get started.

Network: a pattern, reticulated and decussated at equal intervals with interstices between the intersections.

Neurotic: 1. a person who has discovered the secret of perpetual emotion. **2.** a person who, when you ask how she is, tells you. **3.** a woman who calls a doctor when all she wants is an audience. **4.** one who believes the world owes him a loving. **5.** a person who can't leave being well-enough alone. **6.** a person just like you, except that he worries about it. **7.** a person who worries about things that didn't happen in the past—instead of worrying about something that won't happen in the future, like normal people.

New baby: an event similar to an opera—full of grand marches and loud cries for the author every night.

New hair-do: a way to get your husband to appreciate the old one.

News: the same thing happening today that happened yesterday, but to different people.

News commentator, Over-optimistic: See **Over-optimistic news commentator.**

Newspaper: **1.** a circulating library with high blood pressure. **2.** a portable screen behind which man hides from the woman who is standing up in a streetcar. **3.** a publication that condemns gambling on the editorial page and prints racing tips on the sports page.

New Year resolution: something that proves most of our weaknesses are too strong for us.

New Yorker: one who gets acquainted with his neighbor by meeting him down in Florida.

Night club: **1.** a place where the tables are reserved and the guests are not. **2.** a place where they get away with murder and you face the charges. **3.** a place where they take the rest out of restaurant and put the din in dinner.

Night clubs: where people with nothing to remember go to forget.

Nitrate: a special price after six o'clock.

No-account: the man without a bank account.

Nonchalance: the ability to look like an owl when you have behaved like an ass.

Non-churchgoer: a Seven Day Absentist.

Non-conformist: a person who keeps gloves in the glove compartment.

Nostalgia: **1.** longing for the place you wouldn't move back to. **2.** a long, lingering regret that things were never what they used to be. **3.** laughing over a beating you got sixty years ago.

Notes, Research: See **Research notes.**

Novel, Historical: See **Historical novel.**

Nudism: **1.** a back to the form movement. **2.** a person who goes coatless and vestless, and wears trousers to match. **3.** one suffering from clothestrophobia. **4.** the only person with less pocket space than a sailor.

Nudists: folks who grin and bare it.

Nuisance: the right person in the wrong place.

Nurse, Practical: See **Practical nurse.**

Nurse, Private: See **Private nurse.**

Nursery: bawlroom.

Nursery school: where small children go to catch colds from each other so they can stay home.

Nylon hose: sheer today and gone tomorrow.

O

Oats: a grain, which in England is generally given to horses, but in Scotland supports the people.

Obesity: a surplus gone to waist.

Oboe: an ill wood-wind which nobody blows good.

Obstacles: those frightful things you see when you take your eyes off the goal.

Obstinacy: the strength of the weak.

Ocean: huge body of water surrounded entirely by rumors of everlasting peace.

Ocean voyage: when days are both gorgeous and disgorgeous.

Octogenarian: a man who is old enough to know better, but too old to care.

Off-day: the day after a day off.

Office, Doctor's: See **Doctor's office.**

Office drinking fountain: old faceful.

Official, High government: See **High government official.**

Old age: **1.** when you find yourself using one bend-over to pick up two things. **2.** when all girls look good to you. **3.** when one gives up any idea of making home runs and is happy not to be struck out. **4.** when you pay more attention to pampering your wild corns than to sowing your wild oats. **5.** the time when men pay more attention to their food than they do to the waitresses. **6.** when you do more and more for the last time and less and less for the first time. **7.** that time of life when a man flirts with girls but can't remember why.

Old college classmate: someone who's gotten so bald and fat that he sees you at a class reunion and doesn't recognize you.

Old-fashioned girl: 1. one who has never been kissed—and admits it. **2.** one who says, "I don't intend to be married till I'm thirty," while her modern sister says, "I don't intend to be thirty until I'm married." **3.** one who removes the cigarette from her mouth before putting her nightie on over her head.

Old-fashioned town: one that's lighted by electricity only during a thunderstorm.

Old maid: 1. a debutante who overdid it. **2.** a girl who has been looked over and then overlooked. **3.** a girl who knows all the answers but is never asked the questions. **4.** a girl who regrets she had so much sense when she was young. **5.** a girl who spends too much time chinning and not enough time necking. **6.** a "yes" girl who never had a chance to talk. **7.** slipping beauty. **8.** a woman in the prim of life. **9.** a singular being.

Oldster: one who remembers when child guidance was something parents were expected to administer, not submit to.

Old-timer: 1. a fellow who remembers when rockets were just part of a fireworks celebration. **2.** a man who can remember when a careless driver, out with his girl, let the horse stop to graze. **3.** a man whose summer vacation was one day at the county fair. **4.** a man who turned out the gas while courting, instead of stepping on it. **5.** a person who can remember when he could remember. **6.** a real old-timer can remember when Sunday drivers let off steam by shaking their buggy whips at each other. **7.** one who can recall when a bureau was a piece of furniture. **8.** one who can recall when a shoemaker stuck to his last and wives stuck to their first. **9.** one who can remember when callers rang the doorbell instead of blowing the horn. **10.** one who can remember when folks sat down at the dinner table and counted their blessings instead of calories. **11.** one who can remember when grand-pap wore his suspenders the way modern gals wear a one-strap evening dress. **12.** one who can remember when the woman he left behind stayed there. **13.** one who can remember when there were not deductions in his pay until he got home. **14.** one who can remember when there were no gags beginning "An old-timer is one who can remember . . ." **15.** one who can remember when women had no figure to speak of. **16.** one who can remember when you couldn't eat a dollar's worth at a cafeteria. **17.** one who has never been able to figure out why women still take as much time to dress as they did when they wore clothes. **18.** one who remembers when a baby sitter was called a mother. **19.** one who remembers when a child had more brothers and sisters than fathers. **20.** one who remembers a housewife putting food into cans, instead of taking it out. **21.** one who remembers when a dishwashing machine had to be married, not bought. **22.** one who remembers when a man did his own withholding on his take-home pay. **23.** one who remembers when charity was a virtue and not an organization. **24.** one who remembers when dancing was done with the feet. **25.** one who remembers when he could buy a pound of steak for a dime, but forgets he had to work an hour to earn the dime. **26.** one who remembers when, if a woman told how many quarts and pints she had on the shelf, she meant canned fruit. **27.** one who remembers when it cost more to run a car than to park it. **28.** one who remembers when marriage problems were solved, not dissolved. **29.** one who remembers when modern meant being up to the minute, instead of years and years ahead. **30.** one who remembers when only fighting men died with their boots on. **31.** one who remembers when people were more intelligent than machines. **32.** one who remembers when people who wore blue jeans worked. **33.** one who remembers when the medicine man used to come to town on a wagon instead of a television signal. **34.** one who remembers when the only people who paid income taxes were those who could afford to. **35.** one who remembers when the only problem about parking was to get the girl to agree to it. **36.** one who remembers when we just laughed at the fellow who thought he was going to set the world on fire. **37.** you're an old-timer if you can remember when any man who washed dishes worked in a restaurant. **38.** one who didn't know a poor fish was one who had no big fins on his car. **39.** one who remembers when there was a faster way of throwing money down the drain than by calling a plumber. **40.** a person who remembers when a sensational novel contained asterisks. **41.** a person who can remember when the only dirty books in a library were the dusty ones. **42.** one who remembers when a girl didn't care whether a spinning wheel had whitewall tires or not. **43.** one who remembers when parents cut switches instead of rugs. **44.** a man who can remember when you saw less of a woman on the beach than you see on the street today. **45.** a person who remembers when your coffee breaks came with your meals. **46.** a fellow who has made the last payment on his house. **47.** one who remembers when the telephone was a convenience. **48.** one who remembers when the moon inspired only romance instead of space travel. **49.** one who can remember when a man could tell a risqué story in mixed company without boring the ladies present. **50.** one who remembers when a kid who got a licking at school was in for another when he got home. **51.** one who remembers when the best music heard on radio wasn't in the commercials. **52.** one who remembers when eight-forty was the time the play started, not the price of the ticket. **53.** one who can recall when the law suspended crooks instead of sentences. **54.** one who remembers when movie serials and breakfast cereals both were silent. **55.** one who remembers when the only skin diver was a mosquito. **56.** a man who lived in an era when the day was done before he was. **57.** one who remembers when a fellow who blew his horn was a braggart, instead of a Sunday driver. **58.** one who remembers when the papers talked about millions for defense. **59.** a fellow who can remember when an automobile salesman said "500," he was referring to price, not horsepower. **60.** one remembers when you could promise a child the moon without having to buy him a space suit. **61.** one who can remember when an allergy was just an itch and all you did was scratch it. **62.** one who can remember when virtue was a virtue and not a vice. **63.** one who can remember when a child who misbehaved to get attention—got it. **64.** one who can remember when a woman didn't have to be old to be middle-aged. **65.** one who can recall when a fellow wasn't considered a good driver just because he hadn't killed anybody. **66.** one who remembers when the national income was smaller than the present federal budget. **67.** one who can remember when the "5 and 10 cent" store meant just that. **68.** one who can remember when a baseball game was called on account of darkness. **69.** one who can remember when church collection plates got most of the money golf courses now get on Sundays. **70.** one who can remember when people worried about dying broke instead of living that way. **71.** one who can remember when a businessman spent his time trying to corner the market instead of his secretary. **72.** one who recalls when radio activity was mostly static. **73.** one who can remember when a fellow wondered where his next dollar was coming from instead of where it had gone. **74.** one who can remember when a girl married a man for his money instead of divorcing him for it. **75.** one who remembers when you didn't add another room on the house until you had three more children. **76.** one who remembers when a woman who had equal rights didn't think she was underprivileged. **77.** one who can remember when "setting the world afire" was merely a figure of speech. **78.** one who remembers when only small boys feared consequences when they smoked cigarettes. **79.** one who remembers when time was marching on instead of running out. **80.** one who remembers when the sky was the limit. **81.** one who can remember when parents worried about an adolescent's interest in the corset section of a mail order catalog. **82.** one who can remember when a do-it-yourself kit consisted of a pair of hands. **83.** one who can remember when the word "fallout" was only a barber's expression. **84.** a person who can remember when a job was the first thing you went steady with. **85.** one who can remember when a woman looked the same after washing her face. **86.** one who can recall when a wife would rather boil her husband's shirt than cook his goose. **87.** a guy who remembers when "tight money" was something you saved to get drunk on. **88.** one who remembers when only Italians ate pizza. **89.** one who remembers when dad gave you a quarter to go to the movie, for popcorn, and told you to stop on your way home and pick up a loaf of bread and to bring back the change. **90.** one whose income tax is higher than his salary used to be. **91.** one who can remember when a charger was something a man rode instead of married. **92.** one who remembers when a juvenile delinquent was a youngster who owed a few cents on an overdue library book. **93.** one who remembers when the housewife had to haul the wash water from the well—but she didn't have to sit up nights figuring out how to meet the payments on the bucket. **94.** one who can recall when it was the crook who was hung instead of the jury. **95.** one who remembers when the wonder drugs of the day were castor oil and camphor. **96.** one who remembers the assurance that relief measures would be abandoned when prosperity returned. **97.** one who can remember when a woman who touched up her hair had neighbors whose comments were enough to curl it. **98.** one who remembers when the midnight oil was burned in lamps instead of transmissions. **99.** one who remembers when "on time" meant being punctual rather than an accepted way of making a purchase. **100.** one who can recall when wives rocked the cradle instead of the boat. **101.** one who remembers when the law was quoted "according to Blackstone" instead of according to Perry Mason. **102.** a man who used to save up instead of paying down. **103.** one who can remember when there were other hand-me-downs for the children beside money. **104.** one who can remember when a man in public life could safeguard his privacy by being elected vice-president. **105.** one who can remember when Russia was known for its caviar instead of its bull. **106.** one who remembers when all a boy needed to take pictures was a camera. **107.** a man who can remember when both panhandlers and restaurant owners only asked a nickel for a cup of coffee. **108.** one who remembers when it was printed like this: D—n. **109.** one who remembers when fathers got out of school before their children started. **110.** one who is clad in overshoes and furs from head to foot and claims we don't get severely cold winters like we did years ago.

Oleomargarine: the food of people who haven't seen butter days.

Open mind: **1.** a mind in which convictions go out as fast as they come in. **2.** one that is too porous to hold a conviction.

Opera: where a guy gets stabbed in the back and instead of bleeding he sings.

Opera, Soap: See **Soap opera.**

Operation: a surgical job taking minutes to do and years to describe.

Operation, Minor: See **Minor operation.**

Opinionated people: little rotund islands of complacency anchored in a sea of prejudice.

Opinion, Public: See **Public opinion.**

Opinions, Concrete: See **Concrete opinions.**

Opportunism: the ability to park on the other fellow's nickel.

Opportunist: 1. a person who, finding himself in hot water, decides he needs a bath anyway. **2.** one who meets the wolf at the door and appears the next day in a fur coat. **3.** a manufacturer who, knowing the world is going to the dogs, starts a dog food factory. **4.** the man that makes hay of the grass you let grow under your feet. **5.** a girl who, after eloping by using knotted sheets, remembers to take the sheets with her. **6.** a man who listens carefully to what you say you'd like to do, then does it himself. **7.** one who sees his duty and gets someone else to perform it. **8.** a guy who is always able to land on somebody else's feat. **9.** the chap who keeps up with the Joneses by selling them new cars.

Opportunity: 1. a favorable occasion for grasping a disappointment. **2.** that which, if you have not thought out what it means, you cannot recognize when it comes. **3.** something a fool waits for but a wise man runs down the road to meet.

Optimism: 1. a cheerful frame of mind that enables a tea kettle to sing though in hot water up to its nose. **2.** the noble temptation to see too much in everything. **3.** waiting for a ship to come in when you haven't sent one out. **4.** the digitalis of failure.

Optimist: 1. a fellow who believes a housefly is looking for a way to get out. **2.** a fellow who goes into a hotel without baggage and asks to have his check cashed. **3.** a fellow who is always talking about what a fool he used to be. **4.** a girl who mistakes a bulge for a curve. **5.** a guy who starts putting on his shoes when the speaker says, "And now, in conclusion . . ." **6.** a happychondriac. **7.** a hope addict. **8.** a man who is just starting to shovel out a long driveway; Pessimist: one who has been working at it for five minutes. **9.** a man who marries his secretary—thinking he'll continue to dictate to her. **10.** a man who thinks a woman in a phone booth will be right out when he hears her starting to say good-by. **11.** a man who thinks his wife has stopped smoking cigarettes when he finds cigar butts around the house. **12.** a man who, while waiting for a woman, keeps his motor running. **13.** a middle-aged man who believes that the cleaners have been shrinking the waistband of his pants. **14.** a person who puts a 3¢ stamp on a letter and marks it "rush." **15.** a single man contemplating marriage; Pessimist: a married man contemplating it. **16.** a woman who leaves the dinner dishes because she will feel more like washing them in the morning. **17.** one who already has his bad breaks relined. **18.** one who calls a spade two spades. **19.** one who doesn't care what happens—so long as it doesn't happen to him. **20.** one who makes the best of conditions, after making the conditions the best possible. **21.** one who says his glass is half-full, while the pessisimist says his is half-empty. **22.** one who thinks humorists will some day run out of definitions of an optimist. **23.** someone who tells you to cheer up when things are going his way. **24.** someone who thinks he has a new definition of one. **25.** the man who thinks his wife has given up when she has given in. **26.** the sort of man who marries his sister's best friend. **27.** someone who thinks that love is a game of chance. **28.** a person who drops a quarter in the collection plate and expects a $5 sermon. **29.** a man who believes his wife won't buy a new hat, just because she doesn't see one she likes. **30.** a man who does the best he can under all circumstances. **31.** a proponent of the theory that black is white. **32.** a father who is willing to let his teen-age son take the brand new car on a date; Pessimist: one who isn't; Cynic: one who did. **33.** a man who, instead of feeling sorry he can't pay his bills, is glad he isn't your creditor. **34.** a fellow who takes the cold water thrown on his ideas, heats it with enthusiasm, makes steam, and pushes ahead. **35.** a guy who can always see the bright side of other people's troubles. **36.** a man who thinks that when his shoes wear out he will be back on his feet. **37.** a grown-up man who decides to take up ice-skating again, with a bottle on his hip. **38.** a ninety-year-old man who is getting married and wants to buy a home near a school. **39.** one who thinks that betting on horses is gambling. **40.** a bridegroom who thinks he has no bad habits. **41.** a fellow who realizes right now that some day these will be the good old days. **42.** the fellow who waits for his ship to come in—when he hasn't sent one out. **43.** a man who sees a light that is not there; a pessimist is the fool who tries to blow it out. **44.** one who believes everything he reads on the jacket of a new book. **45.** a guy who buys a lifetime pen and expects it to last at least a month. **46.** a fellow who looks for a room to rent with a trombone under his arm. **47.** one who thinks that peace comes when a war ends. **48.** a person who saves the pictures in the seed catalog to compare them with the flowers he grows. **49.** a man who thinks he can build a $12,000 house for $12,000. **50.** a man who idles the motor in front of his house while he waits for his wife. **51.** a neurotic person with gooseflesh and teeth a-chatter, trying hard to be brave. **52.** one who sees an opportunity in every calamity. Pessimist: one who sees a calamity in every opportunity. **53.** one who plays out the futile farce of life, never realizing it is a farce.

Oration: a flood of words and a drought of reason.

Orator: **1.** a man who's willing to lay down your life for his country. **2.** a public speaker whose audience would be much better off if he were addressing envelopes.

Orator, Best: See **Best orator.**

Oratoreador: an orator who specializes in throwing the bull.

Oratory: **1.** eloquence accompanied by a Prince Albert. **2.** the art of making deep noises from the chest sound like important messages from the brain. **3.** the power to talk people out of their sober and natural opinions.

Organ recital: two or more persons discussing their operations.

Originality: **1.** undetected imitation. **2.** the art of remembering what you hear and forgetting where you heard it.

Orthopedist: a marrow-minded doctor.

Osteopath: a man who works his fingers to your bones.

Our national air: carbon monoxide.

Outdoor man: a fellow who hammers on the radiator for more heat while he is dressing to go skiing.

Outlaws: a menace to society, but in-laws are worse.

Out of bounds: a tired kangaroo.

Overeating: **1.** what makes you thick to your stomach. **2.** the destiny that shapes our ends.

Over-optimistic news commentator: pollyanalyst.

Overprivileged child: a gimme pig.

Overweight: just desserts.

P

Pacifist: a fellow who could attend a peace conference without getting into a fight.

Pain: nature's policeman.

Pal, Broadway: See **Broadway pal.**

Pal, Hollywood: See **Hollywood pal.**

Panelist: someone with an ability to think on his seat.

Panic: a sudden desertion of us, and a going over to the enemy of our imagination.

Paper, Fly: See **Fly paper.**

Paper napkin: its only ambition is to get down off your lap and play on the floor.

Par (golf): mathematical perfection, usually attained with a soft pencil and a softer conscience.

Paragon: the model man a woman regrets she gave up for the one she mistakenly married.

Parasite: one who goes through a revolving door on another's push.

Paratrooper: **1.** a soldier who climbs down trees he never climbed up. **2.** the only man who gets up in the world by falling down on the job.

Parent: **1.** a person who believes the words "progeny" and "prodigy" are interchangeable. **2.** (collegiate definition) the kin you love to touch.

Parent, Modern: See **Modern parent.**

Parents: **1.** one of the hardships of a minor's life. **2.** persons who spend half their time worrying how a child will turn out, and the rest of the time wondering when a child will turn in. **3.** people who always think their children would behave if they didn't play with the kids next door. **4.** people who lie awake wondering if daughter's dreamboat is one of those ships that make a pass in the night. **5.** people who bear infants, bore teenagers and board newlyweds.

Parent, Wise: See **Wise parent.**

Park drinking fountain: old faceful.

Parking meter: a snitching post.

Parking space: 1. an unfilled opening in an unending line of cars near an unapproachable fire plug. 2. an unoccupied area along the curb on the other side of the street. 3. something you see when you haven't got your car. 4. that area that disappears while you are making a U-turn.

Parlor, Beauty: See **Beauty parlor.**

Parlor, Dental: See **Dental parlor.**

Partner, Bridge: See **Bridge partner.**

Partner, Senior: See **Senior partner.**

Party, Bachelor: See **Bachelor party.**

Party, Big: See **Big party.**

Party, Cocktail: See **Cocktail party.**

Party, Modern: See **Modern party.**

Passport photo: a way to see yourself as others see you.

Past: something often forgotten for a present.

Patience: 1. a minor form of despair, disguised as a virtue. 2. the ability to idle your motor when you feel like stripping your gears. 3. the ability to stand something as long as it happens to the other fellow. 4. the quality that is needed most, just as it is exhausted.

Patient man: one who can put up with himself.

Patient, Psychoanalyzed: See **Psychoanalyzed patient.**

Patriot: 1. a man who loves his country and wants to make as much out of it as possible. 2. one who is sorry because he has only one income to give to his country. 3. a citizen who can whistle "The Star Spangled Banner" while the tax collector is examining his books. 4. a person who saves enough of his salary each week to pay his income tax.

Patriot, California: See **California patriot.**

Patriotic American: one who never orders from a menu anything he can't pronounce.

Patriotism: 1. realization that this is a nation and not a denomination. 2. your conviction that this country is superior to all others because you were born in it. 3. the willingness to make any sacrifice so long as it won't hurt business.

Patron: commonly a wretch who supports with insolence, and is paid with flattery.

Pauper: a poor fish without a fin.

Paving, City: See **City paving.**

Pawnbroker: 1. a guy who lives on the flat of the land. **2.** one who hopes people will see him at their earliest inconvenience.

Pay, Take-home: See **Take-home pay.**

Peace: 1. a period in which men toil to meet the expense of the war preceding and succeeding. **2.** a short pause between wars for enemy identifications. **3.** in international affairs, a period of cheating between two periods of fighting. **4.** the luxury you enjoy between the children's bedtime and your own. **5.** goodwill effectively asserted against greed. **6.** a blessing that can be made perpetual if nations will agree not to make new wars until they have paid for the old ones.

Peace conference: a meeting to find out who won't win the next war.

Pedal-pushers: a kind of pants worn as a compromise by a woman whose husband can't decide whether she looks worse in slacks or Bermuda shorts.

Pedestrian: 1. a car owner who has found a parking space. **2.** a fellow whose wife beats him to the garage. **3.** a guy who counted on his wife to put some gas in the car. **4.** a guy with three good tires. **5.** a man who falls by a wayside. **6.** a man who thought there still were a couple of gallons of gas left in the tank. **7.** a man with a son in high school and only one car in the family. **8.** street-walking object invisible to the motorist. **9.** the most approachable chap in the world. **10.** a guy who knows there are still several gallons of gas in the tank when the gauge shows empty. **11.** a man who has two cars, a wife, and a daughter. **12.** a person who can't find the place where he parked his car.

Pedestrian–Jaywalker: a pedestrian is one who walks when you are walking; a jaywalker is one who walks when you are driving.

Pedestrian–Walker: a man in danger of his life; Walker: a man in possession of his soul.

Peeping Tom: one who climbs the ladder of success stare by stare.

Pen-pal: the fellow who signs your paycheck.

Pension: in England, understood to mean pay given to a state hireling for treason to his country.

Pentagon: a building with five sides—on every issue.

People, Best: See **Best people.**

People, Opinionated: See **Opinionated people.**

Perfect bridge lamp: light enough to see by, too heavy to throw.

Perfect gentleman: a man of high principle and no interest.

Perfect guest: one who makes his host feel at home.

Perfect husband: one who is convinced he has a perfect wife.

Perfectionist: **1.** one who takes infinite pains, and often gives them to other people. **2.** a person who chooses a picnic site as if it were to be his permanent home. **3.** one who never quite finishes what he started out to do.

Perfect lady: a woman who makes it easy for a man to be a perfect gentleman.

Perfect man: a wife's first husband.

Perfect timing: getting to the first tee just ahead of a feminine foursome.

Perfect traveler: See **Good traveler.**

Perfect wife: **1.** one willing to help her husband with the housework. **2.** one who will sit up with you when you are ill, and put up with you when you're not.

Perfect woman: one who can hit the right male on the head.

Perfume: **1.** any smell that is used to drown a worse one. **2.** chemical warfare.

Perfume counter: a place where people talk scents.

Perpetual motion: the family upstairs.

Perseverance: a lowly virtue whereby mediocrity achieves an inglorious success.

Person, Average: See **Average person.**

Person, Clever: See **Clever person.**

Person, Educated: See **Educated person.**

Person, Level-headed: See **Level-headed person.**

Person, Strong-minded: See **Strong-minded person.**

Person, Well-adjusted: See **Well-adjusted person.**

Personality 1. the name we give to our own little collection of funny habits. **2.** what a person has when he makes you feel the same way about him as you do about yourself.

Personal liberty: that which a man exchanges for a wife.

Personal taxes: the unkindest cut of all.

Pessimist: 1. a man to whom an optimist owes money. **2.** an optimist on the way home from the horse races. **3.** an optimist who endeavored to practice what he preached. **4.** a woman driver who's sure she can't park her car in a tight place; Optimist: a man who thinks she won't try. **5.** one who blows out the light to see how dark it is. **6.** one who feels bad when he feels good for fear he'll feel worse when he feels better. **7.** one who is always building dungeons in the air. **8.** one who, of two evils, chooses them both. **9.** one who sizes himself up and then gets sore about it. **10.** one who thinks everybody's as nasty as himself, and hates them for it. **11.** a sentimental optimist who expected too much. **12.** the fellow who financed an optimist. **13.** a person, who when smelling flowers, looks around for the funeral. **14.** one who thinks all is lost because he is not running it. **15.** a gloomy person who passes all his days in constant expectation of the unexpected. **16.** a guy who fills up every time he sees a gas station; Optimist: one who believes the gasoline mileage promises of the salesman who sold him the car. **17.** a former optimist who taught the lady folks in his family how to drive. **18.** a man who thinks the whole world is against him—and, what's more, he's right. **19.** one who has to live with an optimist. **20.** a man who gets mad while taking stock of himself. **21.** someone who likes to listen to the patter of little defeats. **22.** a person who suffers seasickness during the entire journey of life. **23.** a person who paints a window black and then tries to look through it. **24.** a person who is happy when he is wrong. **25.** one who expects nothing on a silver platter except tarnish. **26.** a man who looks at the world through morose colored glasses.

Pessimist–Optimist: Pessimist: a man who thinks all women are bad; Optimist: a man who hopes they are.

Petition: a list of people who didn't have the nerve to say "no."

Pheasant under glass: a small bird with a large bill.

Philanderer: a man who considers himself too good to be true.

Philanthropist: 1. a man who atones openly for the wrong which he has done secretly. **2.** one who gives away what he should be giving back.

3. one who returns to the people publicly what he steals from them privately. 4. a rich old gentleman who has trained himself to grin while his conscience is picking his pocket.

Philosopher: 1. a fellow who always knows what to do until it happens to him. **2.** a man who can get the "fun" out of "defunct." **3.** a person wearing a blindfold, in a dark room, looking for a black cat—which wasn't there. **4.** a person who says he doesn't care which side his bread is buttered on, because he eats both sides anyway. **5.** one who, instead of crying over spilt milk, consoles himself with the thought that it was over four-fifths water. **6.** a fellow who can enjoy a blonde's golden curls even when he knows the roots are black. **7.** a fool who torments himself while he is alive, to be talked about after he is dead.

Philosophers: people who talk about something they don't understand, and make you think it's your fault.

Philosophical: a cheerful attitude assumed by everybody not directly involved in the trouble.

Philosophy: 1. a route of many roads leading from nowhere to nothing. **2.** a study which enables man to be unhappy more intelligently. **3.** something that enables the rich to say there is no disgrace in being poor. **4.** unintelligible answers to insoluble problems. **5.** a filter turned upside down, where what goes in clear comes out cloudy.

Phony: a guy who tries to cut his throat with an electric razor.

Photograph albums: the strange views people take of things.

Photographer: 1. one who can make an ugly girl as pretty as a picture. 2. one who always insists on accentuating the negative. 3. a person who takes your picture and makes you pay to get it back.

Photographer, Amateur: See **Amateur photographer.**

Photo, Passport: See **Passport photo.**

Physical education: what a young boy gets when he goes down to the beach.

Physician: a man who pours drugs of which he knows little into a body of which he knows less.

Piggy banks: pennytentiaries.

Pink elephant: a beast of bourbon.

Pink tea: giggle, gabble, gobble, git.

Pin money: bowling fee.

Pioneer: anyone who settled there before they raised the taxes.

Pioneer, Modern: See **Modern pioneer.**

Pipe: a thing that makes a man think—he thinks it's lit when it isn't.

Plan: something abandoned or unfinished.

Planned economy: where everything is included in the plans except economy.

Platform, Political: See **Political platform.**

Platitude: **1.** a truth we are tired of hearing. **2.** a dull old saw that everyone borrows, but no one sharpens. **3.** an old saw that has lost its teeth.

Platonic friendship: **1.** play for him and tonic for her. **2.** one that half the town says isn't.

Platonic love: **1.** all of the pleasures with none of the responsibilities. **2.** the gun you didn't know was loaded.

Platonic lover: a man who holds the eggshells while somebody else eats the omelette.

Play: *loving* to do things; Work: *having* to do things.

Playboy: **1.** a man who summers in the Alps, winters in Miami, and springs at blondes. **2.** one who is very good at being no good. **3.** a good-time Charlie who dishes out the sweet stuff to his little sugar and ends up paying a lump sum. **4.** a guy who believes it's never too late to spend.

Playboy, Reformed: See **Reformed playboy.**

Player, Bridge: See **Bridge player.**

Plays, Modern: See **Modern plays.**

Pleasingly plump: a girl with a shape like a figure ate.

Pleasure trip: any trip that your wife can put in the memory book—and you can put on the expense account.

Pneumonia: a slight cold handled by a public relations man.

Poet: one who makes his living the bard way.

Poetry: religion which is no longer believed.

Poise: **1.** an acquired characteristic which enables father to buy a new pair of shoes at the same time he is ignoring a hole in his sock. **2.** the ability to keep talking while somebody else picks up the check. **3.** the ability to remain calm and at ease in a barber chair, with your mouth full of lather, while the porter tries to give your new hat to another fellow. **4.** the act of raising the eyebrows instead of the roof. **5.** looking like an owl after behaving like a donkey.

Poker: it's darkest just before you've drawn.

Policy: a common substitute for good judgment.

Policy, Foreign: See **Foreign policy.**

Policy, Insurance: See **Insurance policy.**

Politeness: **1.** the art of choosing among your thoughts. **2.** the most acceptable hypocrisy. **3.** an inexpensive way of making friends.

Political bedfellows: men who usually use the same bunk.

Political campaign: **1.** a matter of mud, threats and smears. **2.** when a politician quits work and goes around making speeches about all the work he intends to do.

Political convention: a gathering at which factions speak louder than wards.

Political economy: two words that should be divorced on grounds of incompatability.

Political machine: a united minority working against a divided majority.

Political platform: a platform like that on the front of a streetcar—not meant to stand on, just to get in on.

Political promises: those that go in one year and out the other.

Political timber: what you'll find on the stump during an election year.

Political war: one in which everyone shoots from the lip.

Politician: **1.** a career that's most promising. **2.** a fellow who borrows your pot in which to cook your goose. **3.** a fellow who's got what it takes to take what you've got. **4.** a man who divides his time between running for office and running for cover. **5.** a man who shakes your hand in the hope of shaking your purse. **6.** a man who spends half his time making laws, and the other half helping friends evade them. **7.** a man who stands for what he thinks others will fall for. **8.** a person who can talk in circles while standing foursquare. **9.** one who promises the people a car in every garage when he runs for office and after he is elected proceeds to erect parking meters. **10.** one who when he comes to the parting of the ways goes both ways. **11.** a fellow who loves a wordy cause. **12.** a fellow who approaches every question with an open mouth. **13.** someone who shakes your hand before the election and your confidence afterward. **14.** a guy who contrasts his wings and halo against his opponent's horns and tail. **15.** one who succeeds by playing both ends against the taxpayer. **16.** an animal who can sit on a fence and yet keep both ears to the ground.

Politician, Honest: See **Honest politician.**

Politician, Practical: See **Practical politician.**

Politicians: **1.** people who get in the public eye by getting in the public chest. **2.** something like poor relatives, you only see them when they need help.

Politician, Successful: See **Successful politician.**

Politics: **1.** a simple matter of either passing the buck or passing the doe. **2.** be sure you're in right, then go ahead. **3.** one party trying to get into office and the other party trying to stay in. **4.** the art of looking for trouble, finding it everywhere, diagnosing it incorrectly, and applying the wrong remedies. **5.** the art of obtaining money from the rich and votes from the poor on the pretext of protecting each from the other. **6.** the only profession for which no preparation is thought necessary. **7.** where people work hard to get a job and do nothing after they get it. **8.** a balancing act between people who want to get into it and people who don't want to get out of it. **9.** a game in which some men are self-made but most are machine-made. **10.** the conduct of public affairs for private advantage. **11.** the science of who gets what, when and why.

Polls: places where you stand in line for a place to decide who will spend your money.

Polygamy: an endeavor to get more out of life than there is in it.

Poor distribution: a bald-headed man with a mustache.

Poor man: **1.** a man who has nothing but money. **2.** one who keeps spending enough to prevent his neighbors from guessing how little he really has.

Popularity: to be gifted with the virtue of knowing a whole lot of uninteresting people.

Popular song: one that has the happy virtue of making all of us think we can sing.

Positive: being mistaken at the top of one's voice.

Posterity: **1.** what the founding fathers would not have talked about so glowingly if they had known we were going to be it. **2.** what an author writes for after the publishers turn him down.

Potomac fever: that hideous disease which causes one to swell without growing.

Poverty: a state of mind sometimes induced by a neighbor's new car.

Powder: something that may cause an explosion if found on the lapel.

Power: to know, and to know that you know.

Practical engineer: one who perpetuates the errors of his predecessors.

Practical nurse: one who marries her rich patient.

Practical politician: a man who shakes your hand before election and your acquaintance afterwards.

Praise: **1.** what you receive when you are no longer alive. **2.** something a person tells you about yourself that you've suspected all along.

Prejudice: **1.** a lazy man's substitute for thinking. **2.** a vagrant opinion without visible means of support. **3.** being down on something you're not up on. **4.** merely bad manners raised to an intolerable degree. **5.** the dislike of the unlike. **6.** weighing the facts with your thumb on the scale. **7.** being positive about something negative. **8.** an unwillingness to be confused with the facts. **9.** when you decide some fellow is a stinker before you even meet him.

Prescription, Doctor's: See **Doctor's prescription.**

Present: something which around Christmastime is more important than past or future.

Press agent: one who has hitched his braggin' to a star.

Pretzel: a drinking man's filter.

Preview, Motion-picture: See **Motion-picture preview.**

Pride, Ancestral: See **Ancestral pride.**

Pride, Civic: See **Civic pride.**

Primitive country: one that has no taxes to handle juvenile delinquency, in case it gets civilized enough to achieve it.

Principal: a man who takes children into his office and hits them with the Board of Education.

Prison: a place where you do without the things you stole money to buy.

Prisoner: one who doesn't mind being interrupted in the middle of a sentence.

Private nurse: too cute for wards.

Problems: opportunities in work clothes.

Procrastination: the art of keeping up with yesterday.

Procrastinator: 1. one who puts off until tomorrow things he's already put off until today. 2. a person who can't put away the garden tools until the snow thaws.

Prodigies, Infant: See **Infant prodigies.**

Prodigy: a child who plays the piano when he ought to be asleep in bed.

Producer: a man who stands in the back of the theatre on opening night and wishes he were dead.

Producer, Associate: See **Associate producer.**

Profanity: the well-known signature of a simple mind.

Professional bachelor: one who realizes he's stuck with himself for life and can't do a thing about it.

Professor: 1. a man whose job it is to tell students how to solve the problem of life which he himself has tried to avoid by becoming a professor. 2. a textbook wired for sound. 3. one who talks in someone else's sleep.

Professor, College: See **College professor.**

Professor emeritus: a teacher who has had it.

Professors: those who go to college and never get out.

Profit: that which foretells the future.

Progress: **1.** a state of human development where a man pays a laundry for destroying his shirts and collars. **2.** something that's achieved by man's innate desire to live beyond his means. **3.** swapping old troubles for new. **4.** the slow business of falling in line with the schemes of minorities. **5.** what an inactive committee always reports. **6.** when you're just getting used to something and somebody invents something better that you won't have time to get used to before somebody invents something better. **7.** the art of making bigger and bigger circles to run around in.

Progressiveness: looking forward intelligently, looking within critically, and living on incessantly.

Prohibitionist: a fellow who thinks that what you drink is going to hurt him.

Promise, Breach of: See **Breach of promise.**

Promises, Political: See **Political promises.**

Promoter: a man who will furnish the ocean if you will furnish the ships.

Propaganda: **1.** baloney disguised as food for thought. **2.** the other side's case put so convincingly that it annoys you. **3.** an opinion with which you do not agree.

Proposal: **1.** a figure of speech ending in a sentence. **2.** a girl listening faster than a man can talk.

Proposal, Marriage: See **Marriage proposal.**

Prosperity: **1.** being able to pay a little more for things we shouldn't buy anyway. **2.** something the businessman created for the politicians to take credit for. **3.** that short period between the final installment and the next purchase. **4.** the sweet buy and buy.

Proverb: a short sentence based on long experience.

Proverbs: **1.** the wisdom of many and the wit of one. **2.** short sentences drawn from long experiences.

Prune: a plum that has seen better days.

Psychiatrist. **1.** a fellow who goes to a burlesque show to watch the audience. **2.** a guy who makes you squeal on yourself. **3.** a man who doesn't have to worry as long as other people do. **4.** a mind sweeper. **5.** one who tries to find out whether an infant has more fun in infancy than an adult in adultery. **6.** a guy who tells you all the things you should do to get better and then takes all your dough so you can't afford to. **7.** a fellow who convinces you that your parents were failures because you turned out to be a louse. **8.** a physician who hates the sight of blood. **9.** a man who profits from your experience. **10.** the last guy you talk to before you start talking to yourself. **11.** a man you pay to ask you questions your wife asks for nothing.

Psychiatry: **1.** the art of analyzing ouches on couches. **2.** old-fashioned cracker barrel philosophy, modernized, at a price.

Psychoanalysis: **1.** panned parenthood. **2.** the disease it purports to cure.

Psychoanalyzed patient: altered ego.

Psycho-ceramic: a crackpot.

Psychologist: **1.** a man who, when a good-looking girl enters a room, watches everybody else. **2.** a man you pay to ask you questions your wife asks you for nothing.

Psychologist, Child: See **Child psychologist.**

Psychology: the science that tells you what you already know in words you can't understand.

Psychology, Child: See **Child psychology.**

Psychology, Feminine: See **Feminine psychology.**

Psychology, Mass: See **Mass psychology.**

Public golf course: a place where you hit a ball . . . and a *picnic* runs out and grabs it.

Public interest: a term used by every politician to support his ideas.

Public opinion: **1.** private gossip which has reached the proportions and virulence of an epidemic. **2.** what people think other people are thinking. **3.** that mysterious variable of political calculation. **4.** private opinion that makes enough noise to attract attention.

Public relations: **1.** the letter you don't write when you're mad and the nice letter you write to the so-and-so the next day after you've regained your sense of humor. **2.** the art of giving you the benefit of the dirt. **3.** performing the right act at the right time—and getting credit for it.

Public speaking: the art of diluting a two-minute idea with a two-hour vocabulary.

Pugilist: 1. a person who believes that it is better to give than to receive. **2.** a guy who makes money hand over fist.

Pun: the lowest form of humor—when you don't think of it first.

Punctuality: 1. a grandstand play in an empty ball park. **2.** the art of guessing how late the other fellow is going to be. **3.** the art of wasting only your own time. **4.** waiting around for other people. **5.** a bad habit of the people who send out bills.

Puncture: a little hole in a tire found a great distance from a garage or gas station.

Punishment, Capital: See **Capital punishment.**

Puppy: a little waggin' without wheels.

Puppy love: the beginning of a dog's life.

Puritan: a person who pours righteous indignation into the wrong things.

Push-button warfare: competition for the use of an automatic elevator.

Puttering: woman's word for man's work.

Putting green: great oaths from little acorns grow.

Pyromaniac: a landlord's description of a tenant who asks for heat.

Q

Quartet: 1. four guys who think the other three sing off-key. **2.** the sum of two pints.

Question: a thing with two sides so long as it does not concern us personally.

Quiet: what home would be without children.

R

Rabbit: 1. a small animal that's hare today and mink tomorrow. **2.** a small animal that grows fur for which other animals get credit when it appears in the form of a coat.

Racehorse: 1. a fast means of redistributing wealth. 2. the only animal that can take several thousand people for a ride at the same time.

Racetrack: 1. a place where a man is washed up as soon as he loses his shirt. 2. a place where windows clean people. 3. where thousands of people can go for a ride on the same horse. 4. a place where you can lose your dough window shopping. 5. a place where people look for the right odds to get even.

Radical: 1. a conservative out of a job. 2. anyone whose opinion differs from ours. 3. a man with both feet firmly planted in the air.

Radio announcer: a man who talks until you have a headache, then tries to sell you something to relieve it.

Radio City: the tower of babble.

Radio commercial: the pause that depresses.

Radio story: one to which you can always give a happy ending by a turn of the dial.

Raise: the increase in pay you get just before going into debt a little further.

Raisin: a worried grape.

Rare antique: an object that has wormed its way up.

Rare volume: a borrowed book that comes back.

Rationing: less and less of more and more oftener and oftener.

Raving beauty: the girl who finished second in a beauty contest.

Reactionary: a somnambulist walking backward.

Reading: thinking with someone else's head instead of one's own.

Readjustment: when your neighbor loses his job; Recession: when you lose your job; Depression: when your wife loses her job.

Reality: dirty dishes in the sink that are still there when you come home.

Recess: teacher's coffee break.

Recession: See also **Readjustment.** 1. a period in which you tighten your belt; Depression: a period in which you have no belt to tighten. 2. when you lose *your* job; Depression: when I lose *mine.* 3. a period when sales are down 5 per cent and staff meetings are up 25 per cent.

4. when prices are reduced to where you could afford them if you were still enjoying prosperity.

Recession, Business: See **Business recession.**

Recital, Organ: See **Organ recital.**

Reckless driver: one who passes you on the highway, in spite of all you can do.

Red light: the place where you catch up with the motorist who passed you at 60 m.p.h. a mile back.

Redskins: people on the American bathing beaches.

Reducing: wishful shrinking.

Reducing expert: a person who lives on the fat of the land.

Reducing salon: a good place to shoo the fat.

Reformed playboy: a cut-down cut-up.

Reformer: **1.** a man who rides through a sewer in a glass-bottomed boat. **2.** one who insists upon his conscience being your guide. **3.** one who, when he smells a rat, is eager to let the cat out of the bag. **4.** one who's business is what's none of his business. **5.** a member of the meddle class. **6.** a person the world needs because there is always the work of some former reformer to be undone.

Reform–Revolution: Reform: a correction of abuses; Revolution: a transfer of power.

Reform school: a brat trap.

Regret: insight that comes a day too late.

Relations: **1.** a tedious pack of people who haven't the remotest knowledge of how to live nor the smallest instinct about when to die. **2.** people who come to visit you when the weather is too hot to cook their own meals. **3.** people whom we inherit and who wish to inherit from us.

Relations, Public: See **Public relations.**

Relative: See also **Relations.** inherited critic.

Relative humidity: those times when you think your rich uncle is all wet.

Relatives, Rich: See **Rich relatives.**

Reliable source: the guy you just met; *informed source:* the guy who told the guy you just met; *unimpeachable source:* the guy who started the rumor originally.

Relief, Comic: See **Comic relief.**

Religion: 1. fairy tales for grown-ups. **2.** insurance in this world against a fire in the next. **3.** an infectious disease, the rapid spread of which is due to the social instincts of mankind.

Remark, Chance: See **Chance remark.**

Remark, Futile: See **Futile remark.**

Remarriage: the triumph of hope over experience.

Remorse: a miscalculation of the chances of detection.

Reno: 1. large inland seaport in America with the tied running in and the untied running out. **2.** residence of the bitter half. **3.** the land of the free and the grave of the home. **4.** where the cream of society goes to be separated. **5.** grounds for divorce. **6.** a city where ladies are presented at court. **7.** city of otherly love.

Reno cocktail: marriage on the rocks.

Reno-vated: divorced in Nevada.

Repartee: 1. an insult with its dress-suit on. **2.** knowing what to say after you've just missed your chance to say it. **3.** what a person thinks of after he becomes a departee. **4.** what you wish you had said.

Repentance: to be sorry enough to quit.

Representative government: that which elects six men in favor of a thing and six against it, and then wonders why something isn't done.

Reputation: 1. a bubble which man bursts when he tries to blow it for himself. **2.** a personal possession, frequently not discovered until lost. **3.** character minus what you've been caught doing. **4.** something to live up to in your youth and to live down in old age. **5.** a bubble which others can blow up or burst by what they say behind your back.

Research: 1. an organized method for keeping you reasonably dissatisfied with what you have. **2.** to see what everybody else has seen, and think what nobody has thought.

Research notes: things you keep for thirty years, then throw away the day before you need them.

Resistance, Sales: See **Sales resistance.**

Resolution, New Year: See **New Year resolution.**

Resort: 1. a place where the tired grow more tired. **2.** a place where they charge you enough to make up for the nine months you are not there.

Resort, Luxury: See **Luxury resort.**

Resort, Summer: See **Summer resort.**

Respectability: the offspring of a liaison between a bald head and a bank account.

Restaurant: an eating place that does not sell drugs.

Restricted: a piece of inside news you get from a civilian.

Reticence: knowing what you're talking about but keeping your mouth shut.

Retirement: when you awaken in the morning with nothing to do and retire without doing it.

Retribution: when a talkative barber marries a gabby woman.

Return, Income tax: See **Income tax return.**

Reunion, Class: See **Class reunion.**

Revolution: See **Reform–Revolution.**

Revolution (in politics): an abrupt change in the form of misgovernment.

Rhubarb: celery with high blood pressure.

Rhumba: a fox trot with the backfield in motion.

Riches: a burden on those who have them and a greater burden on those who haven't them.

Rich man: 1. one who isn't afraid to ask the clerk to show him something cheaper. **2.** nothing but a poor man with money.

Rich relatives: the kin we love to touch.

Righteous indignation: your own wrath as opposed to the shocking bad temper of others.

Ring, Engagement: See **Engagement ring.**

Ring, Wedding: See **Wedding ring.**

Rising generation: a generation which is fond of sitting.

Risk, Calculated: See **Calculated risk.**

Roadhog: a fellow who meets you more than half way.

Road map: a book of etiquette showing motorists which fork to use.

Robber: what a doctor and a TV serviceman call one another.

Robbery, Highway: See **Highway robbery.**

Rock and roll: **1.** a truck loaded with empty tin cans smashing into a greenhouse. **2.** the kind of music we keep hoping will turn into a tune. **3.** catch-as-catch-cancan.

Rolling pin: a night club.

Romance: a form of neckromancy.

Roulette: a wheel that seldom takes a turn for the bettor.

Rudeness: a weak man's imitation of strength.

Rumble seat: a breakfast nook on wheels.

Rummage sale: where you buy stuff from somebody else's attic to store in your own.

Rush hour: when traffic is at a standstill.

Russian: a man who sits on nothing and dances.

Russian delegate: a yes-man who says no.

Rut: a grave with the ends knocked out.

Rye: grain for sowing wild oats.

S

Sadist: one who does kind things for a masochist.

Safety belt: when a gal slaps an eager beaver.

Sagacity: buying a needle instead of hunting for one in a haystack.

Sailor: a man who makes his living on water but never touches it on shore.

Saint: a dead sinner, revised and edited.

Salary: **1.** an unearned income. **2.** a stipend, part of which is withheld biweekly, the balance returnable on April 15. **3.** a thing you can't bank on nowadays. **4.** what a husband commands and his wife commandeers. **5.** an amount of money that, no matter how large it is, some people spend more money than.

Salary, Movie actor's: See **Movie actor's salary.**

Sale, Bargain: See **Bargain sale.**

Sale, Rummage: See **Rummage sale.**

Salesman: one who often needs the wind taken out of his sales.

Salesman, Falsie: See **Falsie salesman.**

Salesmanship: transferring a conviction by a seller to a buyer.

Salesman, Top: See **Top salesman.**

Salesmen: people with both feet on the ground who take orders from people with both feet on the desk.

Sales resistance: the triumph of mind over patter.

Salmon: a fish that lurks in a can and only comes out when unexpected company arrives.

Sandwich: an unsuccessful attempt to make both ends meat.

Sandwich, Honeymoon: See **Honeymoon sandwich.**

Sandwich, Mother-in-law: See **Mother-in-law sandwich.**

Sandwich spread: what you get from eating between meals.

Santa Anita: Spanish for instant poverty.

Savage: a fellow who stalks people without a driver's license.

Saxophone: an ill wind that blows no good.

Scale, Bathroom: See **Bathroom scale.**

Scalper, Ticket: See **Ticket scalper.**

Scandalmonger: **1.** a prattlesnake. **2.** one who puts who and who together and gets whew!

Scared skin diver: chicken of the sea.

Scene stealer: a guy who puts up billboards.

Schedule: that wonderful little gimmick which enables a housewife to do approximately one half of the things she had planned.

School, Art: See **Art school.**

School-bus driver: a man who thought he liked children.

School, Charm: See **Charm school.**

School, Nursery: See **Nursery school.**

School, Reform: See **Reform school.**

School, Sunday: See **Sunday school.**

School teacher: one who takes a lot of live wires and sees to it that they are well grounded.

Science: **1.** an orderly arrangement of what at the moment seems to be the facts. **2.** an allegory that asserts that the relations between the parts of reality are similar to the relations between terms of discourse.

Science friction: the competition in missile development between the armed services.

Science, Military: See **Military science.**

Screen door: something the kids get a bang out of.

Screen, Window: See **Window screen.**

Sculptor: a poor unfortunate who makes faces and busts.

Sculptor, Modern: See **Modern sculptor.**

Seabag: a sailor's girl friend.

Seasickness: traveling across the ocean by rail.

Seasoned troops: soldiers that are mustered by the officers and peppered by the enemy.

Season, Football: See **Football season.**

Seat, Rumble: See **Rumble seat.**

Second marriage: the triumph of hope over experience.

Second story man: the fellow whose wife doesn't believe his first story.

Second wind: what a public speaker acquires when he says, "And, in conclusion."

Secret: **1.** something a woman can keep with a telling effect. **2.** something that is hushed about from place to place. **3.** something that's not worth keeping or in the alternative is too good to keep. **4.** what you ask someone else not to tell because you can't keep it. **5.** something you tell only one person at a time.

Secretary: **1.** an office worker who is obliged to look like a girl, think like a man, and work like a horse. **2.** (undesirable) one that is clock-eyed. **3.** a girl who can tell by a caller's name whether or not the boss is in. **4.** a girl you pay to learn to type while she's looking for a husband.

Secretary, Good: See **Good secretary.**

Secret, Military: See **Military secret.**

Secrets: things we give to others to keep for us.

Secrets, Trade: See **Trade secrets.**

Security, Social: See **Social security.**

Self-control: **1.** when a woman checks out of a market with nothing more than she had on her shopping list. **2.** calling a spade a spade after stubbing your toe on one.

Self-importance: a feeling that is momentarily removed by a walk through the cemetery.

Selfishness: that detestable vice which no one will forgive in others and no one is without in himself.

Self-made man: a horrible example of unskilled labor.

Self-reliance: the name we give to the egotism of the man who succeeds.

Self-respect: the secure feeling that no one, as yet, is suspicious.

Self-restraint: feeling your oats without sowing them.

Senior partner: the fellow who has nothing to do between trips to Florida; Junior partner: the boss' son.

Sense, Business: See **Business sense.**

Sense of humor: being able to laugh at your friends' misfortunes.

Sentence, Suspended: See **Suspended sentence.**

Sentimentality: the name we give to any sentiment we are incapable of feeling.

Separate cover, Under: See **Under separate cover.**

Servant: a woman who's here today and gone tomorrow.

Service: the rent we pay for our room on earth.

Service station: a place where you fill the car and drain the family.

Sewing bee: a place where a bachelor often gets stung.

Sewing circle: 1. where friendship hangs by a thread. 2. a woman's exchange.

Sewing circle, Ladies': See **Ladies' sewing circle.**

Sex appeal: 1. fifty per cent what you've got and fifty per cent what people think you've got. 2. something that makes feminine capital out of masculine interest.

Sexton: someone who minds his keys and pews.

Shakespeare: a dramatist of note who lived by writing things for other people to quote.

Shape: what a bathing suit takes when a girl's in it.

Sharp tongue: the only edged tool that grows keener with constant use.

Shipboard: where four bells means three cocktails.

Shock absorbers: parents.

Shooting script: a letter from a blonde that your wife finds in your pocket.

Shop, Beauty: See **Beauty shop.**

Shop, Gift: See **Gift shop.**

Shopper, Bargain: See **Bargain shopper.**

Shopper, Woman: See **Woman shopper.**

Shopping, Christmas: See **Christmas shopping.**

Short cut: a route on which you can't find anybody to ask where you are.

Short vacation: half a loaf.

Shoulder, Cold: See **Cold shoulder.**

Shoulder strap: a device for keeping an attraction from becoming a sensation.

Show-off: a fellow who's apt to be shown up in a showdown.

Sick kleptomaniac: one who takes things lying down.

Sickness, Car: See **Car sickness.**

Silence: **1.** the only successful substitute for brains. **2.** unbearable repartee. **3.** wisdom in dead storage. **4.** the most perfect expression of scorn. **5.** an ignorant man's most valuable possession but only so long as he keeps it.

Silent film: one where no one in the audience bought popcorn.

Silk: something that can never be worsted.

Sincere friend: one who says nasty things to your face, instead of saying them behind your back.

Singer, TV: See **TV singer.**

Singing: a man's bathright.

Single file: a girl's file of eligible bachelors.

Single fund-raising effort: putting all of your begs in one ask it.

Sinner: a stupid person who gets found out.

Skeleton: a person with the inside out and the outside off.

Skeptic: a fellow who won't take know for an answer.

Skiing: **1.** (Indian's definition) Whoosh! Then walk a mile. **2.** a winter sport that people learn in several sittings.

Skin diver, Scared: See **Scared skin diver.**

Skunk: a streamlined cat with a two-tone finish and a fluid drive.

Slang: **1.** language that takes off its coat, spits on its hands, and goes to work. **2.** the speech of him who robs the literary garbage cans on their way to the dump. **3.** sports-model language stripped down to get more speed with less horsepower.

Sleep: something that always assumes more importance the morning after than it did the night before.

Sleeping bag: a nap sack.

Slogan: a good old American substitute for facts.

Small business: one that has never been investigated by a congressional committee.

Small talk: patter of little feats.

Small town: **1.** a place where everybody knows the troubles you've seen. **2.** a place where everybody knows whose check is good. **3.** where everybody is interested in what the Joneses will name the latest baby, while a big city is where they worry about what the zoo will call the new elephant. **4.** where you chat on the phone for an hour or so, even when you get the wrong number. **5.** where you pinch a girl and everybody squeals. **6.** a place where the street lights dim when you plug in your electric razor. **7.** a place where everybody knows what everyone else is doing, but still reads the local papers to see if they got caught at it. **8.** a place where the news gets around before the newspaper does. **9.** a place where the fellow with the black eye doesn't have to explain to anybody—*they know.* **10.** where you never know what you've been up to until the gossip gets back to you. **11.** a place where, if you see a man dining with a girl young enough to be his daughter, she is. **12.** a place where babies never arrive unexpectedly. **13.** where Sunday papers can be lifted with one hand.

Smart bride: one who quits playing ball after she makes a good catch.

Smart girl: **1.** one who can get her way without half crying. **2.** one who can tell the difference between being bitten by a love bug and a louse. **3.** one who can lie convincingly enough to make a man believe that he's as smart as he thinks he is. **4.** one who can hold a man at arm's length without losing her grip on him.

Smart man: **1.** one who hasn't let a woman pin anything on him since he was a baby. **2.** one who doesn't give the same advice once. **3.** a husband who thinks twice before saying nothing.

Smart woman: **1.** one who can keep a man pursuing her even after she lets him catch her. **2.** one who will let you wind her around your little finger as long as she knows she has you under her thumb.

Smile: **1.** radiant lighting. **2.** a curve that can set a lot of things straight. **3.** something that adds to *your* face value.

Smog: the air apparent.

Smoker, Chain: See **Chain smoker.**

Smoker, Inveterate: See **Inveterate smoker.**

Smokers: people who claim the more they fume, the less they fret.

Snack: the pause that refleshes.

Snappy comeback: something you think of twelve hours after you were tongue-tied by somebody else's wisecrack.

Snob: **1.** one who in climbing the ladder of success kisses the feet of the one ahead of him and kicks the head of the one following him. **2.** one who talks as though he had begotten his own ancestors. **3.** a person who wants to know only the ones who don't want to know him. **4.** a person born with a lifted face. **5.** one so wrapped up with those above him that he can't see a thing in the people on his own level. **6.** one who is just one notch from being snubbed.

Snobbery: pride in status without pride in function.

Snobbishness: high-hattitude.

Snob, Intellectual: See **Intellectual snob.**

Snoring: sheet music.

Snow tires: those wonderful things that you put on just after the first blizzard of the late autumn and take off just before the last one of the early spring.

Snuff maker: a man who puts his business in someone else's nose.

So-and-so: the fellow driving the other car.

Soap opera: corn on the sob.

Socialized medicine: when women get together at a card party to talk about their operations.

Social security: **1.** when a boy has the only football or baseball in the neighborhood. **2.** where the government guarantees you a steak in your old age—when your teeth are gone.

Social success: the infinite capacity for being bored.

Social tact: the ability to make your guests feel at home though you wish they were.

Society: **1.** that which some folks are born in, other are taken in, but most folks pay to get in. **2.** where every woman wants to enlarge her sphere but not her circumference.

Society folks: the upper crust, made from crumbs and held together by dough.

Solemnity: a trick of the body to hide the faults of the mind.

Son, Boss': See **Boss' son.**

Song: the licensed medium for bawling in public things too silly or sacred to be uttered in ordinary speech.

Song, Love: See **Love song.**

Song, Popular: See **Popular song.**

Sophistication: **1.** knowing enough to keep your feet out of the crack of the theatre seat in front of you. **2.** liking something you don't like. **3.** the art of admitting that the unexpected is just what you anticipated. **4.** the art of recognizing a new joke and then acting as if it's an old one.

Sorority: a group of girls living in one house, with a single purpose . . . to get more girls to live in one house, with a single purpose.

Sound barrier: what you should have between the rumpus room and the rest of the house.

Source, Reliable: See **Reliable source.**

Source, Unimpeachable: See **Reliable source.**

Spa: a place where people drink their bath water.

Space, Parking: See **Parking space.**

Space suit: maternity dress.

Spanking: a process which takes less time than reasoning and penetrates sooner to the seat of memory.

Spare tire: the one you check the day after you have a flat.

Speaker, After-dinner: See **After-dinner speaker.**

Speaking, Public: See **Public speaking.**

Specialist: **1.** a doctor whose patients are expected to confine their ailments to office hours. **2.** a doctor who diagnoses your case by feeling your purse.

Spectacular, TV: See **TV spectacular.**

Speculator: a man who observes the future and acts before it occurs.

Speech, Free: See **Free speech.**

Speech, Good: See **Good speech.**

Speeches, After-dinner: See **After-dinner speeches.**

Spell: something that if a stenographer can, she'll never be out of work for too long a.

Spender, Big: See **Big spender.**

Spendthrift: **1.** one who grows poor by seeming rich. **2.** a neighbor who makes more money than you do. **3.** one who makes his heirs grey.

Spinster: **1.** a lady in waiting. **2.** a lady frequently guilty of contempt of courting. 3. a woman who is unhappily unmarried. **4.** a girl with a wait problem.

Spiritualist: a trance-guesser.

Sponsors: people who make television programs possible and impossible at the same time.

Sport, Good: See **Good sport.**

Sport, Minor: See **Minor sport.**

Spring: **1.** the season of balls—golf, tennis, base and moth. **2.** the time of the year when farmers and golfers start their spring plowing. **3.** the time of year when motorists drain the anti-freeze from their radiators two weeks too soon. **4.** when a young man's fancy lightly turns to what the girl has been thinking about all winter. **5.** when boys begin to feel gallant and girls begin to feel buoyant. **6.** that glorious time of the year when your neighbor comes by with an invitation for golf just as you have your hands full of storm windows. **7.** the mating season for everything but the golf socks one put away last autumn.

Spring fever: a seasonal disorder, often accompanied by depression, and believed by many to be caused by tax bite.

Square: teen-age title for guys they don't like to have round.

Stable government: one with plenty of horse sense.

Stagnation: a country without women.

Stale-mate: a husband with one joke.

State, Totalitarian: See **Totalitarian state.**

State, Welfare: See **Welfare state.**

Statesman: **1.** an ex-politician who has mastered the art of holding his tongue. **2.** a politician who is held upright by equal pressure from all directions. **3.** a politician away from home. **4.** a man who can solve grave problems which wouldn't exist if there were no statesmen. **5.** a successful politician, who is dead.

Statesman, Elder: See **Elder statesman.**

Statesman–Politician: a statesman is a person who wants to do something for his country, and a politician is one who wants his country to do something for him.

Static: Nature's way of protecting us from certain radio pragrams.

Station wagon: something a city person uses when he moves to the country so the country people will know he's from the city.

Statistician: a man who draws a mathematically precise line from an unwarranted assumption to a foregone conclusion.

Statistics: **1.** mendacious truths. **2.** the art of drawing a crooked line from an unproved assumption to a foregone conclusion.

Status symbol: anything you can't afford, but did.

Steak, Chopped: See **Chopped steak.**

Steam: water turned crazy with the heat.

Stockbroker: a man who can take a bankroll and run it into a shoestring.

Stockings: an article of wearing apparel that covers a multitude of shins.

Stomach: a bowl-shaped cavity containing the organs of indigestion.

Stooge: a guy who lives by the wrong side of the cracks.

Store detective: counter spy.

Stork: **1.** a bird with many things charged against it which should have been blamed on the lark. **2.** a bird with a big bill.

Storyteller, Good: See **Good storyteller.**

Straight actress: 36–36–36.

Straight face: what you try to put on when you know that the other fellow is crooked.

Strapless gown: **1.** when a woman won't shoulder the responsibility. **2.** a compromise between the law of decency and the law of gravity.

Strategy: usually darn poor judgment that happens to work out all right.

Strip teaser: a skin diva.

Strong-minded person: one who doesn't NO his own mind.

Struggle, Eternal: See **Eternal struggle.**

Stucco: what a lot of house hunters are getting these days.

Students: children whom parents send to college either because they themselves went or didn't.

Substitute: the right article made of the wrong material.

Subtlety: the art of saying what you think and getting out of range before it is understood.

Suburb: **1.** a place where, by the time you've finished paying for your home there, the suburbs have moved 20 miles out. **2.** where the houses are further apart and the payments are closer together. **3.** a place where people wait for the kids to grow up so they can move back to the city.

Suburbanite: **1.** a man who hires someone to mow his lawn so he can play golf for exercise. **2.** a yard man with bedroom privileges.

Suburbs: where the station wagons are bigger than the stations.

Success: **1.** failure with a fresh coat of paint. **2.** getting what you want; Happiness: wanting what you get. **3.** making more money to meet obligations you wouldn't have if you didn't make so much money. **4.** self-expression at a profit. **5.** the ability to hitch your wagon to a star while keeping your feet on the ground. **6.** the art of making your mistakes when nobody is looking. **7.** the one unpardonable sin committed against one's fellows. **8.** the degree to which other people envy you. **9.** something that always comes faster to the man your wife almost married. **10.** when a man's wife takes most of the credit and the government takes most of the cash. **11.** the proper ratio between what one contributes and what one derives from life. **12.** the ability to get along with some people—and ahead of others.

Success, Howling: See **Howling success.**

Success, Social: See **Social success.**

Successful business executive: **1.** a man who has an infinite capacity for taking planes. **2.** one who can delegate all the responsibility, shift all the blame, and appropriate all the credit.

Successful comedian: one who has succeeded in making a complete asset of himself.

Successful cookout: one at which the host pulls up steaks before the fat is in the fire.

Successful farmer: one who has the summer stock company hold over in his barn an extra week.

Successful gossip columnist: top man on the quote 'em pole.

Successful man. **1.** a man who so lives that when he dies even the undertaker is sorry. **2.** one who earns more than his wife can spend. **3.** one who can carry out five per cent of the good intentions he had when he left school. **4.** one who looks for work after he has found a job. **5.** usually an average man who either had a chance or took a chance. **6.** one who spends more time taking the bull by the horns than shooting it. **7.** one who does what he has to do at the time he hates to do it most. **8.** one who failed repeatedly until he succeeded. **9.** one who has a wife who tells him what to do, and a secretary who does it.

Successful marriage: **1.** where the wife is the boss and doesn't know it. **2.** one in which the husband knows when to remember and the wife knows what to forget. **3.** one composed of three complete volumes: the Prayer Book, the Check Book and the Cook Book.

Successful politician: **1.** a person who can take a popular economic fallacy and make a major plank for his party. **2.** one who can get in the public eye without irritating it.

Successful woman: one who finds such a man.

Sugar daddy: a form of crystallized sap.

Suicide blonde: one who dyed by her own hand.

Suit, Bathing: See **Bathing suit.**

Suitcase: something you sit on while waiting for the train.

Suit, Modern bathing: See **Bathing suit, Modern.**

Summer: **1.** the season when children slam the doors they left open all winter. **2.** the time of year when the highway authorities close the regular roads and open up the detours. **3.** when the four-color pictures in the seed catalog turn into four-hour backaches in the garden. **4.** the topsy-turvy season when the goldfish have to be boarded out while the family goes on a fishing trip. **5.** that season of the year when everything that is supposed to stick together comes apart, and everything that is supposed to stay apart sticks together. **6.** when you ride bumper to bumper to get to the beach where you sit the same way. **7.** the time when it's too hot to do the things it was too cold to do in the winter. **8.** the time of the year when mothers need a teacher's patience.

Summer camps: those places where little boys go for mother's vacation.

Summer, Indian: See **Indian summer.**

Summer resort: **1.** a place where a waiter expects a 25-cent tip when he presents a 60-cent bill for a 35-cent bottle of beer. **2.** a place where the natives live on your vacation until the next summer. **3.** a pleasant strutting ground where nobody knows how unimportant you are at home.

Summer resort, Ideal: See **Ideal summer resort.**

Sunbather: a fry in the ointment.

Sunburn: **1.** getting what you basked for. **2.** the red menace.

Sunday drive: **creeping up with the Joneses.**

Sunday driver: one who doesn't drive any better during the week.

Sunday night: weak end of the week-end.

Sunday school: a prison in which children do penance for the evil consciences of their parents.

Sunday School teacher: a person whose job is to welcome a lot of live wires and see that they are well grounded.

Superiority: the feeling you get when riding on an express train and pass a local.

Supermarket: **1.** a place where you travel farther than your money. **2.** a place where you can find anything you want except the kids when you're ready to leave.

Super-salesman: one who can sell a double-breasted suit to a man with a Phi Beta Kappa key.

Superstition: the error of putting faith in the wrong things.

Surgeon, Tree: See **Tree surgeon.**

Surprise: opening your laundry to see what you get.

Suspended sentence: one where the prisoner is hanged.

Suspicion: trying to find out what you'll wish later you didn't know.

Swearing apparel: a stuck zipper.

Sweater: a garment worn by a child when his mother feels chilly.

Sweater girl: one who pulls your eyes over the wool.

Swell-head: nature's frantic effort to fill a vacuum.

Swimming instructor: a hold-up man.

Swimming pool: a crowd of people with water in it.

Swimming pool, Family: See **Family swimming pool.**

Swish: a guy with delusions of gender.

Symbol, Status: See **Status symbol.**

Sympathizer: a fellow that's for you as long as it doesn't cost anything.

Sympathy: **1.** what one girl offers another in exchange for details. **2.** your pain in my heart. **3.** two hearts tugging at one load.

Syncopation: a lively movement from bar to bar.

Synonym: a word you use when you can't spell the other one.

T

Tabloid: a newspaper with a permanent crime wave.

Tabloids: fast reading for the slow-thinking.

Tact: **1.** the ability to arrive at conclusions without expressing them. **2.** the ability to change a porcupine into a possum. **3.** the ability to describe others as they see themselves. **4.** the ability to give a person a shot in the arm without letting him feel the needle. **5.** the ability to hammer home a point without hitting the other fellow on the head. **6.** the ability to make your guests feel at home when you wish they were. **7.** the ability to put your best foot forward without stepping on anybody's toes. **8.** the ability to shut your mouth before someone else does. **9.** the art of knowing how far one may go too far. **10.** the knack of making a point without making an enemy. **11.** the unsaid part of what you think. **12.** to lie about others as you would have them lie about you. **13.** the ability to convince a man who's sure he's never wrong that he is occasionally right. **14.** the art of lying out of it gracefully. **15.** what a guy has when he won't change his mind—but can change the subject. **16.** something a girl uses to make a slow man think he's a fast worker. **17.** the ability to get the fleece off the flock without a flinch.

Tact, Feminine: See **Feminine tact.**

Tactful wife: one who makes sure that her husband can't afford another woman.

Tactlessness: saying what everybody else is thinking.

Tact, Social: See **Social tact.**

Tainted money: tain't yours and tain't mine.

Take-home pay: 1. a 19th century custom, now outmoded by the tax laws. 2. so-called because it's not big enough to get there by itself.

Talent: wanting something bad enough to work for it.

Talker, Convincing: See **Convincing talker.**

Talker, Good: See **Good talker.**

Tangerine: a loose-leaf orange.

Tarnished lady: one that is not bright.

Taxation: 1. the process by which money is collected from the people to pay the salaries of the men who do the collecting. The surplus is used to pay the salaries of the men the people elect to decide how much shall be collected from them. 2. the art of plucking the goose to secure the greatest amount of feathers with the least amount of squawking.

Tax collector: a political office that seeks the man.

Taxes: a method used by the government to artificially induce the rainy day everybody has been saving for.

Taxes, Personal: See **Personal taxes.**

Tax expert: a legal-beagle who saves you the amount of his fee.

Tax–Fine: See **Fine–Tax.**

Taxi: that which when you want one there ain't any of.

Taxidermist: a man who knows his stuff.

Taximeter: a device for showing how fast you aren't getting there.

Tax, Income: See **Income tax.**

Taxpayer: **1.** a government worker with no vacation, no sick leave and no holidays. **2.** a person who has the government on his payroll. **3.** incompooped. **4.** one who does not have to pass a civil service test for the government.

Tea, Pink: See **Pink Tea.**

Teacher: a person who swore she would starve before teaching and who has been doing both ever since.

Teacher, Ballet: See **Ballet teacher.**

Teacher, Elementary: See **Elementary teacher.**

Teacher, First grade: See **First grade teacher.**

Teacher, Good: See **Good teacher.**

Teacher, Kindergarten: See **Kindergarten teacher.**

Teacher, Sunday School: See **Sunday School teacher.**

Tears, Women's: See **Women's tears.**

Technocracy: communism with spats.

Teen age: **1.** the interval between pigtails and cocktails. **2.** when youngsters aren't bright enough to realize their parents couldn't be that stupid. **3.** the years between the time people are too young to do the things they would like to do, and the time when they are too old to do them. **4.** the time in life when girls begin to powder and boys begin to puff.

Teen-ager: **1.** one of a crowd who are alike in many disrespects. **2.** a gawky-talkie.

Teen-agers: **1.** people who express a burning drive to be different by dressing alike. **2.** people who get hungry again before the dishes are even washed.

Teen-age talk: idol gossip.

Telegram: a form of correspondence sent by a man in a hurry and delivered by a boy in his sleep.

Telephone: **1.** a contrivance for letting us talk to people whom we don't want to meet. **2.** an invention of the devil which abrogates some of the advantages of making a disagreeable person keep his distance.

Telephone booth: a vertical coffin where sweet dispositions and good humor are buried.

Television: **1.** a kind of radio which lets people at home see what the studio audience is not laughing at. **2.** a means of getting a baby sitter, so Mom and Dad can get out to the movies. **3.** a medium of entertainment that permits a female singer wide range—from high C to low V. **4.** radio with eyestrain. **5.** something to put on a radio so that folks can see things are really as bad as they heard they were. **6.** summer stock in an iron lung. **7.** vidiot's delight. **8.** when the law of the jingle prevails. **9.** chewing gum for the eyes. **10.** a lot of people with nothing to do watching a lot of people doing it. **11.** a series of commercials interrupted by some entertainment.

Television set: an electronic device which, when broken, stimulates conversation.

Temper: one's only attribute that never gets better with use.

Temperament: temper that is too old to spank.

Temperamental: **1.** easy glum, easy glow. **2.** ninety per cent temper, ten per cent mental.

Temperament, Artistic: See **Artistic temperament.**

Temperance: moderation in the things that are good and total abstinence from the things that are bad.

Temptation: **1.** an irresistible force at work on a movable body. **2.** something which when resisted gives happiness and which when yielded to gives even greater happiness.

Testamentary will: a dead give-away.

Texan: **1.** a person who sends CARE packages to relatives in Scarsdale, New York. **2.** a wealthy man with ranch to ranch carpeting.

Theatre, Burlesque: See **Burlesque theatre.**

Theatre, Drive-in: See **Drive-in theatre.**

Theology: the effort to explain the unknowable in terms of the not worth knowing.

Thermometer: an instrument that can't read the weather forecasts.

Thirty: a nice age for a woman . . . especially after she's forty.

Thrift: **1.** a moss-grown obsession of those primitive men whose accomplishment was to create the United States of America. **2.** the art of buying a complexion to match a hat instead of buying a hat to match a complexion. **3.** an excellent virtue, especially in an ancestor.

Thrift, Modern: See **Modern thrift.**

Thrifty woman: one who saves money in one shop in order to spend it in another.

Ticket scalper: a man who enables you to see one football game for the price of five.

Tightwad: one who has an impediment in his reach.

Timber, Political: See **Political timber.**

Time: **1.** the arbitrary division of eternity. **2.** the only money that cannot be counterfeited. **3.** the stuff between paydays. **4.** that which the average American never seems to have quite enough of and is nearly always behind. **5.** a system of folds which only death can unfold. **6.** that which heroes have the knack of arriving in the nick of.

Time, Double: See **Double time.**

Time-killing: suicide on the installment plan.

Time, Leisure: See **Leisure time.**

Timesaver, Great: See **Great timesaver.**

Timing, Perfect: See **Perfect timing.**

Tips: wages we pay other people's help.

Tire, Spare: See **Spare tire.**

Tires, Snow: See **Snow tires.**

Toastmaster: **1.** a gentleman who introduces a gentleman who needs no introduction. **2.** a man who eats a meal he doesn't want so he can get up and tell a lot of stories he doesn't remember to people who have already heard them. **3.** the man at a banquet whose duty it is to inform you that the best part of the entertainment is over. **4.** the punk that starts things off.

Tobacco: found in many southern states and in some cigarettes.

Today: 1. the tomorrow you worried about yesterday. 2. yesterday shaking hands with tomorrow.

Tolerance: 1. another word for indifference. 2. something parents have to teach a child in the first ten years—so he'll be able to put up with them for the next ten. 3. that uncomfortable feeling that the other fellow might be right after all. 4. the ability to laugh when somebody steps on your mental corns. 5. the ability to keep your shirt on when you're hot under the collar. 6. the oil which takes the friction out of life. 7. the ability to smile when someone else's child behaves as badly as your own. 8. seeing things with your heart instead of with your eyes. 9. the quality of listening with interest to someone telling your favorite story.

Tomboy: a girl who hasn't yet discovered that her strength lies in her weakness.

Tombstone: the only thing that has a good word for a man when he's down.

Tomorrow: a husband's greatest labor-saving device.

Tongue, Sharp: See **Sharp tongue.**

Tongue twister: a phrase that gets your tang all tongueled up.

Tooth, Gold: See **Gold tooth.**

Toothache: a pain that drives you to extraction.

Top salesman: one who sells two milking machines to a farmer with one cow and then takes the cow as a down payment.

Torch singer: a woman who lights a fire that the customers put out with liquor.

Totalitarian state: a place where the people in jail are better than the people who put them there.

Toupee: top secret.

Tourist: 1. a person who stops at filling stations for free air, free water, free crankcase service, free information, and to blame the attendant for the condition of the roads. 2. a person with a heavy tan on his left forearm. 3. a man who travels to see things that are different and then complains when they aren't the same. 4. a person who puts up with any inconvenience in a wild search for all the comforts of home.

Tourists: people who travel thousands of miles to get a picture of themselves standing by the car.

Towel, Dish: See **Dish towel.**

Towel, Guest: See **Guest towel.**

Town, Hick: See **Hick town.**

Town, Home: See **Home town.**

Town, Old-fashioned: See **Old-fashioned town.**

Town, Small: See **Small town.**

Track meet: where a lot of young men suddenly discover that they are in public in their underwear and start running like hell.

Trade secrets: what women do.

Tradition: what a town gets when its residents don't want to build new buildings.

Traffic: a lot of cars moving fast until your car joins them.

Traffic judge: one who has a fine time working on others.

Traffic light: **1.** a little green light that changes to red as your car approaches. **2.** a trick to get pedestrians halfway across the street safely.

Traffic ticket: finale of the policeman's bawl.

Tragedy: getting what one wants—or not getting it.

Train announcer: a misunderstood man.

Training–Experience: training means learning the rules; experience means learning the exceptions.

Travel: **1.** people travel for the same reason as they collect works of art; because the best people do it. **2.** something that broadens people and flattens them at the same time.

Travel, Air: See **Air travel.**

Traveler: one who usually returns brag and baggage.

Traveler, Good: See **Good traveler.**

Traveler, Perfect: See **Perfect traveler.**

Travel folder: a trip teaser.

Travel, Wartime: See **Wartime travel.**

Tree: an object that will stand in one place for years, then jump in front of a lady driver.

Tree, Family: See **Family tree.**

Tree surgeon: a doctor who fell out of his patient.

Trim figures: what women do when they tell their age.

Trip, European: See **European trip.**

Trip, Pleasure: See **Pleasure trip.**

Triumph: umph added to try.

Troops, Seasoned: See **Seasoned troops.**

Trouble: 1. opportunity in work clothes: **2.** something that many are looking for but no one wants.

Trousseau: the clothes a girl wears for the first three years after marriage.

Truck driver: a man who has the opportunity to run into so many nice people.

True concentration: the ability to do your child's homework while he is watching television.

True friend: one who thinks you're a good egg even when you're busted.

True gardener: a fellow who has learned how much was left out of the saying "April showers bring May flowers."

True gossip: a person who talks about things that leave her speechless.

True musician: when one hears a lady singing in the bath, he puts his ear to the keyhole.

Truly happy marriage: one in which a woman gives the best years of her life to the man who made them the best.

Trust: a large body of capitalists wholly surrounded by water.

Trust, Charitable: See **Charitable trust.**

Tune, Haunting: See **Haunting tune.**

Turkey: a big old bird that strutted and got caught.

Turkey in the straw: a flop in summer theatre.

TV celebrity: a person who is very much in the public eye and often gets into the public's hair.

TV singer: a gal with a range from a high C to a low V.

TV spectacular: the bill you get from the repairman.

TV Western actor: one who is quick on the drawl.

Twin beds: under separate cover.

Typewriter: a machine used by stenographers and which can't spell either.

U

Ukelele: a so-called musical instrument which, when listened to, you cannot tell whether one is playing on it or just monkeying with it.

Ulcer, Gastric: See **Gastric ulcer.**

Ulcers: the result of mountain-climbing over molehills.

Umbrella: **1.** a shelter for one and a shower bath for two. **2.** something to put away for a rainy day.

Umpire: an authority on diamonds.

Unaware: what you put on first and take off last.

Uncanny: the way our grandmothers prepared meals.

Uncertainty: the only thing in life that is certain.

Under separate cover: twin beds.

Undertaker: your best friend—at least, the last man to let you down.

Unimpeachable source: See **Reliable source:**

Unimportance: the sensation that comes when you make a mistake and nobody notices it.

United Nations building: a site for sore allies.

United States: where under the Constitution every man may make a fool of himself as he sees fit.

University: **1.** a vast athletic association where some studies are maintained for the benefit of the feeble-bodied. **2.** a place where they have room for 2000 in the classrooms and 50,000 in the stadium. **3.** where the girls go out for facts and the boys go in for figures.

Untold wealth: that which does not appear on income tax returns.

Upper berth: where you rise to retire and get down to get up.

Upper crust: a bunch of crumbs stuck together with their own dough.

Up-to-date house: one with wall-to-wall carpeting, wall-to-wall windows, and back-to-wall financing.

Used car: **1.** a car in first crash condition. **2.** not what it's jacked up to be.

Usher: **1.** a guy who can really put you in your place. **2.** one who takes a leading part in a theatre.

Utopia: conditions that will prevail when Americans enjoy 1958 wages, 1926 dividends, 1932 prices, and 1910 taxes.

V

Vacation: **1.** a period during which people find out where to stay away from next year. **2.** a sunburn at premium prices. **3.** a trip to put you in the pink—and leave you in the red! **4.** three weeks on the sands—the rest of the year on the rocks. **5.** what you take when you can't take what you've been taking. **6.** a time when you get away from the people and places you love best so that you can put up with them when you get back. **7.** a period of travel and recreation when you take twice the clothes and half the money you need.

Vacation menace: sabotourists.

Vacation, Short: See **Short vacation.**

Vacation time: **1.** that period when the flowers in the home garden are at their best and only the neighbors are around to enjoy them. **2.** that season of the year when a man stops doing what the boss tells him to do and does what his wife wants.

Valentine Day: the day when men figure that one bottle of cheap perfume is supposed to cover up for the stinkers they've been all year.

Vegetable: a substance used to ballast a child's plate while it's carried to and from the table.

Verse, Free. See **Free verse.**

Vicious circle: one radio comedian stealing gags from another radio comedian.

Violinist: a man who is always up to his chin in music.

Virgin forest: a place where the hand of man has never set foot.

Virtue: 1. insufficient temptation. **2.** in the female, lack of temptation —in the male, lack of opportunity.

Virus: 1. a Latin word used by doctors to mean "your guess is as good as mine." **2.** a word coined by someone who couldn't spell pneumonia. **3.** when the doctor doesn't know what else to call it; allergy: when he knows what to call it but doesn't know how to get rid of it.

Vision: the telescope in the observatory of opportunity.

Vocabulary: something which permits a man to describe a shapely girl without using his hands.

Voting: a process of standing in line for the opportunity to help decide which party will spend your money.

Voyage, Ocean: See **Ocean voyage.**

Vulgarity: the conduct of others.

W

Waffle: a pancake with non-skid tread.

Waiter: a man who thinks money grows on trays.

Waiter, Cannibal: See **Cannibal waiter.**

Wallflower: a girl without a gent to her name.

Wall street: a thoroughfare that begins in a graveyard and ends in a river.

War: 1. a monster which will destroy us unless we destroy it. **2.** proceeding that ruins those who win. **3.** a business in which a lot of people watch a few people get killed and are glad it wasn't they.

War, Cold. See **Cold war.**

Ward, Maternity. See **Maternity ward.**

Warfare, Chemical: See **Chemical warfare.**

Warfare, Push-button: See **Push-button warfare.**

War, Political: See **Political war.**

Wartime travel: the most uncomfortable distance between two points.

Washington: 1. hubbub of the universe. 2. the city beautiful. 3. the city with a heart—and somebody else's pocketbook. 4. where the skeletons in the closets are ashamed of the people who live in the houses.

Waterworks: a woman's tears.

Weakling: a man who doesn't let his will power get the best of him.

Wealth: 1. a curse when the neighbors have it. 2. any income that is at least $100 more a year than the income of one's wife's sister's husband.

Wealth, Untold: See **Untold wealth.**

Weather: that which the Chamber of Commerce calls unusual and the tourist lousy.

Weather forecaster: someone with whom the weather doesn't always agree.

Wedding: 1. a ceremony at which a man loses complete control of himself. 2. a ceremony where the bridegroom starts kissing the bride and the other fellows stop. 3. a funeral where you smell your own flowers. 4. the point at which a man stops toasting a woman and begins roasting her.

Wedding, Hollywood: See **Hollywood wedding.**

Wedding license: a certificate that gives a woman the legal right to drive a man.

Wedding ring: 1. the smallest handcuff in the world. 2. a one-man band.

Weed: a plant whose virtues have not been discovered.

Weekend: when you slow down to let the strain go by.

Weekend, Lost: See **Lost weekend.**

Welcome: something that can't be reconditioned after it's worn out.

Welfare state: one run for the benefit of everyone but the taxpayer.

Well-adjusted person: **1.** one who can play golf and bridge as if they were games. **2.** one whose intake of pep pills overbalances his consumption of tranquilizers just enough to leave him sufficient energy for a weekly trip to the psychiarist.

Well-informed man: one whose wife has just told him what she thinks of him.

Well-informed person: one who has opinions like yours.

Well-informed woman: one who's on a party line.

Western, Adult: See **Adult western.**

White collar worker: one who carries his lunch in a briefcase instead of a pail.

Wickedness: a myth invented by good people to account for the singular attractiveness of others.

Widower: the only man who has an angel for a wife.

Widow, Grass: See **Grass widow.**

Widowhood: the only compensation that some women get out of marriage.

Wife: **1.** a dish jockey. **2.** a former sweetheart. **3.** a person who can look into the top drawer of a dresser and find a man's handkerchief that isn't there. **4.** a person who may suffer in silence but who usually has a lot to say about it later. **5.** a woman who sticks with her husband through all the troubles he never would have had if he hadn't married her. **6.** a person who sits up with you when you are sick and puts up with you when you are not. **7.** a person who can ride through the most magnificent scenery in the world with her eyes glued to the speedometer. **8.** an ingenious device for detecting lies. **9.** one who is sorry she did it but would undoubtedly do it again. **10.** what a man blames things on, that he can't blame on the government. **11.** a woman who keeps breaking things, like fives, tens and twenties. **12.** a woman who can turn an old rake into a lawn mower. **13.** the one person in the car who saw the parking space 50 yards back on a one-way street.

Wife, Ambitious: See **Ambitious wife.**

Wife, Dominant: See **Dominant wife.**

Wife, Experienced: See **Experienced wife.**

Wife, Good: See **Good wife.**

Wife, Ideal: See **Ideal wife.**

Wife, Modern: See **Modern wife.**

Wife, Perfect: See **Perfect wife.**

Wife, Tactful: See **Tactful wife.**

Will: See **Testamentary will.**

Will power: **1.** the ability, after you have used three-fourths of a can of paint and finished the job, to close the can and clean the brush, instead of painting something else that really doesn't need it. **2.** the ability to eat one salted peanut. **3.** the ability to stick to a diet for two days in a row. **4.** what every man has until he tries to give up smoking.

Window screen: a device to prevent the escape of insects.

Window shopper: a store-gazer.

Winter: **1.** the season when we try to keep the house as hot as it was in the summer, when we complained about the heat. **2.** when it is so cold even the wind howls about it.

Wisdom: **1.** common sense in an uncommon degree. **2.** knowing when to speak your mind and when to mind your speech. **3.** the ability to stop wanting somebody as soon as you know you can't get her.

Wisdom, Modern: See **Modern wisdom.**

Wisecrack: what results from a good opening.

Wise husband: one who buys his wife such fine china she won't trust him to wash the dishes.

Wise man: **1.** one who is smarter than he thinks he is. **2.** one who thinks all he says; fool: one who says all he thinks. **3.** one who seldom blows his knows.

Wise parent: one who knows which side his brood should be battered on.

Wise woman: one who makes her husband feel as if he's head of the house when actually he's only chairman of the entertainment committee.

Wizard, Financial: See **Financial wizard.**

Wolf: **1.** a fellow who wants his hands on a girl but doesn't want a girl on his hands. **2.** a guy who strikes while the eyein' is hot. **3.** a man with a community chest. **4.** a wild animal on two legs, with a pair of eyes on two other legs. **5.** frequently a fine fellow once you get to no him. **6.** one who enjoys life, liberty, and the happiness of pursuit. **7.** a guy who knows all the ankles. **8.** a man of single purpose and double talk. **9.** a man who wants an "aye" for an eye. **10.** a man who is waiting for the right girl to come along. **11.** a guy who believes in wine, women and so-long. **12.** a man who tries to make life a bed of ruses. **13.** a character whose bark is worse than his bite. **14.** a modern cleaner who works fast and leaves no ring. **15.** a guy who is ready, villain and able.

Wolf, Elderly: See **Elderly wolf.**

Woman: **1.** a creature who dresses for men's eyes and women's eyebrows. **2.** a creature whom God made beautiful that man might love her; and unreasonable that she might love man. **3.** a person who can hurry through a drug store aisle 18 inches wide without brushing against the piled-up tinware and then drive home and still knock off one of the doors of a 12-foot garage. **4.** a person who can't change her opinion and won't change the subject. **5.** a person who goes to a football game to look at mink coats. **6.** a person who needs a shoe larger inside than outside. **7.** a person who's always ready to take what's becoming to her. **8.** a person who stands 20 minutes talking at a door because she hasn't time to come in. **9.** a person who tells what somebody said about somebody without even pausing every 15 minutes for station announcements. **10.** a person who will spend $20 on a beautiful slip and then be annoyed if it shows. **11.** one who generally speaking, is generally speaking. **12.** someone who reaches for a chair when answering the telephone. **13.** the only one who can skin a wolf and get a mink. **14.** the opposition sex; the weeper sex; a species of creatures known for untold ages. **15.** a creature that is expensive when picked up, but explosive when dropped. **16.** the female of the speeches. **17.** a thing of beauty and a jaw forever. **18.** a creature smart enough to understand a man yet silly enough to admire him. **19.** a demon that makes us enter Hell through the door of Paradise. **20.** an illogical creature who uses her intelligence to find a reason to use her intuition. **21.** one who is always ready to give a man the benefit of the debt. **22.** the species that can remember a hat she bought 20 years ago but not what's trumps.

Woman, Career. See **Career woman.**

Woman, Conscientious: See **Conscientious woman.**

Woman driver: **1.** a person who drives the same way a man does—only she gets blamed for it. **2.** one who doesn't let her right hand know what her left hand has signaled.

Woman, Fallen: See **Fallen woman.**

Woman, Frustrated: See **Frustrated woman.**

Woman, Married: See **Married woman.**

Woman, Modern: See **Modern woman.**

Woman motorist: one who, when she holds her hand out, you can be certain is either going to turn to the right, turn to the left, or stop.

Woman, Nagging: See **Nagging woman.**

Woman, Perfect: See **Perfect woman.**

Woman's club: **1.** a place where they knock after they enter. **2.** a room full of loose tongues and tight girdles.

Woman shopper: one who returns an article for credit, buys something that costs twice as much, and figures she has saved half the amount.

Woman, Smart: See **Smart woman.**

Woman, Successful: See **Successful woman.**

Woman, Thrifty: See **Thrifty woman.**

Woman, Well-informed: See **Well-informed woman.**

Woman, Wise: See **Wise woman.**

Women: **1.** people who are biased—"buy us this" and "buy us that." **2.** people who need a shoe larger inside than outside. **3.** the sex that believes that if you charge it, it's not spending, and if you add a cherry to it, it's not intoxicating. **4.** the weeper sex. **5.** the plural of whim.

Women's clothes: go to extremes, but seldom to extremities.

Women's tears: water power.

Wonder drug: a medicine that makes you wonder whether you can afford to get sick these days.

Wood: that remarkable material which burns so easily in a forest and with such difficulty in a fireplace.

Word: something you must keep after giving it to another.

Work: **1.** a tonic which contains no habit-forming drugs. **2.** something that has never killed anybody but seems to scare some people half to death.

Work days: an unfortunate lapse of time occurring somewhere between paid holidays and sick and annual leave.

Worker, White collar: See **White collar worker.**

Work, Hard: See **Hard work.**

Working girl: one who quit her job to get married.

World: **1.** a big ball which revolves on its own taxes. **2.** a place so full of a number of things, and they all seem piled on our desk.

Worry: **1.** interest paid on trouble before it falls due. **2.** putting today's sun under tomorrow's cloud. **3.** a rocking chair which gives you something to do, but doesn't take you very far from your problems. **4.** a circle of inefficient thought whirling about a pivot of fear. **5.** stewing without doing.

Wrinkle: the nick of time.

Writers, Ghost: See **Ghost writers.**

Y

Yawn: **1.** a silent shout. **2.** the only time some married men ever get to open their mouths. **3.** silence with an exclamation mark. **4.** an opening made by a bore.

Yes-man: **1.** a yes-sir who has been promoted. **2.** one who stoops to concur.

Yes-men: fellows who hang around the man whom nobody noes.

Yom Kippur: instant Lent.

Younger generation: a group that is alike in many disrespects.

Young man: one whose hardest problem is to find a girl attractive enough to like, but dumb enough to like him.

Youth: **1.** that brief period, as distinguished from childhood or middle age, when the sexes talk to each other at a party. **2.** the first fifty years of your life; the first twenty of anyone else's. **3.** that time of life when you can be a college track star during the day, but can't go to the corner drug store at night without the family car.

Youthful figure: something you get when you ask a woman her age.

Z

Zeal: a certain nervous disorder afflicting the young and inexperienced.

Ziz-zag line: the shortest distance between two joints.

Zombie: something some men drink and other men marry.

Zoo: a place devised for animals to study the habits of human beings.

Subject Index

(Numbers in the index refer to selections in the text, *not to page numbers.*)

C

D

G

H

I

J

K

M

N

P

Q

R

S

T

Author and Source Index

(Numbers in the index refer to selectioı in the text, *not to page numbers.*,

D

G

H

M

Mc

N

S

T

U

V

W

Index to Names and Personalities Referred to in Main Text

(Numbers in the index refer to selections in the text, *not to page numbers.*)